Questions & Answers

Law of Contract

Questions & Answers Series

Series Editors: Rosalind Malcolm and Margaret Wilkie

The ideal revision aid to keep you afloat through your exams

Q&A Company Law
Stephen Judge

Q&A Criminal Law
Mike Molan

Q&A Employment Law
Richard Benny, Michael Jefferson,
and Malcolm Sargeant

Q&A Equity and Trusts
Margaret Wilkie, Rosalind Malcolm,
and Peter Luxton

Q&A EU Law
Nigel Foster

Q&A Evidence
Maureen Spencer and John Spencer

Q&A Family Law
Ruth Gaffney-Rhys, with Chris
Barton, Mary Hibbs, and Penny
Booth

Q&A Human Rights and Civil Liberties
Steve Foster

Q&A International Law
Susan Breau

Q&A Land Law
Margaret Wilkie, Peter Luxton,
and Rosalind Malcolm

Q&A Law of Contract
Adrian Chandler with Ian Brown

Q&A Law of Torts
David Oughton and Barbara Harvey

Q&A Public Law
Richard Clements and Philip Jones

- **advice on exam technique**
- **summary of each topic**
- **bullet-pointed answer plans**
- **model answers**
- **diagrams and flowcharts**
- **further reading**

Questions & Answers

Law of Contract

EIGHTH EDITION

Adrian Chandler

LLB, LLM, PhD
Professor of Contract Law,
Bristol Law School,
University of the West of England, Bristol

with

Ian Brown

LLB, DPhil
Former Reader in Law, Bristol Law School,
University of the West of England, Bristol

2011 and 2012

OXFORD
UNIVERSITY PRESS

OXFORD
UNIVERSITY PRESS

Great Clarendon Street, Oxford OX2 6DP

Oxford University Press is a department of the University of Oxford.
It furthers the University's objective of excellence in research, scholarship,
and education by publishing worldwide in

Oxford New York

Auckland Cape Town Dar es Salaam Hong Kong Karachi
Kuala Lumpur Madrid Melbourne Mexico City Nairobi
New Delhi Shanghai Taipei Toronto

With offices in

Argentina Austria Brazil Chile Czech Republic France Greece
Guatemala Hungary Italy Japan South Korea Poland Portugal
Singapore Switzerland Thailand Turkey Ukraine Vietnam

Oxford is a registered trade mark of Oxford University Press
in the UK and in certain other countries

Published in the United States
by Oxford University Press Inc., New York

© Adrian Chandler and Ian Brown 2011

The moral rights of the author have been asserted

Crown copyright material is reproduced with the permission of the Controller, HMSO
(under the terms of the Click Use licence)

Database right Oxford University Press (maker)

Fifth edition 2005
Sixth edition 2007
Seventh edition 2009

British Library Cataloguing in Publication Data

Data available

Library of Congress Cataloging in Publication Data

Data available

Typeset by Laserwords Private Ltd, Chennai, India
Printed in Great Britain on acid-free paper by
Ashford Colour Press Limited, Gosport, Hampshire

ISBN 978-0-19-959993-6

10 9 8 7 6 5 4 3 2

Contents

The Q&A Series

Key features

The Q&A series provides full coverage of key subjects in a clear and logical way.

This book contains the following features:

- Questions

- Commentary

- Bullet-pointed answer plans

- Diagrams

- Suggested answers

- Further reading suggestions

online resource centre

www.oxfordtextbooks.co.uk/orc/qanda

Every book in the Q&A series is accompanied by an Online Resource Centre, hosted at the URL above, which is open-access and free to use.

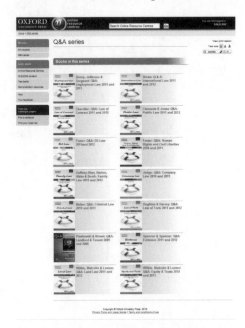

The Online Resource Centre for this book contains revision and exam advice, a glossary of contract law terms, and links to websites useful for the study of contract law.

Preface

New questions and answers have been added to this edition, or existing ones significantly amended, in order to reflect recent case law or statutory developments. Recent cases, amongst others, that have been incorporated include: *Granville Oil & Chemicals Ltd v Davis Turner & Co. Ltd* [2003] EWCA 570, [2003] Lloyds 356 (excluding liability for fraud), *ChipsAway International Ltd v Kerr* [2009] EWCA Civ 320, [2009] All ER (D) (restraint of trade clauses and the rules of severance), *Pratt v Aigaion Insurance Co. SA* [2008] EWCA Civ 1314, [2009] 1 Lloyd's Rep 225 (contract interpretation and the relevance of the parties' background knowledge), *Berkeley Community Villages Ltd v Pullen* [2007] EWHC 1330, [2007] EGLR 101 (the meaning of words used in a contract), *Attorney-General of Belize v Belize Telecom Ltd* [2009] UKPC 10, [2009] 1 WLR 1988 (implied terms and the construction test), *Chartbrook Ltd v Persimmon Homes Ltd* [2009] UKHL 38, [2009] 3 WLR 267 (addressing obvious mistakes in a contract), *Office of Fair Trading v Abbey National plc and others* [2009] UKSC 6, [2010] 1 All ER (Unfair Terms in Consumer Contracts Regulations 1999), and *Office of Fair Trading v Foxtons Ltd* [2009] EWCA 288, [2009] 3 All ER 697 (the effect of 'general' OFT challenges on fairness of clauses at the level of the individual contract).

As in previous editions, this book seeks to provide guidance on the best ways of answering examination questions on areas within a standard Contract Law syllabus. Always consider *both* sides of an argument when answering a question in an examination, with any reasoned conclusion simply *inclining* to one side. It is readily admitted that the length of some of the answers makes their precise replication under examination conditions almost impossible. However, as higher marks are traditionally awarded for answers that contain greater analytical depth of a limited range of issues (rather than superficial coverage of *every* conceivable issue), it is vital that every point raised within a question is subjected to comprehensive analysis and explanation.

I hope that you find that this new edition continues to offer questions and answers of a critical and thought-provoking nature, whilst maintaining a balanced, logical approach so vital to any understanding and analysis of the law.

Adrian Chandler, July 2010

Table of Cases

Table of Statutes

1

Offer and acceptance

Introduction

The rules of offer and acceptance enable a court to ascertain the precise moment at which a binding contract is formed between the offeror (O) and the offeree (A) as O's clear offer must be followed by A's similarly unequivocal acceptance. Thus, in *New Zealand Shipping Co. Ltd v AM Satterthwaite & Co. Ltd (The Eurymedon)* [1975] AC 154, Lord Wilberforce was prepared to state:

> It is only the precise analysis . . . into the classical offer and acceptance . . . that seems to present difficulty . . . English Law, having committed itself to a rather technical and schematic doctrine of contract, in application takes a practical approach, often at the cost of forcing the facts to fit uneasily into the marked slots of offer, acceptance and consideration.

In practice, the complexities of modern business, the greater use of intermediaries, and the dramatic increase in methods of communication, often make it difficult to identify the moment when an offer has actually been accepted. Indeed, there are relatively simple situations in which the finding of an enforceable contract cannot be equated satisfactorily with the rules of offer and acceptance (see *Brogden v Metropolitan Ry Co.* (1877) 2 App Cas 666; *Clarke v Earl of Dunraven and Mount-Earl, The Satanita* [1897] AC 59; *Blackpool & Fylde Aero Club Ltd v Blackpool Borough Council* [1990] 1 WLR 1195). Thus, Lord Denning suggested that the sole test should be whether the parties had reached agreement rather than 'forcing the facts' into the template of offer and acceptance (see *Butler Machine Tool Co. Ltd v Ex-cell-O Corp. (England) Ltd* [1979] 1 WLR 401; *Gibson v Manchester City Council* [1978] 1 WLR 520 (CA)). However, this approach was unanimously rejected by the House of Lords in *Gibson* ([1979] 1 All ER 972) and it is arguable that its adoption would substitute uncertainty for the prescriptive rigidity, yet comparative predictability, of the rules of offer and acceptance.

Structure

Most contract law exam papers contain an orthodox problem question on offer and acceptance, demanding an analysis of whether offers have been made, their possible termination, and the validity of acceptances. The best approach would be to pose five questions.

First, has an offer been made? An offer is a specific and definite proposition manifesting the offeror's clear intention to be bound. Such statements must be contrasted with mere invitations to treat (ITT) which lack any contractual significance, such as goods displayed in a shop window (e.g. *Fisher v Bell* [1961] 1 QB 394) or goods placed on shelves in a self-service shop (e.g. *Pharmaceutical Society of Great Britain v Boots Cash Chemists (Southern) Ltd* (1953) 1 QB 401). At present, there is a strong presumption that an advert constitutes an ITT because: (a) the advert will often lack specific details (e.g. sale of a car where the mileage is omitted), (b) the advert is often couched in eulogistic terms (e.g. 'a chance to win the opportunity of a lifetime'), (c) the responsibility for making an offer may be firmly placed on the enquirer (e.g. '£1,000 or nearest offer'); and (d) a reasonable person would not intend to expose himself to limitless actions for breach of contract where a limited supply of goods has become exhausted (e.g. one bicycle offered for sale followed by ten acceptances). Nevertheless, there are situations where an advertisement contains all the necessary ingredients of an offer. For example, in *Carlill v Carbolic Smoke Ball Co. Ltd* [1893] 1 QB 256 the advertisement was specific and definite ('£100 reward *will* be paid . . . to anyone contracting influenza') and demonstrated the requisite intent to be bound ('£1000 has been deposited with the Alliance Bank . . . showing our sincerity in this matter'). *Carlill* emphasizes the vagaries of offer and acceptance in this area: it cannot be certain whether a statement constitutes an offer or an ITT. This will depend upon the circumstances and the specificity of the language employed, so never attempt to be too dogmatic in your answer (compare *Bigg v Boyd Gibbins Ltd* [1971] 1 WLR 913 with *Harvey v Facey* [1893] AC 552 and *Bowerman v Association of British Travel Agents Ltd* (1995) NLJ Rep 1815).

Secondly, if an offer has been made, has the offeree unequivocally accepted this offer? In particular: (a) does the purported acceptance contain any new terms? If so, it may constitute a counter-offer, requiring the other's acceptance before a contract is formed (see *Hyde v Wrench* (1840) 3 Beav 334); (b) does the acceptance display the requisite degree of intent? For example, there is a strong presumption in land law that accepting 'subject to contract' creates no contractual liability (but see *Alpenstow Ltd v Regalian Properties plc* [1985] 1 WLR 721 and, more generally, *Branca v Cobarro* [1947] KB 854); (c) has the conduct of the offeree clearly established the fact of acceptance? Silence rarely constitutes acceptance, unless the offeree has agreed to that method of acceptance (e.g. *Re Selectmove Ltd* [1995] 1 WLR 474), but actions sometimes speak louder than words (e.g. *Brogden v Metropolitan Ry Co.* (1877) 2 App Cas 666); (d) has the acceptance been authorized and communicated by the offeree or his agent (see *Powell v Lee* (1908) 99 LT 284)? It will be seen that this is a far stricter rule than the communication of an offer's revocation through a third party; and (e) when email is the mode of communication, has the offeree incorporated his/her name within the body of the email? The sending of an email where the ISP adds the sender's name *after* transmission may be insufficient proof of an intention to accept an offer or, separately, to make an offer in the first place (see *J Pereira v Fernandes SA v Mehta* [2006] EWHC 813, [2006] 1 WLR 1543 and, generally, the Electronic Communications Act 2000, s. 7).

Thirdly, has the acceptance been communicated effectively? In particular: (a) is the acceptance effective on receipt or must it be actually read and understood by the offeror? Traditionally, communication has implied more than mere receipt (see various *obiter* comments in *Entores Ltd v Miles Far East Corp.* [1955] 2 QB 327) but there is recent authority for suggesting that receipt may be sufficient in commercial dealings if it equates with the intentions of the parties or achieves a just solution having regard to the allocation of risks (see *The Brimnes* [1975] QB 929, *Brinkibon Ltd v Stahag Stahl et al* [1983] 2 AC 34). This might have far-reaching consequences for acceptances recorded on answering machines or faxes received outside office hours (see *Mondial Shipping & Chartering BV v Astarte Shipping Ltd* [1995] CLC 1011, (1996) 146 NLJ 549); (b) has the offeree used the correct mode of communication? If a particular mode is prescribed by the offeror and the offeree uses an alternative means the acceptance will not be valid unless the alternative mode is equally expeditious (compare *Eliason v Henshaw* (1819) 4 Wheat 225 with *Tinn v Hoffmann & Co.* (1873) 29 LT 271); (c) does the postal rule apply to the acceptance? The rule states that a postal acceptance is effective on posting but this will be subject to a test of reasonableness and the express reservations contained within the offer (see *Quenerduaine v Cole* (1883) 32 WR 185; *Holwell Securities Ltd v Hughes* [1974] 1 WLR 155). Note that where the postal rule applies there is a preponderance of persuasive authority favouring the view that any withdrawal of the acceptance is ineffective after the acceptance has been posted (see *A to Z Bazaars (Pty) Ltd v Minister of Agriculture* (1974) 4 SA 392). Is any other view logical? and (d) if dealing with more modern forms of technological communication, how has the common law approach to 'communication' been affected by the Electronic Commerce (EC Directive) Regulations 2002, SI No. 2013, and the Consumer Protection (Distance Selling) Regulations 2000, SI No. 2334, and 2005, SI No. 2005/689?

Fourthly, at the moment when the acceptance is *deemed* to have been effective, is the offer still open? In particular: (a) has the offer lapsed? Expiry of a specified acceptance period, death of the offeror, and rejection of the offer are just some of the circumstances where the offer may no longer be capable of acceptance (see *Ramsgate Victoria Hotel & Co. v Montefiore* (1866) LR 1 Exch 109, *Bradbury v Morgan* (1862) 1 H & C 249; and (b) has the offer been revoked? Revocation is effective at any time before the date of effective acceptance, provided it is communicated to the offeree personally or through a reliable third party source (see *Byrne v Van Tienhoven* (1880) 5 CPD 344, *Dickinson v Dodds* (1876) 2 Ch D 463), and is judged by the normal standards of objectivity; for example, if A makes B an offer and then sends a further offer to B, in what circumstances would B be expected to realize that the subsequent offer was an implicit withdrawal of the earlier offer (see *Pickfords Limited v Celestica Limited* [2003] EWCA Civ 1741, [2003] All ER (D) 265)?

Finally, is there any precedent for suggesting a departure from the aforesaid rules of offer and acceptance? Two important issues may arise in this context. First, there is a growing number of cases where courts have been prepared to modify the traditional rules in the light of the parties' clear intention to enter into formal contractual arrangements (see *Blackpool & Fylde Aero Club Ltd v Blackpool Borough Council* [1990] 1 WLR 1195 and the Court of Appeal's decision in *Gibson v Manchester City Council* [1978] 1 WLR 520 reversed by the House of Lords [1979] 1 All ER 972). Similarly, where a transaction has been *executed*, it is easier for the courts to dispense with the formalities of offer and acceptance (see *G Percy Trentham Ltd v Archital Luxfer Ltd* [1993] 1 Lloyd's Rep 25). See also **Chapter 2** which deals with agreements that lack the required degree of certainty (e.g. *Hillas & Co. Ltd v Arcos Ltd* (1932) 147 LT 503). Secondly, if an *offer* of a unilateral contract has been made the offeror may be unable to revoke the offer even though the potential offeree has not yet accepted (see the extended commentary in **Question 4**). In particular, there is authority for the suggestion that once the offeree has embarked upon a course of performance leading ultimately to a completed act of acceptance the offeror cannot withdraw the offer (see *Carlill v Carbolic Smoke Ball Co. Ltd, Daulia Ltd v Four Millbank Nominees Ltd* [1978] Ch 231, *Errington v Errington and Woods* [1952] 1 KB 290—cf *Luxor (Eastbourne) Ltd v Cooper* [1941] AC 108).

Conclusion

The rules of offer and acceptance were largely formulated in the nineteenth century so there is scope for their adjustment if they are found to be ill-suited to modern business conditions, or, more importantly, are insufficiently flexible to cope with technological change. Moreover, always remember that the application of these rules to new factual situations will rarely result in definitive conclusions. Thus, your prime focus must be the *analytical processes* by which any tentative conclusion can be justified. It is vital to keep an open mind when attempting an offer and acceptance question by considering all the possible variations. For example, if a statement potentially represents either an offer or an ITT consider the justifications for *both* propositions—if there are plausible arguments on both sides, adopt a flow diagram approach, identifying the various possible conclusions resulting from either argument proving successful. This approach is demonstrated in the diagram below.

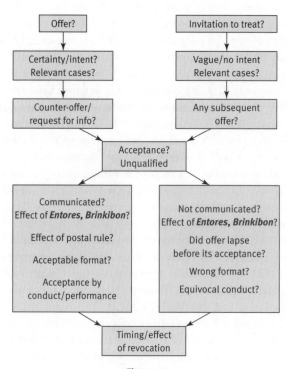

Figure 1

Question 1

Andrea has decided to sell her caravan. She parks it outside her house with a notice on the front windscreen stating: 'For sale. Pristine example—one owner. £4,750 or near offer. Please call at number 34 or tel: 713850, only. First person to agree a price WILL get the caravan.'

On Monday at 9.00 am, Bernice sees the caravan, but as she is late for the dentist, she telephones Andrea from work at 10.00 am, and makes an offer of £4,500 which Andrea says she would like to consider. Bernice says that she will assume Andrea has accepted unless she hears from her by 9.00 pm that evening, a proposal to which Andrea agrees.

At 11.00 am on Monday, Curtis calls at Andrea's house but Fenella, Andrea's daughter, is the only person there. He therefore leaves a note reading: 'Monday 11.00 am. Please keep caravan for me—here is a cheque for £4,750, Curtis.' Fenella leaves the note on a desk in Andrea's study.

At 2.15 pm on Monday, David sees the notice and, within a few minutes, has posted a letter of acceptance and cheque for £4,750, using the post-box at the end of the street. Unfortunately, David misaddresses his letter so it only arrives on Friday.

At 3.00 pm on Monday, Andrea decides to accept Bernice's offer and posts a letter to Bernice's business address saying: 'I agree to sell on your terms. Because of the lower price can you pay in cash?'

At 9.30 pm on Monday, Andrea reads Curtis's acceptance and immediately telephones Bernice's business address, leaving a message on the recorded answering service: 'Ignore the letter you will receive—deal off. Andrea'. Bernice is away on business and only listens to the tape on Wednesday evening.

Advise each party as to their legal position.

Commentary

This is a very traditional offer and acceptance question which deals with a variety of standard, technical issues. These include: identification of an offer, the definition of a counter-offer, the use of silence as a means of communicating acceptance, the moment at which a recorded message of acceptance becomes effective, the limitations to the postal rule of acceptance, and the relevance of specifying the anticipated mode for communicating acceptance.

One of the difficulties in answering this question is how one interprets the first paragraph—is the windscreen notice an offer or an ITT? You can circumvent this difficulty by giving reasons for and against the advert constituting an offer and then employing appropriate sub-headings as a means of demonstrating a logical structure to the examiner. This will clarify the issues in your own mind and will also send a clear signal to the examiner that you do not expect answers in this type of examination to be clear-cut, with only one possible solution.

Answer plan

- Is Andrea's advertisement sufficiently clear to constitute an offer, or will a court follow the standard approach of treating it as an invitation to treat?
- Assuming Bernice's statement is an offer and/or counter-offer, what is the effect of Andrea's agreeing to silence as a means of communicating her acceptance?

- Is Andrea's eventual acceptance unqualified and, if so, when was it communicated?
- If the original advertisement was an offer, has Curtis accepted that offer by calling at the house and leaving his note? Has this resulted in an immediate communication of his acceptance?
- Does the postal rule apply to David's purported acceptance?

Suggested answer

The first issue is whether the windscreen notice constitutes an offer or an ITT, for if it is an ITT Curtis and David's offers are never accepted. Does the notice demonstrate a clear willingness to be bound without any need or desire to prolong negotiations? An affirmative answer might suggest that the notice constitutes an offer. On the one hand the notice states a definite price, the caravan is subject to an external inspection and there is a prescribed method of communication. Use of the word 'WILL get the caravan' demonstrates clear intent and is not dissimilar to the following cases where an offer was held to have been made: *Harvela Investments Ltd v Royal Trust Co. of Canada (CI) Ltd* [1986] AC 207 ('we bind ourselves to accept') and *Carlill v Carbolic Smoke Ball Company Ltd* [1893] 1 QB 256 ('as a matter of sincerity'). Moreover, the stipulated methods of communication allow Andrea to vet each acceptance personally and thereby avoid any confusion as to who is the 'first person'.

Conversely, the price stated invites different bids ('or near offer'), it is unlikely that a buyer would come forward without an *internal* inspection of the caravan and test-drive, and an advertisement is normally considered to be a means of generating interest rather than a final stage before a contract is concluded. Following *Partridge v Crittenden* [1968] 1 WLR 1204, there is a presumption that where individuals attempt to conclude private contracts they will prefer to make the final decision as to whom they will sell, particularly where there is a limit on available stock (although Andrea's comment that only the 'first person gets the caravan' potentially eliminates this problem). Moreover, is a notice on a windscreen any different from a displayed price in a shop window (e.g. *Fisher v Bell* [1961] 1 QB 394)?

Consequently, as the contractual status of the notice is debatable, the answer below will assume that either proposition is valid.

Assuming the windscreen notice is an ITT

Andrea v Bernice

Bernice is clearly making an offer to Andrea to buy the caravan for £4,500. Andrea attempts to accept this offer by posting a letter in which she states that payment must be made in cash. What is the effect of this letter? First, by introducing this new requirement of payment in cash, Andrea's response may be classified as a *qualified* acceptance, i.e. a counter-offer. If so, the counter-offer destroys Bernice's original offer (*Hyde v Wrench* (1840) 3 Beav 334) and Bernice would need to accept this counter-offer before any contract came into existence (of which there is no evidence). Moreover, Andrea's subsequently recorded telephone message would effectively revoke this counter-offer, at the very latest when Bernice listened to it on Wednesday morning. Is there an alternative view? By specifying that payment should be made in cash, Andrea may simply be clarifying the position. How else would Bernice pay, especially as payment by cheque is considered to be equivalent to payment in cash (*D & C Builders Ltd v Rees* [1966] 2 QB 617)?

Assuming Andrea's acceptance to be unqualified, when is it effective? As the letter is posted, it may attract the postal rule, whereby acceptance is effective on posting (*Adams v Lindsell* (1818) 1 B & Ald 681). If so, existing case law authority would lean towards Andrea's subsequent retraction being ineffective (e.g. *Wenkheim v Arndt* (1873) IJR 73 (NZ)). However, one should question the reasonableness of using the postal rule in these circumstances. The notice on the caravan required would-be purchasers to visit Andrea's home or telephone her personally. An instantaneous communication is clearly contemplated by the parties, lest other people show an interest in the caravan whilst a letter is in transit. In these circumstances a court might well declare the postal rule inapplicable, particularly as B (the offeror) would not have expected a posted response. If so, the letter cannot be effective prior to its receipt, making the final result dependent upon whether the letter was delivered *before* or *after* Bernice listened to Andrea's recorded message on Wednesday. (NB you might also wish to consider whether Andrea's retraction is effectively communicated when it was recorded or only when Bernice heard it—see extended analysis of this point in **Question 2**.)

One final possibility must also be considered, rendering most of the above paragraphs irrelevant! When Bernice offered to pay £4,500 she stated that unless Andrea responded by Monday 9.00 pm she would assume that her offer had been accepted. Imposing silence as a means of acceptance is not normally permissible (see *Felthouse v Bindley* (1862) 11 CB NS 869) and should therefore leave Andrea free to sell to anyone else. However, in the later decision of *Re Selectmove Ltd* [1995] 1 WLR 474, the Court of Appeal recognized, in a very strong *obiter* comment, that if an offeree *agrees* to silence being a means of acceptance then failure to communicate with the offeror is equivalent to acceptance. On this basis, as Bernice did not *receive* any further communication from Andrea before Monday 9.00 pm, a court is entitled to conclude that Bernice had bought the caravan at that moment in time.

Andrea v Curtis

If the windscreen notice is only an ITT, Curtis will be making an offer to Andrea to buy her caravan for £4,750. As there is no evidence that Andrea has communicated her acceptance, no contract can yet exist. Certainly Andrea's mental acceptance of Curtis's offer is insufficient, unless Curtis dispensed with the need to communicate acceptance. (NB arguably if Andrea cashed Curtis's cheque this might constitute effective communication, provided Curtis's bank was acting as agent for its customer when clearing the cheque, but there is no evidence that this occurred here.)

Andrea v David

David is in the same position as Curtis, assuming the windscreen notice to be an ITT. There is no evidence that Andrea has accepted his offer.

Assuming the windscreen notice is an offer

Andrea v Bernice

Whether Andrea's notice was an offer or an ITT makes very little difference to Bernice's position. Assuming that the notice was an offer, Bernice's reply would clearly constitute a counter-offer as she offered a lower price. On this basis, Andrea's subsequent request for payment in cash would either be a counter counter-offer, in which case no contract would yet exist, or an acceptance of that counter-offer. If the latter, the final result would be determined by the following two points: (i) whether Andrea's acceptance was *communicated* to Bernice before her attempted retraction, or afterwards (see previous coverage of this issue), and (ii) whether Andrea's failure to communicate with Bernice before Monday 9.00 pm resulted in a contract coming into existence anyway on grounds of acceptance by conduct (following *Re Selectmove Ltd*).

Andrea v Curtis

Curtis has accepted Andrea's offer without qualification. When is his acceptance effective? Is it when the letter arrives at Andrea's house (i.e. receipt) or when Andrea reads it (i.e. comprehension)?

Two arguments could be advanced in support of the receipt theory: (i) Fenella is Andrea's agent, thus communication takes place when Curtis delivers his acceptance into her hands (see *Powell v Lee* (1908) 99 LT 284). In fact, this is an unlikely result as it is doubtful whether a daughter would have the authority to act as an agent or, (ii) Curtis complied with the terms of the notice, visiting Andrea's house personally and has now left his acceptance. There is nothing to suggest that Andrea's notice required face-to-face communication. If either argument is successful then a contract is formed at 11.05 am Monday, leaving other prospective purchasers with no redress as Andrea's offer will have impliedly lapsed in accordance with the notice on the caravan which specified 'first person'. (NB it is unlikely that Curtis could rely upon any *obiter dictum* in *The Brimnes* [1975] QB 929 to the effect that a letter that has been delivered will normally be deemed to have been opened within a reasonable time as this applies to communications with businesses rather than with private individuals.)

If the above arguments fail, Curtis's acceptance will only be effective when it has been communicated to Andrea (presumably when she read it on Monday at 9.30 pm). By this time Andrea has potentially formed a contract with Bernice (e.g. the postal rule applies to Andrea's 'acceptance' sent at 3.00 pm on Monday, or Andrea is deemed to have accepted Bernice's offer by not communicating with Bernice before Monday 9.00 pm). If so, Andrea's advertised offer will either have impliedly lapsed (the notice only states 'first person') or, if a court felt that the offer remained in force until it had been positively withdrawn, Andrea would be in breach of contract to Curtis by selling the caravan to Bernice (thereby allowing Curtis to claim damages based upon the loss of bargain suffered).

Andrea v David

If the notice is an offer, David will argue that his posted acceptance has created a contract with Andrea. Two questions are worth posing: (i) does the postal rule apply to his letter of acceptance? and (ii) by using a different means of communication is his acceptance valid?

For the postal rule to apply, the acceptance must be properly addressed, the rule must not be excluded by the terms of the offer (e.g. *Holwell Securities Ltd v Hughes* [1974] 1 WLR 155), and the post must be a reasonable means of communication. In the present case David fails on all three counts. First, he has misaddressed his letter. Secondly, the terms of the offer stipulate a personal visit or a telephone call (see below). Thirdly, as the situation presumably requires direct communication between the parties (in order to avoid unknown acceptances in the post creating unexpected liabilities) it would appear unreasonable for the postal rule to apply.

The inapplicability of the postal rule does not necessarily exclude the remote possibility that David's letter might be effective when it is delivered on Friday (assuming for some reason that neither Bernice nor Curtis have formed a contract with Andrea). Is this arguable? The general rule is that the offeree must adhere to the prescribed mode provided it is explicit and dogmatic, otherwise the acceptance is invalid (e.g. *Eliason v Henshaw* (1819) 4 Wheat 225), whereas if the offeror's intentions are at all ambiguous the offeree may choose an equally expeditious means of communication (*Tinn v Hoffmann & Co* (1873) 29 LT 271). In the present case, Andrea has used the word 'only' in her offer, thereby excluding use of the postal service, so David's acceptance is unlikely to be valid on receipt. Moreover, even if alternative forms of communication were not excluded by the terms of the offer, one would still expect an instantaneous means of communication to be used. As the post is not as fast as the telephone, nor as immediate as a personal visit, David's attempted acceptance should therefore remain invalid.

In conclusion, unless Curtis can successfully argue that the original notice in the caravan was an offer and that he had effectively communicated his acceptance by delivering it to A's daughter, it seems that B has the best chance of securing the caravan at a price of £4,500, with the contract probably being formed at Monday 9.00 pm on the basis of A's failure to contact B before that time with a rejection of the offer.

Question 2

Margaret, the sales director at TechMech, is approached by Philip, a local businessman, who outlines the size and nature of his business enterprise and asks Margaret to quote a price for the installation of TechMech's new accounts software system. Margaret, realizing that her monthly sales quota has not yet been reached, replies: 'I am sure that for a business of your size we can guarantee a price of £3,000, covering all installation costs and appropriate staff training. But please get back to me quickly, I cannot hold that price for more than a week.'

Later that day, Philip receives an advertisement by email from CostPlus Ltd which states: 'We can offer "state-of-the-art" accountancy software for small businesses at a price guaranteed not to exceed £2,500.' He immediately telephones CostPlus and places an order. However, after discussing the matter further with a CostPlus representative, it becomes apparent that the actual costs of installation would exceed £4,000. Philip thereupon withdraws his order.

Next day, Philip telephones TechMech. He leaves a message on the answering machine accepting the offer of £3,000 made by Margaret, at the same time asking whether the cost could also include on-site training for any new staff he takes on over the next six months.

Subsequently, Philip has second thoughts and telephones TechMech to cancel his order. The secretary, now on duty, points out that she has passed all the answering service tapes over to Margaret who would be listening to them shortly, but that she would make a note of his wishes.

Advise Philip whether he has concluded a contract with TechMech and/or CostPlus and, if so, on what terms?

Commentary

This question incorporates a number of well-known principles such as the contractual effect of advertisements, the termination of an offer, and the communication of acceptance and/or its withdrawal. Adopting a logical structure for your answer may be quite difficult so consider the possibility of using sub-headings, thereby avoiding unnecessary confusion for the examiner.

Although a technical, schematic approach is demanded, there is considerable scope for better students to demonstrate their analytical abilities. For example, the average student will apply the general rule of communication of acceptance in *Entores v Miles Far East Corp.* [1955] 2 QB 327 whereas the good student will explain the limitations possibly imposed upon this principle by the subsequent decisions in *The Brimnes* [1975] QB 929 and *Brinkibon Ltd v Stahag Stahl und Stahl* [1983] 2 AC 34.

Answer plan

- Does the CostPlus advertisement demonstrate sufficient intent and clarity to constitute an offer or is it merely an invitation to treat?
- If an offer, will CostPlus be in breach of contract in attempting to increase the price after Philip has placed an order?
- Is Margaret's response to Philip's enquiry an offer or an invitation to treat?

- Does Philip's attempted acceptance constitute a counter-offer, a request for information, or an acceptance subject to a preferred dispensation?
- If Philip's recorded message constitutes an unqualified acceptance, when was it actually communicated to TechMech?
- Did Philip revoke his 'acceptance' in time?

Suggested answer

There are two possible contracts that Philip may have entered into: a contract negotiated personally with Margaret (of TechMech) and a contract with CostPlus. The question is whether Philip is contractually bound to purchase the relevant accounts software from either of the two firms. Naturally, if two contracts are found to have been concluded, Philip will automatically be in breach of contract regarding one of those agreements unless, of course, he is willing to pay twice!

CostPlus Advertisement

Clearly the original terms of the advertisement are extremely advantageous to Philip but did it constitute an offer or an invitation to treat (ITT). Whereas an ITT merely represents a preliminary stage in negotiations, an offer is a definite proposition by the offeror signifying a willingness to be bound by the terms stated therein as soon as it has been accepted by the offeree. The basic distinction between an offer and an ITT is that an ITT lacks the required objective intent and specificity to transform it into an offer. Traditionally, courts have preferred to view an advertisement as an opening gambit in future negotiations (i.e. an ITT) for two reasons. First, the wording of the advertisement is often too vague (cf *Grainger & Son v Gough* [1896] AC 325). Here the advertisement simply states a maximum price that presumably means that a lower price might be negotiated; moreover, no precise details are included about the software specifications, nor its inherent limitations or performance targets relevant to its intended business use. Secondly, sound business sense may dictate that a business 'supplier/seller' would prefer to choose its customers so as to avoid being inundated with acceptances that could not be fulfilled from existing stock (see *Partridge v Crittenden* [1968] 1 WLR 1204). Finally, there seems little difference between shops advertising goods in windows or on shelves, either of which are normally viewed as ITTs (see *Fisher v Bell* [1961] 1 QB 394, *Pharmaceutical Society of Great Britain v Boots Cash Chemists (Southern) Ltd* (1953) 1 QB 401) or advertising them via some other medium. The above reasoning points to the advertisement's being an ITT, reinforced by the subsequent conversation which demonstrates that CostPlus required further information before it could actually quote a definite price. Indeed, if the advert was an offer, what *is* the price at which Philip is accepting—£2,500, or less? The fact that no definite answer can be given again suggests that the advert lacked the certainty required of an offer—drawing an analogy with the facts of *Harvey v Facey* [1893] AC 552 would reinforce this argument.

However, there are two points that might arguably alter the position here. First, in *Partridge v Crittenden* Parker LJ, in a strong *obiter dictum*, excluded manufacturers' catalogues from the presumption that an advert represented an ITT. Should this approach be extended to the supplier of specialist software who quotes a definite upper limit? Secondly, in *Carlill v Carbolic Smoke Ball Company Ltd* [1893] 1 QB 256 an advert was held to be an offer because the clarity of its wording, linked with an intention to be bound as evidenced by the deposit of money with the bank, demonstrated the required degree of intent and specificity. Similarly, does CostPlus's advert incorporate a statement of clear intent or is it a mere advertising puff? One might emphasize, for example, that the words 'price guaranteed not to exceed £2,500' demonstrates a clear contractual intent and that any further discussions will result in a lower price being agreed.

In the end, the argument that an ITT was made initially is probably stronger, in which case no contract will result (at any price). What is important here is that if the advertisement does constitute an offer, Philip has accepted its terms before CostPlus increased its quote (i.e. offer) to £4,000. Specifically, the normal rule is that an offer can be accepted, subject to the need for communication, at any time before notice of its withdrawal has reached the offeree (see *Byrne v Van Tienhoven* (1880) 5 CPD 344). Thus, if a contract was formed when Philip placed his order, any post-contractual attempt by CostPlus to increase the quote would represent a breach of contract.

Discussions with TechMech

Does Margaret's statement of price represent an offer or an ITT? Adopting the analysis in the previous section, the required degree of intent and clarity of language must be isolated. Crucially, Margaret has used the words 'I am sure', suggesting a clear intent to be bound. Compare this with *Gibson v Manchester City Council* [1979] 1 All ER 972 where the defendants' statement that they 'may be prepared to sell' was viewed by the House of Lords as an ITT—especially when linked with the later statement in the letter inviting the tenant to 'make a formal application'. In our facts, a specific price has been given, with a definite time limit. It is therefore more likely that the price constitutes an offer. (Note: if it was definitely an ITT, the remainder of the question would have no purpose.) One final point is that the offer can be withdrawn at any time before acceptance, unless Philip has provided consideration for the offer to be kept open (e.g. payment).

Unqualified Acceptance?

Has Philip unequivocally accepted the terms of TechMech's offer? At first glance he appears to have added a new term; namely that the cost includes the training of new staff recruited over the next six months. If this represents a counter-offer then the placing of his order cannot constitute an acceptance—TechMech can choose to accept or reject this counter-offer (see generally *Hyde v Wrench*).

Could Philip argue that he was simply requesting information in order to clarify the position, i.e. is it clear that the quoted price applied only to the training of existing employees? This seems a weak argument as Philip's recorded message is not really phrased as a question of clarification, but rather as a favour. However, he may find greater support from *Society of Lloyds v Twinn* (2000) The Times, 4 April where the Court of Appeal recognized that there was no reason why an offeree should not unconditionally accept an offer whilst, at the same time, making a separate offer collateral to the original offer. If the collateral offer was rejected then the unconditional acceptance of the original offer still created a binding agreement. On the facts, Philip's acceptance seems unconditional with his plea for indulgence regarding the training of subsequently recruited staff representing a collateral offer that TechMech is free to accept or reject.

Communication of Acceptance

Philip attempts to accept by telephone. The general rule is that acceptance must be communicated to the offeror or his agent in order to be effective. In this case Philip's acceptance has been recorded on an answering machine: is it effective when recorded or when it has been listened to? In *Entores* the Court of Appeal suggested that communication was equivalent to understanding, e.g. if the offeror does not hear the acceptance it is not effective. On this basis no contract has yet come into existence. But, as ever, there are arguable alternatives.

First, it is possible that the answering machine is a mechanical agent (see *Thornton v Shoe Lane Parking Ltd* [1971] 2 QB 163). If so, a contract has been formed and Philip has no chance of withdrawing from it.

Secondly, more recent decisions may have tempered the effect of *Entores*. In *The Brimnes*, the plaintiffs exercised their right to withdraw from the contract. The question was whether the plaintiffs' telex, incorporating the withdrawal, was effective when it was received during designated office hours or when it was read the following morning. The Court of Appeal concluded that the telex was effective on receipt as the plaintiffs had been told that it was the defendants' ordinary practice to read such telexes immediately. Whether one can apply this reasoning to communications of acceptance is, at present, a moot point. If it were applicable the following arguments might be advanced: (i) if the answering service implied that recorded messages would be listened to before the end of normal business hours of that day then acceptance would have been effectively communicated at some time during that day and a contract would come into existence, subject to the timing of Philip's attempted withdrawal; (ii) if the answering service suggested that messages would be listened to on the following day then it would seem that Philip's revocation would have already become effective, i.e. no contract would come into existence (see *Mondial Shipping & BV v Astarte Shipping Ltd* [1995] CLC 1011).

A first class answer *might* even elaborate on the suggestion, in *The Brimnes*, that a court could employ the indeterminate time between the receipt of a letter or telex, and its reading, to secure a just result; e.g. should TechMech be entitled to argue that a message is effective at the moment of its recording when the obvious consequence of using an answering service is to delay the actual time when communication is intended to take place? Such flexibility was supported by the House of Lords in *Brinkibon Ltd v Stahag Stahl und Stahl* [1983] 2 AC 34: the time at which a telexed acceptance was effectively communicated would depend on the intentions of the parties, sound business practice, and even a judgement as to where risks should lie. Is the receipt of a telexed acceptance similar to the telephone recording of an order? If so, can one assume that the intention of the parties was that Philip's order would only be communicated when his recorded message was heard, thereby allowing him the freedom to withdraw the order until that time? Conversely, does the use of an answering machine imply that a busy company does not wish to miss any opportunity to receive an order and that tapes will be listened to as quickly as possible, thereby suggesting that recording is tantamount to communication? Either argument is possible, again showing the inherent flexibility which the courts enjoy when applying the normal rules of offer and acceptance.

To summarize: if Philip's acceptance is effective only when his message has been listened to then his revocation is effective—an offeree can withdraw any acceptance provided the withdrawal is communicated prior to the acceptance (see *Byrne v Van Tienhoven*). If his acceptance is effective when recorded then a contract is immediately created, preventing him from attempting a revocation.

Question 3

On Wednesday Oftmark Ltd offers to sell 100 tonnes of steel to Aftercool Ltd at £500 per tonne. The offer to Aftercool states: 'Please telephone or email an acceptance by noon today. Delivery will take place next Monday.'

Aftercool Ltd faxes an acceptance at 10.00 am, the fax machine informing the clerical assistant that the message has been properly relayed to Oftmark. Unfortunately, the Oftmark fax machine has not been fitted with a new printing cartridge so the acceptance is not received. Moreover, as Aftercool Ltd believes that a firm contract exists, it enters into a binding contract with Torquecar Ltd to produce car body panels, using the anticipated delivery of steel on Monday.

Advise Aftercool Ltd whether there is a binding contract with Oftmark Ltd.

Would your advice differ in the following circumstances?

(a) Aftercool emailed a withdrawal of its acceptance before noon, but the email was accidentally deleted by an Oftmark employee.

(b) Aftercool telephoned an acceptance to Oftmark in the afternoon.

(c) Instead of a telephoned acceptance Oftmark's offer had specified: 'Please notify us of your acceptance by first class registered post sent before noon.' Aftercool sent a letter of acceptance before noon by unregistered post which was never received by Oftmark Ltd.

Commentary

This question is concerned with the problems of adapting the rules of offer and acceptance to new developments in communications technology. Communicating an acceptance by hand-delivered note or by post, or simply by using the telephone, has been overtaken in recent years by the ubiquitous telex and fax machines. Their advantages are clear: they combine speed and low operating costs with the benefits of a written record of any exchange of correspondence. Moreover, in these days of transnational negotiations and attendant time-zone difficulties, they provide commercial organizations with a means of immediate access to the offices of foreign clients. However, these forms of communication create their own difficulties. What happens if the recipient's telex machine is not permanently supervised? What if the equipment is improperly maintained? The House of Lords' decision in *Brinkibon v Stahag Stahl und Stahl* [1983] 2 AC 34 provided some guidance on how courts should approach such difficulties, emphasizing the importance of the parties' intentions and current business usage as well as requiring the court to make a judgment as to where the *risks* should lie.

To provide a complete answer to the above question, students must have a reasonable knowledge of the decisions in *Entores Ltd v Miles Far East Corp.* [1955] 2 QB 327, *The Brimnes* [1975] QB 929, and *Brinkibon v Stahag Stahl*. In particular, the *obiter* comments made in the judgments will address the problem of Oftmark's fault in not maintaining the fax machine properly and the reliance of Aftercool Ltd in entering into a contract with Torquecar Ltd.

Answer plan

- What is the effect of Aftercool Ltd's employing a mode of acceptance different from that stipulated by Oftmark Ltd?
- As Aftercool Ltd has used an instantaneous means of communication, when is its acceptance effective? What flexibility does *Brinkibon* offer either party in these circumstances?
  - (a) At what point was Aftercool Ltd's emailed acceptance effective: when it was capable of being accessed or only when it was actually read?
  - (b) When did Oftmark Ltd's offer lapse, thereby negating any subsequent acceptance?
  - (c) Did Oftmark Ltd impliedly exclude the postal rule?

Suggested answer

It would appear that the requirements of an offer have been made out in that there is sufficient certainty (price and quantity) and intention (business context).

The significant feature here is that the offeror has clearly prescribed a mode of acceptance. The general rule is that the offeree must adhere to the prescribed mode provided it is explicit and dogmatic, and if he does not, the acceptance is invalid (*Eliason v Henshaw* (1819) 4 Wheat 225). However, if this degree of precision is absent the offeree may choose an equally expeditious means of communication (*Tinn v Hoffmann & Co.* (1873) 29 LT 271). Into which category does this offer fall? On the one hand, the mode of acceptance is clearly specified but, on the other hand, use of the word 'please' suggests a degree of informality rather than a curt prescription. It is arguable that there is considerable room for manoeuvre here and, perhaps, the offeree is placed in a difficult position—does O want speed or a particular mode? If speed is of the essence then A has clearly complied with O's wishes by an immediate near-instantaneous communication which should have the added benefit of a permanent record (i.e. the printed fax). However, if the telephone or email mode is an absolute requirement then Aftercool's acceptance is invalid.

Assuming A has employed a valid mode of acceptance, has a contract been formed? When does the acceptance take place? The general rule is that acceptance is only effective once it has been 'communicated' to O (*Entores v Miles Far East Corp.*); normally this means its understanding and/or receipt by O. In the instant case O does not receive any acceptance because of the malfunctioning fax machine. Does this mean that the acceptance is invalid?

Entores is a strong and sensible rule but it is not inflexible. The rule can be modified in various situations, e.g. if O is at fault with his defective communications equipment (turning off his 24-hour telex machine) then acceptance may be deemed to occur at the moment when it would have been received (see generally *Brinkibon v Stahag Stahl und Stahl* and *The Brimnes*). If this is the case then A may argue that, as O was at fault in failing to replace the printing cartridge on his fax machine, acceptance was deemed to be effective at 10.00 am (subject to the comments below). As fault and business usage are the determining factors, a different answer might be forthcoming if A clearly recognized that the fax had not been properly transmitted.

There is a further line of argument based on estoppel. In *Entores*, Lord Denning considered the possibility of O's telex machine running out of ink and, therefore, being incapable of receiving A's acceptance. His Lordship suggested that if an offeree reasonably believed that the acceptance had been received, and the offeror was at fault, then the latter would be estopped from saying that the acceptance was not received. This estoppel might be more easily established on the present facts as Aftercool Ltd relied to its *detriment* upon the assumed communication by entering into a binding agreement with Torquecar Ltd (cf *Argy Trading Development Co. Ltd v Lapid Developments Ltd* [1977] 1 WLR 444 where it was questioned whether a promissory estoppel could operate without a *pre-existing* contract).

Difference with (a)

There is as yet no definitive case authority dealing with the use of email communication in the context of offer and acceptance. One must therefore extrapolate relevant principles from existing authority that might be appropriate to deal with the current situation. The basic principle stays the same: to be effective the revocation of an offer must be communicated prior to the time when any effective acceptance has become valid. In the context of faxes we have seen that communication normally occurs on receipt (*Entores*) but that this rigid rule is subject to flexible interpretation (*Brinkibon*). Treating the email like a fax would mean that Aftercool could argue that: (i) communication had taken place on receipt (relying on *Entores*); (ii) no estoppel could operate in Oftmark's favour as Aftercool's actions could not have induced any alteration of position; and (iii) even if communication of Aftercool's original acceptance had occurred, neither party should be allowed to take advantage of their own fault in order to create or prevent the formation of a contract (see *The Brimnes*).

However, one important difference between a fax and an email is that the latter often requires some positive action by the offeror before the acceptance can be read whilst the former is simply received in printed form. In particular, apart from switching on a PC, the offeror needs to access the email. In many ways, opening an email is very similar to opening an envelope in order to read its contents. Seen in this light, email communication is not instantaneous and may not be governed by the *Entores* principles. If so, consider *The Brimnes* where the Court of Appeal, *obiter*, suggested that a letter (that is not protected by the postal rule) delivered during normal business hours is assumed to have been read a reasonable time after its delivery. If the same can be said of emails Aftercool could argue that the email was presumptively read a reasonable time after its 'delivery'. Indeed, a similar approach is adopted in Regulation 11(2) of the E-commerce (EC Directive) Regulations 2002, SI No. 2013 (applicable to internet contracting rather than email exchanges) which assumes that communications over the internet take place once the recipients 'are able to access them'. (NB it is highly unlikely that a court would contemplate adopting this approach to emails sent outside office hours.)

Difference with (b)

What is the effect of A's telephoning an acceptance after the noon deadline? An offer will lapse in accordance with its terms or, if this is unclear, a reasonable time after it has been made (see *Ramsgate Victoria Hotel Co. v Montefiore* (1866) LR 1 Exch 109). 'Reasonable' will depend on the circumstances, such as the implicit need for urgency displayed in *Quenerduaine v Cole* (1883) 32 WR 185 and the nature and perishability of the goods. On the present facts O has stipulated a reply before noon by telephone or email. It would seem, therefore, that the offer has impliedly lapsed by the time A attempted to accept the terms of the offer.

(Note: the offeror would have expected to receive an acceptance before noon.) Another possible argument is that A, by not complying with the conditions of the offer, has made a counter-offer which was not accepted by O (*Wettern Electric Ltd v Welsh Development Agency* [1983] QB 796).

Difference with (c)

Two issues arise to be discussed. First, does the postal rule apply? The post is clearly contemplated as the expected medium for communicating acceptance. However, the postal rule can be excluded by express contrary intent, provided it is specified in the terms of the offer. For example, when completing a football pools' coupon there is a clear statement that the coupon must be received by a certain time before any liability ensues. The present facts are similar to *Holwell Securities Ltd v Hughes* [1974] 1 WLR 155 where the offeree was requested to exercise his option by 'notice in writing'. These words were held to exclude the postal rule as the offeror was specifying the need to see the acceptance (i.e. have 'notice' of it) before any contract was formed. Equally, O appears to be imposing a similar condition. If so, no contract would come into existence as the postal acceptance never reached O.

The alternative argument is that the court in *Holwell* was applying the provisions of s. 196 of the Law of Property Act 1925 in which, *inter alia*, the exercise of an option by post was deemed effective 'at the time at which the . . . letter would in the ordinary course be delivered'. Thus, *Holwell* is limited to contracts affecting interests in land. Moreover, whereas 'notice in writing' implies delivery, notification by post might suggest that the act of posting is sufficient; in particular, only O can 'notice' an acceptance, but only A can notify it. If this argument were accepted the postal rule would be applied: the acceptance would be effective on posting irrespective of its subsequent loss.

Secondly, by using unregistered post has Aftercool sent a valid acceptance? Previous comments have suggested that this will depend upon the contents of the offer. If registered post is a pre-condition for acceptance, no contract will exist, whereas if any equally expeditious means of communication is acceptable, a contract should be formed as registered and unregistered delivery have the same time scale for delivery. Moreover, what is the purpose of stipulating registered post? It cannot help O as the acceptance is either delivered, in which case it is known, or it is not delivered, in which case it remains unknown. In *Yates Building Co. Ltd v RJ Pulleyn & Sons (York) Ltd* (1975) 119 Sol Jo 370, the court concluded that the instruction to use registered post was intended to protect the offeree, so if A took a risk by using unregistered post (thereby lacking proof of transmission if the letter was lost in transit) his acceptance would still remain valid on proof of delivery.

In conclusion, if the postal rule applied then A's acceptance is effective on posting, provided there is sufficient evidence that the letter was actually posted. If the postal rule does not apply, no communication of acceptance has taken place so no contract can exist.

Question 4

Sweatshirt Ltd, which manages a chain of sports fitness centres, places the following advertisement on its website, dated 5 January:

Pay for one year's standard membership at a Sweatshirt Fitness Centre, and swim 400 consecutive lengths in one of our pools by 10 January, and you will be rewarded with a free one-year membership for your spouse. Happy Swimming and Good Luck!

Owing to bad publicity, resulting from some if its new members suffering heart attacks in its swimming pools, on the morning of 8 January Sweatshirt Ltd placed a prominent notice on its website withdrawing the promotional membership campaign contained on its website.

Discuss the legal position of the parties in the following *separate* situations:

(a) Andrew paid for a year's membership at his local Sweatshirt Fitness Centre on 7 January. The following day he logged on to the Sweatshirt website and noticed the revocation. Nevertheless, he attempted to swim the 400 lengths that afternoon but found that he did not have the stamina to complete more than 25 lengths.

(b) Bernice applied for a year's membership on the morning of 10 January. Whilst arranging for payment of her membership fee she was informed of Sweatshirt Ltd's promotion. As Bernice was a long-distance swimmer, she immediately rushed into the changing rooms to prepare for the challenge. However, before entering the pool, she was told of Sweatshirt Ltd's revocation by the pool attendant.

(c) Cathy received free membership at the Sweatshirt Fitness Centre, Bristol, on 6 January, having won a competition run by a local supermarket. She successfully swam 400 lengths, which was reported on local television, but was subsequently refused free membership for her spouse as she had not paid for her own membership.

Commentary

This problem concerns the particularly controversial issue of formation and performance of unilateral contracts. There are very few rules to guide the student in this area so you must be prepared to balance the various arguments and recognize that there will rarely be a definitive answer to such a question.

Whereas a bilateral contract entails an exchange of promises between the parties, the essence of a unilateral contract is that the offer is accepted by the offeree's actual performance of an act. The word 'unilateral' is used to denote that only the offeror is bound initially, with the offeree being free to decide whether or not to commence performance of the stipulated act of acceptance. In *Daulia Ltd v Four Millbank Nominees Ltd* **[1978] Ch 231** such undertakings were described by Goff LJ as 'if' contracts. For example, if a reward is offered for the first person to swim the English Channel tomorrow, no person is contractually bound to respond, nor will any person who undertakes this challenge (but withdraws before its completion) incur any liability to the offeror. Finally, it seems clear that communication of acceptance is generally not required—the simple performance of the stipulated act (of acceptance) is sufficient in itself. The paradigm unilateral contract is therefore best illustrated by *Carlill v Carbolic Smoke Ball Co. Ltd*

[1893] 1 QB 256 where the acceptance necessarily involved a course of conduct (viz. to complete the course of treatment).

Two difficulties are immediately apparent. First, when is an act of acceptance sufficiently clear and unequivocal to create a binding contract? Whilst the offeree may wish to establish commencement of the stipulated act as an acceptance, the offeror's response will inevitably be that he bargained for nothing short of a completed performance. Consider how you would apply these two different perspectives to *Carlill*: did Mrs Carlill complete the required act when she purchased the smoke ball, or when she finished the course of treatment, or only when she succumbed to influenza? Secondly, can the offer be revoked legitimately once the offeree has commenced performance? The general rule is that revocation of an offer is permissible at any time prior to its acceptance, but strict adherence to this rule might appear inequitable in unilateral contracts once the offeree has begun to perform the stipulated act (and potentially incurred expenditure on the faith of the offer remaining open). Should the offeree be afforded some measure of protection against a premature revocation?

Answer plan

- Is Sweatshirt Ltd's advertisement an offer of a unilateral contract or an invitation to treat? Can you draw an analogy with *Carlill*?
- If it is an offer, what act must be performed in order to accept it?
- At what point is it too late for Sweatshirt Ltd to revoke its offer: once performance of the required act has commenced or at any time before completion?
- When is notification of a revocation by a third party effective? Does *Dickinson v Dodds* suggest that the third party must be reliable?
- What difficulties emerge when attempting to compensate the offeree for the offeror's revocation of his offer of a unilateral contract?
- Can Cathy accept the 'offer' when she did not pay for a one-year membership?

Suggested answer

This problem focuses on the difficulties inherent in the formation and subsequent revocation of a unilateral contract.

Before dealing with any of the specific incidents that took place, we must first ask whether the advertisement of Sweatshirt Ltd (S) was an offer or an invitation to treat (ITT). An ITT is predominantly an opening gambit in negotiations and is therefore incapable of acceptance, whereas an offer is an unequivocal proposition made with an intention to be legally bound. The advertisement contains the necessary specificity and, arguably, as it emanates from a business the court may be more inclined to construe it as an offer (see *Carlill v Carbolic Smoke Ball Co. Ltd* [1893] 1 QB 256). It would be difficult for S to argue that the advertisement's tone suggested a lack of relevant intent as it incorporates both an immediate benefit and detriment: earn free membership for a spouse in return for paying for your own membership and enduring the physical challenge of swimming 400 lengths. Consequently, the advertisement appears to represent a unilateral offer of a contract which will be converted into a binding contract once an appropriate act of acceptance has occurred. Note that if the advertisement was held to be an ITT, none of the parties would have any realistic prospect of claiming the reward as their swimming feats would simply be viewed, at most, as the making of an offer, leaving S with an unfettered discretion as to whether to allocate free membership to any of the parties' spouses.

Andrew (A)

Assuming that the original advert was an offer, when does A's acceptance occur? The presumption in unilateral contracts is that only the completion of the stipulated act can amount to acceptance as, in the majority of cases, this is what the offeror bargained for. In our facts, Sweatshirt (S) does not therefore appear to be under any liability to A as he failed to complete the 400 lengths, nor was there any suggestion that S would compensate for any failed attempts. Support for this conclusion can be found in *Luxor (Eastbourne) Ltd v Cooper* [1941] AC 108 where the client (the offeror) agreed to pay the estate agent (the offeree) £10,000 if he could find a purchaser for two cinemas at a minimum price of £185,000. The estate agent introduced a prospective purchaser who agreed, subject to contract, to pay that price. The client ignored this offer and, instead, sold the cinemas to a third party. The House of Lords held that any acceptance would necessarily entail a completed sale to the purchaser introduced by the estate agent and, accordingly, the client was free to revoke his offer at any time before that acceptance had been completed. Moreover, the House refused to imply a term that the client would not revoke his offer in the above circumstances as this was not necessary to give business efficacy to both parties' intentions (see **Chapter 4** for an explanation of this test). This appears to undermine any argument by A that S was prevented from withdrawing its offer.

However, A possesses a very strong counter-argument. In *Errington v Errington and Woods* [1952] 1 KB 290 a father promised his son and daughter-in-law that, if they paid the existing and future mortgage instalments on his house as they fell due, the house would belong to them. Various *obiter* statements in the Court of Appeal suggested that the father's promise was irrevocable once the couple had 'entered on performance of the act' but that this limitation disappeared if they left it 'incomplete and unperformed'. Indeed, whereas in *Luxor* the extravagant commission (£10,000 on a sale price of £185,000) demonstrated the estate agent's acknowledgment of both the risk of not finding a purchaser and the client's right to revoke before completion, in *Errington* the couple would have never assumed an equivalent *business* risk whilst diligently paying off the instalments (see also *Ward v Byham* [1956] 1 WLR 496 where a refusal to countenance any revocation by the father could be similarly justified). Moreover, the couple conferred a *tangible benefit* on the father with every payment made, thereby making any attempted revocation more inequitable as time progressed. Surely the payment of membership fees provides an equally important benefit to S?

In conclusion, the court will need to balance three competing interests in reaching a satisfactory conclusion: *reliance* of the offeree (payment of fees in order to secure the advertised benefit), *benefit* conferred on the offeror (receipt of fees), and the inherent *risk* being accepted by the offeree (who may be unable to complete the stipulated challenge). The current weight of authority (e.g. *Daulia Ltd v Four Millbank Nominees Ltd*) is that once the offeree has 'embarked upon a course of performance' that is intended to lead to completion of the required act, the offeror will be prevented from revoking the offer (see also *United Dominions Trust (Commercial Ltd) v Eagle Aircraft Services Ltd* [1968] 1 All ER 104). On the facts it must surely be the case that A did embark upon the required course of performance once he had signed a contract to pay membership fees for one year. Consequently, the subsequent revocation will not have an immediate effect as A will have until the end of 10 January to improve his swimming performance and comply fully with the terms of the offer!

Bernice (B)

B's position is different from that of A's. In S's favour is the uncertainty of whether B entered a contract of membership before being told of S's advertisement. The general rule is that one cannot accept an offer without knowledge of it (e.g. *Williams v Carwardine* (1833) 5 C&P 566). In our facts, B was informed of the promotion 'whilst arranging for payment of her membership fee'. If knowledge of the promotion was acquired *after* the offer and acceptance had taken place, S would rely upon *Williams* to argue that B had no right to claim free membership for her spouse, even if she had actually completed the required number of lengths. B's only defence would be to cite *Gibbons v Proctor* (1891) 64 LT 594 which suggests that, where an offer of reward is advertised, a person can claim the reward provided he/she was informed of this offer *before completion* of the required act. As B was notified of the reward *before* embarking upon her marathon swim she may yet succeed on this point. At present the law is very unclear on these matters (especially as *Gibbons* has been doubted) so a definitive answer is not possible

If the decision in *Gibbons* prevails, and B is entitled to accept S's offer, she will presumably adopt the same argument as Andrew with regard to the timing of S's revocation; namely, that she had already embarked upon performance before being notified of any attempted revocation. However, B can strengthen this argument by pointing to the manner in which S's revocation was communicated to her. It was held in *Shuey v US* (1875) 92 US 73 (a US decision and therefore of only persuasive authority) that an offer of reward was revocable by giving the revocation 'the same notoriety' as that given to the offer, even if the offeree A had no actual knowledge of it. This is justifiable where the offeror does not know the potential offerees (in *Shuey* the offer was made to the public) but S will have a record of all of its new members (names, addresses, and telephone numbers presumably). Indeed, B was actually present in the fitness centre when signing up for membership. In such circumstances the court may decide that S should have communicated directly, and individually, with all of its new members, including B. If B failed on this point her case would be fatally undermined as it was recognized in *Dickinson v Dodds* (1876) 2 Ch D 463 that a reasonable third party may communicate the offeror's revocation even though not authorized by the offeror to perform this task. One must assume that knowledge of revocation acquired from a paid employee of S would be covered by the same principle.

Finally, there is the problem of the measure of damages. If B is entitled to accept S's offer, and S's revocation is ruled ineffective, how should B be compensated now that she has been discouraged from swimming the required lengths within the stipulated time? No contract can exist until B has completed all of the stipulated acts, so S cannot be in breach of contract. In the light of B's manifest ability to comply with the swimming challenge, the court may consider S to be in breach of a collateral contract not to revoke. Alternatively, perhaps a compromise can be reached which allows S to revoke its offer subject to an obligation to reimburse B to the extent of her justifiable reliance on the offer. Whilst not a perfect solution, in that it leaves open the question of how reliance is to be quantified, it would enable a court to *apportion* loss rather than take the all-or-nothing approach evidenced in *Errington* and *Luxor* respectively (see also certain *obiter* comments regarding a *quantum meruit* raised in *Morrison SS Co v Crown* (1924) 20 Ll LR 283).

Cathy (C)

Cathy will presumably argue that her swimming exploits attracted television publicity that proved advantageous to S. Surely the whole purpose of S's promotion campaign was to raise its visibility amongst the public? The added media coverage merely reinforces the commercial advantage derived by S and is similar to that achieved in *Esso Petroleum Co. Ltd v Commissioners of Customs & Excises* [1976] 1 WLR 1 where the public were encouraged to buy petrol from the plaintiff's petrol stations in exchange for free World Cup coins. In that case, two Law Lords stated, *obiter*, that it was wrong for the plaintiff to derive a huge commercial advantage from its advertising campaign without some correlative duty to provide the coins on request. In our facts S would appear to receive a 'windfall' unless ordered to pay compensation to C.

However, S possesses a very strong counter-argument which should prove conclusive. Using the 'mirror-image' principle, an offeree's acceptance must exactly match the terms of the original offer. In unilateral contracts this presumably entails performance of the conditions stipulated by the offeror. As C did not purchase a one-year membership at a Sweatshirt Fitness Centre, it appears that she is not complying with the terms of the offer and, thus, is actually making a counter-offer by seeking to claim free membership for her spouse purely in return for swimming 400 lengths. If so, this will destroy S's original offer and S is entitled to reject B's counter-offer (see *Hyde v Wrench* (1840) 3 Beav 334). An alternative way of phrasing this argument is that S only directed its offer to those who paid for a one-year membership (i.e. C is not a potential offeree). Surely S's primary motive for advertising was to increase membership revenues? On this basis, a court would hold that only the payment of a membership fee would amount to an unequivocal beginning of performance (thereby preventing any subsequent revocation), a requirement which C clearly fails to satisfy.

Further Reading

Case-notes

Bowerman v ABTA Ltd (1995) NLJ Rep 1815
McMeel, 'Contractual Intention: The Smoke Ball Strikes Back' (1997) 113 LQR 47

Blackpool & Fylde Aero Club Ltd v Blackpool Borough Council [1990] 1 WLR 1195
Davenport, 'Obligation to Consider Tenders' (1991) 107 LQR 201
Brown & Chandler, 'Intent and Contract Formation' [1991] Conv 149

Brinkibon Ltd v Stahag Stahl, etc [1983] 2 AC 34
Woodward, 'Contracts and Communications' (1982) 41 CLJ 236

Butler Machine Tool Co. Ltd v Ex-cell-O Corp. (England) Ltd [1979] 1 WLR 401
Rawlings, 'The Battle of Forms' (1979) 42 MLR 715

Pharmaceutical Society of Great Britain v Boots Cash Chemists (Southern) Ltd (1953) 1 QB 401
Unger, 'Self-service Shops and the Law of Contract' (1953) 16 MLR 369

Articles

Coote, 'The Instantaneous Transmission of Acceptances' (1971) 4 New Zealand UL Review 31

Hill, 'Flogging a Dead Horse—The Postal Acceptance Rule and E-mail' (2001) 17 JCL 151

Howarth, 'The Meaning of Objectivity in Contract' (1984) 100 LQR 265

McKendrick, 'The Battle of the Forms and the Law of Restitution' (1988) 8 OJLS 197

2

Certainty of terms and intention

Introduction

Contractual Certainty

If businessmen are often not overly-concerned with the niceties of offer and acceptance it follows that their contracts may not be complete in every respect. The parties may reach an agreement *in principle* but prefer to rely on experience from previous dealings, business practice and goodwill to determine their respective rights and liabilities, rather than on the precise wording of a formal, written, and all-embracing contract. Accordingly, the law's overall policy has been to uphold bargains where possible, rather than being 'too astute or subtle in finding defects' (*Hillas & Co. Ltd v Arcos Ltd* (1932) 147 LT 503, 514, *per* Lord Wright).

Nevertheless, the law will expect the parties to fix the boundaries of their own obligations rather than intervening to *create* a contract on their behalf. This potentially creates a rebuttable presumption that if an essential term is missing from an agreement negotiations remain ongoing, i.e. the parties have not yet shown an intention to be legally bound. For example, in *Baird Textile Holdings Ltd v Marks & Spencer plc* [2001] EWCA 274, [2002] 1 All ER (D) 352 the two parties had established a long-standing relationship of dealing with each other which the defendants had unexpectedly terminated. The claimant argued that the defendants were contractually obliged to purchase garments from them 'in quantities and at prices which in all the circumstances were reasonable'. However, in the absence of any objective criteria for assessing that quantity or price, the Court of Appeal concluded that no such contract existed (see also *British Steel Corporation v Cleveland Bridge & Engineering Co Ltd* [1984] 1 All ER 504).

In seeking to clarify and enforce agreements the law must therefore tread a middle line, avoiding wanton destruction of agreements on one side or the imaginative creation of bargains on the other (compare *Hillas* (*supra*) with *Scammell (G) & Nephew*

Ltd v Ouston [1941] AC 251). At present, in line with the general policy of upholding bargains, the courts have tended to (a) ignore meaningless clauses if they add nothing to an otherwise complete agreement (see *Nicolene Ltd v Simmonds* [1953] 1 QB 543), (b) enforce an agreement where one party is under a duty to resolve the uncertainty (see *David T Boyd v Louis Louca* [1973] 1 Lloyd's Rep 209), (c) refer to previous dealings and trade practices (see *Hillas* (*supra*)), and, (d) resolve vagueness by reference to custom (see *Shamrock SS Co. v Storey & Co.* (1899) 81 LT 413).

The real difficulty arises where the parties insert a variable provision into their agreement, e.g. date of payment and delivery to be fixed from 'time to time in the future'. Such a provision may be regarded by the courts as 'an agreement to agree' and be so uncertain as to be incapable of enforcement (see *May & Butcher v R* [1934] 2 KB 17n; *Smith v Morgan* [1971] 1 WLR 803). Nevertheless, as the courts are reluctant to strike-down provisions which are intended to have legal effect, they may uphold some 'agreements' even if further terms are to be agreed by the parties (see *British Bank for Foreign Trade v Novinex* [1949] 1 KB 623), especially where they have inserted a binding arbitration clause lest they fail to reach agreement on those terms (see *Foley v Classique Coaches Ltd* [1934] 2 KB 1) and/or agree the criteria for resolving any uncertainty (see *Brown v Gould* [1972] Ch 53). On this latter point, more recent case law has introduced a certain degree of confusion. In *Sudbrook Trading Estate Ltd v Eggleton* [1983] 1 AC 444 the relevant mechanism for resolving the price within a lease agreement broke down—the price was to be determined by two valuers, one nominated by each side, but the lessor refused to nominate a valuer. By this time a substantial part of the contract had been performed. The House of Lords held that since the nomination of valuers was only a *mechanism* for fixing a fair price (rather than an essential *criterion* for determining the price), the court could substitute its own machinery for calculating a fair price. In truth, separating the process for ascertaining the contract price from the criteria being used in that process is fraught with difficulties as the two so often overlap. Consequently, it is not surprising to find that subsequent courts have sought to distinguish *Sudbrook*. For example, in *Gillatt v Sky Television Ltd* [2000] 2 BCLC 103 the disposal of a shareholding was to occur at 'the open market value . . . as determined by an independent chartered accountant' (who was never appointed). The Court of Appeal held that the machinery was integral and essential to the final determination of price (as there was no definition of 'open market value'); in addition, it had failed because the claimant had not acted in accordance with its terms and so could not thereupon claim that the machinery meant nothing and should be replaced by an assessment of the court. This reasoning was followed by the Court of Appeal in *Infiniteland Ltd v Artisan Contracting Ltd* [2005] EWCA Civ 758, [2005] All ER (D) 236.

Letters of intent cause problems with certainty. Here the sender of the letter states that he intends to contract with the recipient and the latter may act in reliance on the letter in commencing performance. It is quite possible to establish a certain, binding contract in such cases (see *Trollope & Colls Ltd v Atomic Power Constructions Ltd* [1963] 1 WLR 333; *Wilson Smithett & Cape (Sugar) Ltd v Bangladesh Sugar and Food Industries*

Corporation [1986] 1 Lloyd's Rep 378). Similarly, letters of comfort may be either bind-ing contracts or vague assurances resting entirely upon business goodwill (see *Kleinwort Benson Ltd v Malaysia Mining Corporation Berhad* [1989] 1 WLR 379).

Finally, in *Walford v Miles* [1992] 2 AC 128, the House of Lords considered the status of a 'contract to negotiate' the sale of a business in which the parties were 'locked out' from negotiating with any other parties. It was held that no contract existed as there was no specified length within which negotiations were to be concluded (see *May & Butcher, supra*); nor could this uncertainty be resolved by implying a duty to negoti-ate in good faith as this ran counter to the adversarial nature of contract negotiations. Nevertheless, the argument that the *Walford* decision implicitly recognized that a purely negative lock-out arrangement, *for a specific period of time*, constituted an enforceable contract was subsequently recognized in *Pitt v PHH Asset Management Ltd* [1993] 4 All ER 961. Moreover, in *Petromec Inc v Petroleo Brasiliero SA Petrobas (No. 3)* [2005] EWCA Civ 891, [2006] I Lloyd's Rep 121, where a contract already existed, it was held that an express duty to negotiate (in good faith) the additional costs of upgrading the agreed level of performance was enforceable as the contract provided for an explicit right to such upgrading.

Contractual Intent

As well as the other elements required for the formation of a contract, there must be an intention to create legal relations (ICLR), this being assessed objectively. In commercial contracts there is a presumption of ICLR and the onus is on the party who asserts that no legal effect is intended to rebut the presumption. The parties may expressly deny any intent but, in the absence of such an express denial, rebuttal is extremely difficult (see *Edwards v Skyways Ltd* [1964] 1 WLR 349; *Rose & Frank Co. v J R Crompton & Bros Ltd* [1923] 2 KB 261; *Kleinwort Benson Ltd v Malaysia Mining Corporation Berhad* [1989] 1 WLR 379).

Conversely, many social and domestic agreements lack sufficient intent to make them legally binding (see *Balfour v Balfour* [1919] 2 KB 571), although this presumption can be rebutted, where spouses have reached an agreement, on proof of the requisite legal intent (see *Pearce v Merriman* [1904] 1 KB 80; *Merritt v Merritt* [1970] 1 WLR 1211). Similarly, other domestic arrangements can involve difficulties of intention (see *Jones v Padavatton* [1969] 1 WLR 328; *Simpkins v Pays* [1955] 1 WLR 975; *Parker v Clark* [1960] 1 WLR 286). However, more recently, the Court of Appeal has questioned whether the presumptions regarding commercial and domestic agreements represent the correct starting point, preferring to concentrate on the 'seriousness' of any promise as the primary indicator of intent (see *Edmonds v Lawson* [2000] QB 501). Finally, a statement inducing a contract may be a 'mere puff', with the test being one of intention (see *Weeks v Tybald* (1605) Noy 11; *Carlill v Carbolic Smoke Ball Co. Ltd* [1893] 1 QB 256). Similarly, intention determines whether a statement is a term of the contract or a 'mere representation' (see *Heilbut, Symons & Co. v Buckleton* [1913] AC 30).

Question 1

It is a basic axiom of English law that, although the courts cannot make a contract for the parties, they will strive to uphold a bargain wherever possible.
  Discuss.

Commentary

This question calls for an understanding of certainty of terms and, to a lesser extent, intention to create legal relations. Students must be able to make an accurate analysis of the lengths to which the courts will go in enforcing contracts. The decisions tend to make technical distinctions but students should be aware of the important substantive issues raised in *Kleinwort Benson Ltd v Malaysia Mining Corporation Berhad* [1989] 1 WLR 379 and *Walford v Miles* [1992] 2 AC 128.

Answer plan

- What is meant by the rule that a contract must have certainty of terms?
- To what extent will the courts strive to uphold a bargain and seek to clarify the terms of the contract?
- To what extent can the parties leave a term of the contract to be agreed upon in the future?
- Do recent decisions adopt a more rigorous approach than formerly in demanding that intent and certainty must unite to forge an intelligible and enforceable undertaking?

Suggested answer

It is the parties who make their own contract and fix its boundaries whilst the courts enforce the bargain thus created. It follows that if the agreement is uncertain and imprecise the courts will be unable to enforce it and may decide that it also lacks the requisite intention to create legal relations. For example, in *Scammell (G) & Nephew Ltd v Ouston* [1941] AC 251 there was an agreement to acquire goods 'on hire-purchase terms' but the House of Lords held that this could not be a binding contract as it was 'so vaguely expressed that it cannot, standing by itself, be given a definite meaning' (see also *Jacques v Lloyd D George & Partners* [1968] 1 WLR 625).

Nevertheless, the courts have traditionally sought to uphold bargains where possible and, as Lord Wright emphasized in *Hillas & Co. Ltd v Arcos Ltd* (1932) 147 LT 503, have not been 'too astute or subtle in finding defects', even where the commercial agreement has been crudely drafted by businessmen. In *Hillas*, the plaintiffs agreed to buy from the defendants a quantity of Russian softwood timber of a particular quality, the agreement containing an option for the plain-tiffs to buy more timber at a later date but with no particulars of size or quality. When the plaintiffs sought to exercise the option, the defendants objected that the clause was vague and indeterminate and provided, at best, a basis for future negotiations. The House of Lords held that, having regard to previous dealings, there was sufficient intention to be bound and the agreement could be rendered certain by referring to the parties' previous dealings and the normal practice in the timber trade. *Hillas* is illustrative of the courts willingness to imply terms that make commercial sense of the agreement, but an alternative method of resolving uncertainty is to delete a meaningless, subsidiary provision, leaving the remainder of the contract complete and enforceable. In *Nicolene Ltd v Simmonds* [1953] 1 QB 543, the defendant agreed to sell a quantity of steel bars to the claimant on terms which were clear except for the statement that 'we are in agreement that the usual conditions of acceptance apply'. It was held that the words were meaningless, thereby leaving the core of the obligation intact. As Denning LJ com-mented, if the opposite conclusion had been reached in *Nicolene* defaulters would be 'scanning their contracts to find some meaningless clause on which to ride free'. However, the *Nicolene* principle cannot function if the meaningless clause is intended to govern an undertaking *central* to the agreement, for such uncertainty would potentially vitiate the whole agreement.

The courts also look favourably on agreements which, although leaving some issue to be resolved in the future, provide the machinery or criteria for its resolu-tion. Thus, an agreement will not fail simply because it provides for the resolution of outstanding issues by arbitration, and, in *Brown v Gould* [1972] Ch 53, an option to renew a lease 'at a rent to be fixed having regard to the market value of the premises' was binding in that it provided a criterion, albeit somewhat elusive, for resolving the vagueness. This approach was extended in *Sudbrook Trading Estate Ltd v Eggleton* [1983] 1 AC 444 where a lease gave the tenant an option to purchase the premises 'at such price as may be agreed upon by two valuers' who were to be appointed by each party. The landlord refused to appoint a valuer but the House of Lords held that the option did not fail for uncertainty. The sub-stance of the undertaking was an agreement to sell at a reasonable price, to be determined by valuers, and the extra stipulation that each party should nominate a valuer was 'subsidiary and inessential'. But a note of caution should be added here. Whilst a court may choose to follow this analysis and substitute its own pro-cedures for resolving uncertainty where the original machinery breaks down (e.g. ascertaining the price with the help of expert evidence—(see *Re Malpas* [1985] Ch 42), the more recent Court of Appeal decisions in *Gillatt v Sky Television Ltd* [2000] 2 BCLC 103 and *Infiniteland Ltd v Artisan Contracting Ltd* [2005] EWCA Civ 758, [2005] All ER (D) 236 suggest that such discretion is severely circumscribed as it is not always easy to separate the process by which an agreed price is to be reached (e.g. *Sudbrook*), from the essential criteria for determining that price (which remain inviolate in accordance with *May & Butcher v R* [1934] 2 KB 17—*infra*).

Finally, the courts have not been deterred from clarifying uncertainty where there is a clear intention to form a binding contract but the vagueness in question has related to a fundamental obligation which the parties have deliberately left open-ended. This may occur where both parties are reluctant to enter into a final-ized contract for a lengthy period of time, preferring to leave questions such as the price and manner of payment for later consideration and agreement. Are such agreements enforceable? In *May & Butcher v R* [1934] 2 KB 17n, an agreement for the sale of tentage provided that the price, dates of payment, and manner of delivery should be agreed 'from time to time'. On these facts, the House of Lords held that the agreement was incomplete as it amounted to nothing more than an agreement to agree in the future. If the agreement had been silent on these issues, the House thought that s. 8(2) of the Sale of Goods Act 1893 (now Sale of Goods Act 1979, s. 8(2)) might have led to a reasonable price being payable, but the parties had shown that this was not their intention by providing for a further agreement. However, *May & Butcher* has been distinguished in several cases and, although it is difficult to make generalizations in this area, it seems that if the courts identify substantial agreement between the parties (referring to existing commercial practice where relevant) some points may be left for future resolution without vitiating the agreement. For example, in *Foley v Classique Coaches Ltd* [1934] 2 KB 1, the plaintiff owned a petrol station and adjoining land which he agreed to sell to the defendants on condition that they should agree to buy all the petrol for their coach business from him. The agreement regarding the petrol was executed and provided that it was to be supplied 'at a price to be agreed by the parties in writing and from time to time'. The land was conveyed and the petrol agreement was acted on for three years but the defendants then repudiated it arguing that it was incomplete in relation to the price of the petrol. The Court of Appeal held that the agreement was enforceable and that, consequently, the defendants must pay a reasonable price for the petrol. The most influential factors in the decision appeared to be that the contract had been acted upon for several years (see also *Trentham Ltd v Archital Luxfer* [1993] 1 Lloyd's Rep 25) and that the petrol agreement formed part of a linked bargain with the sale of the land, the defendants paying a price for the land which no doubt reflected the fact that they would buy their petrol from the plaintiffs.

However, more recent decisions have cast doubt upon the whole notion that the courts, as described above, will strive to uphold the parties' bargain where pos-sible. In *Kleinwort Benson Ltd v Malaysia Mining Corporation Berhad* [1989] 1 WLR 379 the defendant issued a letter of comfort to the plaintiff in respect of a loan of £10 million to one of the defendant's subsidiary companies. Com-fort letters possess varying degrees of formality but here the letter was negotiated between the parties and contained the statement by the defendant that it was its 'policy to ensure that the business of [the subsidiary] is at all times in a position to meet its liabilities to you under the above arrangements'. The defendant argued that neither party intended this statement to be contractually binding. At first instance, it was held that the plaintiff should succeed as: (a) the presumption of intention to create legal relations which applies to commercial contracts had not been rebutted by the defendant; (b) the wording was unambiguous and 'crystal clear'; and (c) the undertaking was of crucial importance and the plaintiff had acted in reliance on it in advancing the loan. The Court of Appeal reversed the decision and held that the wording of the undertaking did not amount to a contractual promise and thus the question of rebutting the presumption of intention to create legal relations never arose. Moreover, the court considered that the statement was only one of present intention in that the defendant's 'policy' could change in the future. The Court of Appeal's reasoning appears to ignore the presumption of intention and, if that presumption has not been rendered redundant by the decision, it is very difficult to ascertain in which circumstances it will apply. The second decision, *Walford v Miles* [1992] 2 AC 128, concerned the enforceability of a contract to negotiate. The plaintiff and defendant were negotiating the sale of the defendant's business and an agreement was reached by which the plaintiff would provide the defendant with a letter of comfort from the plaintiff's bankers confirming that a loan would be granted to the plaintiff. In return, the defendant agreed to terminate any negotiations with third parties and not to consider any alternative offers. The comfort letter was provided but the defendant withdrew from the negotiations and sold the business to a third party. The House of Lords held that the plaintiff's action must fail. The House considered that it was possible to have an enforceable lock-out contract (i.e. an agreement *not* to negotiate with third parties) provided the duration of the 'lock-out' was specified expressly, but that the parties could never be 'locked in' by such an arrangement to negotiate positively as this would amount to an uncertain and unenforceable contract to negotiate.

Kleinwort and *Walford* illustrate perfectly the *laissez-faire* principles of self-reliance and judicial non-interventionism. It is suggested that the decisions ignore English law's basic tenet that agreements should be validated wherever possible and, in so doing, potentially encourage bad faith in commercial transactions. Consequently the Court of Appeal decision in *Petromec Inc v Petroleo Brasiliero SA Petrobas (No. 3)* [2005] EWCA Civ 891, [2006] 1 Lloyd's Rep 121 is to be welcomed. The facts involved a provision within an *existing* contract that required the parties to negotiate in *good faith* the costs of upgrading that contract (note that the possibility of upgrading was permitted and acknowledged within the contract). This provision was held to be enforceable. Longmore LJ was not put off by the difficulty of determining the result of 'good faith' negotiations (i.e. in calculating the costs of upgrading) as this would be a relatively easy task. Moreover, whilst withdrawing from negotiations in 'bad faith' (i.e. a potential breach of contract) would be difficult to ascertain, to ignore that possibility would unfairly undermine the expressed and reasonable intentions of the parties. Thus, whilst the traditional notion that courts seek to uphold rather than destroy contracts has, to some extent, come under attack in recent times, the sentiments expressed in the original question still retain great resonance in the law today.

Further Reading

Case-notes

Walford v Miles [1992] 2 AC 128
Brown, 'The Contract to Negotiate: A Thing Writ in Water' [1992] JBL 353

Kleinwort Benson Ltd v Malaysia Mining Corp. Bhd [1989] 1 WLR 379 (CA)
Brown, 'The Letter of Comfort: Placebo or Promise?' [1990] JBL 281

Articles

Hedley, 'Keeping Contract in its Place—*Balfour v Balfour* and the Enforcement of Informal Agreements' (1985) 5 OILS 391

Hepple, 'Intention to Create Legal Relations' [1970] CLJ 122

Gilliker, 'Taking Comfort in Certainty: To Enforce or Not to Enforce the Letter of Comfort' [2004] LMCLQ 219

Steyn, 'Contract Law: Fulfilling the Reasonable Expectations of Honest Men' (1977) 113 LQR 433

3

Consideration

Introduction

Whilst the enforcement of all promises is theoretically possible, practical and evidential constraints demand that the law imposes certain limits on their enforceability. For example, current rules regarding the *form* the contract must take (e.g. by deed or in writing) draw unequivocal boundaries and prescribe detailed formalities in certain circumstances (e.g. the requirements of the **Consumer Credit Act 1974**). However, it would clearly be impossible to demand writing for every contract and so a more general test of enforceability is required. What are the possible bases for such a test? First, the agreement might involve an *exchange* of values (i.e. a bargain). Here, A would not be bound unless he received *consideration* from B in the form of a return promise or actual performance of the undertaking. Secondly, B's *reliance* on A's promise might simultaneously establish both a nexus between the parties and a justifiable reason for enforcing their agreement (see **American Restatement (Second) of Contracts, section 90**).

The proponents of the reliance theory suggest that if B has relied to his detriment on A's promise he has a stronger claim to redress than if he merely gives a return promise without any actual performance. Whilst this appears to be theoretically logical, it lacks practical merit as a universal ground of liability. How, exactly, can reliance be ascertained? If A promises to give £100,000 to B, a charity operating in Africa, and two weeks later B replenishes its store of emergency food and grain, does this provide unequivocal evidence of B's reliance on A's promise? What if the alleged reliance is negative in nature; for example, is a promise not to act in a particular way proven by lack of such action? Consequently, the test of reliance has found no overall favour in English law, although there are clearly elements of justifiable reliance which the courts recognize (see Estoppel, *infra*). Instead, it is the exchange model that has been adopted as the *dominant* test of enforceability and is referred to as the doctrine of consideration (with the one notable exception being an agreement under seal which need not be supported by consideration). This '*exchange of values*', with its overtones of profitable contracts being negotiated in a free-market economy, became a cornerstone of nineteenth-century *laissez-faire* ideals.

Types: Consideration is said to be *executory* when it is present in an exchange of promises and *executed* when it is a promise in return for an act. With either type, the essence of bargain is demonstrated by two distinct rules. First, consideration must move from the promisee, meaning that a party must provide consideration if he is to sue on a promise (see *Tweddle v Atkinson* (1861) 1 B & S 393). Note, however, that the Law Commission, in its 1996 Report on Privity of Contract (Law Com. No. 242, 1996, Cm 3329), interpreted the decision in *Tweddle* as simply demonstrating that consideration must be provided by the main contracting parties in order to support the exchange of promises, but did not require the third party to furnish *additional* consideration (see now **Contracts (Rights of Third Parties) Act 1999**). Secondly, consideration cannot be *past*, referring to those situations where a promise follows a completed act. For example, if B rescued A from a car accident, without any prior encouragement, and A later promised to reward B for his bravery, this promise would be unenforceable as A's promise was made *after* B had acted, rather than *in advance of B's rescue* (see *Eastwood v Kenyon* (1840) 11 A & E 438; *Roscorla v Thomas* (1842) 3 QB 234; *Re McArdle* [1951] Ch 669). It is often said that an exception to this rule occurs where A, without a prior, *express* promise to pay, requests that B perform services for him and, on completion, promises to reward B (see *Lampleigh v Brathwait* (1615) Hob 105). The better view is, however, that the subsequent promise merely *quantifies* the amount owing to B, as payment is implicit in A's original request (see *Re Casey's Patents* [1892] 1 Ch 104). Certainly if the rule were otherwise many business arrangements would be unenforceable as an account is often only sent on completion of services rendered.

Adequacy of Consideration

The law does not seek to value the parties' exchange, or ensure that it is fair, provided that there is something promised or exchanged which amounts to consideration. Confusingly, this is expressed in the rule that consideration must be *sufficient* but need not be *adequate*, two words that are often used interchangeably in everyday language. This adage is best interpreted as meaning that the consideration furnished by both parties must have a recognizable *value in the eyes of the law* (sufficiency) but need not be of *equal* value (adequacy). This finds its clearest illustration in those bargains where the consideration is a mere token but is nevertheless regarded as adequate (see *Bainbridge v Firmstone* (1838) 8 A & E 743; *Haigh v Brooks* (1839) 10 A & E 309; *Thomas v Thomas* (1842) 2 QB 851; *De La Bere v Pearson* [1908] 1 KB 280; *Chappell & Co. Ltd v Nestlé Co. Ltd* [1960] AC 87). The rule allows gratuitous promises to become binding simply by the addition of a nominal consideration (a 'peppercorn bargain') but whilst this amounts to a tangible consideration, it is arguable that it is really evidence of serious intent.

Sufficiency of Consideration

However, there are certain actions, or promises thereof, which the courts do not recognize as containing any value 'in the eyes of the law'. For example, what value does A, the creditor, receive when he promises B, the debtor, that part-payment of an existing debt from B will extinguish the remainder of the debt? The orthodox view is that as B is under an existing obligation to perform the completed act, payment of only part of a debt is neither a *legal* detriment to him nor a legal benefit to A. Yet there may well be a *factual* benefit and detriment: B's part-payment may be more onerous to him than the risk of being sued by A, and the partial settlement may be more beneficial to A than receiving nothing. Similarly, where A promises to pay B more money in order to secure complete performance of an existing duty, A may prefer to incur this additional cost rather than suffer the *factual* inconvenience of finding somebody else to perform the said duty, while B might calculate that the *factual* detriment of performance is only outweighed by the promised additional payment. Nevertheless, in both sets of circumstances, the courts have traditionally concentrated upon the legal benefit/detriment accruing to the parties, as opposed to any factual one, thereby assuming the absence of consideration (compare *Stilk v Myrick* (1809) 2 Camp 317 and *Hartley v Ponsonby* (1857) 7 E & B 872, demonstrating the difference between *performing* an existing duty and *exceeding* that duty).

Similar reasoning was adopted by the House of Lords in *Foakes v Beer* (1884) 9 App Cas 605 where a debtor claimed that part-payment of an existing debt was binding upon the creditor once the latter had acknowledged extinction of that debt. It was held that the debtor would not be released as his performance had fallen short of the contractually specified level (see below for various exceptions to this principle).

However, other decisions have established that an agreement to perform an existing contractual duty for extra payment will be enforceable *provided* that there is no duress and the new arrangement results in a factual benefit, or obviates a disbenefit (see *Williams v Roffey Bros & Nicholls (Contractors) Ltd* [1990] 2 WLR 1153). Equally, in the seminal decision of *Central London Property Trust Ltd v High Trees House Ltd* [1947] KB 130 (see later) the rules of Equity were used to limit the unreasonable withdrawal of a promise to modify an existing contract (i.e. to pay a reduced rent) even though no consideration was given in return for the promise.

The present rules of sufficiency of consideration can therefore be distilled into the following propositions:

(a) *Performance of an existing public duty* does not constitute sufficient consideration for any additional payment unless the promisee has agreed to exceed that duty. See *Collins v Godefroy* (1831) 1 B & Ad 950 and *England v Davidson* (1840) 11 Ad & E 856 for the effect of performing an existing duty, and *Glasbrook Brothers Ltd v Glamorgan County Council* [1925] AC 270, *Ward v Byham* [1956] 1 WLR 496, and *Harris v Sheffield United FC Ltd* [1988] QB 77 for the effect of exceeding that duty.

(b) *Performance of an existing contractual duty* does not normally constitute sufficient consideration for any additional payment, unless the promisee has agreed to exceed that duty (compare *Stilk v Myrick* (1809) 2 Camp 317 and *Hartley v Ponsonby* (1857) LR 3 CP 47—see also (d) below).

(c) *Third party consideration*: If A and B are contractually bound and C promises A an extra amount if A will simply perform his contract with B, a court will allow A to enforce payment against C. It would seem that by accepting C's promise A gives up any right to vary his contract with B (see *Shadwell v Shadwell* (1860) 9 CB (NS) 159; *Scotson v Pegg* (1861) 6 H & N 295; *New Zealand Shipping Co. Ltd v AM Satterthwaite & Co. Ltd (The Eurymedon)* [1975] AC 154; *Pao On v Lau Yiu Long* [1980] AC 614).

(d) *Practical benefit from performance of an existing duty*: In *Williams v Roffey Bros & Nicholls (Contractors) Ltd* [1990] 2 WLR 1153 the Court of Appeal held that performing an existing duty (e.g. in exchange for additional payment) which results in the promisor receiving a *practical benefit* (and/or obviating a disbenefit) constitutes sufficient consideration. Note that the *Roffey* principle will not apply if the contract modification resulted from the promisee applying some form of economic duress.

(e) *Where the parties agree to rescind an existing agreement* and replace it by a new agreement, the consideration for the rescission agreement is represented by the parties' mutual surrender of their rights under the old agreement. This clearly places further limitations upon *Stilk v Myrick*, although it is essential that *both* parties had duties under the rescinded agreement yet to be fully performed (see *Compagnie Noga D'Importation et D'Exportation SA v Abacha (No. 2)* [2003] EWCA Civ 1100; [2003] 2 All ER (Comm) 915).

(f) *In principle, the part-payment of a debt is insufficient consideration* (see *Pinnel's Case* (1602) 5 Co Rep 117a; *Foakes v Beer* (1884) 9 App Cas 605; *D & C Builders Ltd v Rees* [1966] 2 QB 617). This principle was re-affirmed in *Re Selectmove Ltd* by the Court of Appeal's refusal to extend the reasoning of *Williams v Roffey* to cases involving the part-payment of debts (but see below for exceptions).

(g) *The part-payment of debt principle is subject to numerous exceptions*, resulting from the courts' refusal to enquire into the adequacy of the parties' respective contributions. These exceptions require the agreement of the creditor to the part-payment extinguishing the original debt: (i) compromise of an existing debt which has been either disputed in good faith by the debtor (see *Re Warren* (1884) 53 LJ Ch 1016) or represents an unliquidated sum (see *Ibberson v Neck* (1886) 2 TLR 427), (ii) part-payment at an earlier date (see *Pinnel's Case, supra*) or place (see *Vanbergen v St. Edmund's Properties Ltd* [1933] 2 KB 233), (iii) part-payment plus the delivery of a chattel, or 'payment' by chattel alone (see *Pinnel's Case*), (iv) part-payment by a third party (see *Welby v Drake* (1825) 1 C & P 557—debtor's father paid half of debt in full satisfaction of claim), and (v) a composition agreement with creditors, i.e. all creditors agree to accept less (see *Good v Cheesman* (1831) 2 B & Ad 328). These exceptions rightly weaken a rule that has often been criticized as arbitrary and divorced from commercial reality (see *Couldery v Bartrum* (1881) 19 Ch D 394).

Promissory Estoppel

The principle of estoppel is that if one party has induced another to act in a certain way he may subsequently be prevented from denying that fact and is thus said to be estopped. A variation of a contract normally requires consideration, but in those situations where a variation benefits one party only, Equity focuses upon the conduct of the party granting the forbearance (i.e. the promise to modify the contract) and its effect on the other party. It may therefore be inequitable for A to revoke a serious promise made to B, particularly where B has acted upon it to his detriment (see *Hughes v Metropolitan Ry* (1877) 2 App Cas 439; *Central London Property Trust Ltd v High Trees House Ltd* [1947] KB 130).

In identifying promissory estoppel within an exam question, the following questions require affirmative answers:

(a) Do the parties have an existing contractual relationship or, possibly, any relationship which gives rise to rights and duties?

(b) Has there been a clear and unequivocal promise by words or conduct that existing rights will not be enforced (see *Scandinavian Trading Tanker Co. AB v Flota Petrolera Ecuatoriana (The Scaptrade)* [1983] QB 529)?

(c) Has the promisee relied upon the promise? Originally, reliance involved some element of *detriment*, or, at the very least, an 'alteration of position' (see, generally, *Ajayi v RT Briscoe (Nigeria) Ltd* [1964] 1 WLR 1326), but nowadays it appears that the promisee must simply 'act upon the promise' (see *Alan (WJ) & Co. Ltd v El Nasr Export & Import Co.* [1972] 2 QB 189; *Société Italo-Belge pour le Commerce et l'Industrie v Palm & Vegetable Oils (Malaysia) Sdn Bhd (The Post Chaser)* [1981] 2 Lloyd's Rep 695; and the interesting analysis of Arden LJ in *Collier v P & MJ Wright (Holdings) Ltd* [2007] EWCA Civ 1329, [2008] 1 WLR 643).

(d) Is it inequitable for the promisor to revoke his promise (see *D & C Builders Ltd v Rees* [1966] 2 QB 617; *The Post Chaser, supra*; *Re Selectmove Ltd* [1995] 1 WLR 474)? The points raised in (c) and (d) are often inextricably linked: (i) the greater the reliance on the promise, the more inequitable it will be to permit its revocation, and (ii) reliance that is beneficial to the promisee may prove particularly detrimental if revocation of the promise is permitted.

(e) Is the promisee using the doctrine as a shield rather than a sword? Estoppel is defensive in nature in that the promisee's reliance on a gratuitous promise excuses his non-performance of an existing obligation rather than creating new causes of action (see *Combe v Combe* [1951] 2 KB 215), otherwise, the requirement of consideration would be abolished (see *Brikom Investments Ltd v Carr* [1979] QB 467).

If an estoppel has been established what are its effects? Normally it will suspend rights which can be revived by giving reasonable notice (see *Tool Metal Manufacturing Co. Ltd v Tungsten Electric Co. Ltd* [1955] 1 WLR 761) but it can extinguish rights if it is impossible for the promisee to resume his position (see *Birmingham & District Land Co. v L & NW Ry* (1888) 40 Ch D 268) or if it is inequitable to insist that he should so resume it (e.g. *Nippon Yusen Kaisha v Pacifica Navegacion SA (The Ion)* [1980] 2 Lloyd's Rep 245).

The following diagram may prove helpful in demonstrating the potential enforceability of promises to modify existing contracts.

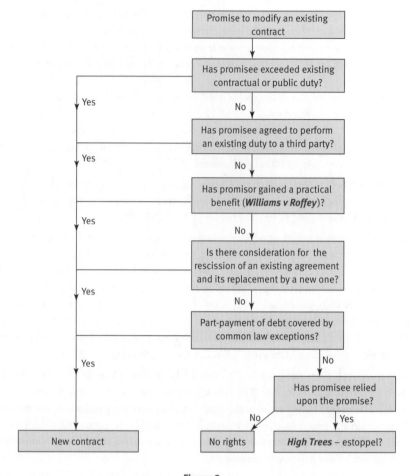

Figure 2

Question 1

Gayle is a successful IT consultant who is about to launch a new business, RoboNut, that specializes in the sale and supply of 'intelligent industrial robots' to the manufacturing sector. She hires a stand at the prestigious World Industrial Technology Exhibition (WITE), London, in order to demonstrate the range and capabilities of these robots.

Exprop contracts with Gayle to erect the exhibition stand for £10,000. Moreover, Tech Weekly, a new London-based publication that is seeking to raise its profile amongst the business community, agrees to advertise the presence of RoboNut's exhibition stand for free.

Gayle is determined that her WITE exhibition stand projects the right image so she pays Exprop an extra £2,000 to make sure 'it has a wow factor'. Moreover, she promises to pay

£1,000 to Securefest, a company employed by WITE to provide security for the exhibition, if its employees can keep a 'watch' on her stand.

The RoboNut stand is a great success but Gayle refuses to pay Exprop the extra £2,000, nor Securefest its £1,000. Tech Weekly is being pursued by some creditors so Gayle promises to pay it £3,000 for the advertising of her exhibition stand. However, she later withdraws her promise to Tech Weekly after looking at the state of her private finances, despite Tech Weekly having already incurred additional costs in anticipation of receiving that money.

Discuss the legal position of all the parties involved.

Commentary

This question covers most of the issues thrown up by the rules of consideration, in particular highlighting the problems caused by the parties changing their existing contractual arrangements once performance has begun. As with some of the problem questions in offer and acceptance, where a number of parties are involved in a complex factual scenario, the use of sub-headings to separate out the various relationships seems justified.

Answer plan

- Was Exprop performing its existing contractual duty to Gayle or did it furnish additional consideration for the promised £2,000?
- Was Securefest performing its duty to the WITE organizers in maintaining a close eye on Gayle's stand? If so, did it provide consideration for the £1,000 promised by Gayle?
- Was Gayle's promise to compensate Tech Weekly for its advertising costs an example of past consideration in that the promise was made after the journal had performed its services, or do the conditions in *Lampleigh v Brathwait* and *Re Casey's Patents* apply?
- Finally, is Gayle estopped from withdrawing her promise to pay Tech Weekly the £3,000?

Suggested answer

This question concerns sufficiency of consideration, past consideration, third party consideration, and promissory estoppel. It is proposed to divide the question in accordance with the various contracts that have been entered into.

Gayle (G) v Exprop (E)

G and E clearly entered into an enforceable contract: intention to create legal relations will be presumed where two businesses have reached an agreement, whilst E's promise to pay G £10,000, in return for the erection of the stand, clearly constitutes consideration on both sides. Does this enable E to claim the additional £2,000?

Courts do not normally enquire into the adequacy of the consideration furnished by either party provided there is clear evidence that both have contributed *something of value in the eyes of the law* to their bargain. However, where A performs an existing contractual duty to B it is normally assumed this does not represent sufficient consideration for any additional payment from B, particularly as A has not suffered any further legal detriment in so acting. For example, in *Stilk v Myrick (1809) 2 Camp 317*, some crew members deserted during a voyage so the captain promised to share their wages amongst the remaining crew if they stayed on board until they reached their final destination. It was held that the sailors had not provided additional consideration as they were merely performing their existing contractual duty (NB there was also a public policy dimension to *Stilk* in that it discouraged HM sailors from threatening mutiny in order to increase their wages—see the alternative report of *Stilk* by Espinasse, (1809) 6 Esp 129). However, if the promisee *exceeds* his contractual duty (or promises to do so) a court will treat this as sufficient consideration for an additional payment. In *Hartley v Ponsonby* (1857) 7 E & B 872 the scale of desertion by the crew was so great (36 reduced to 19) that it became dangerous to continue the voyage. This freed the sailors from their existing contractual commitments and enabled them to negotiate a new contract with increased remuneration. In our facts it is unclear whether E has exceeded its existing contractual duty. In one sense E is simply performing an existing contractual duty in erecting the exhibition stand, but if it incurs extra costs beyond those itemized within the contract and/or exceeds the level of performance stipulated (in order to give the stand a 'wow factor'), it will be entitled to claim the additional £2,000.

Assuming E fails on the above point, what other options might it pursue? More recent case law has suggested that if E (the promisee) has incurred a *factual* detriment and G (the promisor) has obtained a factual benefit, enforcement of the bargain is acceptable in that it is acknowledging this commercial reality and the underlying intentions of the parties (an approach originally proposed by Lord Denning in dealing with the performance of existing *public duties*—see *Ward v Byham* [1956] 1 WLR 496; *Williams v Williams* [1957] 1 WLR 148). For example, in *Williams v Roffey Bros & Nicholls (Contractors) Ltd* [1991] 1 QB 1, the defendant building contractors were refurbishing a block of flats. The carpentry work was sub-contracted to the plaintiff who subsequently encountered financial difficulties and was unable to complete the work. The defendants offered the plaintiff an additional £10,000 to complete the work on time, thereby potentially avoiding payment of any liquidated damages for late completion of the overall contract or the need to hire alternative carpenters. As there was no evidence of economic duress the Court of Appeal concluded that the defendants had obtained a factual benefit from the arrangement, making payment of the additional £10,000 enforceable. In our problem, three possible conclusions emerge: (i) applying *Roffey* might suggest that G has secured a factual benefit from taking possession of an exhibition stand that matches her enhanced expectations, even though it falls within the original specification of the original contract (i.e. E has not exceeded its contractual duties). If so, her promise to pay an additional £2,000 may be enforceable; (ii) alternatively, if the exhibition stand conforms to the original contract and G secures no other factual benefit (e.g. early completion) E will be unable to claim the extra money; or (iii) if the stand exceeds the contract specification G will have secured a legal benefit, entitling E to rely on *Hartley v Ponsonby* and claim the extra money (see previously). The final decision will therefore depend on the court's interpretation of the actual wording used in the contract to describe the exact features of the desired exhibition stand.

Gayle (G) v Securefest (S)

When G promises to pay S £1,000 for taking extra precautions over the security of her exhibition stand she is, in effect, paying S to perform an existing contractual duty that it owes to WITE (a third party). Has S furnished sufficient consideration to support this separate contract? Surprisingly the answer is yes. Assuming the court decides that the 'agreement' between G and S was sufficiently clear and intended to be legally binding, it will almost certainly follow the decisions in *New Zealand Shipping Co. Ltd v AM Satterthwaite & Co. Ltd (The Eurymedon)* [1975] AC 154 and *Pao On v Lau Yiu Long* [1980] AC 614 and find the presence of consideration: S has suffered a detriment by making itself potentially liable to two different parties if it fails to perform its security duties and G has secured a benefit by being able to sue S directly. On this basis G must pay S the £1,000.

Gayle (G) v Tech Weekly (TW)

The doctrine of consideration demands a contemporaneous exchange of consideration by the parties; thus, where one party performs an act constituting consideration *before* any promise to pay for it has been given, the consideration is said to be 'past' and unenforceable (see *Roscorla v Thomas* (1842) 3 QB 234—a promise that a horse was 'sound' *after* it had been sold was treated as past consideration). In our facts G promised to pay TW *after* it had advertised her exhibition stand. However, there is one major exception to the above rule, the relevant conditions being set out in *Lampleigh v Brathwait* (1615) Hob 105 and *Re Casey's Patents* [1892] 1 Ch 104. First, the promisor must have requested the promisee to perform the act. Secondly, it must reasonably be assumed that the promisee would be remunerated. Finally, the payment must have been legally enforceable had it been promised in advance. If these three conditions apply, the subsequent promise becomes enforceable. Unfortunately, on this basis TW is unlikely to succeed as it offered to perform the act (i.e. advertise G's stand) rather than being asked by G, and TW explicitly offered to act without payment, thereby undermining any argument that it expected to be remunerated.

TW's alternative argument is that G is estopped from withdrawing her promise of payment. The decision in *Central London Property Trust Ltd v High Trees*

House [1947] KB 130 suggests that the promise which forms the basis of an estoppel must be: (i) clear and intended to be binding, (ii) not inequitably extracted by the promisee, (iii) acted upon by the promisee, (iv) relate to the modification of an existing contract, and (v) not of itself form a cause of action. The first three conditions are easily met: G's promise is very specific, there is no suggestion that TW has unfairly forced G to pay this money, and TW 'acts upon' the promise by incurring additional expense in anticipation of receiving the money.

The next condition requires the presence of an initial, legally binding contract that the promisor was promising to modify. In our facts TW advertised G's exhibition standing for free, suggesting that G provided no consideration (and therefore no contract existed). However, when courts consider sufficiency of consideration by both parties they tend to adopt a reasonably flexible approach to the matter. Consider *De La Bere v Pearson* [1908] 1 KB 280 where the defendant owners of a newspaper invited readers to submit letters requiring the advice of a financial expert. The plaintiff sent in a question that was printed, received some advice, acted upon said advice, and lost money as a consequence. The court found that there was sufficient consideration to support a contract. The plaintiff had allowed his letter to be published, thereby receiving the benefit of some advice. The defendant had benefited from being able to print readers' letters, which might have improved the circulation of its newspaper. Applying this reasoning to our facts suggests a similar outcome. G received consideration via the free publicity of her exhibition stand whilst TW potentially raised its profile amongst potential advertisers and thereby gained an important commercial advantage. If a contract did exist, G's subsequent promise of payment is clearly modifying her *existing contract* with TW.

Finally, promissory estoppel is not a principal cause of action but is primarily a defensive measure. A party cannot be sued for estoppel (see *Combe v Combe* [1951] 2 KB 215 which referred to estoppel as 'as a shield, not a sword'). Thus, if G had paid TW the £3,000 and thereupon sought to recover the money (i.e. revoke her promise) TW might use estoppel as a means of defending that action, at least temporarily. However, as G never paid the £3,000, TW cannot use estoppel to compel G to pay the money (as this would be tantamount to using estoppel as cause of action), thus it would seem TW will be unable to demand payment of the £3,000.

Question 2

Cheatham & Steele wish to expand the productivity and efficiency of their manufacturing processes. They borrow £100,000 from Grabbit and Runne, merchant bankers. The agreed period of the loan is five years: £20,000 to be repaid each year together with interest at 40% on the capital outstanding.

After repayment of £20,000 with interest, Cheatham & Steele suffer a lengthy industrial dispute which makes it impossible for them to pay the next £20,000 due. The difficulties of Cheatham & Steele are so acute that there is a possibility that the company may become insolvent. Cheatham & Steele draw the attention of Grabbit & Runne to this and the consequential risk to their unsecured loan. With this in mind, Grabbit & Runne agree to the postponement for a year of payment of the £20,000 due and the waiver of all interest payable.

However, four months later, Grabbit & Runne also experience severe financial problems and request Cheatham & Steele to pay the outstanding instalment and interest owing without further delay. Cheatham & Steele refuse to do this and suggest that only £10,000 of the loan could be paid but that this would cause them severe hardship in the circumstances.

Advise Grabbit & Runne.

Commentary

This problem relates to promissory or equitable estoppel. Students commonly find estoppel perplexing. This may be because having just mastered an arcane but somewhat mechanistic world of offer and acceptance, they have to contend with metaphysical notions of reliance and inequity. In fact, estoppel is the simplest of notions in the abstract but more difficult to apply in reality. When has B relied on A's promise? Why is it inequitable for A to revoke his promise? It is this balance of interests which students must make in order to understand estoppel and answer a question on this topic satisfactorily. A mechanical reiteration of the requirements of estoppel with little or no application to the problem will result in a poor mark.

Throughout the law, there is no substitute for reading the primary materials but this is particularly true here. Many of the leading decisions contain judgments by Lord Denning which should be read for their chronological symmetry and clarity of exposition.

Answer plan

- Cheatham & Steele (C&S) provide no consideration for the variation of the contract of loan which is agreed with the lenders, Grabbit & Runne (G&R). May G&R therefore demand the repayment of the loan in accordance with the contract terms or, alternatively, might they be estopped from doing so?

- What is meant by the principle of promissory estoppel and what are the requirements of this doctrine?

- Have C&S relied on the promise of G&R regarding the variation of the contract's terms?

- Is it inequitable for G&R to revoke that promise?

- Is the effect of the estoppel to suspend the rights under the original contract which can thus be revived if G&R give reasonable notice to C&S or, alternatively, might those rights be extinguished?

Suggested answer

Cheatham & Steele (C&S) clearly have a contract with Grabbit & Runne (G&R) which is varied so as to confer a benefit on C&S only. Thus C&S provide no consideration to G&R for the postponement of the loan instalment and, although there might be some factual benefit to G&R in that their unsecured loan is still subsisting, there is no legal benefit as they have a pre-existing contractual right to full and prompt payment. With payment of debts the rule is unequivocal that a creditor is not bound by a promise to accept a partial payment in full settlement and may claim the remainder from his debtor (see *Pinnel's Case* (1602) 5 Co Rep 117a; *Foakes v Beer* (1884) 9 App Cas 605). The rule has been much criticized as being divorced from commercial reality (see *Couldery v Bartrum* (1881) 19 Ch D 394) but, although numerous exceptions surround it, its core remains intact and was reaffirmed in *Re Selectmove Ltd* [1995] 1 WLR 474. However, the unbending rigour of *Pinnel's Case* is mitigated by principles of promissory estoppel.

The basic notion of estoppel, which permeates many areas of the law, is that A makes certain representations or promises to B upon which B relies or acts in some way. Should A wish to change his mind and deny any efficacy to the representations, he may be prevented or estopped from doing so. In *Central London Property Trust Ltd v High Trees House Ltd* [1947] KB 130, Denning J introduced the notion of promissory estoppel to the law of contract by way of the equitable principles in *Hughes v Metropolitan Ry* (1877) 2 App Cas 439. In *High Trees*, the plaintiffs leased a block of flats to the defendants in 1937 at a ground rent of £2,500 per annum but in 1940 agreed to reduce this rent by half because few of the flats were let in the wartime conditions. At the start of 1945 most of the flats were let again but the defendants were still paying the reduced rent. Accordingly, the plaintiffs demanded the full rent, testing their claim by suing for the last two quarters of 1945. It was held that the claim should succeed as the agreement of 1940 was only intended as a temporary arrangement for wartime conditions and it had ceased to operate early in 1945. Most importantly, Denning J also said that, although the defendants had provided no consideration for the plaintiffs' promise to reduce the rent, the plaintiffs could not have recovered the full rent for the period covered by the 1940 agreement. The plaintiffs would thus be estopped from denying the force of the 1940 agreement where the promise was 'intended to be binding, intended to be acted on and in fact acted on' (*per* Denning J).

The requirements for promissory estoppel to operate are as follows: (i) the parties must have a legal relationship which gives rise to rights and duties between them. C&S and G&R have a contractual relationship which is the paradigm of this requirement; (ii) there must be a promise or representation that the promisor will not insist on his strict legal rights. This promise must be clear and unequivocal but it can be implied or made by conduct (e.g. *Hughes v Metropolitan Ry*) and need not be express. In the problem, this requirement is satisfied in an unambigu-ous, express promise; (iii) unlike proprietary estoppel, the *High Trees* principle does not ground a cause of action but is defensive in nature only. In *Combe v Combe* [1951] 2 KB 215, it was established that promissory estoppel may be used 'as a shield but not a sword' (*per* Birkett LJ) but in the problem C&S are only defending themselves and may thus plead the equitable principle; and finally, (iv) the promisee must have relied or acted upon the representation in some way and it must be inequitable for the promisor to revoke his promise.

Regarding reliance and equity, there is no longer a need for the promisee to have acted to his detriment (see *High Trees* where the promisee was clearly not worse off as a result of the promised reduction in rent). Lord Denning consistently argued (see *WJ Alan & Co. Ltd v El Nasr Export & Import Co.* [1972] 2 QB 189; *Brikom Investments Ltd v Carr* [1979] QB 467) that repudiation of the promise was, in itself, inequitable. In *Post Chaser, The* [1981] 2 Lloyd's Rep 695, Robert Goff J emphasized that a promisor will not be allowed to enforce his original contractual rights 'where it would be inequitable having regard to the dealings which have thus taken place between the parties', and that even if a promisee *benefited* from the promise it might still be inequitable to revoke. Consequently the court held that it was not inequitable to revoke the promise two days after it had been made because, as a question of fact, the promisee had not suffered prejudicially in so short a period of time. In our problem, C&S clearly benefit immediately from the postponed pay-ment but suffer hardship when it is revoked, suggesting that such revocation might be inequitable. Conversely, G&R can point to their own dire financial position as a valid reason to retract the promise, leaving the court to balance G&R's alleged ability to withdraw against C&S's plea of estoppel. In concluding, it is worth not-ing that the need to act equitably applies to the promisee as well as the promisor. Should the promisee extract the promise by duress it will not be inequitable for the promisor to resile. The promisee's conduct must therefore be blameless if he is to be afforded equitable protection for 'he who comes to equity must come with clean hands'. In *D & C Builders Ltd v Rees* [1966] 2 QB 617, the plaintiffs agreed to accept £300 from the defendant in settlement of £482 principally because of their desperate financial position, there being evidence that the defendant knew of this and took advantage of it in securing the plaintiffs' promise. Accordingly, it was not inequitable for the plaintiffs to withdraw the promise. In our facts there is no clear evidence of duress. Although C&S 'draw the attention of G&R' to their financial position and the possible risk to G&R's loan, this is unlikely to be viewed unfavour-ably by the court assuming they were telling the truth.

The final question raised by the problem is the effect of the *High Trees* doctrine on the obligations owed by the parties. It is usually said that promissory estoppel suspends rights rather than extinguishing them and that, accordingly, the promi-sor may revive his normal rights provided that he gives reasonable notice to the promisee of his intention to do so—as in *Tool Metal Manufacturing Co. Ltd v Tungsten Electric Co. Ltd* [1955] 1 WLR 761. The suspensive nature of the doctrine can be seen in the *High Trees* case itself but it may have an extinctive effect if it is impossible for the promisee to return to the previous position and perform the original obligation, as in *Birmingham & District Land Co. v L & NW Ry* (1888) 40 Ch D 268. Indeed, there is authority that the doctrine may be extinctive, even though such performance is not impossible, if it would be inequitable to revoke the promise. In *Collier v P & MJ Wright (Holdings) Ltd* [2007] EWCA Civ 1329, [2008] 1 WLR 643, the majority of the Court of Appeal was controversially prepared to argue that a promise to accept part-payment of a debt in full satisfaction of the whole debt created a *permanent* estoppel, as reviving the remainder of the debt would invariably have been inequitable for the promise in the circumstances. Nevertheless, if the court decides that any estoppel is only suspensive it is not entirely clear what effect this might have on a continuing obligation such as a payment of rent or a debt in instalments. If there is an agreed reduction in the debt coupled with a postponement, on expiry of the notice can the promisor claim the full amount for the future only or is he entitled to future payments and the balance of those which fell due during the period of postponement (in *High Trees* the former solution was preferred in the circumstances)? Much depends on the intentions of the parties and it would appear that in the problem there is only an agreed postponement of time with an intended revival of full rights on its expiry but it is arguable that the right to interest on one year's payment might be extinguished.

In conclusion, the court must balance the equities of the parties, i.e. deferment of payment against insistence on an immediate reinstatement of existing contractual rights. This balance can normally be achieved by requiring the promisor to give reasonable notice before his rights can revive, thereby reconciling the rule in *Foakes v Beer* with the doctrine of estoppel in that the creditor's rights are not extinguished but merely suspended. However, the preliminary decision in *Collier* suggests that certain judges are now prepared to go further by, in effect, using promissory estoppel as another 'common law' exception to *Foakes*.

Question 3

Consideration is often a mere fiction devised to make a promise enforceable and, as such, serves little purpose. It would be advantageous to abolish consideration and leave the more satisfactory requirement of intention to create legal relations as the test of an agreement's enforceability.

Discuss.

Commentary

In order to answer such an essay question well, it is imperative that students *think* about the quotation and *discuss* it. This appears to state the obvious but all too often students take such a question as a *carte blanche* to reiterate all they know about consideration. Examiners are very familiar with a regurgitation of case law followed by the trite conclusion 'thus it can be seen that it would/would not be advantageous to abolish consideration'. The 'would/would not' are often used interchangeably with no difference in the essay's content. Moreover, students proliferate examination myths (e.g. the essay title must be agreed/disagreed with) when, in fact, the examiner looks for an answer which shows that its author can *think*, *criticize* and reach *sensible conclusions*.

Answer plan

- What rules *could* a legal system adopt as tests for the enforceability of agreements?
- What is meant by the doctrine of consideration in English law and what is the test of enforceability demanded by this doctrine?
- Are there any illogicalities in the principles of consideration and any rules which should be amended or abrogated?
- Would it be more logical to substitute intention to create legal relations as the sole test for an agreement's enforceability?
- What difficulties might be encountered if intent was the sole test of enforceability?
- Are there signs that the common law is beginning to place greater emphasis on intent in contract formation?

Suggested answer

Offer, acceptance, and certainty are the requirements which prescribe the skeletal structure of a contract's formation while consideration and intent relate to its body and substance. Any legal system may adopt one of a variety of options as a requirement for the enforceability of contracts. First, in order to be enforceable, all contracts might require a degree of form such as writing or a deed. Such a rule undeniably provides the requisite degree of certainty, deters fraud, and embodies as a necessity that the parties intend legal relations but it would be virtually impossible to insist upon form for *all* contracts in the twenty-first century. Form is demanded in exceptional cases, most importantly that contracts for the sale of land must be in writing and that strict formalities are sometimes necessary where the potential exists for one party to abuse the other's inexperience and lack of bargaining power, e.g. hire-purchase and consumer credit. At the other extreme, it is theoretically possible to make *all* agreements enforceable but this notion is as untenable and impractical as the opposite rule which might stipulate a form for all contracts. Other options might look to the seriousness of intent alone or evidence of reliance on the promise or a combination of both. If A makes a serious promise to B upon which it can reasonably be assumed that B will rely, possibly to his detriment, there are clearly good grounds both morally and legally to enforce A's promise. In principle, many European countries adopt the stance that all lawful and serious agreements are contracts. On the other hand, English law uses consideration as its test for a contract's enforcement and, in so doing, is said to look for a bargain or exchange between the parties. The difference of approach between the English and European systems is traceable to historical development: the remedy of *assumpsit* in English law was based upon commercial needs and the element of bargain, whereas continental law developed in the middle ages and was much influenced by canon law and notions of good faith. However, in addition to consideration English law demands intention to create legal relations as a separate requirement for a contract's enforcement (see *Balfour v Balfour* [1919] 2 KB 571). Consequently, the role played by consideration must be ascertained and it should be asked whether intention might perform it better.

The dominant theory of consideration, at least in the nineteenth and twentieth centuries, was that of a bargained-for exchange between the parties: A must show that he has bought B's promise. But the overall influence of *laissez-faire* and freedom of contract meant that, although some consideration was necessary (i.e. sufficiency of consideration), it need not be adequate. Bargains might thus be grossly unequal, this being a pre-requisite of the free-market economy where capitalism was to flourish. In *Thomas v Thomas* (1842) 2 QB 851 for example, rent of £1 per annum was regarded as adequate consideration and it was emphasized in *Chappell & Co. Ltd v Nestlé Co. Ltd* [1960] AC 87 that a contracting party may stipulate for whatever consideration he desires, even if it is valueless. It is evident that consideration does not ensure fairness of bargains and it is even questionable whether such nominal bargains should be classified as bargains in the true sense of the word. The doctrine of consideration thus distinguishes onerous from gratuitous promises by stipulating for a token exchange. Furthermore, Professor Atiyah has argued (*Essays on Contract, Consideration: A Restatement*) that consideration was originally the *reason* for the enforcement of a promise, i.e. those considerations which were relevant in assessing this issue. It is a small step to see the token element in bargains as merely evidence that both parties take the agreement seriously, in other words, as evidence of intention to create legal relations. One advantage in the token agreement is that it provides concrete evidence of intention and it was, therefore, particularly apt for administering the less sophisticated contracts of earlier centuries. Viewed thus, consideration is simply one test of enforceability and serves the same function as intent. But does it perform the function as efficiently as intent? What would happen to the established problems within consideration if intent were the sole yardstick for enforcement?

The underlying purposes behind many of the orthodox rules of consideration are clear and yet they have become obscured by language such as 'sufficiency' and 'adequacy' which admit the uninitiated into the twisting doctrinal corridors. In relation to adequacy of consideration, it is arguable that in supporting the notion of unequal consideration the law may wrongly invest an act of duress with the legitimacy of a so-called 'bargain'. Adequacy of consideration assumes there is a valid consideration where A sells his Rolls Royce car to B for a token amount, but it is perhaps more reasonable to infer the opposite and consider that some duress or blackmail might lie at the root of such an arrangement. In sufficiency of consideration, the cases which establish that performance of an existing contractual duty are insufficient consideration (e.g. *Stilk v Myrick* (1809) **2 Camp 317**; *Hartley v Ponsonby* (1857) 7 E & B 872) are really concerned with protecting the creditor from the economic duress of his debtor. The rule is carried to a logical conclusion in *Foakes v Beer* (1884) **9 App Cas 605**, that part-payment of a debt cannot amount to consideration which would discharge the debtor, thereby leaving the creditor free to claim the amount owing. Similarly, the cases on performance of a public duty such as *Collins v Godefroy* (1831) **1 B & Ad 950** seek to curb possible extortion and corruption in public life. Consideration thus achieves a purpose but at what cost? The price paid is that, at its worst, the rigidity of consideration prevents the desirable contract, worthy of enforcement, being distinguished from the undesirable and unworthy. Thus *all* part-payments of debts are invalidated, even those where a freely-negotiated, sensible business arrangement is sought by both parties. It is extraordinary that the serious discharge of a debt by simple payment of a lesser amount cannot be accommodated within consideration. Certainly the decision in *Re Selectmove Ltd* [1995] **1 WLR 474**, strongly suggests that the decision in *Foakes v Beer* should be reconsidered by the House of Lords or abrogated by legislation.

At its best, consideration spawns innumerable technical exceptions to its rigid code, such as the rule that part-payment of money plus the addition of a chattel will discharge the debt. If intention to create legal relations became the sole test, the courts would be free to examine and enforce legitimate bargains and invalidate those that are illegitimate as having been exacted through improper threats or pressure. Whereas it was necessary to retain the rules of consideration in the absence of any coherent rules regarding economic duress, this necessity has disappeared with the evolution of that doctrine and an awareness that duress must be distinguished from commercial hard-bargaining.

Concern is often expressed that gifts would become enforceable as serious promises if intention were the sole test of a contract's enforceability. This seems to be an illusory concern. Intent would simply become the test for the formation of *contracts* and the parties would still not intend that most social and domestic gifts became binding contracts. However, the courts would have the ability to examine factors other than consideration in deciding whether promises should be enforceable. Much would depend on the nature of the promise and the promisee's response to it; the presence of writing or other formalities, for example, might be paramount. The promisee's direct reliance on the promise would also clearly assume significance in some situations.

Similarly, it is sometimes said that the rules of intention would have to be devised by the courts in order to cope with new problems but, again, this criticism is unfounded because intention is an existing and established requirement for the formation of a contract. Atiyah (above) argues that it is 'nonsensical' to talk of the abolition of consideration as the courts would 'have to begin all over again the task of deciding what promises are to be enforceable' but he concedes that there is 'something to be said' for beginning again whilst questioning whether intention would work any better as a formula. But why should intention not become the dominant requirement, with the essence of consideration being preserved but becoming subservient to intent? The courts would not have to 'begin again' but would be required merely to adjust the concept of a bargain within the more logical rules of intention. It is arguable that such an approach would simply modernize consideration whilst preserving its vitality. If the parties genuinely intended a token bargain it would not cease to be enforceable, yet a freely-negotiated part-payment of a debt, for example, would become enforceable provided there was intention manifested in the mutual benefits received.

The decision in *Williams v Roffey Bros & Nicholls (Contractors) Ltd* [1991] 1 QB 1 seems to point the way ahead. The defendants were building contractors who had a contract to refurbish a block of flats, the carpentry being subcontracted to the plaintiffs who were in financial difficulties and falling behind with the work. Delays might have resulted in the defendants paying liquidated damages under the refurbishment contract and, accordingly, they offered the plaintiffs an extra amount to complete the work on time. The Court of Appeal held that the plaintiffs should succeed, emphasizing that, although the plaintiffs were only performing their existing contractual duty, the defendants obtained a factual, real benefit and there was no duress tainting the bargain. *Stilk v Myrick* was thus subjugated to the rules of intent and the freely-negotiated variation was enforced by the court, while the essence of consideration was preserved by focusing on the benefit received. Perhaps the most significant fact is that the court could almost certainly have found consideration in the revised methods of payment which were introduced by the parties (e.g. a re-structuring of the payments' schedule). The decision might thus have accorded with established doctrine but the Court of Appeal deliberately chose the more radical route of its actual decision.

Williams v Roffey has the potential to revolutionize the rules of consideration or, alternatively, remain limited to variations of existing contracts where a realistic benefit is obtained. Although the court in *Re Selectmove Ltd* was constrained by the House of Lords' decision in *Foakes v Beer*, Peter Gibson LJ saw 'the force of the argument' in extending *Roffey* to part-payment of debts. Some critics have already argued that it is undesirable to substitute the vagaries of intent and duress for the certainty of consideration. This timid approach would presumably wish to see the opposite conclusion reached on the facts of *Roffey* but it is artificial and outmoded to justify such an outcome in the context of the modern law. Why is there such apprehension regarding intent in this context when, for example, criminal law is almost totally reliant on the concept? Indeed, the doctrine of promissory estoppel already functions well with the notions of intent, reliance, and inequity. It is therefore strongly arguable that intent should become the dominant principle in the formation of contract, with the essence of consideration preserved within a re-adjusted perspective of a freely-negotiated bargain.

Question 4

Build-High has a contract to build a new housing estate for Fields Trust. Each of the houses on the estate will have a conservatory and the erecting of these has been sub-contracted to Clearview. Work begins but within two months Clearview is unable to pay the wages of its employees owing to a cash flow problem. The employees refuse to continue working until this problem has been resolved. Build-High, who have been informed of this strike, are already concerned about the progress of Clearview in erecting the conservatories, especially as the Fields Trust recently disclosed that long delays might result in the loss of prospective buyers for the newly-built houses. Build-High enter into a new contract to pay Clearview an additional £10,000, thereby avoiding the inconvenience of finding an alternative builder to finish the conservatories. Clearview pays its employees all outstanding wages, and the employees return to work and complete two more conservatories. At this point Build-High refuse to pay the extra £10,000 as the Fields Trust has gone into liquidation.

Clearview's financial problems have been exacerbated by their dealings with another house builder, Lakeland. Clearview had been sub-contracted by Lakeland to build conservatories for a number of recently completed houses, at a total price of £100,000. Lakeland now admits that it is encountering difficulties in selling these houses and therefore proposes to reduce their sale prices. However, this requires its sub-contractors to agree to a reduction in their own previously agreed levels of remuneration. A number of the sub-contractors, including Clearview, agree to reduce their outstanding claims by 20%, thereby enabling Lakeland to reduce the sale price of its houses, a number of which are thereupon sold.

Discuss.

Commentary

This problem question covers two of the more difficult aspects of consideration; namely, performance of an existing contractual duty and promissory estoppel. In particular, the latter area refers to the more metaphysical issues of reliance and fair dealing which are important characteristics of Equity but are much less significant at common law. The question refers to two separate contractual arrangements, Clearview/Build-High and Clearview/Lakeland, and it therefore appears sensible to deal separately with each contractual relationship. However, you will need to make appropriate cross-references as there is a danger of undue repetition in answering such questions, particular as regards the relevance of promissory estoppel and the treatment of **Williams v Roffey Bros and Nicholls (Contractors) Ltd [1991] 1 QB 1**. Finally, you will find that the diagram located at the end of the introduction to this chapter will prove especially useful to you.

Answer plan

- Is the extra payment of £10,000 to Clearview intended to ensure the continued performance of existing contractual duties, or is Clearview now being expected to exceed these duties in any way?

- Alternatively, has Build-High gained some practical benefit from paying Clearview the extra money in order to secure continuing performance of its contractual duties?

- If a new contract was entered into, what is the consideration for increasing the contract price by £10,000, or can Clearview simply use the principles of promissory estoppel to compel payment of the additional £10,000?

- Does Clearview have a right to claim full payment of its debt with Lakeland? What is the effect of other contractors also agreeing to accept a lesser sum in full satisfaction of their own debts?

- Can Lakeland argue that Clearview received a practical benefit from the new arrangement? Will this make any difference?

- Is Clearview estopped from claiming the remainder of the unpaid debt?

Suggested answer

The old adage that 'Consideration must be sufficient but need not be adequate' has particular resonance in answering this question. Cases such as *Thomas v Thomas* (1842) 2 QB 851 demonstrate that the respective contributions of the parties may be grossly disproportionate, yet provided both have supplied value recognized by the law the contract will be enforced. The major obstacle to Clearview's success is that it does not appear to have done anything extra in return for the payment of £10,000 promised by Build-High, whilst Lakeland's challenge is to circumvent the part-payment rule established in *Pinnel's Case* (1602) 5 Co Rep 117a which drastically limits the ability to extinguish existing debts unless full payment has been made. If either party fails on these primary issues then recourse to the principle of promissory estoppel may offer the only alternative argument.

Clearview (C) v Build-High (B)
First, does C's performance of its existing duty (the erection of the conservatories) provide sufficient consideration for the additional £10,000 payment from B. The

decision in *Stilk v Myrick* (1809) 2 Camp 317, suggests that performance of a contractual duty must be exceeded if sufficient consideration is to be established for any additional payment (e.g. *Hartley v Ponsonby* (1857) 7 E & B 872). In our facts, did C agree to perform its contractual duties differently, or complete them earlier, or even use a different standard of materials? On the facts it appears not—C simply continued to perform its normal contractual duties and, therefore, appears unable to claim the additional sum of money.

However, C possesses a second argument based on *Williams v Roffey Bros and Nicholls (Contractors) Ltd* [1991] 1 QB 1, a case that primarily imposed some important limitations on the *Stilk v Myrick* principle. Aside from exceeding its duties, if C can show that B received a 'practical' benefit' (or obviated a recognizable disbenefit) from C's continuing to perform its existing contractual duty then any promise of additional payment by B may become enforceable. In *Roffey* it was held that the main contractor (operating similarly to B) had received the following practical benefits by promising to pay the plaintiffs an additional £10,000 in order to secure their continued performance of the contract: they had avoided the inconvenience of finding other carpenters to complete the work (and the possibility of being charged more), circumvented the possible enforcement by their employers of a penalty clause for late completion, and agreed a different method for paying the plaintiffs. On our facts only the first point appears relevant here—there is no suggestion that Fields Trust has an enforceable penalty clause which can be used against B for late completion, nor even that there is a set completion date beyond which damages for breach of contract may be obtainable. (NB the existence of a set completion date would certainly strengthen C's argument as timely performance by C would avoid any claim by Fields Trust against B for late completion.) Whether the avoidance of inconvenience is a sufficient 'practical benefit' for the decision in *Roffey* to be invoked must remain a moot point for the following reasons: (i) it is unclear whether the court in *Roffey* would have accepted that *each* of the benefits received by the main contractor was sufficient in its own right to demonstrate sufficient consideration or whether it was their totality that proved crucial, (ii) the facts of our question require further clarification as to whether B could be sued by Fields Trust for late completion (avoidance of the penalty clause in *Roffey* was probably the most influential factor), and (iii) there is always the possibility that C subjected B to some form of economic duress, thereby undermining any reliance upon *Roffey* and its requirement of a practical benefit (although this seems unlikely as, similar to *Roffey*, it was B who offered the additional payment, rather than responding to any demand from C).

Thirdly, did the parties formally rescind their original agreement and replace it with a new contract in which C would be paid more? In *Compagnie Noga D'Importation et D'Exportation SA v Abacha (No. 2)* [2003] EWCA Civ 1100; [2003] 2 All ER (Comm) 915, the Court of Appeal held that in such circumstances it is not the old agreement which compels the performance of any revised obligations but the new agreement. Consequently, the principle established in *Stilk v Myrick* is inapplicable if (i) the old agreement was rescinded, and (ii) either the rescission agreement was underpinned by consideration or the new agreement contained consideration. In our facts, point (ii) applies as both parties had further duties to perform under the original agreement (B was required to complete the conservatories and C to pay for them)—the mutual surrender by B and C of their rights to enforce the performance of each other's executory promises will constitute consideration. Moreover, the decision in *Compagnie Noga* also recognized that consideration can be provided not only by the mutual promises contained in a new agreement but also by the mutual release from the earlier agreement. Unfortunately, point (i) is more difficult to establish as the facts do not explicitly state whether the parties agreed to rescind the old agreement and replace it by a new agreement. If the *extra* payment is only signified by an *additional* agreement (or by the variation, rather than formal rescission, of the existing agreement) the above principle cannot be used.

Finally, if C fails on all of the above points, the only remaining argument is that B is estopped from revoking its promise to pay an additional £10,000. Following the decision in *Central London Property Trust Ltd v High Trees House Ltd* [1947] KB 130, C would need to establish that it had relied upon the payment to continue working, that it had not acted inequitably in obtaining B's promise (e.g. that the reason for the stoppage in erecting the conservatories was not misrepresented), that B's promise to pay was clear and intended to be binding, and that it was now too late to revoke the promise as some of the conservatories had been completed. Unfortunately for C, although these conditions are met, the courts have stressed that promissory estoppel cannot create entirely new rights (see *Combe v Combe* [1951] 2 KB 215); rather, it is a defensive measure to prevent inequitable conduct by the promisor. Consequently, C will be unable to rely upon estoppel to claim the £10,000 as this would be equivalent to *enforcing* the additional payment by B.

Clearview (C) v Lakeland (L)

The principal issue involves the part-payment of debt principle, as first established in *Pinnel's Case* (1602) 5 Co Rep 117a and subsequently confirmed by the House of Lords in *Foakes v Beer* (1884) 9 App Cas 605. In the latter case, the creditor had mistakenly thought that the debtor had repaid the whole of an outstanding debt in full. In fact, as it was a judgment debt, the debt had attracted additional interest which had not yet been repaid. The House of Lords ruled that a creditor is not bound by either a promise to accept a smaller sum or its actual payment by the debtor. Such a promise amounts to nothing more than a promise to perform or performance of *part* of an existing duty owed to the creditor, the debtor consequently providing no consideration. The position is thus similar to *Stilk v Myrick* (1809) 2 Camp 317 except that in part-payment of debts the debtor is seeking to *discharge* an existing obligation rather than offering extra payment for its *performance*. On this basis, it seems that C has a very strong argument for claiming an entitlement to the full contract price (i.e. a sum equivalent to the amount by which the debt had been reduced). However, there are a number of exceptions to the part-payment rule, such as part-payment at an earlier time than the due date, or part-payment plus delivery of a chattel (see *Couldery v Bartrum* (1881) 19 Ch D 394). One possible exception that might apply here is that of a 'composition agreement by creditors'. There is a suggestion that the creditors of L have agreed to reduce their debt claims against L. If all the creditors agreed with *each other*, and with L, they may well be bound by any ensuing debt-reduction arrangement (see *Good v Cheesman* (1831) 2 B & Ad 328). However, the evidence is ambiguous on this point as it is possible that L approached only some of its creditors (on an individual basis), rather than all of the creditors agreeing with each other to the debt reduction.

If C is not bound by any 'composition agreement', L's next argument would be that C derived a practical benefit from the agreed part-payment: surely if L sells more of its properties C will have a greater chance of recovering the majority of its outstanding debt rather than none at all? However, the Court of Appeal decision in *Re Selectmove* forestalled this line of enquiry by stressing that the decision in *Williams v Roffey* cannot be used to undermine the part-payment of debt principle accepted by the House of Lords in *Foakes v Beer*. Here again we see the inutility of this principle. As Lord Blackburn pointed out in *Foakes v Beer*, it is often more beneficial for the creditor to receive a part-payment than insist on his strict legal rights.

Consequently, L's final argument must be that C is estopped from recovering the full debt. Using the principle established in *High Trees*, L is able to show that C made a clear promise which was intended to modify an existing contract, that L relied upon C's promise to accept less (i.e. L reduced the sale prices of its properties), and that there is no evidence of inequitable dealing by L. The last point might cause some problems as there is a suggestion that L was unfairly pressurizing its various sub-contractors into subsidizing the proposed price reduction (see *South Caribbean Trading Ltd v Trafigura Beheer BV* [2004] EWHC 2676; [2005] 1 Lloyd's Rep 128 where an estoppel claim failed owing to the unfair pressure placed upon the promisor by the promisee). Nevertheless, if an estoppel is established, the court must decide whether it is of permanent or only limited duration. The normal principle is that estoppel is suspensory rather than extinctive, and that once the promisor (C) has given reasonable notice the original contract will once again be enforceable (e.g. *Tool Metal Manufacturing Co. Ltd v Tungsten Electric Co. Ltd* [1955] 1 WLR 761). The only exceptions to this are where the promisee (L) would find it impossible to resume its original position (e.g. *Birmingham & District Land Co. v L & NW Ry* (1888) 40 Ch D 268) or it would be inequitable to insist upon such resumption in the circumstances (e.g. *Nippon*

Yusen Kaisha v Pacifica Navegacion SA (The Ion) [1980] 2 Lloyd's Rep 245), in which case the promisor's original rights will be permanently extinguished. In our facts, L has already sold some properties at a discounted price and it therefore seems too late for C to withdraw its promise to accept part-payment from L. C's only possible counter-argument is to question whether the *High Trees* principle can be used to circumvent the House of Lords' decision in *Foakes v Beer*? Whilst the principle of promissory estoppel has been subsequently accepted by the House of Lords (e.g. *Tool Metal Manufacturing Co. Ltd v Tungsten Electric Co. Ltd* [1955] 1 WLR 761) it remains a moot point whether the principle can be relied upon to protect a straightforward part-payment of debt issue. There is, as yet, no definitive answer to this point, although the preliminary ruling in *Collier v P & MJ Wright (Holdings) Ltd* [2007] EWCA Civ 1329, [2008] 1 WLR 643 suggests a preparedness to employ estoppel in this way.

Further Reading

Case-notes

Central London Property Trust Ltd v High Trees House Ltd [1947] KB 130
Cheshire & Fifoot, 'Central London Property Trust Ltd v High Trees House Ltd' (1947) 63 LQR 283

Selectmove Ltd Re [1995] 1 WLR 474
Peel, 'Part Payment of Debt is No Consideration' (1994) 110 LQR 353

Williams v Roffey Bros & Nicholls (Contractors) Ltd [1991] 1 QB 1
Brown & Chandler, 'Consideration and Contract Modification' [1990] Conv 209
Coote, 'Consideration and Variations: A Different Solution' (2004) 120 LQR 19 (New Zealand approach)
Halson, 'Sailors, Sub-Contractors and Consideration' (1990) 106 LQR 183

Articles

Adams & Brownsword, 'Contract, Consideration and the Critical Path' (1990) 53 MLR 536

Bennion, 'Want of Consideration' (1958) 16 MLR 441

Cooke, 'Estoppel and the Protection of Expectations' (1997) 17 LS 258

Halson, 'The Offensive Limits of Promissory Estoppel' [1999] LMCLQ 257

Hooley, 'Consideration and the Existing Duty' [1991] JBL 19

O'Sullivan, 'In Defence of *Foakes v Beer*' (1996) 55 CLJ 219

4

Terms of the contract

Introduction

The terms of a contract define both its content and the scope of the parties' mutual rights and obligations. In a contract for the sale of goods, for example, the price of the goods, date of delivery, mode of payment, and requisite standard of quality which must be met are all likely to be contractual terms. As a breach of contract primarily involves breach of a term, two distinct levels of enquiry emerge: (i) the need to ascertain the precise terms of the contract and, (ii) the need to classify and thereby determine the relative importance of those terms.

There are four principal difficulties in ascertaining the terms of the contract. First, the parties' negotiations may have been particularly wide-ranging, and taken place over an extended period of time. Which, if any, of the promises and statements made during those negotiations should be treated as part of the concluded contract? Secondly, the *general* rule is that a contract need not adopt a particular form, so it can be a deed (specialty), in writing, recorded digitally/electronically, or simply involve an oral agreement (i.e. a parol contract). If the contract is embodied in a deed or wholly in writing, might evidence be adduced to establish that other oral statements were also terms or is the writing a final manifestation of intent? Thirdly, apart from the express terms upon which the parties have agreed, there may be *implied* terms derived from a variety of sources, including statute law, that might be automatically incorporated into the contract (e.g. **s. 14** of the **Sale of Goods Act 1979** (**SGA 1979**) prescribes the minimum standards of quality in a sale of goods contract). Fourthly, the contract may contain exclusion clauses that enable one party to exclude or limit an existing liability owed to the other. To what extent should special rules govern the incorporation of such onerous clauses in the contract or prohibit their use completely? Exclusion clauses, and general rules of incorporation, are considered separately in **Chapter 5**.

The rules regarding the ascertainment of terms originally demonstrated a rigid adherence to freedom of contract and the *implementation* of the parties' intentions. However, more recently, the imposition of a just solution through judicial and legislative interventionism is beginning to take hold.

Ascertainment of the Express Terms of the Contract

The first task is to distinguish terms of the contract from mere representations. A truthful representation (e.g. an honest opinion expressed by an amateur) is legally valueless but if it is factual and untrue it becomes a misrepresentation for which there are now potent remedies (see **Chapter 6** on misrepresentation). Differentiating a term from a mere representation involves ascertaining the *intention* of the maker of the statement (*Heilbut, Symons Co. v Buckleton* [1913] AC 30). Was the accuracy and truth of the statement clearly warranted or was it merely a legitimate 'puff' praising and enhancing the contract's subject matter? The test of intention gives the courts considerable latitude in answering this question. Whereas many of the earlier decisions reflected a *laissez-faire* attitude (e.g. *Heilbut*), more modern cases have increasingly used an objective test to ascertain the effect of the statement on the other party and whether reliance upon it was justified (see *Oscar Chess Ltd v Williams* [1957] 1 WLR 370; *Bentley (Dick) Productions Ltd v Harold Smith (Motors) Ltd* [1965] 1 WLR 623; *Esso Petroleum Co. Ltd v Mardon* [1976] QB 801). Although the cases are necessarily ambivalent, some clear guidance is possible.

Where an agreement is embodied in a deed or reduced to writing, a court will not allow parol (or other extrinsic) evidence to add to, vary, or contradict the writing (known as the *parol evidence rule*). This rule sought to implement the finality of the parties' intentions as expressed in their all-embracing written contract but it is now surrounded by so many exceptions that it has become subsumed within the overall test of intention. A written contract is therefore only one pointer, albeit an important one, to the parties' intent. In 1976, the Law Commission considered that the parol evidence rule might be abolished (WP No. 70) but the final report in 1986 decided that no reform was needed as the rule was not as troublesome and extensive as traditionally expounded (Law Com. No. 154, Cmnd 9700). Indeed, many of the exceptions are understandable when it is realized that their *raison d'être* was the need to avoid this technical and arbitrary rule (e.g. parol evidence can be relied upon to prove the *invalidity* of a contract as this does not *alter* its *content*).

Subject to the above, in seeking to implement the parties' intentions and decide whether a statement is a term or a mere representation, the courts will take into account the following: (a) the shorter the lapse of time between the making of the statement and the contract's formation, the more likely the statement will be treated as a term (see *Schawel v Reade* [1913] 2 IR 64; *Routledge v McKay* [1954] 1 WLR 615); (b) if the maker of the statement had specialist knowledge or was in a better position than the other party to verify the statement's accuracy it is more likely that the statement will be treated as a term (see *Harling v Eddy* [1951] 2 KB 739; *Oscar Chess Ltd v Williams Ltd supra*; *Bentley (Dick) Productions Ltd v Harold Smith (Motors) Ltd*); (c) if the importance of the statement's accuracy was a significant factor in finalizing the contract it will normally be treated as a term (see *Bannerman v White* (1861) 10 CB (NS) 844, *Esso Petroleum Co. Ltd v Mardon supra*); (d) if the statement was omitted in a later, formal written contract it is less likely to be treated as a term (see *Gilchester Properties Ltd v Gomm* [1948] 1 All ER 493; *Birch v Paramount Estates* (1956) 16 EG 396) and, (e) the relatively modern concept of 'collateral contracts' can be used to cloak an oral statement with contractual force. This last possibility arises where a court identifies both a *primary* and *secondary* collateral contract, the consideration for the latter being entry into the primary contract, e.g. 'If you take a lease of this property, I will confirm that the drains are sound'. In *Strongman (1945) Ltd v Sincock* [1955] 2 QB 525, the ambit of the collateral contract was widened even further: an enforceable collateral contract was established even though the primary contract was *unenforceable* for illegality. In *Inntrepreneur Pub Co. (GL) v East Crown Ltd* [2000] 2 Lloyd's Rep 611 Lightman J highlighted the difficulty of finding a collateral contract where the relevant statement was followed by further negotiations (and a written contract that did not contain any term corresponding to the statement), or where there had been an extended lapse of time between the statement and the making of the formal contract, or where the statement referred to a future fact or future forecast, as opposed to an existing fact.

Collateral contracts have proven to be useful where: (a) the parol evidence rule would have unfairly barred a statement's inclusion in the final contract (see *Mann v Nunn* (1874) 30 LT 526)—note that the collateral contract is being used to *contradict* the written terms in the primary contract (see *City and Westminster Properties (1934) Ltd v Mudd* [1959] Ch 129); (b) an exclusion clause in the written contract is seeking to invalidate the collateral promise (see *Andrews v Hopkinson* [1957] 1 QB 229; *Evans (J) & Son (Portsmouth) Ltd v Andrea Merzario Ltd* [1976] 1 WLR 1078); (c) the statement does not qualify as a misrepresentation (see *Andrews*, above: 'It's a good little bus, I would stake my life on it'); and (d) the primary contract was made between the claimant and a third party but the defendant had made a collateral promise to one of them (see *Andrews*, above; *Shanklin Pier Ltd v Detel Products Ltd* [1951] 2 KB 854). However, the first three advantages, referred to above, have been somewhat nullified by the increased use of 'entire agreement' clauses which seek to denude any potential collateral contract of legal effect (see *Inntrepreneur Pub Co. (GL) v East Crown Ltd supra*).

Ascertainment of the Implied Terms of the Contract

There are two broad categories of implied term. First, there are *implied terms in fact* where, traditionally, the courts have attempted to implement the unexpressed intention of the parties, the resultant term being necessary and not inconsistent with the express terms of the contract. A term may be implied in this first category if (a) it is *necessary* to give *business efficacy* to the contract (see *The Moorcock* (1889) 14 PD 64); (b) it is so obvious that *both* parties must have intended it to be part of the contract, i.e. the 'officious bystander' test (see *Shirlaw v Southern Foundries* (1926) Ltd [1939] 2 KB 206); or (c) there is a custom of a trade or locality which is certain, notorious, reasonable, and lawful (see *Hutton v Warren* (1836) 1 M & W 466; *Les Affréteurs Réunis Société Anonyme v Walford* [1919] AC 801). However, in light of *Attorney-General of Belize v Belize Telecom Ltd* [2009] UKPC 10, [2009] 1 WLR 1988, it is now clear that these tests simply represent different methods by which a court will construe the contract objectively, having access to all of the readily available background knowledge, so as to elicit its true meaning (i.e. the parties' intentions). There is no question of imposing a solution or attempting to make the contract *more* reasonable.

The second broad category is predicated on the notion that in certain standard relationships (e.g. landlord and tenant) and contracts (e.g. sale of goods) the law sees merit in imposing a model or standardized set of terms on the parties as a form of judicial regulation—(often referred to as terms implied in law). Naturally, these terms are subject to an express contrary agreement between the parties, unless stated otherwise in a statute (see generally *Liverpool City Council v Irwin* [1977] AC 239; *Shell UK Ltd v Lostock Garage Ltd* [1976] 1 WLR 1187 and Lord Denning MR's adoption of a similar system of classifying implied terms). In *Scally v Southern Health and Social Services Board* [1992] 1 AC 294, for example, the House of Lords implied into a contract of employment that certain employees had to be notified of their entitlement to certain benefits (or changes thereof), whilst in *Mahmud v Bank of Credit and Commerce SA* [1998] AC 20 a term was implied that an employer would not conduct a dishonest or corrupt business.

The final category involves terms implied by statute. Parliament (and the EU) increasingly dictates what terms should be implied into contracts, thereby seeking to maintain minimum standards of performance. Historically, statutory intervention has been linked to the parties' assumed intentions particularly where the common law was being codified (e.g. Sale of Goods Act 1893), but such a tenuous connection is becoming increasingly unrealistic, especially in those situations where a particular statutory provision prohibits exclusion of the statutorily implied obligations (e.g. ss. 6 and 7 of the Unfair Contract Terms Act 1977 which restrict the exclusion of implied terms referred to in the SGA 1979, ss. 13 and 14). It is clear, therefore, that when it comes to consumers dealing with businesses, the law is often imposing a paradigm contract by way of implied terms.

As indicated above, the most common example of statutory implied terms in the law of contract relates to sale of goods contracts. A working knowledge of this area is important as it has a significant impact on the next chapter; viz. the possible exclusion of liability for breach of these terms by businesses dealing with consumers. The primary implied terms are found in ss. 12–15 of the SGA 1979, as subsequently amended. Section 12 implies a condition that the seller has the right to sell the goods, s. 13 implies a condition that in a sale of goods by description the goods will correspond with that description, s. 14 implies conditions that ensure that the goods sold are of satisfactory quality and, where relevant, fit for purpose, and s. 15 implies a condition that where there is a sale by sample the bulk must correspond with the sample in terms of quality and is free of defects not apparent from a reasonable inspection of the sample. Similar arrangements apply for contracts involving the supply of services; see **Supply of Goods and Services Act 1982**. Finally, the **Sale and Supply of Goods to Consumers Regulations 2002, SI No. 3045**, has taken consumer protection to new levels, perhaps ringing the final death knell for the principle of freedom of contract (see **Question 2** for more detail).

Classification and Determination of the Relative Importance of Terms

Traditionally, terms of the contract are classified as either *conditions* or *warranties* representing, respectively, the contract's major and minor stipulations. Where a breach of condition occurs, the innocent party can *either* treat himself as discharged from further performance or affirm the contract and claim damages, whereas a breach of warranty only gives rise to a claim for damages. The consequences flowing from a breach of condition or warranty are often said to be based upon the intention of the parties as manifested in their agreement (see *Bentsen v Taylor, Sons & Co.* [1893] 2 QB 274; *Schuler (L) AG v Wickman Machine Tool Sales Ltd* [1974] AC 235). This existing common law classification can be supplemented by statute law that might provide that a particular implied term is either a condition or a warranty (e.g. the SGA 1979, ss. 12–15).

It follows that if the parties have expressly agreed upon their obligations, the ensuing contract will set out the appropriate remedy for each breach, thereby avoiding the need to consider the seriousness of that breach or its consequences. Thus, a trifling breach of condition might allow repudiation of the entire contract (see *Arcos Ltd v EA Ronaasen & Son* [1933] AC 470), although in non-consumer contracts for the sale of goods, the SGA 1979, s. 15A now provides that the buyer cannot reject the goods for a 'slight' breach of the conditions implied in ss. 13–15 of the 1979 Act.

However, in *Hongkong Fir Shipping Co. Ltd v Kawasaki Kisen Kaisha Ltd* [1962] 2 QB 26, the Court of Appeal recognized that many complex contractual undertakings can be breached in ways that might be catastrophic or merely inconvenient. For example, all charterparties contain the condition that a ship must be 'seaworthy', but this could be breached by the ship having a leaky hull, or at the other extreme, by the ship's first-aid box being inadequately stocked. The court concluded that such undertakings, referred to as *innominate* terms, were not classifiable at the date of contract formation; rather, the *consequences of the breach* should dictate the appropriate remedy. Thus, if the breach deprived the innocent party substantially of the intended benefit under the contract a court would allow that party to repudiate and claim damages, whereas if the breach was of lesser effect the innocent party would only be awarded damages. Note that the innominate (or intermediate) term is only 'classified' by the courts at the date of breach and therefore does not require any retrospective investigation of what damages the parties would have reasonably foreseen flowing from the breach if they had been asked at the time of contract formation (e.g. *Cehave NV v Bremer Handelsgesellschaft mbH, The Hansa Nord* [1976] QB 44 and *Reardon Smith Line Ltd v Yngvar Hansen-Tangen* [1976] 1 WLR 989). Although the innominate term is capable of universal application, considerable scope still remains for a court to adopt the orthodox classification of conditions and warranties, particularly in mercantile contracts where certainty is at a premium. For example, precedent strongly suggests that stipulations as to the time of performance (see *The Mihalis Angelos* [1971] 1 QB 164; *Bunge Corporation v Tradax Export SA* [1981] 1 WLR 711; cf *Universal Bulk Carriers Pte Ltd v Andre et Cie SA* [2001] EWCA 588, [2001] 2 Lloyd's Rep 65) and the precise description of unascertained future goods (e.g. a sale of commodities) are normally treated as conditions, thereby entitling the innocent party to repudiate in the event of a breach (see *Barber v NWS Bank plc* [1996] 1 All ER 906).

Finally, the above classifications relate to *promissory conditions* but there may also be *contingent conditions* which either suspend or cancel contractual liability. A *condition precedent* generally means that the contract will not become binding unless a condition

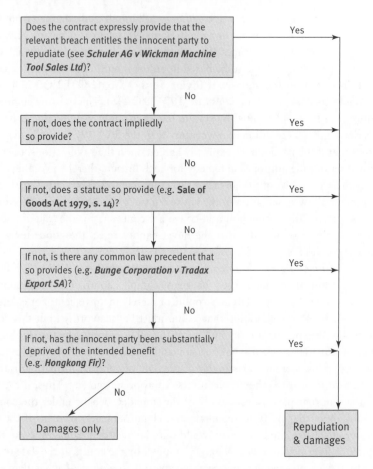

Figure 3 Breach of contract: entitlement to repudiate

is fulfilled (see *Aberfoyle Plantations Ltd v Cheng* [1960] AC 115) and a *condition subsequent* involves a contract which is binding immediately but which may cease to bind the parties or allow one party the option to cancel on the operation of the condition (see *Head v Tattersall* (1871) LR Ex 7).

Interpretation of Contracts

There are many instances where the words used by the parties in their written contract causes interpretational difficulties. Perhaps there is a contradiction between one clause and another, or the use of a particular word differs from one clause to another, or the parties disagree on the meaning of a particular word, or the words themselves are inherently ambiguous. What rules should the courts follow in interpreting the relevant section in the contract? Historically, in resolving such ambiguities, the courts have avoided looking at the parties' negotiations leading up to the contract's formation (see *Prenn v*

Simmonds [1971] 1 WLR 1381), or the manner in which they subsequently performed the contract (with the possible exception of contracts that are partly written and partly oral—see *Maggs (T/A) BM Builders v Marsh* [2006] EWCA Civ 1058, [2006] BLR 395). This approach was justified on two grounds: the parties might change their minds during negotiations (only the final contract represents their true consensus), and third parties might be adversely affected if they relied on the existence of a contract only to be told that its meaning could only be gleaned from pre-contract negotiations from which they were excluded.

In *Investors Compensation Scheme Ltd v West Bromwich Building Society* [1998] 1 WLR 898 Lord Hoffmann offered a five-prong set of rules, as interpreted by subsequent case law: (a) contract interpretation involves ascertaining the meaning that a document would convey to a reasonable person possessing all the background knowledge reasonably available to the parties at the time of contract formation (see *Pratt v Aigaion Insurance Co SA* [2008] EWCA Civ 1314, [2009] 1 Lloyd's Rep 225); (b) this background knowledge (often referred to as the 'matrix of fact') includes 'absolutely anything' that might affect the way in which a reasonable person interpreted the document (excluding facts/knowledge not reasonably available to the parties at the time); (c) the contents of the previous negotiations that took place between parties are nearly always excluded, but where the parties have attributed a specific meaning to a word(s) during their negotiations, yet the contract does not appear to contain a definition or explanation of that word(s), a court is entitled to adopt the meaning used in the negotiations (see *Berkeley Community Villages Ltd v Pullen* [2007] EWHC 1330, [2007] EGLR 101); (d) the meaning of words in a contractual document is determined by what the parties would reasonably have understood them to mean, with the aid of their background knowledge, rather than the linguistic definitions provided by dictionaries and the standard rules of grammar; and, (e) words should be given their 'natural and ordinary meaning' as one will normally assume that the parties have not incorporated linguistic mistakes into their formal documents (see *Bank of Credit and Commerce International SA v Ali* [2001] UKHL 8, [2001] 2 WLR 735). Moreover, having read the document and recognized its background and context, where an obvious mistake has been made it must be clear what correction ought to be made in order to cure that mistake (see *Chartbrook Ltd v Persimmon Homes Ltd* [2009] UKHL 38, [2009] 3 WLR 267).

Question 1

It is illogical and unjust for the law to classify contractual obligations as either conditions or warranties *at the time of* contract formation as this prevents the remedies for a breach of contract from properly reflecting the actual consequences of that breach.
   Discuss.

Commentary

This essay question requires a *critical* examination of conditions and warranties, the consequences of their breach and the development of the innominate term. In particular, students must be able to make both a close analysis of the leading cases and display a critical awareness of the problems which have shaped the new developments in the law. In conclusion, an appraisal should be undertaken of the relative merits of orthodox conditions and warranties as compared with the innominate term.

Answer plan

- Explain what is meant by the classification of contract terms as either conditions or warranties.
- How, and when, is the differentiation made between conditions and warranties? Do the consequences of the breach of contract play any part in this evaluation?
- Explain what is meant by an 'innominate term'. Has the development of this term brought greater flexibility to this area of the law of contract?
- Are there any instances where a prior classification of contract terms as either conditions or warranties may still have significance?

Suggested answer

The promissory obligations of a contract are its terms, classified as either conditions or warranties. Conditions are the important and fundamental obligations whereas warranties are less important, subsidiary promises. In the nineteenth century 'warranty' was often used by the judges to encompass all contract terms and the strict, two-fold demarcation is relatively recent, having been expedited by a definition of these phrases in the Sale of Goods Act 1893 (see now the Sale of Goods Act 1979 (SGA 1979), ss. 11(3) and 61). Most importantly, a breach of condition allows the innocent party to repudiate or affirm the contract and claim damages in either case whereas a breach of warranty allows only a claim in damages. The overriding notion of freedom of contract means that the court must assess the parties' intentions in order to decide whether a particular statement or clause in a written contract is a condition or a warranty. Alternatively, statute may dictate that certain implied terms are conditions as in the SGA 1979, ss. 12–15. The distinction is a crucial one as the right to repudiate is of such importance: an unscrupulous party must not be allowed to use a breach of condition as a sham, enabling him to evade his contractual obligations with the concomitant opportunity of entering into a more profitable contract with a third party. It is vital to establish how the differentiation is made between the two types of term and whether the courts will always pay paramount attention to the parties' intentions.

The orthodox theory is that conditions and warranties are identifiable at the date the contract was formed. This approach has two peculiarities. First, it is based upon the assumption that there is some essential substance which defines these obligations in the abstract and, secondly, it takes no account of the seriousness of the breach and its consequences. It is arguable that the only reason which justifies one party's repudiation is a breach by the other party which goes to the root of the contract, meaning that further performance is futile. Nevertheless, many undertakings have become definitive conditions by virtue of commercial usage, the operation of the doctrine of precedent and statutory implied terms which are expressly declared to be conditions. In *Arcos Ltd v EA Ronaasen & Son* [1933] AC 470, the contract was to sell wooden staves of half-an-inch thick for making cement barrels. Only a small percentage conformed to the specification but the remainder were nearly all less than nine-sixteenths of an inch thick. Although this made no difference to the manufacture of cement barrels (i.e. the goods were merchantable and fit for their purpose) it was held that the buyer was entitled to reject the entire consignment for breach of the implied condition of description in s. 13 of the Sale of Goods Act 1893, even though there was evidence that the motive for the buyer's rejection was that the market price of timber had fallen. A similar conclusion was reached regarding a breach of condition occasioning no loss in *Re Moore & Co. and Landauer & Co.* [1921] 2 KB 519, where Scrutton LJ pointed out that the breach *might* have had drastic consequences. With respect, such a hypothesis did nothing to justify the repudiation where there was no loss on the facts. This tunnel vision has little to commend it and developments in recent years are infinitely preferable.

First, where the contract labels its terms as conditions or warranties the court must attempt to implement the parties' intentions, but it is clear that the form of the contract should not be allowed to dictate its substance or injustice would surely follow. *Schuler (L) AG v Wickman Machine Tool Sales Ltd* [1974] AC 235 concerned a 'condition' in a four-and-a-half-year distributorship agreement that the distributor, Wickman, should visit six named customers once a week to solicit orders. This entailed an approximate total of 1,400 visits during the subsistence of the contract. Clause 11 of the contract provided that either party might determine it if the other committed 'a material breach' of its obligations. The House of Lords refused to accept the contention that a single failure to make a visit should allow Schuler to repudiate the entire contract. Lord Reid said that the House was trying to discover intention as disclosed by the contract as a whole and whilst the use of 'condition' was a strong indication of intention, it was not conclusive. He considered that 'the fact that a particular construction leads to a very unreasonable result must be a relevant consideration. The more unreasonable the result the more unlikely it is that the parties can have intended it'.

Secondly, the development of the innominate or intermediate term introduces a more logical flexibility to this area of law. In *Hongkong Fir Shipping Co. Ltd*

v Kawasaki Kisen Kaisha Ltd [1962] 2 QB 26, the Court of Appeal emphasized that the orthodox division of conditions and warranties could be rigid
and inflexible in operation, meaning that a negligible breach of condition might
allow repudiation whilst only damages would be available for a catastrophic
breach of warranty. The condition that a ship should be seaworthy could thus be
breached across a spectrum of possibilities from inconsequential inconveniences
at one extreme to calamities involving substantial loss at the other. Diplock
LJ held that such undertakings could not be categorized as conditions or warranties but that the legal consequences of the breach should 'depend upon the
nature of the event to which the breach gives rise and . . . not . . . from a prior
classification'.

The *Hongkong* reasoning has been endorsed in subsequent decisions. In *Cehave
NV v Bremer Handelsgesellschaft mbH, The Hansa Nord* [1976] QB 44, the
contract was for the sale of citrus pulp pellets for use in animal food. The contract price was £100,000, an express term being that the goods should be shipped
'in good condition'. The buyer sought to reject the goods for a relatively minor
breach. In fact, the market in such goods had fallen dramatically at the delivery date and the buyer eventually bought the same goods from a third party for
£30,000 *and* used the pellets for cattle food. The buyer argued that rejection was
permissible under both the statutory implied condition of merchantability and
the express condition relating to quality. The court held that the Sale of Goods
Act did not exhaustively define all obligations as either conditions or warranties
and that the express provision was an innominate term, breach of which, on the
facts, did not permit rejection of the goods. The court assumed that merchantability was an immutable statutory condition but that, on the facts, the sellers
were not in breach of that condition. The notion of the innominate term was
similarly approved by the House of Lords in *Reardon Smith Line Ltd v Yngvar
Hansen-Tangen* [1976] 1 WLR 989 with Lord Wilberforce casting doubt upon
the decisions in *Arcos* and *Re Moore*, considering them 'excessively technical' and
probably applicable only to their facts.

Although the innominate term is an attractively logical proposition, there may
nevertheless be instances where the necessity for commercial certainty and predictability demand that the parties should be able to allocate the risks of the contract at the time of its formation. This is particularly so if there is no disparity of
bargaining strength between them. Provisions relating to *time* are often crucial as
are the precise descriptions of unascertained, future goods, such as a sale of commodities. In *The Mihalis Angelos* [1971] 1 QB 164, for example, a stipulation as
to when a ship should be 'expected ready to load' under a charterparty was held
to be a condition and, likewise, a notice of readiness to load in *Bunge Corporation v Tradax Export SA* [1981] 1 WLR 711 (cf *Universal Bulk Carriers Pte Ltd
v Andre et Cie SA* [2001] EWCA 588, [2001] 2 Lloyd's Rep 65).

Thirdly, the SGA 1979, s. 15A now provides that where the buyer 'does not deal as consumer' and the breach of any of the implied conditions in ss. 13–15 is 'so slight that it would be unreasonable for him to reject [the goods]', the breach 'is not to be treated as a breach of condition but may be treated as a breach of warranty'. The principal target of s. 15A is thus the decision in *Arcos Ltd v EA Ronaasen & Son*, referred to earlier (see also the SGA 1979, s. 30(2A)). However, s. 15A(2) allows the parties to exclude expressly the operation of s. 15A.

In conclusion, there is still room to implement the definitive intentions of the parties expressed as conditions and warranties. Lord Wilberforce dissented vigorously in *Schuler* and would not assume 'contrary to the evidence, that both parties to this contract adopted a standard of easygoing tolerance rather than one of aggressive, insistent punctuality and efficiency'. Such tensions will always be present where freedom of contract meets policy-interventionism but combining innominate terms with the orthodox classification of conditions and warranties allows the courts to tread a middle path between rigid, and sometimes unjust rules on one side, and indeterminate flexibility on the other.

Question 2

In contracts for the sale of goods, the development of the statutory implied terms relating to the description, quality and fitness for purpose of the goods sold has reflected changing social needs and recognized the vulnerable position of the consumer buyer. However, the latest amendments to the Sale of Goods Act 1979 (SGA 1979) carry consumer protection to new heights.
  Discuss.

Commentary

The essay title calls for knowledge of the development of the statutory implied terms in sales of goods from the **Sale of Goods Act 1893** to the present **1979 Act**. As the question mentions 'changing social needs' it invites a discussion of the way the implied terms have been adapted throughout a period of 100 years to cope with disparity in bargaining power. A knowledge of the extent to which the implied terms may be excluded is also clearly very important to the answer. The question seeks a broad, critical awareness of the problems in this area, rather than intimate detail concerning the *substance* of the implied terms. An appraisal of the revolutionary amendments made to the **SGA 1979**, is also required.

Answer plan

- Explain the purpose and scope of the implied terms relating to description, quality, and fitness for purpose in the (original) **Sale of Goods Act 1893**.

- Originally, these implied terms could be freely excluded or varied: was this just and realistic in 1893?

- What were the changing commercial conditions which rendered this policy of unrestricted exclusion unjust and unrealistic?

- How does current legislation ensure that consumers are protected from the exclusion of the implied terms whilst business buyers and sellers are at liberty to apportion risks under their contract?

- What are the latest, dramatic amendments that have been made to the **SGA 1979**?

Suggested answer

The Sale of Goods Act 1893 was a radical piece of legislation in that it attempted to codify the common law concerning the sale of goods. During the nineteenth century the courts had developed the notion of *caveat emptor* (let the buyer take care) but, significantly, the 1893 Act introduced statutory implied terms relating to the description, quality and fitness for purpose of the goods sold. The object of the Act was to draw a distinction between specific goods and those bought by description. In relation to specific goods the rules did not favour the buyer as, normally, he could inspect the goods and make his own judgement as to their quality. *Caveat emptor* therefore applied to specific goods, there being no implied term as to their quality. However, the buyer could make his specific purpose known to the seller and, if he did so, there was an implied condition that the goods should be reasonably fit for that purpose. In relation to a 'sales by description' however, there was an implied condition that the goods should reach a standard of 'merchantable quality'. In fact, as neither of those terms was defined by the Act, over a period of time the courts broadened their meaning and ambit, thereby ensuring protection for both commercial buyers and the increasingly common phenomenon in the twentieth century of the private 'consumer' buyer.

Reflecting *laissez-faire* philosophy, s. 55 of the 1893 Act allowed the implied conditions to be freely 'negatived or varied by express agreement or by the course of dealing between the parties, or by usage', providing the parties with freedom to allocate risks under their contract. However, *laissez-faire* ideals could not foresee the changed nature of commerce which developed in the twentieth century. Large retailers selling to private consumers began to deploy written standard-form contracts with ample exclusion clauses negating or restricting the Sale of Goods Act implied terms. The so-called *contract of adhesion*, primarily facilitated by a gross inequality of bargaining power, meant that the aspect of freedom of contract which began to dominate was the freedom to exploit the weaker party. It was with the Supply of Goods (Implied Terms) Act 1973 that radical provisions were introduced restricting the seller's ability to exclude the implied terms. In relation to consumer buyers, attempts at excluding the implied terms relating to quality and fitness were rendered void, but those implied terms could be excluded between two businesses provided the exclusion clause could pass a 'reasonableness' test.

By 1973 the function of the implied terms had thus changed in recognition of social needs. For the consumer, the implied terms provided a strict code of standards which could not be excluded, a development which could not possibly have been envisaged by the 1893 Act. Yet there were still thought to be weaknesses in the buyer's protection: the 1973 Act did not *prevent* the attempted exclusion of the implied terms. Unscrupulous sellers thus continued to display exclusion clauses and deploy them in contracts until the practice was rendered a criminal offence by the Consumer Transactions (Restrictions on Statements) Order 1976 made under the Fair Trading Act 1973. The basic scheme of the Supply of Goods (Implied Terms) Act 1973 was re-enacted in the Unfair Contract Terms Act 1977, ss. 6 and 12, the latter section providing a comprehensive definition of 'dealing as consumer'.

However, a word of warning. The statutory protection referred to above is not foolproof as it is predicated, to some extent, on the courts being able to identify clauses that attempt to exclude liability in the first place. What if a seller seeks to *define* his principal obligations from the outset (commonly known as 'shrinking the core') by for example, warning that the buyer should examine the goods and rely on his own judgement. The extent of the seller's obligations may thus be *shaped* rather than excluded or restricted. In *Harlingdon and Leinster Enterprises Ltd v Christopher Hull Fine Art Ltd* [1991] 1 QB 564, the seller had two paintings by Gabriele Münter for sale which were examined by the buyer. The seller told the buyer that he did not like the paintings and had never before heard of the artist. A price of £6,000 was agreed and an invoice supplied with the artist's name and lifespan. Although the picture was subsequently revealed to be a forgery, the Court of Appeal held that this was not a sale by description within s. 13 of the SGA 1979, as the buyer had not *relied upon* any description. Stuart-Smith LJ dissented and particularly warned against the practice of allowing vague statements as to the limited expertise and knowledge of the seller to nullify the protection of the statutory implied condition within s. 13.

Nevertheless, the implied terms of the SGA 1979 have performed an excellent function in protecting the consumer buyer whilst allowing business buyers and sellers the requisite degree of freedom to contract on equal terms. This equality was more recently reinforced by the substantial amendments made to the SGA 1979 resulting from the EU Directive (99/44/EC, 25 May 1999) on *Certain Aspects of the Sale of Consumer Goods and Associated Guarantees*. The Sale and

Supply of Goods to Consumers Regulations 2002, SI No. 3045, which came into force on 31 March 2003, amended the SGA 1979 and injected some revolutionary concepts into English law. These provisions apply only where one party 'deals as consumer' (see the **Unfair Contract Terms Act 1977, s. 12**), 'consumer' being defined in reg. 2 as 'any natural person who, in contracts covered by these Regulations, is acting for purposes which are outside his trade, business or profession'.

Regulation 3 amends the SGA 1979, s. 14(2), relating to satisfactory quality, and inserts new ss. **14(2D) and (2E)**. Section 14(2D) alters the law fundamentally in providing that 'if the buyer deals as consumer . . . the relevant circumstances mentioned in subsection (2A) above include any public statements on the specific characteristics of the goods made about them by the seller, the producer or his representative, particularly in advertising or on labelling'. The seller of goods is now clearly liable for any 'public statements' made about the goods but the truly dramatic change here is that consumers can now rely on advertising produced by a *manufacturer* of goods when seeking to render the *seller* liable for unsatisfactory goods supplied under the contract of sale. The reform is long overdue and recognizes modern advertising and marketing practices by which consumers are attracted to brand-name goods because of a manufacturer's claims which are endorsed, explicitly or implicitly, by the retail seller. It is surely not unreasonable to impose such extra liability on a retail seller of goods, especially as there are some legitimate exceptions contained in SGA 1979, s. 14(2E): a public statement is not 'a relevant circumstance for the purposes of subsection (2A)' if the seller shows that (a) at the time the contract was made, he was not, and could not reasonably have been, aware of the statement, (b) before the contract was made, the statement had been withdrawn in public or, to the extent that it contained anything which was incorrect or misleading, it had been corrected in public, or (c) the decision to buy the goods could not have been influenced by the statement.

Regulation 5 inserts a new **Part 5A** into the SGA 1979 comprising ss. 48A–48F. These sections introduce a new set of remedies for consumers but the existing remedies (e.g. rejection of the goods/damages) are (supposedly) not affected by the new regime. Under s. 48B(1), the additional, specified remedies, are repair or replacement. These must be provided 'within a reasonable time but without causing significant inconvenience to the buyer' and the seller must 'bear any necessary costs incurred in doing so' (s. 48B(2)). Under s. 48B(3), repair or replacement are not available where either remedy is (i) 'impossible', or (ii) 'disproportionate in comparison to (*sic*) the other of those remedies', or (iii) 'disproportionate in comparison to (*sic*) an appropriate reduction in the purchase price . . . or rescission . . . '. Under *s.* 48B(4) it is 'disproportionate' if one remedy imposes costs on the seller which, in comparison with those imposed by the other remedy, are unreasonable, taking into account—(a) the value which the goods would have if they conformed to the contract, (b) the significance of lack of conformity, and (c) whether the other remedy could be effected without significant inconvenience to the buyer. In addition, the new provisions introduce remedies relating to reduction of the purchase price or rescission of the contract. These remedies are available, under s. 48C, *only* where the buyer can require neither repair nor replacement, *or* the buyer has demanded either of these remedies and the seller has not complied within a reasonable time and without significant inconvenience to the buyer, under s. 48B(2), above. If the buyer obtains rescission, any reimbursement may be reduced to take account of the use he has had of the goods (s. 48C(3)). A comparison of all four remedies is required in order to decide whether repair or replacement is disproportionate and which remedy is economical and practical. For example, if the defect is major, repair might cost much more than replacement, and the latter would be quicker for the seller and more convenient for the buyer. If the defect is minor, vice versa. In the case of second-hand goods with serious defects, expensive repair might be a disproportionate remedy and replacement impossible; reduction in price or, more likely, rescission would be available. At first glance, these new remedies seem to be very beneficial for consumers but considerable uncertainty is introduced by the notion that they may be 'impossible' or 'disproportionate'. It is inevitable that unscrupulous sellers will assert that repair or replacement are disproportionate and seek to foist a small reduction in price on the consumer who will thus be left with the defective goods. English law has always preserved the important, understandable, right to reject goods for minor defects but this significant remedy seems to be eroded considerably by the new reforms. It remains to be seen how the new raft of remedies will work in practice.

Finally, there are two important provisions which do further consumer protection. First, the SGA 1979, s. 48A(3) provides that, where goods do not conform to the contract of sale at any time within six months starting from the date of delivery to the buyer, they must be taken not to have so conformed at that date. This presumption does *not* apply if (a) it is established that the goods did so conform at that date, or (b) its application is incompatible with the nature of the goods or the nature of the lack of conformity. An example of the presumption's incompatibility because of the 'nature of the goods' is where the goods are perishable, and the 'nature of the lack of conformity' relates to situations where the goods have been mistreated or inadequately maintained by the buyer. Secondly, reg. 15 is a self-standing Regulation which applies to 'consumer guarantees'. A 'consumer guarantee' is defined in reg. 2 as 'any undertaking to a consumer by a person acting in the course of his business, given without extra charge, to reimburse the price paid or to replace, repair or handle consumer goods in any way if they do not meet the specifications set out in the guarantee statement or in the relevant advertising'. Regulation 15(1) provides that 'where goods are sold . . . to a consumer which are offered with a consumer guarantee, the consumer guarantee takes effect at the time the goods are delivered as a contractual obligation owed by the guarantor under the conditions set out in the guarantee statement and associated advertising'.

Regulation 15(2) demands that the guarantor shall ensure that the guarantee sets out 'in plain intelligible language' the contents of the guarantee, the essential particulars for making a claim under it, the duration and territorial scope of it and the name and address of the guarantor. Where a manufacturer had no direct contract of sale with a buyer, considerable legal ingenuity was required to establish the guarantee as a binding contract in that, principally, it was difficult to find any consideration moving from the buyer, particularly where he discovered the guarantee in sealed goods after the purchase had been made. Consequently, reg. 15 is most welcome in providing that consumer guarantees are legally binding.

Question 3

Steven advertises in an antiques journal that he has an aeroplane for sale. The advertisement appears on 1 March and reads:

> A rare opportunity to acquire a collector's item. A bi-plane which belonged to the early flying ace, Sir George Ditcher, has come on the market for the first time. Sir George was an early member of the Royal Flying Corps and was the person upon whom Wiggles, the fictional flying hero, was based. £85,000, or nearest offer.

Boris, the owner of a museum dedicated to items connected with the First World War, contacts Steven on 15 March to discuss the sale. Steven shows Boris a large collection of letters written by Sir George Ditcher which describe an aeroplane of the same type as the one offered for sale as 'my little buzz-bomb'. He also points out numerous letters written to Sir George Ditcher by the author of the Wiggles books. On 10 April, Boris agrees to buy the aeroplane for £85,000 and a brief written contract is entered into which makes no mention of Sir George Ditcher or Wiggles.

Boris displays the bi-plane at his museum describing it as 'previously owned by Sir George Ditcher, the real-life Wiggles'. It has now been established that, although he did fly it, the aeroplane never belonged to Sir George Ditcher and that there were ten other people who had as strong a claim as Sir George Ditcher to be the basis of the Wiggles character.

Advise Boris.

Commentary

This question focuses upon the terms of the contract and their breach. Three broad questions should be answered. First, where is the contract to be found? Secondly, what are its terms? Thirdly, what remedies exist if the seller is in breach of a term of the contract? It is important to keep this chronological progression if a logical and readable answer is sought. There is a large amount of material to include in this question and not all points can be given equal weight—for example, reference should be made to misrepresentation but not in any depth. A good student will show the examiner an overall knowledge of the area and be able to put the law in perspective when delineating the options available to the disgruntled buyer.

Answer plan

- Explain briefly the advantages of establishing a statement as a term of the contract. Might misrepresentation provide an attractive remedy for Boris?
- As there is an advertisement describing the aeroplane, the parties have personal negotiations and a written contract is entered into, where are the terms of this contract of sale to be found? What are the tests for deciding if a statement is a term of the contract?
- Once the terms of the contract have been located, it must be decided whether they are conditions, warranties, or innominate terms. How is this achieved?
- As this is a contract for the sale of goods, might the implied terms of the **Sale of Goods Act 1979 (SGA 1979)** provide the most desirable remedy for Boris or should he seek to establish breach of an express term of the contract?

Suggested answer

This question concerns terms of the contract and remedies for breach of a term. Not all statements are contractual in nature as some may be mere representations or commendatory 'puffs' which, if true, lack any legal value. It is obvious that a seller of goods must be able to praise them *within a certain latitude* without legal consequence but if his statements are untrue statements of fact which induce the buyer to enter into the contract, an action may lie in misrepresentation. If the parties have a contract, it is natural to think of contractual remedies first and misrepresentation second and that was certainly the position prior to the Misrepresentation Act 1967. However, s. 2(1) of that Act introduced potent remedies for negligent misrepresentation and placed the burden of discharging negligence on the representor. This is therefore an attractive remedy but there are still advantages in proving a term. If the contract is in writing the term may be easier to prove than a misrepresentation. Secondly, it is not an essential requirement that a term must *induce* the buyer and, thirdly, although the statement constituting the term is usually one of fact, there is no requirement that it *must* be. Where is the contract to be found between Steven and Boris and what are its terms?

It was established in *Heilbut, Symons & Co. v Buckleton* [1913] AC 30 that *intention* is the overall guide as to whether a statement is a term of the contract. This test emphasizes the intent of the *maker of the statement* in asking if he warranted its truth and accuracy rather than merely expressing an opinion, and it is criticizable in that it does not sufficiently accentuate the effect of the statement on the other party and his justifiable *reliance* upon it. More recent cases have tended to emphasize these factors and in *Evans (J) & Son (Portsmouth) Ltd v Andrea Merzario Ltd* [1976] 1 WLR 1078, Lord Denning, referring to *Heilbut*, said that 'much of what was said in that case is entirely out of date'. Sub-divisions of the single test of intention can be attempted in this context however.

First, a lengthy interval between the making of the relevant statement and the conclusion of the contract may indicate that the statement does not have contractual force. In *Routledge v McKay* [1954] 1 WLR 615 an interval of one week between statement and contract was sufficient to deny any contractual intent to the statement. There it was the sale of a motorcycle but much depends on the facts, and if the contract and its subject matter are complicated, longer time must be allowed in order to verify statements. The interval of some five weeks between advertisement and contract is thus not necessarily fatal to Boris's claim.

Secondly, the courts are influenced in their decision by any special knowledge that the maker of the statement may possess. It is presumed that an owner of goods knows their condition and consequent weight attaches to his statements (see *Harling v Eddy* [1951] 2 KB 739—owner of a heifer who 'absolutely guaranteed' her sound condition) but it is possible that Boris, as an expert on the First World War, knows more than Steven and should have verified the statements in the five weeks before contract. This reasoning was influential in the decision in *Oscar Chess Ltd v Williams* [1957] 1 WLR 370, where it was held that the statement of a car's age made by its owner was not a term of the contract as the plaintiff car dealer had specialist knowledge and could/should have verified the statement. This test may therefore militate against Boris.

Thirdly, it is important to assess the overall importance of the statement in the light of the contract and its effect on the other party. Is the statement both crucial and pivotal in the contract's formation? In *Schawel v Reade* [1913] 2 IR 64 and *Bannerman v White* (1861) 10 CB (NS) 844 this test meant that the statements were terms. In *Schawel*, the buyer stopped his examination of a horse when he was told that it was sound, and in *Bannerman*, a buyer of hops asked whether they had been treated with sulphur adding that he would not bother to ask the price if they had been so treated. Similarly, in *Esso Petroleum Co. Ltd v Mardon* [1978] QB 801 the defendant's doubts as to the plaintiff's forecasted 'throughput' of petrol were quelled by the latter, and the statement was thus held to be a term. It is arguable that the provenance of the aeroplane is the dominant factor in this contract as evidenced by the fact that it is displayed with its history at Boris's museum.

Finally, the presence of a written contract might indicate that the parties' intentions are crystallized therein. The parol evidence rule is surrounded by countless exceptions and it is quite possible to have a contract which is partly written and partly oral *if the parties so intend* (*Couchman v Hill* [1947] KB 554—oral assurance dominated the written sale catalogue). Alternatively, the court might construe the statements regarding the aeroplane's history as a collateral contract, thereby avoiding the parol evidence rule. In *Andrews v Hopkinson* [1957] 1 QB 229, for example, the plaintiff had a primary contract with a finance company to take a car on hire-purchase and a collateral contract with the defendant car dealer that it was 'a good little bus'. It is suggested that Boris may succeed in establishing a term but subject to the *caveat* that he is a specialist/expert buyer who cannot be bothered to provide for his requirements in a written contract. As some prominent decisions show a distinct tendency to revert to nineteenth-century principles of *laissez-faire* (e.g. *Photo Production Ltd v Securicor Transport Ltd* [1980] AC 827) a court might thus castigate Boris's laxity.

If the statements are terms of the contract it must be decided whether they are conditions, warranties or innominate terms. A condition is a major stipulation which allows the innocent party either to repudiate or affirm the contract and claim damages in both cases whereas a warranty sounds only in damages. Again, the distinction between these two types of term depends upon the parties' intentions at the date of contract. As the statements are not in the written contract they cannot be *labelled* as either conditions or warranties and the contract is not one of an established commercial type where precedent may classify certain undertakings as conditions (e.g. insurance or carriage of goods by sea). It is likely that the court would consider the statements regarding the aeroplane to be innominate terms which means that, instead of a prior classification of contract terms, the effects of the breach will provide the necessary yardstick for the court's decision. In *Reardon Smith Line Ltd v Yngvar Hansen-Tangen* [1976] 1 WLR 989, for example, it was held that a different numbering of a ship (showing the yard where it was built) from the one specified in the contract was insufficient to allow rejection of the vessel when it was up to specification in every other respect. It is arguable that the statements regarding the aeroplane cause a serious breach which goes to the root of the obligation thereby allowing Boris to repudiate the contract. On the facts of the problem, damages alone could not compensate Boris for this breach.

It is imperative that Boris attempts to establish an express term of the contract as it would appear that the implied terms of the SGA 1979 will be of little avail. The implied conditions in s. 14 relating to satisfactory quality and fitness for purpose probably do not extend beyond physically defective goods; for example, in *Harlingdon and Leinster Enterprises Ltd v Christopher Hull Fine Art Ltd* [1991] 1 QB 564, a forged painting was held not to be physically defective. Moreover, s. 13 relating to the description of the goods would seem to be equally ineffective on the facts of the problem. The reason for this is that, apart from commercial sales of future, unascertained goods where description is crucial, the courts have restricted s. 13 to descriptive words which *identify the subject matter* of the contract. This involves a metaphysical distinction between the subject matter of the contract and its attributes but, as defective food was still held to be food in *Ashington Piggeries Ltd v Christopher Hill Ltd* [1972] AC 441, it is indisputable that, although the aeroplane lacks many of the professed attributes, it is nevertheless an aeroplane, there being compliance with the essence of the bargain within s. 13.

Further Reading

Case-notes

Bunge Corporation v Tradax Export SA [1981] 1 WLR 711
Carter, 'Classification of Contractual Terms: The New Orthodoxy' (1981) 40 CLJ 219

Attorney-General of Belize v Belize Telecom Ltd [2009] UKPC 10, [2009] 1 WLR 1988
Peters, 'The Implication of Terms in Fact' (2009) 68 CLJ 513
MacDonald, 'Casting Aside Officious Bystander and Business Efficacy' (2009) 26 JCL 97

Articles

Bojczuk, 'When is a Condition Not a Condition' [1987] JBL 353

Clarke, 'Notice of Contractual Terms' (1976) 35 CLJ 51

Peden, 'Concerns Behind Implication of Terms in Law' (2001) 117 LQR 459

Phang, 'Implied Terms, Business Efficacy and the Officious Bystander—A Modern History' [1998] JBL 1

5

Exclusion clauses and unfair terms

Introduction

An exclusion clause is a term of the contract which attempts to exclude or restrict one party's liability which he would otherwise owe to the other. In the nineteenth century, at the high-water mark of freedom of contract, such clauses were regarded as unexceptional, their use being viewed as a legitimate exercise of bargaining power. However, in the twentieth century, the courts began to recognize the inevitable consequences of a growing disparity in bargaining strengths between contracting parties, not least in terms of the potential for consumers to be unfairly exploited by the economic superiority of business. Hampered by the principle of freedom of contract, and consequently unable to prohibit the use of such exclusion clauses, the courts nevertheless developed strict rules relating to their incorporation and interpretation. Unfortunately, such measures were largely procedural in nature and could easily be circumvented by adopting the correct practices, and by employing the most skilled draftsmen. It was therefore left to Parliament to legislate on such matters. A whole raft of statutes emerged which sought to control the unreasonable use of exclusion and limitation clauses, bolstered in no small part by the increasing demands of the European Union to standardize the domestic laws of Member States as regards the use of unfair terms in consumer contracts. The existing legal framework is therefore an amalgamation of three sources: (a) the common law, (b) UK-inspired statute law, and (c) EU-inspired laws.

(a) Common Law Restrictions upon Exclusion Clauses

Signature

A party who signs a document containing an exclusion clause is normally bound by its terms irrespective of the degree of notice given and whether he has read it (see *L'Estrange v F Graucob Ltd* [1934] 2 KB 394). However, should the signature have been exacted by misrepresentation, it will not bind the signatory (see *Curtis v Chemical Cleaning and Dyeing Co.* [1951] 1 KB 805), unless the signature *post*-dated the misrepresentation and the signed document properly explained the true legal position (see *Peekay Intermark Ltd v Australia and New Zealand Banking Group Ltd* [2006] EWCA Civ 386, [2006] 2 Lloyd's Rep 511).

Adequate Notice

Most commonly, the document containing the conditions is handed to one party and, in this case, he must receive adequate *notice* of the terms although he need not have *read* the document in order to be bound by its terms (see *Parker v South Eastern Ry* (1877) 2 CPD 416). Indeed, it is irrelevant if the party receiving the document is illiterate or blind (see *Thompson v L M & S Ry* [1930] 1 KB 41), unless the other party knows of this limitation (see *Geier v Kujawa, Weston & Warne Bros (Transport) Ltd* [1970] 1 Lloyd's Rep 364). Whether adequate notice has been given is a question of fact but cases of inadequate notice include terms obscured by a printed date stamp (see *Richardson, Spence & Co. v Rowntree* [1894] AC 217) and conditions printed on the reverse of a document with no notice of them on its face (see *Henderson v Steven* (1875) LR 2 HL (Sc) 470). If the particular clause relied upon is unusually wide or onerous, it may require unusually explicit notice (see *Thornton v Shoe Lane Parking Ltd* [1971] 2 QB 163; *Interfoto Picture Library Ltd v Stiletto Visual Programmes Ltd* [1989] QB 433).

Pre-Contractual Notice

The exclusion clause must be drawn to the attention of the other party before or at the time the contract is entered into, the courts preserving the maximum discretion as to the moment of the contract's completion (see *Olley v Marlborough Court Ltd* [1949] 1 KB 532; *Thornton*, above).

Contractual Document

The document containing the exclusion clauses must be one which a reasonable man would expect to contain contract terms and, again, the courts preserve a wide discretion in deciding this question in cases, for example, involving tickets and receipts (see *Chapelton v Barry UDC* [1940] 1 KB 532; *Burnett v Westminster Bank* [1966] 1 QB 742; *McCutcheon v MacBrayne (David) Ltd* [1964] 1 WLR 125; *Thornton*, above).

Course of Dealing

The court may infer notice of the exclusion clause from a consistent course of dealing between the parties (see *Spurling (J) Ltd v Bradshaw* [1956] 1 WLR 461; *Hollier v Rambler Motors (AMC) Ltd* [1972] 2 QB 71; *Kendall (Henry) & Sons v Lillico (William) & Sons Ltd* [1969] 2 AC 31). Such an incorporation of terms may be easier where both parties are businesses of equal bargaining power (see *British Crane Hire Corp. Ltd v Ipswich Plant Hire Ltd* [1975] QB 303).

Common Law Rules of Construction and Interpretation

Exclusion clauses must be clear and unequivocal or they will be inoperative, the common law's interpretation being *contra proferentem* (see *Andrews Bros Ltd v Singer & Co. Ltd*

[1934] 1 KB 17; *Houghton v Trafalgar Insurance Co. Ltd* [1954] 1 QB 247). The courts have particularly strict rules of construction where there is an attempted exclusion of liability in negligence and will construe any doubt regarding the ambit of the clause against the *proferens* (see the guidance given in *Alderslade v Hendon Laundry Ltd* [1945] 1 KB 189; *Canada Steamship Lines Ltd v The King* [1952] AC 192; *White v John Warwick & Co. Ltd* [1953] 1 WLR 1285).

These rules of interpretation have undoubtedly become less significant since the advent of the Unfair Contract Terms Act 1977 and the courts have warned against a strained and hostile construction of clauses (see *Bankers Insurance Company Ltd v South* [2003] EWHC 380 (QB), [2003] PIQR P532, where an exclusion clause covering 'any motorised waterborne craft' was held to include a jet ski).

Exclusion Clauses and Fundamental Breach of Contract

There is a clear authority for the notion that certain contractual obligations are fundamental to the entire undertaking such that their non-performance amounts to a failure to perform the *contract itself* (see *Chanter v Hopkins* (1838) 4 M & W 399). The common law initially assumed that such a fundamental breach could not be excluded or restricted in any circumstances as this would amount to giving with one hand and taking with the other (see *Pinnock Bros v Lewis and Peat* [1923] 1 KB 690; *Karsales (Harrow) Ltd v Wallis* [1956] 1 WLR 936). However, this approach was rejected in *UGS Finance Ltd v National Mortgage Bank of Greece* [1964] 1 Lloyd's Rep 446, on the basis that it conflicted with freedom of contract and the intention of the parties; rather, the question of whether a clause could exclude liability for a fundamental breach was a question of construction. The *UGS* case was unanimously approved by the House of Lords in *Suisse Atlantique Société d'Armement Maritime SA v NV Rotterdamshe Kolen Centrale* [1967] 1 AC 361 and the rule of construction put beyond doubt by *Photo Production Ltd v Securicor Transport Ltd* [1980] AC 827.

(b) UK-Inspired Statute Law: the Unfair Contract Terms Act 1977

The Unfair Contract Terms Act 1977 has three broad areas of control: (a) exclusion of liability for negligence, (b) exclusion of liability for breach of contract, and (c) exclusion of liability for breach of certain terms implied by statute in the sale of goods, hire purchase, and supply of goods. Control may take one of two forms: the clause may be rendered absolutely void and ineffective or it may be effective only to the extent that it satisfies the test of reasonableness.

Liability for Negligence

Section 2 restricts the ability of one party to exclude his business liability (see ss. 1(3) and 14) for negligence (see s. 1(1)). He cannot by reference to any contract term or a notice, exclude or restrict his liability for death or personal injury resulting from negligence (s. 2(1)). In the case of other loss or damage, he cannot exclude or restrict his liability *except* in so far as the term satisfies the test of reasonableness (s. 2(2)).

Liability in Contract

Section 3 applies generally to contract liability but one of the contracting parties must 'deal as consumer' (see s. 12) *or* on the other's 'written standard terms of business'. The section specifies that one party cannot, by reference to any contract term, exclude or restrict his own liability for breach of contract or render any performance substantially different from that expected of him, or render no performance at all, *except* in so far as the term satisfies the test of reasonableness.

The Sale of Goods and Hire-Purchase

Section 6 provides that the statutory implied obligations as to quality, fitness for purpose, etc., in sale and hire-purchase contracts cannot be excluded or restricted by reference to any contract term as against a party 'dealing as consumer', but for non-consumers the exclusion is possible *if* the clause passes the reasonableness test. Furthermore, the section stipulates that the statutory implied undertaking as to title *cannot* be excluded in either the consumer or non-consumer category. See s. 7 for the corresponding provisions in other miscellaneous contracts, and s. 12 for the definition of 'deals as consumer' and its application in *R & B Customs Brokers Co. Ltd v United Dominions Trust Ltd* [1988] 1 WLR 321.

Other Major Provisions

Section 5—renders absolutely ineffective provisions in manufacturers' guarantees excluding or restricting liability for loss or damage resulting from the manufacturer's negligence when the goods have proved 'defective' in 'consumer use'.

Section 9—affirms the common law's approach to fundamental breach.

Section 13—gives a wide definition of an exclusion clause and may be useful for invalidating provisions which seek to *define* liability rather than *exclude* it (see *Smith v Eric Bush* [1990] AC 831; *Harlingdon & Leinster Enterprises Ltd v Christopher Hull Fine Art Ltd* [1991] 1 QB 564).

Reasonableness under the 1977 Act

This test emphasizes that exclusion clauses may be *negotiated* between the parties and thus represent their allocation of risks (see *Photo Production*, above) rather than being *imposed* as in contracts of adhesion. Section 11 provides that, for a contract term, reasonableness is assessed at the time *the contract is made*, whereas for a notice excluding liability in tort, and not having contractual effect, the relevant time is when the *liability arose*. The test in contract is, therefore, very strict (see *Stewart Gill Ltd v Horatio Myer & Co. Ltd* [1992] 1 QB 600). Section 11(4) specifies that if liability is restricted to a specific sum of money, regard is to be had to the resources of the person inserting the clause and whether he could have taken out insurance.

Schedule 2 of Unfair Contract Terms Act 1977 (UCTA 1977) also contains a set of 'guidelines' that a court must take into account when assessing the reasonableness of an exemption clause, such as equality of bargaining power, the inducement given to the customer for insertion of the clause, and knowledge of the clause. Although these are not exhaustive, and are only expressly applicable for the purposes of ss. 6 and 7, *they are extremely important and show the balancing exercise which the court must perform.* In business-to-business contracts the courts have also been influenced by whether the relevant clause was generally employed within the industry, or was used as a risk-allocation device so as to avoid the possibility of duplicate insurance. Conversely, in business-to-consumer contracts the courts have been more interventionist, seeking to protect the reasonable and legitimate expectations of consumers where possible (e.g. *Smith v Eric Bush* [1990] 1 AC 831). Reported cases on the reasonableness test remain relatively scarce as the test is *primarily* one of *fact* rather than *law,* but consider the following: *Phillips Products Ltd v Hyland* [1987] 1 WLR 659; *Stewart Gill, supra; St Alban's City and District Council v International Computers Ltd* [1996] 4 All ER 481; *Watford Electronics Ltd v Sanderson CFL Ltd* [2001] EWCA Civ 317, [2001] BLR 143; and *Sterling Hydraulics Ltd v Dichtomatik Ltd* [2006] EWHC 2004, [2007] 1 Lloyd's Rep 8.

(c) EU-Inspired Laws

(i) Unfair Terms in Consumer Contracts Regulations 1999

The original **Unfair Terms in Consumer Contracts Regulations 1994, SI No. 3159** (UTCCR 1994) came into force on 1 July 1995 in order to implement an EC Council Directive (93/13/EEC) Unfair Terms in Consumer Contracts, but the 1999 Regulations, (SI 1999, No. 2083) (UTCCR 1999), which came into force on 1 October 1999, revoke and replace the original Regulations and reflect more closely the wording of the Directive. In particular, the UTCCR 1994 applied only to the business supply of goods and services to consumers under the terms of a standard-form contract, so there was doubt as to whether interests in land were covered. The UTCCR 1999 adopts an amended definition of 'supplier', omitting any reference to goods and services. It is thus clear that standard-form business contracts for the supply to consumers of goods, services, and interests in land, fall within the UTCCR 1999 (see *London Borough of Newham v Khatun* [2004] EWCA 55, [2004] 3 WLR 417).

Regrettably, Parliament made no attempt to dovetail the UTCCR 1999 with UCTA 1977. The result is a complex, overlapping set of rules which is most undesirable in the sphere of consumer protection where remedies should be accessible and understandable (see, however, the Draft Bill on Unfair Terms in Contracts, proposed by the Law Commission, No. 292, which puts forward suggestions for amalgamating UCTA 1977 and UTCCR 1999). The overall effect of the UTCCR 1999 is that an 'unfair term' in a contract concluded between a consumer and a seller or supplier 'shall not be binding on the consumer' (**reg. 8(1)**).

It is important to stress that, ultimately, it is the Directive which is paramount and thus, in interpreting the UTCCR 1999, the court must have regard to the purpose and wording of both the Directive and its recitals (see, generally, *Marleasing SA v La Comercial Internacional de Alimentacion SA,* Case C-106/89 [1990] ECR I-4135).

Scope of the Regulations

The UTCCR 1999, reg. 4(1), broadly defines the scope of the regulations as applying to 'unfair terms in contracts concluded between a seller or supplier and a consumer'.

Sellers, Suppliers, and Consumers

'Seller' and 'supplier' are defined in reg. 3(1) as 'any natural or legal person who, in contracts covered by these Regulations, is acting for purposes relating to his trade, business or profession, whether publicly owned or privately owned'. There is no definition of either 'goods' or 'services'. There is, likewise, no definition of a 'trade, business or profession' in the UTCCR 1999, and no further delineation of when the seller or supplier will be regarded as 'acting for purposes relating to' his trade, business or profession. It remains to be seen how this latter phrase will be defined but its counterpart in the UCTA 1977, s. 12 ('makes the contract in the course of a business') has been interpreted by the common law as requiring a *regularity* of business dealings (see *R & B Customs Brokers Co. Ltd v United Dominions Trust Ltd* [1988] 1 WLR 321).

'Consumer' is defined in reg. 3(1) as 'any natural person who, in contracts covered by these Regulations, is acting for purposes which are outside his trade, business or profession'.

When is a Contract Term Unfair?

An 'unfair term' is defined in reg. 5(1) as:

> A contractual term which has not been individually negotiated shall be regarded as unfair if, contrary to the requirement of good faith, it causes a significant imbalance in the parties' rights and obligations arising under the contract, to the detriment of the consumer.

There are thus four crucial elements in the operation of the UTCCR 1999 unfairness test:

  (i) the contract term must not have been 'individually negotiated' (see reg. 5(2)–(4));

  (ii) an absence of good faith;

  (iii) a significant imbalance in the parties' rights and obligations under the contract;

  (iv) detriment to the consumer.

Assessing Unfairness

Regulation 6(1) provides that:

> Without prejudice to regulation 12, the unfairness of a contractual term shall be assessed, taking into account the nature of the goods or services for which the contract was concluded and by referring, at the time of conclusion of the contract, to all the circumstances attending the conclusion of the contract and to all the other terms of the contract or of another contract on which it is dependent.

It is under reg. 6(1) that the court must assess the factors leading to the contract's conclusion and, having regard to the goods or services themselves, weigh in the balance the contract terms which seek to favour the seller/supplier against those which are advantageous to the consumer. The House of Lords considered the question of unfairness under the UTCCR 1994 in *Director General of Fair Trading v First National Bank plc* [2001] UKHL 52; [2002] 1 AC 481.

Schedule 2: the Indicative List of Unfair Terms

An important feature of the UTCCR 1999 is that reg. 5(5) refers to Sch. 2 as providing 'an indicative and non-exhaustive list of the terms which may be regarded as unfair'. Schedule 2 contains a copious list of 17 potentially unfair terms. It must be stressed that these are merely *examples* of terms which *might* be unfair and it is not practical to list and analyse all the examples provided in Sch. 2. The Office of Fair Trading (OFT) produces regular bulletins on unfair contract terms, with abundant examples of such terms and the amendments ordered by the Director General of the OFT under his powers of enforcement.

Terms Concerning Adequacy of the Price or Defining the Subject Matter of the Contract

One crucial limitation on the scope of the test of unfairness in the UTCCR 1999 is contained in reg. 6(2), which stipulates that:

> In so far as it is in plain, intelligible language, the assessment of fairness of a term shall not relate—
>
> (a) to the definition of the main subject matter of the contract, or
> (b) to the adequacy of the price or remuneration, as against the goods or services supplied in exchange.

Paragraph (a) leaves the parties at liberty to define the subject matter of their contract. An example of such a core term, referred to by the Office of Fair Trading (*Unfair Contract Terms*, Bulletin No. 6, April 1999, para. 1.24 and Case Report 56, p. 49) is that retail 'gift vouchers' may, plainly and intelligibly, state the date upon which they expire and thus become invalid.

Paragraph (b) prevents adequacy of consideration from being challenged *per se*—a contract should not be impugned merely because the consumer has voluntarily made a bad bargain by over-paying for the goods or services requested. However, in *Bairstow Eves London Central Ltd v Smith* [2004] EWHC 263, [2004] EGLR 25, Gross J indicated that reg. 6(2) required a strict interpretation otherwise a 'coach and horses could be driven through the Regulations'. Consequently, it is unlikely that reg. 6(2) can be used to 'shield terms as to price escalation or default provisions from scrutiny under the fairness requirement contained in regulation 5(1)'.

The meaning and scope of reg. 6(2) was most recently considered in *Office of Fair Trading v Abbey National plc and others* [2009] UKSC 6; [2010] 1 All ER by the Supreme Court (known as the House of Lords until 1 August 2009). The case involved the banking practice of levying charges on personal current account customers in respect of unauthorized overdrafts (including unpaid item charges and other related charges). The Supreme Court recognized that banks offer a 'package of services' that includes the collection and payment of cheques, other money transmission services, facilities for cash distribution (mainly by ATM machines either at manned branches or elsewhere), and the provision of statements in printed or electronic form. In return the consideration received by the banks consists of: (i) interest and charges on overdrafts, as well as specific charges for particular non-routine services, and (ii) the interest that customers, whose accounts are in credit, forego by receiving a relatively low rate of interest on it (or sometimes no interest at all). It was held that as the bank charges levied on personal current account customers in respect of unauthorized overdrafts constituted *part of the price or remuneration* for the banking services supplied, no assessment under the UTCCR 1999 of the fairness of those terms could relate to their adequacy as against the services supplied (provided the relevant terms giving rise to the charges were drafted in plain intelligible language).

Assessing Good Faith

The **UTCCR 1994** contained, in **Sch. 2,** a list of four factors to be taken into account in making an assessment of good faith: (a) the strength of the parties' bargaining positions; (b) whether the consumer had an inducement to agree to the term; (c) whether the goods or services were sold/supplied to the special order of the consumer; and (d) the extent to which the seller/supplier had dealt fairly and equitably with the consumer. These factors have been deleted from the body of the **UTCCR 1999** because they are contained in **recital 16** to the Directive and the Regulations sought to reflect more accurately the wording of the main text of the Directive. Accordingly, these four factors remain crucial, with **reg. 5(1)** stipulating that the absence of 'the requirement of good faith' is crucial in assessing the unfairness of a contract term. On the question of good faith, see *Director General of Fair Trading v First National Bank plc* (above).

Prevention of the Continued Use of Unfair Terms

Regulations 10–15 relate to the machinery for challenging unfair terms and the prevention of their continued use. Under **reg. 10(1)**, it is the duty of the Director General of the OFT to consider complaints made to him regarding unfair terms. In *Office of Fair Trading v Foxtons Ltd* **[2009] EWCA 288, [2009] 3 All ER 697** it was held that where a 'general challenge' is made against a term that has been drawn up for general use, the decision of the OFT applies not simply to future contracts but also *existing* contracts, whilst **reg. 12(1)** allows for an application for an injunction against any person using such a term. In deciding whether or not to apply for an injunction, the Director may have regard to any undertakings given to him by the person as to the continued use of the term in question (**reg. 10(3)**).

Intelligibility in Written Contracts

Regulation 7 provides that 'a seller or supplier shall ensure that any written term of a contract is expressed in plain, intelligible language' and that, 'if there is doubt about the meaning of a written term, the interpretation which is most favourable to the consumer shall prevail'. Although the common law might achieve this result by a combination of the rules on reasonable notice and interpretation *contra proferentem*, the express articulation of principle in **reg. 7** is most welcome.

(ii) The Unfair Commercial Practices Directive (2005/29/EC)

The most recent European Union foray into the area of consumer protection relates to the Directive on Unfair Commercial Practices, 2005/29/EC (UCP), with domestic implementing legislation coming into effect from 26 May 2008, in the shape of the Consumer Protection from Unfair Trading Regulations 2008, SI No. 1277 (CPUTR). This new law applies to the advertising, promotion, sale, or supply of any product to a consumer and, unlike its forbears, imposes a standard of *maximum harmonization* on all Member States (i.e. the UCP is designed to prevent any Member State from *exceeding* the protections contained within it, thereby ensuring greater consistency of implementation across the EU).

The UCP (and therefore the CPUTR) aims to prohibit the use of certain types of 'sharp' practice by businesses against consumers, in order to regulate more effectively the internal market for consumers (particularly in terms of stimulating cross-border trade or the provision of a greater range of competing products). Schedule 1, CPUTR, contains a list of practices that are automatically deemed to be unfair in *all* circumstances (e.g. 'claiming that the trader is about to cease trading or move premises when he is not'). Any other practice will be subjected to a case-by-case assessment, with the criteria set out in CPUTR, Part 2 (regs. 3–7) being used as the relevant benchmarks. Regulation 3 has a general prohibition on any type of unfair commercial practice. Regulations 5 and 6 ban misleading actions such as false information contained in advertisements, or purposeful omission of material information, said information referring to the main characteristics of the product, price, taxes, delivery charges, and the existence of a right of withdrawal (if one exists). Equally, reg. 7 prohibits 'aggressive' commercial practices such as harassment and coercion (e.g. 'the use of threatening or abusive language or behaviour').

The CPUTR defines 'unfair' as being contrary to the requirements of 'professional diligence' *and* which materially distorts (or is likely to distort) consumers' economic behaviour with regard to the relevant product, a 'consumer' being someone who is 'reasonably well informed, reasonably observant and circumspect'. 'Professional diligence' is based upon the standards of care and skill that a trader might reasonably be expected to exercise with respect to consumers, and that are commensurate with honest market practice in the trader's field of activity or the general principle of good faith in the trader's field of activity. Hopefully this should put an end to cold-callers who refuse to leave when asked to do so by the homeowner!

Finally, it is disappointing that the CPUTR does not recognize the right of the individual to sue directly for non-compliance, leaving all such matters to the standard enforcement authorities. There is clearly an urgent need to overhaul the existing domestic statutory regulation of unfair contract terms in order to simplify the law for the average consumer, highlighted by the Law Commission's 'Draft Bill on Unfair Terms' which sought to amalgamate UCTA 1977 and the UTCCR 1999.

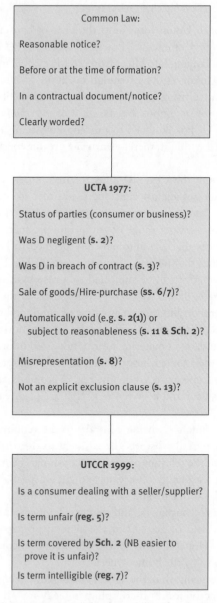

Figure 4 Incorporation and enforceability of exclusion clauses

Question 1

Harvey buys a country mansion in Gloucestershire and decides to have the gardens landscaped. He contacts Capability Ltd after seeing the company's advertisement in the local newspaper stating: 'Paths, fencing and garden maintenance our speciality—also quotations given for larger jobs.' Before concluding any contract, Harvey discovers that there is a local builder, Scrapitt, who offers to do the work at '5% less than whatever price Capability quotes'. Harvey has little confidence in Scrapitt and he therefore decides to enter into a contract with Capability Ltd.

A price of £10,000 is agreed and Harvey is given a document headed 'Memorandum of Terms'. This document sets out the job specification, price, and date of completion. The reverse has the following clauses added by rubber stamp:

Clause 1: The company accepts no responsibility for personal injury to the customer during performance of the contract.

Clause 2: Liability for any damage to the customer's home is limited to the sum of £500, and no liability can be accepted for loss of, or damage to, the customer's goods.

Reckless, employed by Capability Ltd, drives a dumper truck through the wall of Harvey's house. As Harvey returns home that night, he collides with the dumper truck which Reckless has left in the middle of the driveway. The car is completely ruined and Harvey is injured.

Advise Harvey.

Commentary

There are three areas for evaluation in this problem. First, the question of the common law and exclusion clauses: have these clauses been incorporated as terms of the contract? Secondly, the relevant sections of the **Unfair Contract Terms Act 1977** must be considered and, finally, a brief mention must be made of third party liability and exclusion clauses in relation to Reckless, the employee of Capability Ltd.

Answer plan

- Have the exclusion clauses been incorporated as terms of the contract? What are the tests, at common law, for the effective incorporation of exclusion clauses in a contract?

- Explain which provisions of the **Unfair Contract Terms Act 1977** and the **Unfair Terms in Consumer Contracts Regulations 1999 (UTCCR 1999)** apply to these exclusion clauses.

- Explain the legal position of Reckless who is not party to the contract between Harvey and Capability Ltd. Does the **Contracts (Rights of Third Parties) Act 1999** apply to Reckless?

Suggested answer

This question concerns the extent to which Harvey (H) is bound by the attempted exclusion and restriction of Capability Ltd's (C) liability. Like any other term of the contract, an exclusion clause must be an integral part of the undertaking if it is to be effective but, as an exclusion clause attempts to remove a liability that would otherwise exist, there are particularly stringent rules regarding the incorporation of such terms in contracts. If H had signed the contract there would be a strong presumption that he was bound by its terms (*L'Estrange v F Graucob Ltd* [1934] 2 KB 394) but in the absence of a signature, H must be given adequate *notice* of the terms. It was emphasized in *Parker v South Eastern Ry* (1877) 2 CPD 416 that it is notice of the terms which is important, not their actual reading or understanding, and it follows that if the notice is illegible or obscured by a date stamp as in *Richardson, Spence & Co. v Rowntree* [1894] AC 217, it will be ineffective. The clauses in the problem appear to be quite legible but they are on the reverse of the document and there is no notice such as 'See over for conditions' on its face. This may well be fatal to C, for in *Henderson v Steven* (1875) LR 2 HL (Sc) 470 the court held that the absence of a notice on the front of a ticket referring to clauses printed on its back rendered the clauses invalid. Most recently, in *Interfoto Picture Library Ltd v Stiletto Visual Programmes Ltd* [1989] QB 433, the court emphasized that if the clause is particularly stringent, or onerous, extra care must be taken to draw its attention to the other party. Furthermore, the notice that is given must be contemporaneous with the contract's formation (see *Olley v Marlborough Court Ltd* [1949] 1 KB 532; *Thornton v Shoe Lane Parking Ltd* [1971] 2 QB 163). The exclusion clauses in the problem are certainly not presented to H post-contractually as they are given to him *before* the price is agreed and this requirement would therefore appear to be satisfied.

Even if the conditions regarding notice are complied with, there are other demands made by the common law. The document containing the clauses must be a contractual document, i.e. one which a reasonable man would expect to contain the conditions of the contract. In *Chapelton v Barry UDC* [1940] 1 KB 532, a receipt which was given for the hire of a deck chair was not such a contractual document and neither was the front cover of a cheque book in *Burnett v Westminster Bank* [1966] 1 QB 742. The courts preserve great flexibility when deciding this question (see *McCutcheon v MacBrayne (David) Ltd* [1964] 1 WLR 125) and it may be that the 'Memorandum of Terms' in the problem will not suffice. There might be a full, written contract elsewhere which would mean that the court could strike down this 'Memorandum'.

Before leaving the common law, it must be emphasized that, should the clauses be successfully integrated in the contract, any ambiguity will nevertheless be construed against C (i.e. *contra proferentem*). Particularly exacting standards are demanded of clauses which are alleged to exclude all liability for negligence and the law will preserve this head of liability wherever possible (see *Alderslade v Hendon Laundry Ltd* [1945] 1 KB 189; *White v John Warwick & Co. Ltd* [1953] 1 WLR 1285). The question is one of construction of the contract, but if the defendant disclaims liability for 'any loss' the court may consider that he is attempting to exclude all *types* of loss without being sufficiently specific as to their *cause* (see *Price v Union Lighterage Co.* [1904] 1 KB 412). The clauses in the problem certainly make no express reference to negligence and, as such, they will clearly be construed against C following the tests laid down by Lord Morton in *Canada Steamship Lines Ltd v The King* [1952] AC 192. However, the common law's powers to circumvent clauses by deft interpretation are now of less significance in the light of the **Unfair Contract Terms Act 1977**.

Section 2(1) of the 1977 Act invalidates any attempt by a contract term or notice to exclude or restrict liability for death or bodily injury resulting from negligence. It seems indisputable that it was negligent to leave the dumper truck in the driveway and clause 1 of the contract would be ineffective as regards H's claim for his injuries.

Section 2(2) further provides that in the case of 'other loss or damage' a person cannot exclude or restrict his liability for negligence except in so far as the term or notice satisfies the test of reasonableness. This is clearly applicable to C, as is s. 3, which subjects an attempted exclusion of liability for breach of contract to the reasonableness test where one party 'deals as consumer or on the other's written standard terms of business'. Apart from the difficult question of whether C's terms are 'written standard terms' (which the Act does not define and in relation to which there is no judicial guidance), it must be decided whether clause 2 can pass the reasonableness test. Section 11(1) provides that the time for determining whether the clause is reasonable is the time at which the contract is made. This is a very strict test and the seriousness of the loss or damage caused cannot be considered except to the extent to which it was, or ought reasonably to have been, in the contemplation of the parties at the time of contract. Following the interpretation given to s. 11 in *Stewart Gill Ltd v Horatio Myer & Co. Ltd* [1992] 1 QB 600, it seems most unlikely that C could justify the insertion of the exclusion clause in the contract. *Stewart Gill* also decides that the *whole* clause must be reasonable, not merely the part relied upon by the defendant: clause 2 may therefore fail in its entirety and this conclusion is fortified in that deliberate breaches of contract are within the literal wording of the clause (see also *Watford Electronics Ltd v Sanderson CFL Ltd* [2001] EWCA 317; [2001] BLR 143, which would clearly support the view that clauses 1 and 2 were separate for the purposes of applying s. 11 of the **Unfair Contract Terms Act 1977 (UCTA 1977)**. Section 11(4) provides that if the defendant limits liability to a specific sum of money, regard shall be had, in assessing reasonableness, to the resources which he could expect to be available to him for meeting the liability and how far it was open to him to cover himself by insurance. This provision was designed to alleviate undue hardship to small businesses but it is arguable that C could and should have insured against the risk in question and this would certainly be the case if C could insure without any material increase to H in the contract price.

It is also vital to consider the guidelines for assessing reasonableness in **Sch. 2** of the Act. Particularly relevant to this problem is the question of whether the customer was given any inducement to agree to the clause or had the opportunity of doing business elsewhere without having to accept the clause. As C charges more than one of its competitors (Scrapitt would give a 5% discount on C's prices) it is legitimate to ask whether Scrapitt would use any exclusion clauses and, if so, whether they are more or less onerous than C's. C's exclusion clause might, therefore, be condemned using such a comparative assessment.

The decision in *Phillips Products Ltd v Hyland* [1987] 1 WLR 659 is particularly applicable to the problem. There the plaintiff hired an excavator from the second defendants on the latter's standard terms which provided that the driver should be regarded as employed by the plaintiff, the plaintiff thereby remaining liable for any loss arising from the machine's use. The driver negligently damaged the plaintiff's factory whilst carrying out work at the plaintiff's request. It was held that several factors meant that the clause failed to pass the reasonableness test. First, the plaintiff did not regularly hire machinery of this sort whereas the defendants were in the business of equipment hire. Secondly, the clause was not the product of any *negotiation* between the parties: rather it was simply one of the defendant's 43 standard conditions. Thirdly, the hire period was very short and the plaintiff had no opportunity to arrange insurance cover. Finally, the plaintiff played no part in the selection of the driver and had no control over the way in which he performed his job. On balance, it is suggested that C's clause would not be regarded as a reasonable one.

The UTCCR 1999, SI No. 2083, also apply to these facts. C is undoubtedly a business 'supplier', defined in **reg. 3(1)** as 'any natural or legal person who, in contracts covered by these Regulations, is acting for purposes relating to his trade, business or profession, whether publicly owned or privately owned', and H is a 'consumer' who is 'acting for purposes which are outside his trade, business or profession' (**reg. 3(1)**). The Regulations apply only to contract *terms* (**reg. 4(1)**) but, on the facts which are given, the 'memorandum of terms' would appear to contain contractual obligations. Moreover, the clauses added by rubber stamp have certainly not been 'individually negotiated' (**reg. 5(1)**) but, instead, have been 'drafted in advance' (**reg. 5(2)**). The contract between H and C would thus appear to be a 'pre-formulated standard contract' (**reg. 5(3)**) within the scope of the Regulations but, in any event, the remainder of the contract can be viewed as such a standard contract even if a 'specific term' has been individually negotiated, provided that an 'overall assessment of it indicates that it is a pre-formulated standard contract' (**reg. 5(3)**).

Assuming that the UTCCR 1999 apply to the contract between H and C, are any of the contract terms unfair, and thus not binding (see reg. 8(1)), on grounds that they are 'contrary to the requirement of good faith' and cause a 'significant imbalance in the parties' rights and obligations arising under the contract, to the detriment of the consumer'? Recital 16 of the Directive on Unfair Terms in Consumer Contracts (93/13/EEC) refers to several factors in the assessment of good faith. Applying these factors to the problem, there is no obvious disparity in the bargaining strengths of H and C and H has been given no inducement to agree to the term. Moreover, the services supplied by C are to H's 'special order'. However, it is arguable that *a unilateral imposition* of such terms means that C has not 'dealt fairly and equitably' with H and has failed to consider H's 'legitimate interests'. In addition, H may not have had a 'real opportunity of becoming acquainted' with the contract terms before the contract was concluded (Sch. 2, para. 1(i)). In conclusion, these terms may be 'so weighted in favour of the supplier as to tilt the parties' rights and obligations under the contract significantly in his favour' (*Director General of Fair Trading v First National Bank plc* [2002] 1 AC 481, *per* Lord Bingham at 494).

Moreover, Sch. 2 of the Regulations provides an indicative, non-exhaustive list of terms which may be regarded as unfair, and a term excluding liability for death or bodily injury caused by negligence of the supplier heads the list of 17 examples (see clause 1). However, UCTA 1977, s. 2(1), renders such an attempted exclusion of liability totally ineffective and the Act is thus more advantageous to H. Clause 2 would also seem to be unfair under the Regulations for 'inappropriately excluding or limiting the legal rights of the consumer *vis-à-vis* the supplier . . . in the event of total or partial non-performance or inadequate performance by the supplier of any of the contractual obligations' (Sch. 2, para. 1(b)). However, the test of reasonableness under the UCTA 1977 may, once again, prove to be more advantageous to H as, under the UCTA 1977, the burden is on C to prove that the exclusion clauses satisfy that test whereas, under the Regulations, the burden of proving that the terms are unfair is placed on H.

Finally, Reckless (R), who is employed by C, does not appear to be protected by the exclusion clauses and, therefore, will retain personal liability for his actions (see *Adler v Dickinson* [1955] 1 QB 158). In particular, note that R cannot rely upon s. 1 of the Contracts (Rights of Third Parties) Act 1999 as he was not 'expressly identified' in any of the clauses (see s. 1(3)), nor is there any evidence that C and H agreed that R would be entitled to such protection. Ironically, as R's negligent acts were committed in the course of his employment, C will be vicariously liable for H's loss without any concomitant right to rely upon the two exclusion clauses. Furthermore, it would be impossible to argue that C is acting as R's agent for the purpose of bringing R into direct contractual relations with H (see *New Zealand Shipping Co. Ltd v AM Satterthwaite & Co. Ltd (The Eurymedon)* [1975] AC 154).

Question 2

Patrick, a director of Dartsma Ltd, which manufactures computers, decided that the company should purchase a prestigious car which could be used principally for entertaining the company's customers but which would also be suitable for private use by Patrick and the other directors. Accordingly, the company bought a second-hand 'Lynx' car from Dependable Motors Ltd (DM). Patrick managed to negotiate a 15% 'trade discount' on the price of the car. The lengthy contract for the sale of the car, which Patrick signed, contained the following clause on page 10: 'DM Ltd will refund the price of any defective goods provided that such defects are communicated to the company in writing no later than 3 days after the contract of sale is concluded but the Company shall not otherwise be liable for any loss or damage caused by defects in the goods.'

Before leaving DM, Patrick noticed that the car's windscreen-wiper blades needed replacing. He therefore purchased two new blades from the parts department of DM Ltd, fitting them himself. The sales invoice contained the same exclusion clause as that in the contract for the sale of the car and was also signed by Patrick. After using the car for two weeks, Patrick had a minor accident whilst driving the car in wet weather and the car was damaged. He discovered that the rubber wiper blades had perished and had consequently failed to clear the windscreen of rain. In the third week of using the car, its gearbox seized up and was ruined. DM Ltd had failed to refill the gearbox with oil during the pre-delivery service of the car.

Advise Patrick.

 Commentary

This question involves a consideration of the extent to which the implied terms of the **Sale of Goods Act 1979 (SGA 1979)** relating to description, quality, and fitness for purpose of the goods can be excluded in consumer and business sales. **Sections 6 and 12** of the **Unfair Contract Terms Act 1977 (UCTA 1977)** must be considered together with the courts' interpretation of those sections. It is also crucial to consider the **Unfair Terms in Consumer Contracts Regulations 1999 (UTCCR 1999)**.

 Answer plan

- Is Dependable Motors Ltd, the seller of the car, in breach of the implied terms of the **SGA 1979** relating to satisfactory quality and fitness for purpose?

- Have the exclusion clauses been incorporated as terms of the contract?

- Is Patrick classifiable as a business buyer ('dealing otherwise than as consumer') or a consumer buyer ('dealing as consumer') within **ss. 6** and **12** of the **UCTA 1977**? What is the relevance of these distinctions in relation to exclusion clauses? How is a consumer buyer distinguished from a business buyer?

- Are any of the provisions of the **UTCCR 1999** applicable to Patrick? Does **UCTA 1977** provide better remedies in this context than those available in the **1999 Regulations**?

Suggested answer

This problem involves a consideration of whether the exclusion clauses in issue protect DM from breach of the implied terms of the Sale of Goods Act 1979 (SGA 1979), ss. 13–15, which cover the description, quality and fitness for purpose of the goods sold. First, it is almost certain that DM is in breach of s. 14 of the SGA 1979. Both the car and the wiper blades were sold 'in the course of a business' by DM (see *Stevenson v Rogers*, below) and the goods are both unsatisfactory and unfit for their purpose. Secondly, there can scarcely be any dispute regarding the integration of these exclusion clauses as terms in the contracts of sale as they are advanced by DM at the moment of the formation of both contracts (see *Olley v Marlborough Court Ltd* [1949] 1 KB 532) and both documents are probably contractual in nature (see *Chapelton v Barry UDC* [1940] 1 KB 532). There might only be some doubt in this respect regarding the 'sales invoice' for the wiper blades but the problem does not provide enough information to decide the issue. More importantly, both documents are signed by Patrick (P) and, in the absence of any misrepresentation or duress, the exclusion clauses will almost certainly be integrated as terms of the contract (see *L'Estrange v F Graucob Ltd* [1934] 2 KB 394). It is arguable, therefore, that at common law these exemption clauses would bind P.

However, UCTA 1977, ss. 6 and 12 restrict dramatically the extent to which ss. 13–15 of the SGA 1979 may be excluded. Section 6 provides that 'as against a person dealing as consumer' liability for breach of obligations arising from the SGA 1979, ss. 13–15 'cannot be excluded or restricted by reference to any contract term', but as against a person 'dealing otherwise than as consumer' liability can be excluded but 'only in so far as the term satisfies the requirement of reasonableness'. Section 12 defines a consumer sale stipulating three requirements. First, that one party does not make the contract 'in the course of a business' nor 'holds himself out as doing so'. Secondly, that the other party *does* make the contract in the course of a business and, thirdly, that the goods 'are of a type ordinarily supplied for private use or consumption'. Section 12 was subsequently amended (by the Sale and Supply of Goods to Consumer Regulations 2002, SI No. 3045, reg. 14(2)) and s. 12(1A) now provides that if the consumer is 'an individual', the third requirement in s. 12 must be ignored. Consequently, the consumer buyer, who is an individual, may now purchase goods which are *not* of a type ordinarily supplied for private use or consumption (e.g. a pantechnicon) and, nevertheless, seek the protection conferred by ss. 6 and 12. It is clear, from the common law's interpretation of 'dealing as consumer' (see below), that a limited company can so deal and thus be within ss. 6 and 12 but, in this event, the company would have to buy goods of a type ordinarily supplied for private use or consumption. Applying this to the problem, it is the company, Dartsma Ltd, which buys the car but, almost certainly, the purchase of a single car would be classified as a type of goods ordinarily supplied for private use or consumption. Whilst wiper blades for cars might, formerly, have posed a problem for Patrick in that such goods could be regarded, typically, as 'trade goods' (but note that the test also relates to *use/consumption* of the goods), this is no longer a difficulty as Patrick clearly buys the blades in his capacity as an individual and he is thus within s. 12.

It must now be asked whether the remaining requirements of s. 12 are met: does one party 'make the contract in the course of a business' whilst the other does not do so and, consequently, 'deals as consumer'? There are two possible interpretations of the former phrase. First, a business or person may contract in this way by, for example, purchasing goods for the business even though the business does not deal in the type of goods which have been purchased and the sale is thus not a normal and regular part of the business activity which is carried on, e.g. a solicitor who buys an electric fire for use in the office. It is plain that the definition is wide enough to encompass this example and it was arguably the intent of the legislature to cast the net very widely. Moreover, in *Stevenson v Rogers* [1999] QB 1028, the Court of Appeal held that the phrase 'sells goods in the course of a business' in the SGA 1979, s. 14(2), must be given a literal interpretation. In *Stevenson*, the defendant had an established business as a fisherman and he sold a fishing vessel which he used in the course of his business, replacing that vessel with a new one. The defendant's business was thus not that of buying and selling ships or boats. The Court of Appeal ruled that, having regard to the legislative history of the SGA 1979, the wording in s. 14(2) of the Act had been deliberately changed to widen the protection conferred upon a buyer of goods from a business seller. Thus, it was held that s. 14(2) must be construed at face value and the sale of the fishing vessel was in the course of a business: the wording of the section did not demand any element of regularity of dealing and so there was no reason 'to re-introduce some implied qualification, difficult to define, in order to narrow what appears to be the wide scope and apparent purpose of the words' (p. 623, *per* Potter LJ). The second possible interpretation of the UCTA 1977, s. 12 is that, to be in the *course* of a business, the goods in question must be bought for some definite business purpose with a degree of regularity. In contrast with the example, above, of the solicitor who buys an electric fire for his office, the regularity argument would mean that only a trader whose business is to purchase electric fires for resale would be making the contracts in the course of a business.

The courts are clearly adopting this second interpretation for s. 12. In *Rasbora Ltd v JCL Marine Ltd* [1977] 1 Lloyd's Rep 645, a private buyer of a boat substituted the plaintiff company as buyer for the purposes of avoiding payment of VAT. On her maiden voyage, the boat caught fire and sank. Lawson J held that this was a consumer sale (under SGA 1893, s. 55(7)) and, more importantly, that even if the company had been the *original buyer* the sale would still have been a consumer sale on the basis that the boat was to be used by the company's majority shareholder and not chartered to third parties. This approach has been confirmed by the Court of Appeal in *R & B Customs Brokers Co. Ltd v United Dominions Trust Ltd* [1988] 1 WLR 321 where a director of the plaintiff company decided that the company should buy a new car and trade in its existing car in part-exchange, his intention being that the car would be used both for company and personal use. The car proved to be defective but, again, because the company was only an irregular purchaser of cars, it was held that it was acting as a consumer and the exclusion clauses were ineffective. Moreover, the court dismissed the argument that there was any holding-out that the contract was made in the course of a business under s. 12. These decisions are criticizable in that they evaluate the *purpose* for which the goods are bought and the *regularity of dealing*, neither of these factors being present in the objective statutory definition.

Although at first glance it appears unnecessary to have these conflicting interpretations, a moment's thought reveals the justice underlying them. If the regularity requirement is held to apply to business sellers, the buyer has no protection under the implied conditions in the SGA 1979, s. 14, where the seller sells goods which are not his stock-in-trade, as in *Stevenson v Rogers*. Equally, if the regularity stipulation did *not* apply on the facts of *R & B Customs Brokers*, and the buyer was thus characterized as acting in the course of a business, the exclusion clauses would not be declared void but would be subject to the reasonableness test only. In short, protection is secured for the buyers in both *Stevenson v Rogers* and *R & B Customs Brokers*.

In view of these decisions, it would seem that both the sale of the car and the wiper blades would fall within the consumer classification and *Rasbora* indicates that the 15% discount obtained by P would not alter this conclusion. The exclusion clauses would thus be ineffective. Finally, the damage to the car resulting from the defective wiper blades would almost certainly be a recoverable consequential loss, being reasonably in the contemplation of the parties at the time the contract was made. In sales of goods, the courts have treated such claims in the buyer's favour (see *Parsons (Livestock) Ltd v Uttley, Ingham & Co. Ltd* [1978] QB 791).

If the purchases in the problem are regarded as made in the course of a business, the exclusion clauses would be subject to the reasonableness test, but it is most unlikely that they would pass that test. Having regard to the guidelines concerning reasonableness in **Sch. 2** of the UCTA 1977, the parties have roughly equal bargaining power and P has been given a 15% discount both of which favour DM. However, it is likely that P could have bought the same model of car elsewhere without such a restrictive clause but with as generous a discount. Similarly, perhaps P ought not reasonably to have known of the existence of the term in this lengthy document at page 10 and it seems that the time limit of three days for notifying defects could not be justified at the date the contract was entered into, this being the time that an evaluation is made under the UCTA 1977, s. 11. It is quite unreasonable to expect defects to manifest themselves and then be notified within three days (see *R W Green Ltd v Cade Bros Farms* [1978] 1 Lloyd's Rep 602). Furthermore, in *Rees Hough Ltd v Redland Reinforced Plastics Ltd* (1984) 1 Const L J 67, a clause in a contract between two businesses was held to be unreasonable because it provided that the sellers of piping excluded all liability unless notified of complaints within three months.

It is clear that the UTCCR 1999 cannot apply to the sale of the car as, although DM are clearly business sellers of goods within reg. 3(1), it is the *company* (Dartsma Ltd) which has bought the car and the definition of a 'consumer' in reg. 3(1) applies only to a 'natural person'. Provided that the 'sales invoice' given to P contains contract terms, the 1999 Regulations will apply to the sale of the wiper blades. P buys them in his capacity as a 'natural person' and, almost certainly, he is 'acting for purposes which are outside his trade, business or profession' (reg. 3(1)). Moreover, it is indisputable that the terms in the invoice have not been 'individually negotiated' (reg. 5(1)) but, instead, have been 'drafted in advance' (reg. 5(2)). This contract would thus appear to be a 'pre-formulated standard contract' (reg. 5(3)) within the scope of the Regulations. It is very likely that the terms are unfair and thus not binding upon P (reg. 8(1)) as being 'contrary to the requirement of good faith' and causing a 'significant imbalance in the parties' rights and obligations arising under the contract, to the detriment of the consumer' (reg. 5(1)). In particular, the terms in the problem have been imposed unilaterally, meaning that DM has not 'dealt fairly and equitably' with P and has failed to consider his 'legitimate interests' (Directive 93/13/EEC, Recital 16). Similarly, P does not appear to have had a 'real opportunity of becoming acquainted' (UTCCR 1999, Sch. 2, para. 1(i)) with the terms before the contract was concluded. Moreover, the time limit of three days for notifying defects plainly has the effect of 'excluding or hindering the consumer's right to take legal action or exercise any other legal remedy' (Sch. 2, para. 1(q)). There is little doubt that these terms are unfair as being 'so weighted in favour of the supplier as to tilt the parties' rights and obligations under the contract significantly in his favour' (*Director General of Fair Trading v First National Bank plc* [2002] 1 AC 481, 494 *per* Lord Bingham). However, as mentioned earlier, both sales in the problem are, almost certainly, within the UCTA 1977, ss. 6 and 12 and, consequently, there is a total ban on excluding the implied conditions relating to description, satisfactory quality, and fitness for purpose of the goods within the SGA 1979, ss. 13 and 14. The provisions of the UCTA 1977 are thus obviously much more advantageous to P than his having to prove the unfairness of the contract terms under the UTCCR 1999.

Question 3

The statutory framework for policing the enforceability of exclusion clauses and unfair terms in contracts requires a thorough overhaul if it is to provide clear, effective, and comprehensive protection for the vulnerable in society.

To what extent do you agree with this statement in the light of the recommendations of the Law Commission and its Draft Bill on Unfair Terms in Contracts.

Commentary

This question requires a reasonable knowledge of the main provisions contained in the **Unfair Contract Terms Act 1977 (UCTA 1977)** and the **Unfair Terms in Consumer Contracts Regulations 1999 (UTCCR 1999)**. Your answer must highlight some of the main differences between these two pieces of legislation as regards their policing of exclusion clauses and unfair contract terms, the terminology that they adopt to achieve their aims, and the different ways in which they interpret similar, or even identical, legal terms. By drawing upon such examples, you will inevitably justify the need for greater clarity within the existing regulatory framework. Finally, you will need to summarize the main recommendations of the Law Commission's Draft Bill on Unfair Terms in Contracts, adding some personal comments on whether these proposals will actually clarify and improve the existing legal framework.

Answer plan

- What is the basic approach of the **UCTA 1977** and what are its main provisions?
- How wide ranging is the **UCTA 1977** in proscribing the use of unfair contract terms?
- In what ways do the **UTCCR 1999** provide greater protection for consumers in entering contracts?
- Give examples of how the **UCTA 1977** and **UTCCR 1999** treat the same set of facts differently?
- To what extent would the Law Commission's Draft Bill on Unfair Terms in Contracts improve the current regulatory framework, especially in terms of protecting consumers against unfair business practices.

Suggested answer

The statutory framework for overseeing the enforceability of exclusion clauses and unfair terms within contracts is primarily governed by the UCTA 1977 and the UTCCR 1999. Both operate independently of one another but their spheres of influence overlap considerably. The potential for conflict and confusion is exacerbated by their different styles and approaches. Whilst UCTA 1977 acknowledges and builds upon the important heritage of the common law, using tests which would clearly be part of the vocabulary of any English contract lawyer (e.g. the 'reasonableness' test contained in s. 11), the UCCTR adopt a much more European approach, placing alien concepts such as 'good faith' at the heart of its regulatory design. For the consumer who is caught in the middle, recourse to specialist legal advice becomes a necessity.

The types of contracts covered by UCTA 1977 include consumer, business, and employment contracts, albeit with numerous limitations; for example, where businesses contract with each other, the general section on breach of contract (s. 3) only applies to the extent that one party deals on the other's 'standard terms'. More importantly, the title of UCTA 1977 is misleading insofar as it suggests that the reasonableness or validity of *any* term can be the subject of litigation. The reality is that UCTA 1977 focuses on a relatively narrow range of clauses; in particular, those seeking to exclude or limit common law or statutory liability for negligence (see s. 2) or breach of contract (see ss. 3, 6, and 7), or which assert a right to 'render a contractual performance substantially different from that which was reasonably expected' (see s. 3). Where the Act is applicable, the relevant term will either be automatically unenforceable (e.g. s. 2(1)) or will only be adjudged valid if found to be fair and reasonable (see s. 11 for the applicable test). Finally, UCTA 1977 is written in a dense style that makes its understanding by lawyers, let alone the average consumer, somewhat problematic. As the Law Commission recently noted: 'Pity the poor adviser who has to work out that s. 6 applies to exemption clauses in two types of contract (sale and hire-purchase) in four possible patterns: business to consumer, consumer to business, business to business, and 'private' contracts where neither party acts in the course of a business.' Add to this that there are specific parts of UCTA 1977 that are limited exclusively to Scotland and we clearly have a recipe for confusion.

The UTCCR 1999, on the other hand, apply to all types of consumer contracts, but not to business or private contracts. Apart from the main subject matter or the price, they cover all terms that have not been individually negotiated. Any term that is found to contravene the overriding precept of 'good faith' and which 'creates a significant imbalance' between the parties is declared invalid. The UTCCR 1999 contains an indicative list of terms that are potentially considered unfair, but, unlike UCTA 1977, no term is automatically considered invalid. Finally, the Office of Fair Trading (OFT) and other bodies are empowered to prevent unfair terms from being used by businesses against consumers, unlike the provisions of UCTA 1977 which apply only as between the parties.

The overlap between UCTA 1977 and the UTCCR 1999 is considerable, and the potential for confusion undoubted, especially where the same words or concepts are being used in both instruments. For example, in both UCTA 1977 and the UTCCR 1999, to qualify as a 'consumer' a party to the contract must not be acting in the course of his or her business, yet current case law suggests that the meaning of 'consumer' differs in important respects. As regards UCTA 1977, the Court of Appeal, in *R & B Customs Brokers Co Ltd v United Dominions Trust Ltd* [1988] 1 WLR 321, recognized that a business might be treated as a 'consumer' where the contract (to purchase a car for the personal and business use of its directors) was incidental to the main activity of that business. Naturally, there are limits to this approach as witnessed in *Chester Grosvenor Hotel Co v Alfred McAlpine Management* (1991) 56 BLR 115 where the plaintiffs, owners of a hotel, used the defendant construction company as management consultants for the purposes of refurbishing the hotel. It was held that the transaction had been made in the course of business as it was 'integral' to the plaintiff's business even though it was of a type not regularly entered into by the plaintiffs. Consequently, it is the *nature* of the transaction rather than its regularity which seems more important to a business acting as a consumer. In contrast, the UTCCR 1999 only recognizes a 'natural person' as being a consumer, so the above issues appear to be resolved. Nevertheless, as the 'person' must still be 'acting for purposes which are outside his trade, business or profession', we encounter similar difficulties when dealing with the activities of sole traders. Does the accountant who buys a computer primarily for personal entertainment, but may use it for business purposes when working from home, act as a consumer under the UCTTR?

There are also major differences in the way UCTA 1977 and the UTCCR 1999 approach the use of 'standard terms' in consumer contracts. The latter apply only to terms that have 'not been individually negotiated' (see reg. 5), thereby referring to those terms that have been drafted in advance or where their substance has not been influenced by the consumer. Conversely, the application of UCTA 1977 to consumer contracts is rarely affected by whether the term was influenced by the consumer (the reference to 'standard terms' in s. 3 only relates to contracts between businesses), although it might affect how the reasonableness test is applied. Is the UTCCR 1999's approach sensible when the average consumer rarely has the ability, knowledge or experience, to make any pre-contract negotiation meaningful? Indeed, assuming that one can identify those circumstances where a term has actually been individually negotiated (e.g. is it essential that the initially proposed term was amended in some way?), one is left with the distinct impression that when dealing with consumers, businesses would be better advised to substitute one unfair term with a differently constituted, albeit equally unfair, term (e.g. surrender the right to be paid the whole contract price in advance but, instead, negotiate a 99% advance payment). This would enable the business to argue that the term was 'individually negotiated'!

The above two examples are simply symptomatic of a huge range of linguistic and interpretational differences that presently exist between UCTA 1977 and the UTCCR 1999. Even the burden of proof is different under UCTA 1977 and UTCCR 1999: the former either renders a clause totally unenforceable, or requires the party seeking to rely upon it to establish its reasonableness, whereas under UTCCR 1999 the consumer must prove the term is 'unfair'. Consequently, in an effort to reduce this existing confusion, the Law Commission produced a Draft Bill on Unfair Terms in Contracts, February 2005 (No. 292), which seeks to combine UCTA 1977 and the UTCCR 1999, thereby providing a more unified system for the regulation of all unfair terms in contracts used within the UK. The Draft Bill adopts the use of simple terminology wherever possible, manages to avoid any reduction in consumer protection (e.g. the automatic invalidity of certain terms under UCTA 1977 is preserved), and contains totally separate parts for consumer contracts, business-to-business contracts, employment contracts, and 'private' contracts. In a break from the UTCCR 1999, all terms are required to satisfy a 'fair and reasonable' test (apart from subject matter and price) irrespective of whether they have been individually negotiated—reference to any test of 'good faith' has therefore been deleted. Moreover, it reinforces the need for all terms to be couched in plain intelligible language, thereby diminishing the importance of any separate common law *contra proferentem* test. With regard to the previously highlighted differences between UCTA 1977 and the UTCCR 1999, the Commission proposed that (i) the definition of a 'consumer' should only refer to a person acting 'for purposes unrelated to his or her business', in order to circumvent the decision in *R & B Customs Brokers Co Ltd v United Dominions Trust Ltd*, whilst also recommending that the identification of a consumer in a 'mixed transaction' (e.g. the purchase of goods for business and private purposes) should be determined by the main, or predominant, purpose of the contract, and (ii) that any unified regulatory framework should apply equally to both negotiated and non-negotiated terms.

However, the Draft Bill goes beyond the simple unification of existing laws by recognizing that consumers are not the only vulnerable elements of society. 'Small' business is equally subject to various forms of exploitation by 'big' businesses and often does not have the resources available to risk lengthy, expensive, and protracted litigation. The Law Commission, therefore, proposed a limited extension of the UTCCR 1999 to small businesses. This represents a radical departure from the *laissez-faire* economics of the common law and heralds a new era of state intervention in commercial activities, albeit that the Draft Bill imposes important limits upon this 'micro-business' exception. For example, it will only apply to businesses with nine or less employees (and excludes those that are 'associated' with larger businesses), the transaction value of the relevant contract must not exceed £500,000 (financial services contracts are excluded) and, most importantly, only applies to standard terms that have not been individually negotiated (assuming it was not a 'core' term such as the price).

In conclusion, the law on unfair contract terms, which affects ordinary people in their everyday lives, is unnecessarily complicated and difficult to understand. It leads to widespread confusion among consumers, businesses, and their advisers, which was simply exacerbated by the implementation in May 2008 of the EC Directive on Unfair Commercial Practices (2005/29/EC) via the Consumer Protection from Unfair Trading Regulations 2008, SI No. 1277 (CPUTR). The UK Law Commission has sought to address these existing problems through the creation of a unified regulatory framework which eliminates the need for litigants to *choose* whether to sue under UCTA 1977 or the UTCCR 1999. Moreover, in proposing a dramatic increase in those situations where business-to-business contracts are subjected to judicial scrutiny, it has started to recognize that vulnerability is not determined simply by the status of the parties (business or consumer) but also by the disparity of bargaining power that exists between contracting parties. Indeed, if the Draft Bill becomes law it may well represent the death knell for the *laissez-faire* principles of freedom of contract devised by the common law courts during the nineteenth century.

Question 4

Both the radical concepts employed in the Unfair Terms in Consumer Contracts Regulations 1999 (UTCCR 1999) and the scope of the Regulations suggests that the law's approach to the use of exclusion clauses in consumer contracts is undergoing a radical transformation.
   Discuss.

Commentary

Whilst this question demands an overall knowledge of the **UTCCR 1999** and the scope of their operation, it also calls for a critical analysis of the notion of unfairness and the concept of good faith and transparency of dealing in commercial contracts. Where relevant, there is scope to compare the **UTCCR 1999** with the **Unfair Contract Terms Act 1977 (UCTA 1977)**.

Answer plan

- What is the scope of the **UTCCR 1999**?
- What are the central concepts employed in the **1999 Regulations**? Explain the notions of good faith and fairness which are utilized by the Regulations.
- How did the House of Lords interpret these Regulations in *Director General of Fair Trading v First National Bank plc* [2001] UKHL 52; [2002] 1 AC 481 and *Office of Fair Trading v Abbey National plc and others* [2009] UKSC 6; [2010] 1 All ER?

Suggested answer

The UTCCR 1999, SI No. 2083 implement an EC Council Directive (93/13/EEC) on Unfair Terms in Consumer Contracts. The UTCCR 1999 revoke and replace the original Regulations (SI 1994, No. 3159) and reflect more closely the wording of the Directive. The Regulations have been clarified and the powers of enforcement granted by them have been extended considerably. The overall effect of the UTCCR 1999 is that an 'unfair term' in a consumer contract 'shall not be binding on the consumer' (**reg. 8(1)**).

The range of standard form consumer contracts (the contract term must not have been 'individually negotiated' (**reg. 5(1)**) to which the UTCCR 1999 apply is immense. **Regulation 4(1)** provides that ' . . . these Regulations apply in relation to unfair terms in contracts concluded between a seller or supplier and a consumer'. UTCCR 1994 applied only to the business supply of goods and services to consumers under the terms of a standard form contract, and there was doubt as to whether interests in land were covered. However, the amended definition of a 'seller or supplier' in reg. 3(1) omits any reference to goods and services, stating that a 'seller or supplier' is 'any natural or legal person who, in contracts covered by these Regulations, is acting for purposes relating to his trade, business or profession, whether publicly owned or privately owned'. It is thus clear that standard form business contracts for the supply to consumers of goods, services and interests in *land*, are within the 1999 Regulations (see *London Borough of Newham v Khatun* [2004] EWCA 55, [2004] 3 WLR 417). Moreover, certain contracts were expressly exempted from the operation of UTCCR 1994, namely 'any contract relating to employment . . . , succession rights . . . , rights under family law . . . and the incorporation and organization of companies or partnerships' (UTCCR 1994, Sch. 1). This list of excluded contracts has been deleted from UTCCR 1999. It must be assumed that the rationale underpinning the deletion is that, in the recitals to the Directive (93/13/EEC, Recital 10), this group of contracts is said to be excluded from the ambit of the Directive itself and UTCCR 1999 have sought better to embody the wording of the Directive. It must be asked, therefore, whether these contracts fall within or outside of UTCCR 1999. The purposive construction which must be adopted when interpreting the Directive dictates that full consideration must be given to the recitals and, consequently, it seems that this group of contracts will continue to be excluded from the operation of the UTCCR 1999. However, employers regularly supply goods such as tools, equipment and materials to employees in the course of their employment and an employer's provision of training contracts for his employees might easily be regarded as a supply of services. If onerous, unfair conditions were to be attached to these undertakings for the supply of goods or services to employees, it is difficult to see, at least in principle, why the UTCCR 1999 should not render them unenforceable. Moreover, there is recent authority that the UCTA 1977, s. 3, can apply to contracts of employment (see *Brigden v American Express Bank Ltd* [2000] IRLR 94).

The 'consumer' is defined in reg. 3(1) as 'any natural person who, in contracts covered by these Regulations, is acting for purposes which are outside his trade, business or profession'. Although this definition applies only to 'natural' persons and does not include limited companies (cf the UCTA 1977 and *R & B Customs Brokers Co. Ltd v United Dominions Trust Ltd* [1988] 1 WLR 321, where limited companies can be regarded as consumers), there is no restriction on the type of goods or services to be supplied (cf the UCTA 1977, s. 12(1)(c), where consumer goods must be 'of a type ordinarily supplied for private use or consumption').

The principles utilized in the UTCCR 1999 are both broad and radical. Three pivotal elements feature in the definition of an 'unfair term' in reg. 5(1), namely: (i) an absence of good faith; (ii) a significant imbalance in the parties' rights and obligations under the contract; and (iii) detriment to the consumer. These factors are, potentially, much broader than the notion of 'reasonableness' in the UCTA 1977, and it is plain that English law must begin to develop the precept of good faith and fair dealing in consumer contracts (see also the **Consumer Protection from Unfair Trading Regulations 2008, SI No. 1277** which again refers to the concept of 'good faith' (see reg. 2(1)). In the UTCCR 1999 good faith encompasses both a *substantive* test of fairness and the more accessible, *procedural* test of fairness in contract formation (e.g. misrepresentation, duress, and the notion that contract terms must be legible and understandable). The Office of Fair Trading (*Unfair Contract Terms*, Bulletin No. 2, September 1996, para. 2.22) has emphasized that, in assessing good faith, it takes account of the availability and use of explanatory pre-contractual brochures and whether, having signed a contract, consumers are given a reasonable 'cooling-off' period in which they may cancel the contract without penalty.

The House of Lords considered the question of unfairness under the UTCCR 1994 in *Director General of Fair Trading v First National Bank plc* [2002] 1 AC 481. The agreement under scrutiny was a standard form loan agreement regulated by the **Consumer Credit Act 1974 (CCA)**. Clause 8 provided that, should the borrower default on his repayments, interest continued to be payable at the contract rate on the outstanding principal plus accrued interest unpaid, until any judgment obtained by the bank was discharged. Interest thus continued to be payable before and after judgment until that judgment was discharged by payment. The Director General's contention was that cl. 8 would operate unfairly where (a) judgment was obtained against the borrower; (b) an order was made to pay the debt by instalments, e.g. a time-order under the CCA, s. 129; but (c) no order was made under the CCA, s. 136 to amend the agreement, with the result that interest would continue to accrue notwithstanding the due payment of the instalments ordered. The Court of Appeal had held ([2000] QB 672) that the clause had not been drawn to the borrower's attention at or before the conclusion of the contract and he would not be given notice of it at any later time prior to the making of an order nor in the order itself. The Court thus considered that cl. 8 was unfair in that it created 'unfair surprise'. That decision was reversed by the House of Lords. The House recognized that a 'significant imbalance' would occur if a term was so weighted in favour of the supplier as to tilt the parties' contractual rights and obligations in his favour and that 'good faith' connoted fair and open dealing. Accordingly, terms had to be expressed fully and clearly and suppliers could not take advantage of the consumer's weaker bargaining position. As regards the fairness of cl. 8, the House held that the borrower's obligation to repay the principal in full together with interest was unambiguously and clearly expressed in the contract and contained nothing unbalanced or detrimental to the consumer. It was also pertinent to note that the CCA had not prohibited the use of a term such as that in cl. 8 and neither was there any scheme in the CCA under which notice of the protective provisions in ss. 129 and 136 had to be drawn to the borrower's attention at the date of contract (a position which has been remedied by the Consumer Credit (Disclosure of Information) Regulations 2004, SI No. 1481, reg. 4). This meant that the borrower's difficulties stemmed from the lack of procedural safeguards which would bring the relief available to his attention. Lord Bingham had no doubt that this situation was 'unacceptable' (p. 496) but it did not indicate that the term was unfair *per se*.

As well as injecting into the mainstream of English law the radical concepts discussed above, there are certain other aspects of the UTCCR 1999 which add to their utility. First, Sch. 2 contains an 'indicative and non-exhaustive list of the terms which may be regarded as unfair' (reg. 5(5)), the list comprising 17 potentially unfair terms. Secondly, under reg. 10(1), it is the duty of the Director General of Fair Trading to consider complaints made to him regarding unfair terms and, under reg. 12(1), he may apply for an injunction against the person using such a term. Regulation 11 extends the power to seek an injunction to other regulatory bodies which are specified in Sch. 1, e.g. the Directors General of Electricity, Gas, and Water. Further, the power to seek injunctions extends to every weights and measures authority in Great Britain and to the Consumers' Association.

It is indisputable that the scope of the Regulations, and the broad notions of fairness, good faith and openness which underpin their operation, mean that businesses using standard form contracts can no longer take advantage of their superior bargaining strengths to abuse consumers and treat them unfairly.

Further Reading

Case-notes

Director General of Fair Trading v First National Bank plc [2001] UKHL 52, [2002] 1 AC 481

Dean, 'Defining Unfair Terms in Consumer Contracts—Crystal Ball Gazing?' (2002) 65 MLR 773

Mitchell, 'Unfair Terms in Consumer Contracts' (2000) 116 LQR 55

Pearce, 'Evolution or Revolution? Unfair Terms in Consumer Contracts' (2002) 61 CLJ 22

Interfoto Picture Library Ltd v Stiletto Visual Programmes Ltd [1989] QB 433
Chandler & Holland, 'Notice of Contractual Terms: Developing Existing Precedent' (1988) 104 LQR 359
McLean, 'Incorporation of Onerous or Unusual Terms' (1988) 47 CLJ 172

R & B Customs Brokers Co. Ltd v United Dominions Trust Ltd [1988] I WLR 321
Price, 'When is a Consumer Not a Consumer?' (1989) 52 MLR 245

St Alban's City & District Council v International Computers Ltd [1996] 4 All ER 481
Bright, 'Winning the Battle Against Unfair Contract Terms' (2000) 20 LS 331

Stewart Gill Ltd v Horatio Myer & Co. Ltd [1992] 1 QB 600
Brown & Chandler, 'Reasonableness and the Unfair Contract Terms Act' (1993) 109 LQR 41

Watford Electronics Ltd v Sanderson CFL Ltd [2001] EWCA Civ 317, [2001] BLR 143
Peel, 'Reasonable Exemption Clauses' (2001) 117 LQR 545

Articles

Adams & Brownsword, 'The Unfair Contract Terms Act: A Decade of Discretion' (1988) 104 LQR 94

Dean, 'Unfair Contract Terms: The European Approach' (1993) 56 MLR 581

Macdonald, 'The Emperor's Old Clauses: Unincorporated Clauses, Misleading Terms and The Unfair Terms In Consumer Contracts Regulations' (1999) 58 CLJ 413

6

Misrepresentation

Introduction

During the course of pre-contractual negotiations a number of statements may be made with a view to inducing the other party to enter into the contract. For example, the seller of a car may describe it as 'a good little runner' or 'accident-free' or as having 'very low mileage'. Chapter 4 explained the circumstances in which such representations might constitute terms of the contract, depending upon the objectively defined intentions of the parties and their respective state of knowledge. If a breach of contract resulted (i.e. the statements proved incorrect) the representee could claim damages and/or repudiation. However, the representee possesses an alternative course of action which is to sue in misrepresentation. Students are well advised to treat these two areas as forming one unit, for whereas damages in contract accentuate loss of bargain, damages for misrepresentation are based on reliance losses. The resulting difference requires close scrutiny when evaluating which course of action offers the greater benefits to a claimant in terms of damages for losses suffered. In particular, recent case law has drawn attention to the advantages of suing under s. 2(1) of the Misrepresentation Act 1967, where applicable, as opposed to pursuing a breach of contract action.

For most purposes the definition of a misrepresentation is as follows: a false statement of fact, made pre-contractually, which is intended to induce the representee to enter into a contract and which has that effect. If an actionable misrepresentation is found to exist a court will then need to consider the available remedies. On this basis, the following structure for answering any problem question on misrepresentation should be adopted.

Is it a Statement of Existing Fact?

As a *general* rule, statements of fact do not include vague or commendatory puffs, opinions, beliefs, statements as to the future, and statements of law. Thus the description of land as being 'fertile and improvable' was held not to give rise to any liability (see *Dimmock v Hallett* (1866) 2 Ch App 21). Note that all cases involving the description of property for sale should be read in the light of the Property Misdescriptions Act 1993 which imposes strict limits on the use of estate agents' flowery jargon.

Even statements which are more precise may not be characterized as statements of *fact*, e.g. the unambiguous opinion of a declared amateur (see *Bisset v Wilkinson* [1927] AC 177). Indeed, where the representor is in no better position than the representee to know the facts, current case law suggests the former need not have objectively reasonable grounds for stating an opinion or belief (see *Economides v Commercial Union Assurance Co. plc* [1997] 3 WLR 1066). Nevertheless, a statement of opinion or belief will generally, by implication, contain a representation that the person making it actually holds the belief or opinion (otherwise it would constitute a 'misrepresentation of the mind'); moreover, where the representor possesses some degree of expertise, the court will assume that any stated opinion or belief was held on reasonable grounds (see *Smith v Land & House Property Corporation* (1884) 28 Ch D 7). On this basis, the greater the expertise of the representor the more likely that a court will assume that any opinion was based on fact (see *Reese River Silver Mining Co. v Smith* [1869] LR HL 64).

Thus, the types of question one should *initially* be considering are:

(a) is the statement too vague?

(b) is it stated as an opinion or as a fact?

(c) how knowledgeable is the representor?

(d) is the representor misrepresenting the state of his mind?

Statements as to the Future

A promise as to the future which is subsequently broken is not an actionable misrepresentation as there is no statement of *existing fact*. For example, obtaining a loan by honestly 'representing' that it *will* be used for one purpose but then deciding to use it for a different purpose creates no problems. However, liability would arise if, when the representation was made, the representor had no intention of using the money for the stated purpose (see generally *British Airways Board v Taylor* [1976] 1 All ER 65 and *Edgington v Fitzmaurice* (1885) 29 Ch D 459: 'The state of a man's mind is as much a fact as the state of his digestion', *per* Bowen LJ).

Statements of Law

It was originally assumed that a representation of law could not found an action merely because it was wrong (unless it had been fraudulent in which case the state of the representor's mind had been misrepresented). In applying this test a court was required to distinguish between *law* and *fact*; for example, a statement as to the effect of a private document such as a will might constitute a fact, and therefore become actionable, insofar as it related to the contents of the document rather than legal interpretation of the will. Fortunately, in *Pankhania v Hackney LBC* [2002] EWHC 2441, [2004] 1 EGLR 135, the High Court has now stated that the distinction between law and fact was illogical and should be ignored.

Silence

In general, *caveat emptor* prevails so there is no duty of disclosure in pre-contractual dealings (see *Keates v Cadogan* (1851) 10 CB 591). However, silence or non-disclosure can lead to an active or implied misrepresentation so always consider the following questions:

(a) Does the defendant's conduct amount to an active concealment of a defect? For example, in *Gordon v Selico Ltd* (1986) 278 EG 53 it was held that painting over dry rot, immediately prior to sale of the property, was a fraudulent misrepresentation (see also *Walters v Morgan* (1861) 3 DF & J 718 which considered the overlap between oral statements and physical behaviour—e.g. 'a nod or a wink').

(b) Does the statement constitute a half-truth? Silence can distort a positive representation by conveying the wrong impression (see *Atlantic Estates plc v Ezekiel* [1991] 35 EG 118; *Gran Gelato Ltd v Richcliff* [1992] Ch 560; and *Spice Girls Ltd v Aprilia World Service BV* [2000] EMLR 478).

(c) Has there been a change in circumstances? A subsequent change in circumstances prior to the contract which falsifies an existing representation should be disclosed (see *With v O'Flanagan* [1936] Ch 575).

(d) Does the defendant's conduct incorporate an implicit guarantee of a factual character? If goods are bought there is an implied representation that they will be paid for, if goods are sold there is an implied representation that, to the seller's knowledge, they exist (see generally *Edinburgh United Breweries v Molleson* [1894] AC 96).

(e) Is there a fiduciary relationship between the parties? If so, a duty of disclosure will be implied (see *Tate v Williamson* (1866) 2 Ch App 55).

(f) Is the contract one demanding *uberrima fides*? Contracts of insurance require utmost good faith as the assured possesses information which is not known to the insurer, and thus the contract can be avoided if material facts are not disclosed.

Is there Evidence of Inducement and Reliance?

A misrepresentation must relate to a *material factor*, i.e. it must be something that would affect the judgement of a reasonable man in deciding whether, and on what terms, to enter a contract (see *Edgington v Fitzmaurice, supra*). However, if fraud is established, a court will *automatically assume* that the representee was induced into the contract provided the misrepresentation was 'actively present' in the misrepresentee's mind when the contract was made (see *Ross River Ltd v Cambridge City Football Club Ltd* [2007] EWHC 2115, [2008] 1 All ER 1005).

Aside from fraud, the issue of inducement raises the following questions:

(a) Was the representee ignorant of the misrepresentation? An uncommunicated misrepresentation is not actionable (see *Horsfall v Thomas* (1862) 1 H & C 90).

(b) Was the misrepresentation ignored by the representee? Note that the misrepresentation need not be the sole reason for entering the contract (see *Attwood v Small* (1838) 6 Cl & F 232; *Gran Gelato Ltd v Richcliff*, above).

(c) Was the representee aware of the true facts? The opportunity to verify the statements will not prevent liability arising provided that representees do not avail themselves of such opportunities (see *Redgrave v Hurd* (1881) 20 Ch D 1), but signing a document which accurately reflects the true position will normally bind the representee (see *Peekay Intermark Ltd v Australia and New Zealand Banking Group Ltd* [2006] EWCA Civ 386, [2006] 2 Lloyd's Rep 511).

What Type of Misrepresentation has been Made?

Fraudulent Misrepresentation

A fraudulent statement is one that is made (a) knowingly, or (b) without belief in its truth, or (c) recklessly, careless whether it be true or false (see *Derry v Peek* (1889) 14 App Cas 337). The litmus test is clearly whether there has been an absence of honest belief, honesty in this context denoting a subjective appreciation of events, i.e. *did* rather than *could* the representor honestly hold that view (see *Akerheilm v Rolf De Mare* [1959] AC 789).

Negligence at Common Law

Since 1963, it has been possible to argue that a contract-inducing negligent statement may give rise to an action for damages in the tort of negligent misstatement (see *Hedley Byrne & Co. v Heller & Partners* [1964] AC 465). Success depends upon proof of a *special relationship* existing between the parties (see *Esso Petroleum Co. Ltd v Mardon* [1976] QB 801).

Section 2(1) of the Misrepresentation Act 1967

Unlike negligence at common law, s. 2(1) does not require representees to establish a duty of care. Moreover, it places the burden on representors to prove that they had 'reasonable grounds to believe and did believe up to the time the contract was made that the facts represented were true'. This burden may be difficult to discharge as shown in *Howard Marine & Dredging Co. Ltd v Ogden & Sons Ltd* [1978] QB 574, although where the representor is a private individual a court might adopt a more lenient approach (see *Cooper v Tamms* [1988] 1 EGLR 257).

Innocent Misrepresentation

This is a statement without any provable fault. Following s. 2(1) we must assume that proof of 'reasonable grounds' is sufficient to demonstrate innocence.

What Remedies are Available?

Fraud

The representee will be entitled to damages in the tort of deceit *and* rescission (subject to exceptions discussed later). The purpose of damages is to restore the victim to the position he occupied before the representation had been made. In *Smith New Court Securities Ltd v Scrimgeour Vickers (Asset Management) Ltd* [1996] 4 All ER 769, the House of Lords stated that in cases of fraud the misrepresentor will be liable for all the damage *directly flowing* from the transaction: the damages need not be foreseeable but must have been caused by the transaction (see *Doyle v Olby (Ironmongers) Ltd* [1969] 2 QB 158). Moreover, in a property transaction the misrepresentee is entitled to recover the full price minus any benefits resulting from the transaction.

Normally such benefits will include the current market value at the date of the transaction, although this might not apply if the continuing effect of the misrepresentation induces the claimant to retain the property, or the circumstances of the fraud are such that he is 'locked into' the property (e.g. a buyer cannot be found). Finally, the misrepresentee must take reasonable steps to mitigate any losses on discovery of the fraud (see also *Standard Chartered Bank v Pakistan National Shipping Corp.* [1999] 1 Lloyd's Rep 747). In the words of Lord Steyn: 'the plaintiff is entitled to recover as damages a sum representing the financial loss flowing directly from his alteration of position under the inducement of the fraudulent representations of the defendants' (see *Smith New Court Securities*).

The above statement demonstrates the wide-ranging nature of damages for fraud. For example, they may include lost opportunity costs representing the loss that the misrepresentee has incurred in relying upon the fraud, and thereby not entering a different and more lucrative transaction with someone else (see *East v Maurer* [1991] 2 QB 297; *Clef Aquitaine SARL v Laporte Materials (Barrow) Ltd* [2000] 3 All ER 493).

Negligence at Common Law

The normal remedies are rescission (discussed below) and damages in the tort of negligence (incorporating a test of reasonable foreseeability).

Section 2(1) of the Misrepresentation Act 1967

This section imposes liability in a rather convoluted manner:

> if the person making the representation would be liable in damages . . . had the misrepresentation been made fraudulently, that person shall be so liable notwithstanding that the misrepresentation was not made fraudulently, unless he proves he had reasonable grounds to believe and did believe up to the time the contract was made that the facts represented were true.

Recent case law has surprisingly assumed that the successful claimant will be entitled to the same remedies as those available in fraud unless the representor discharges the burden of proof (see *Naughton v O'Callaghan* [1990] 3 All ER 191; *Royscot Trust Ltd v Rogerson* [1991] 2 QB 297; *Cemp v Dentsply R&D Corp. (No. 2)* [1991] 34 EG 62). In particular, damages will be based on 'direct consequence' (tort of deceit) rather than reasonable foreseeability (tort of negligence). However, unlike fraud, there is a possibility that damages under s. 2(1) can be reduced by the court if there is evidence that the claimant has been contributorily negligent (see *Gran Gelato v Richcliff* [1992] 1 All ER 865).

Innocent Misrepresentation

At present this area is shrouded in mystery. It would seem that a court may follow one of two lines of authority: award rescission or damages at its discretion under s. 2(2) (consider *Watts v Spence* [1976] Ch 165 and *William Sindall plc v Cambridgeshire County Council* [1994] 1 WLR 1016), or award rescission with an indemnity (see *Whittington v Seale-Hayne* (1900) 82 LT 49 for the limited nature of an indemnity).

Rescission

Although rescission is available for all types of misrepresentation the remedy will be barred by: (a) lapse of time; (b) affirmation; (c) the impossibility of returning the parties to their original position (see *Halpern v Halpern (No. 2)* [2006] EWHC 1728, [2006] 3 All ER 1139; *Crystal Palace FC (2000) Ltd v Dowie* [2007] EWHC 1392, [2007] IRLR 682); and (d) third parties having acquired rights to the subject matter prior to the claimant's avoidance of the contract.

Moreover, under s. 2(2) of the 1967 Act a court can award damages in lieu of rescission, for a non-fraudulent misrepresentation. This discretion will be exercised in accordance with the principles of equity, having regard to the nature of the misrepresentation, the loss that would be caused if the contract were upheld, as well as the loss that rescission would cause to the other party. Initially it appeared that the discretion to award damages in lieu of rescission under s. 2(2) applied even if the right to rescission had been lost (see *Witter (Thomas) Ltd v TBP Industries* [1996] 2 All ER 573), however this now seems unlikely in the light of *Government of Zanzibar v British Aerospace Ltd* [2000] 1 WLR 2333 and *Floods of Queensferry Ltd v Shand Construction Ltd* [2000] BLR 81.

Has Liability for Misrepresentation been Excluded?

Under s. 3 of the Misrepresentation Act 1967 (as amended by the Unfair Contract Terms Act 1977 (UCTA 1977), s. 8) such an exclusion clause must satisfy the test of reasonableness contained in UCTA 1977, s. 11 (e.g. *Walker v Boyle* [1982] 1 WLR 495, *Howard Marine & Dredging Co. Ltd v Ogden & Sons Ltd* [1978] QB 574, and *Smith v Eric S Bush* [1990] AC 831 and the comments in **Chapter 5**). In *Witter (Thomas) Ltd v TBP Industries* [1996] 2 All ER 573 Jacob J assumed that a blanket exclusion of liability for misrepresentation was necessarily unreasonable as it would cover fraud. Consequently, following *Stewart Gill Ltd v Horatio Myer & Co Ltd* [1992] 1 QB 600, the clause would fail in its entirety, irrespective of whether the facts disclosed an innocent misrepresentation. However, this approach was questioned more recently, in *Government of Zanzibar v British Aerospace Ltd* [2000] 1 WLR 2333, where the High Court relied on much earlier authority to the effect that a blanket exclusion clause was not normally apt, on its proper construction, to cover fraud (a similar approach was adopted in *Granville Oil & Chemicals Ltd v Davis Turner & Co. Ltd* [2003] EWCA 570, [2003] Lloyds 356). This suggests that a blanket exclusion clause will need to make an overt reference to some type of fraudulent activity before it can be automatically invalidated in its entirety under the *Stewart Gill* rule.

Table 1 Breach of Contract v **Misrepresentation Act 1967, s. 2(1)**

Offer/Intent	Fact (not Puff/Opinion)
Acceptance of offer	Inducement/reliance
Burden on claimant to establish breach	Burden on defendant to establish 'reasonable grounds'

Repudiation? Is the term a condition, warranty, or an innominate term?	Rescission—subject to bars (e.g. lapse of time) and/or **s. 2(2)** of the **1967 Act**

Damages	*Damages*
Robinson v Harman—protecting the expectation interest	Protecting the reliance interest—but see ***East v Maurer*** and the award of opportunity costs
Remoteness and reasonable contemplation— ***Hadley v Baxendale***	Remoteness and direct consequence test— ***Royscot v Rogerson***
Contributory negligence: strict liability or duty to take reasonable care?	Contributory negligence? Compare ***Redgrave v Hurd*** with ***Gran Gelato v Richcliff***
Limits on recovery of non-pecuniary losses (see ***Farley v Skinner***)	Fraud, and therefore **s. 2(1)**, includes damages for anxiety/distress

Is there a Breach of Contract?

This will depend upon those considerations outlined in **Chapter 4**. If the statement is a term of the contract then the available remedies will depend upon whether the term is classified as a condition, a warranty or an innominate term. In answering a problem question on misrepresentation a student may be expected to consider the remedies available for breach of contract as compared with those available in misrepresentation. See Table 1 for a more detailed comparison.

Question 1

Welton Bogg, a well-known singer, decides to use Bikton Concert Hall (BCH) as the first venue in his 'Round UK Music Tour'. During negotiations the BCH Manager, Jim, informs Welton that '. . . the hall will hold 3,000 people . . . [and] . . . the acoustics are suitable for the performance of your musical repertoire'.

Welton signs the contract of hire which contains the following clause: 'The management reserves the right to restrict the capacity of this Theatre on grounds of public safety and does not accept liability for any statements made by BCH staff concerning the quality of the facilities provided'.

Welton's concert is sold out. However, only 2,500 are admitted on the instructions of the local police, and the acoustics are so bad that a large percentage of the audience demands its money back.

The adverse media publicity affects ticket sales for the remainder of Welton's UK tour.

Advise the parties.

Commentary

Adopting the structure used in the introduction to this chapter you must consider the following questions: Do any of the pre-contractual statements made by Jim constitute statements of fact? If so, did any of these statements induce Welton to enter into the contract? What type of misrepresentation was made? What remedies are available? Do any of the statements constitute contractual terms? If so, what remedies are available for breach of contract? What is the effect of the exclusion clause?

Answer plan

- During the preliminary negotiations, did BCH's manager make any statements of fact, or were all his comments mere puffs/opinions?
- Was BCH's silence on any issue, such as audience capacity, capable of being construed as a 'statement of fact'?
- Were any of these 'statements of fact' sufficiently material to have induced Welton to enter into the contract?
- What type of misrepresentation, if any, was BCH guilty of making?
- Is rescission barred for any reason, such as lapse of time, etc?
- What types of damages can Welton claim, especially under **s. 2(1)** of the **Misrepresentation Act 1967**?
- Would the exclusion clause be regarded as 'reasonable' under **s. 8** of the **Unfair Contract Terms Act 1977 (UCTA 1977)**?

Suggested answer

Welton will need advice on his possible remedies in misrepresentation and for breach of contract. As regards the former, misrepresentation can be defined as a false statement of fact, made pre-contractually by one party (representor), with a view to inducing the other party (representee) to enter into the contract. The statement must have been intended to be acted upon and must actually induce the other party to enter the contract.

Did Jim make any false statements of fact? The first statement concerned the capacity of the hall. There is no suggestion that the statement was phrased as an opinion (see *Bisset v Wilkinson* [1927] AC 177 which presumes that opinions are generally not 'facts'); moreover, even if it were, one would argue that Jim is an expert and that the figure is presumably based upon facts known to him. For example, in *Smith v Land & House Property Corporation* (1884) 28 Ch D 7, the vendor described the sitting tenant as 'desirable and a first class investment'. This constituted a misrepresentation as the only facts known to the vendor were in direct conflict with this summation.

There is, however, a further difficulty. Technically, the capacity of the hall *is* 3,000. Did Jim realize that this figure would be limited by the local police? Perhaps this was a common occurrence when such concerts were held. If so, Jim's silence regarding the safety feature effectively distorts his original statement, thereby conveying the wrong impression to Welton. In common parlance, the statement constitutes a half-truth and, therefore, a misstatement of fact (e.g. *Nottinghamshire Patent & Brick Tile Co. v Butler* (1889) 16 QBD 778).

Jim also states that the 'acoustics are suitable' for the intended performance, a relatively vague and ambiguous comment. In *Scott v Hanson* (1829) 1 Russ & M 128, the description of land as being 'uncommonly rich water meadow' was held only to constitute a misrepresentation with reference to non-meadow land, rather than meadow that was of poor quality. Perhaps, as in the above paragraph, Welton will need to show that Jim had no facts upon which to base his statement (e.g. *Smith v Land & House Property*) in which case he is misrepresenting the state of his mind. As Bowen LJ put it in *Edgington v Fitzmaurice* (1885) 29 Ch D 459, 483: 'The state of a man's mind is as much a fact as the state of his digestion.' Moreover, there is some precedent for suggesting that an actionable misrepresentation may lie where an opinion is stated and the representor is the only person to be in a position to know the true facts (*Brown v Raphael* [1958] Ch 636).

Assuming that a false statement of fact is established, was it intended to induce Welton to enter into the contract and, if so, did Welton rely upon it in this way. In general terms, inducement involves the application of an objective test: would a reasonable man have considered the statement to be a *material* factor? Undoubtedly the answer is yes. The capacity of the hall will influence the hire charge. The standard of acoustics will determine suitability for its intended use.

Has Welton relied upon the statement in entering into the contract? The facts suggest that Welton had already decided to hire the concert hall before negotiations began. However, if Jim had proposed a much greater hire charge or the capacity of the hall was embarrassingly low or the acoustics were only considered suitable for the performance of classical opera, Welton would have presumably withdrawn. Thus, Welton can demonstrate some form of potential reliance.

The remedies for misrepresentation will be determined by the lack of care exercised by the misrepresentor. Traditionally, fraud has attracted the best remedies for the representee but the burden of proof is a heavy one to discharge (e.g. *Derry v Peek* (1889) 14 App Cas 337). Moreover, in the light of case law concerning the Misrepresentation Act 1967, s. 2(1), it is unlikely that Welton would be advised to pursue a claim in fraud unless he had firm evidence that Jim was intentionally lying.

Alternatively, if a special relationship exists between the parties Welton might consider suing in the tort of negligent misstatement (e.g. *Esso Petroleum Co. Ltd v Mardon* [1976] QB 801). Here, Welton must affirmatively establish negligence on the part of Jim in making those pre-contractual statements. However, as we shall see, in view of s. 2(1) of the 1967 Act, it is pointless to pursue this line of argument.

Section 2(1) of the Misrepresentation Act 1967 reverses the burden of proof, requiring Jim to prove that he had 'reasonable grounds' for his belief. This may be difficult to establish, especially in the light of *Howard Marine & Dredging Co. Ltd v A Ogden & Sons (Excavations) Ltd* [1978] QB 574, where the Court of Appeal stated that a party had an 'absolute obligation' not to state facts which he had no reasonable grounds for believing were true. As honest belief is insufficient, it would seem difficult for Jim to argue that he was not expected to know of the theatre's capacity when negotiating the hire charge. Perhaps his only escape route would be if the capacity of the hall had never previously been restricted by police measures and the acoustics had always been found to be suitable at previous concerts of a similar nature. This seems unlikely. In the light of these comments, one could safely ignore the possibility of innocent misrepresentation which, in general terms, refers to false statements made without provable fault.

All misrepresentations attract the remedy of rescission, subject to the standard common law bars such as *restitutio in integrum* being impossible. As the concert has already been performed, it seems that rescission is no longer available (note that the recent flexibility shown in *Halpern v Halpern (No. 2)* [2006] EWHC 1728, [2006] 3 All ER 1139 seems irrelevant here as there is no element of the contract's performance that can be reversed).

Regarding the remedy of damages, Welton would be best advised to pursue his claim under s. 2(1) of the 1967 Act. Recent case law has emphatically stated that damages will be assessed in the tort of deceit, with all its concomitant advantages (e.g. *Royscot Trust Ltd v Rogerson* [1991] 2 QB 297). Welton will be entitled to reclaim all those damages which *directly* flow from his reliance upon the misrepresentation, such as the losses sustained in returning money to dissatisfied customers. This might also include any subsequent losses incurred on the remainder of the tour resulting from the adverse media publicity as well as any personal distress and anxiety suffered by Welton (see generally *Doyle v Olby (Ironmongers) Ltd* [1969] 2 QB 158; *Archer v Brown* [1985] QB 401). Finally, damages may encompass lost opportunity costs such as the profit that Welton would have made if he had booked a different concert hall in the vicinity (see *East v Maurer* [1991] 2 QB 297) or the transaction with BCH had been more favourable but for any proven fraud (see *Clef Aquitaine SARL v Laporte Materials (Barrow) Ltd* [2000] 3 All ER 493).

However, Welton's claim is subject to the enforceability of the exclusion clause. Assuming the clause has been properly incorporated (e.g. adequate notice as demonstrated in *Parker v South Eastern Ry* (1877) 2 CPD 416) one needs to consider the effect of the UCTA 1977, s. 8, which subjects such clauses to a test of reasonableness. Adopting the guidelines in Sch. 2 of the Act, the answer might depend upon what opportunity Welton was given of checking on the capacity, whether he received any inducement for agreeing to the clause, and the respective strength of the parties' bargaining positions. Note that with regard to the last point the House of Lords, in *Photo Production Ltd v Securicor Transport Ltd* [1980] AC 827, suggested that a very hard line would be taken where equality of bargaining power exists; i.e. freedom of contract prevails and the clause will be enforceable. Welton's only escape route would be the Court of Appeal's decision in *Stewart Gill Ltd v Horatio Myer & Co. Ltd* [1992] 1 QB 600, which emphasized that all parts of a clause must be reasonable, irrespective of what reliance is being placed upon each part by either party. If a sub-clause is found to be unreasonable the whole clause fails. On the present facts, although it *might* be reasonable to restrict admission for reasons of public safety, the whole clause might still fail owing to the latter part which seems to absolve BCH from fraudulent statements (see however *Granville Oil & Chemicals Ltd v Davis Turner & Co. Ltd* [2003] EWCA 570, [2003] Lloyds 356 which suggests that a court, wherever possible, will seek to interpret a blanket clause as not covering fraud).

Finally, Welton should consider the alternative possibility of claiming damages for breach of contract. The test for determining whether a pre-contractual statement has become part of the contract is one of objective intent (e.g. *Heilbut, Symons & Co. v Buckleton* [1913] AC 30). The courts have developed a variety of guidelines as aids to identifying the requisite degree of contractual intent. For example, Welton could argue that Jim possessed specialist knowledge (e.g. *Oscar Chess Ltd v Williams* [1957] 1 WLR 370), that he (Welton) attached considerable importance to the statement (e.g. *Bannerman v White* (1861) 10 CB (NS) 844), and that he was not encouraged by Jim to verify the statement. Jim would point out that the statement was not incorporated into the written contract (e.g. *Birch v Paramount Estates (Liverpool) Ltd* (1956) 16 EG 396), that Welton's previous experience of arranging musical venues should be taken into account as it created an equality of expertise between the parties (see generally *Bentley (Dick) Productions Ltd v Harold Smith (Motors) Ltd* [1965] 1 WLR 623) and, finally, that there was no evidence of a collateral contract as Welton did not place any specific emphasis on Jim's statement during the negotiations (unlike in *City and Westminster Properties (1934) Ltd v Mudd* [1959] Ch 129). The decision could go either way but it does seem that the statement lies at the heart of the hire contract and therefore would be intended to have some legal effect, especially with regard to the hall's capacity which is couched in a clear and definite manner.

If the statement constitutes a term of the contract, Welton's primary remedy would be damages. These would depend on whether, at the time of making the contract, they were in the reasonable contemplation of the parties as liable to result from the specified breach (see *Hadley v Baxendale* (1854) 9 Exch 341). For example, should the parties have foreseen the effect of the reduced hall capacity and/or below par acoustics, and their consequential impact on future tour receipts? (Note: it is unlikely that an examiner would expect an extended analysis of damages for breach of contract in a problem question so clearly based on the potential existence of an actionable misrepresentation.)

Question 2

Financial Systems Ltd (FSL) is experiencing intermittent interruptions to its gas supplies and therefore requests a quote from Solheat & Co (S) for the installation of a new solar-powered heating system that will avoid reliance on outside energy suppliers. The sales representative of S delivers the quote to FSL and adds the following comments: 'This system is a world-beater. It achieves the highest "Ecology Rating", based on research by Government environmental agencies. Moreover, I guarantee that you will recover the initial installation costs within five years.' FSL is impressed by these comments.

Two days later FSL signs a contract with S regarding the installation of the new heating system. The contract contains an 'entire agreement' clause which states: 'This written instrument contains all the terms and conditions of the contract. All previous representations made by S's employees are hereby withdrawn.' Moreover, the contract does not incorporate any guarantee of cost recoupment, nor any reference to the system's ecology rating.'

The solar-powered heating system is installed into FSL's offices, with the parties agreeing that the system conforms to the specifications contained within the contract. Two months later FSL discovers that the new heating system had lost its Government approved 'ecology rating' because of superior products coming on to the market, while a recently published report confirms previous research that the start-up costs of solar-powered heating systems can never be recovered by purchasers . FSL demands the removal of the new heating system, a full refund of the original contract price, and the repair of all office walls and partitions caused by the original installation of the new heating system. S refuses to comply with any of these requests.

Advise FSL.

Commentary

This problem relates to contractual terms and representations. The first question to consider is whether FSL has a remedy in breach of contract. In this context the better student will also reflect on the prospects of FSL establishing a collateral contract. Secondly, misrepresentation as a possible remedy must be evaluated, particularly as regards the basis for quantifying damages. Finally, the overall effect of the 'entire agreement' clause must be considered: does it prevent FSL from claiming a breach of contract based on the pre-contractual statements and/or claiming misrepresentation. Good examination technique would strongly discourage a student from dismissing all of FSL's possible breach of contract actions simply on grounds that the 'entire agreement' clause was enforceable. Shortcut methods rarely succeed because the examiner will be looking for the adoption of a systematic method of analysis which covers all issues raised by the facts even if, ultimately, a particular approach is probably doomed to fail. Finally, the answer set out below refers to terms, parol evidence, classification of terms, entire agreement clauses, assessment of damages, misrepresentation, and remedies. Your module tutor will give you some indication of whether this type of 'mixed' question is normally set and, if so, how much depth is required in answering each part.

Answer plan

- Are the statements of the sales representative capable of being terms of the contract or is there scope for them to form a collateral contract?

- Does the parol evidence rule apply here?

- How would you classify any terms that had been broken—condition, warranty, or innominate term?

- Is there an actionable misrepresentation—an untrue statement of fact made pre-contractually that induced FSL to enter the contract?

- What type of misrepresentation has occurred, if any?

- What are the general remedies available to FSL, e.g. rescission and/or damages? What if FSL was considered to have contributed to its own loss?

- What is the effect of the 'entire agreements' clause on FSL's chances of claiming breach of contract or misrepresentation?

Suggested answer

There are three grounds of action which FSL may seek to pursue: breach of contract, or breach of a collateral contract, or misrepresentation. As regards breach of contract, can FSL prove that any pre-contractual statements made by S's sales representative were terms of the contract as opposed to mere representations? As stated in *Heilbut, Symons & Co. v Buckleton* [1913] AC 30, this requires an ascertainment of the parties' objective intention, helped by posing the following subsidiary questions. First, is there a substantial lapse of time between the oral statement and the writing? If the period is short, as occurs on the facts, the court is more likely to consider the oral statement to be a term (e.g. *Routledge v McKay* [1954] 1 WLR 615 in which a period of seven days was crucial), but much will depend on the nature of the goods sold, and the surrounding factual matrix, so no hard-and-fast rule can be established. Secondly, if the sales representative possesses expert knowledge, more weight will be attached to any of his statements (see *Harling v Eddy* [1951] 2 KB 739). On the facts, such knowledge and expertise should not be too difficult to establish. Thirdly, does FSL rely on the relevant statements? Consider *Schawel v Reader* [1913] 2 IR 81 which demonstrates that a statement may have contractual effect if it was clearly of importance to the other party and thus a dominating factor in the contract's formation. The facts suggest this to be the case. Finally, if there is evidence that FSL was asked to verify the statement, this would seriously undermine the statement being a term (see *Ecay v Godfrey* (1974) 80 Ll LR 286; *Leaf v International Galleries* [1950] 2 KB 86). The above analysis strongly suggests that statements made by S's sales representative should be treated as terms of the contract. If so, the applicability of the parol evidence rule, the type of remedy available for any breach, and the validity of the 'whole agreements clause' will become crucial.

The parol evidence rule states that extrinsic evidence may not be adduced to add to, vary or contradict writing. The rule embodies the strong presumption that if the parties have committed their agreement to an all-embracing written contract, it must represent their finalized intent. On the facts there does not seem any evidence that the parties were intending to contract on terms that were partly-written and partly-oral (see *Allen v Pink* (1838) 4 M & W 140) so S will rely on the parol evidence rule to avoid any oral statements being incorporated into the contract. In response, FSL may try to establish a collateral contract. This has the advantage of circumventing the parol evidence rule (if applicable) in that a separate contract is shown to exist, the consideration being entry into the main contract. Surely the statements that were made formed such a contract, particularly if the written undertakings were silent on the material points (see *Mann v Nunn* (1874) 30 LT 526)?

If the statements made by the sales representative were terms of the contract, FSL is potentially entitled to repudiate the contract and claim damages for any breach of condition, or obtain damages for breach of warranty. Alternatively, if the court decided to categorize the terms as being 'innominate', FSL's remedy will depend on whether they were substantially deprived of the intended benefit under the contract (see *Hongkong Fir Shipping Co. Ltd v Kawasaki Kisen Kaisha Ltd* [1962] 2 QB 26). For instance, if the recoupment of installation costs took six rather than five years a court would probably award only damages, equivalent to a breach of warranty. However, such issues appear somewhat academic as it is unlikely that a court would permit FSL to repudiate the contract when the new heating system has already been installed, and the old one has been removed (and disposed of?). Consequently, if the award of damages was the most likely outcome, one would need to apply the standard common law rules of measure, remoteness and mitigation. [Note: You may be expected to consider this point in some depth, depending on the previous guidance of your module tutor. If so, you should point out that the lost ecology rating (assuming it occurred pre-contractually) and the inability to recoup installation costs within five years, would be the primary 'losses' suffered by FSL. Using the standard expectation measure (*Robinson v Harman* (1848) 1 EX 850), or the alternative yardstick of reliance costs (*McRae v Commonwealth Disposals Commission* (1951) 84 CLR 377), in conjunction with the normal rules of remoteness (see *Hadley v Baxendale* (1854) 9 Exch 341), the court would need to identify the objective value attributable to the 'ecology rating', and the pecuniary loss sustained by failing to recoup initial installation costs within the prescribed period.]

In concluding on breach of contract, is the 'entire agreement' clause enforceable? This issue is neatly illustrated in *Inntrepreneur Pub Co. v East Crown Ltd* [2000] 2 Lloyd's Rep 611 where the court concluded that the incorporation of a clause which simply stated that the written contract represented the 'entire agreement' between the parties was sufficient to prevent any express terms arising outside the agreement (including breach of any collateral warranty). If correct, any collateral contract predicated on the oral statements made by S's representative will be denied contractual effect.

FSL's final remedy lies in misrepresentation. A misrepresentation is a false statement of fact made by the representor which is intended to induce and, in fact, does induce the representee to enter into the contract. As regards the first statement (it is a 'world-beater') S will presumably argue that it was too vague statement or couched as an opinion (see *Dimmock v Hallett* (1866) 2 Ch App 21—the words 'fertile' and 'improvable' were considered too vague to constitute 'facts'). However, this argument is easily countered as FSL (or any reasonable person) would have assumed that the opinions of a specialist salesperson were based on some clear supporting evidence (see *Smith v Land and House Property Corporation* (1884) 28 Ch D 7 where use of the word 'desirable' to describe a tenant who was habitually late in paying rent was considered to be a false statement of fact). Note, also, *Brown v Raphael* [1958] Ch 636 which established that an opinion may be actionable as a misrepresentation where the representor is in a much stronger position to ascertain the facts than the representee. This is clearly relevant here.

The comment regarding the ecology rating appears to be an unequivocal, false statement of fact in that the relevant Government agency has withdrawn its top 'ecology rating' for S's product. However, FSL must establish that it was a false statement of *existing* fact (i.e. that the ecology rating was withdrawn *before* FSL entered the contract). Note that if the statement was correct when made, but incorrect at the time the contract was formed, S would have an obligation to inform FSL of this change of circumstances (e.g. *With v O'Flanagan* [1936] Ch 575), whereas if this information was only disclosed post-contractually no liability would arise. The final statement (recoupment of costs) does appear to be a definite misrepresentation: the language used and intention conveyed seems obvious, a clear fact is mentioned, and S is in a superior position to know the truth (e.g. *Smith v Land & House Property*). Moreover, the timing of the research report, referred to in the facts, is immaterial as the statement remains false irrespective of when publication took place (i.e. before or after the contract was made), although the date of its publication might be relevant to the type of misrepresentation made (e.g. innocent or fraudulent).

Assuming a false statement of fact has been identified, FSL must prove that it relied on that statement and was thereby induced to enter the contract. There is no evidence that FSL was given the opportunity to check the truth of the statements before a contract came into existence (e.g. *Attwood v Small* (1838) 6 Cl & F 232), nor would it be sufficient for S to argue that FSL could/ought to have known about previous research on cost recoupment, particularly as *Redgrave v*

Hurd (1881) 20 Ch D 1 established that the *opportunity* to discover untruths is irrelevant as constructive knowledge is insufficient to disprove reliance. So it only remains for FSL to prove that the comments of S's sales representative (particularly as to cost recoupment) might have been a material factor in persuading a reasonable person to enter the contract (see *Edgington v Fitzmaurice* (1885) 29 Ch D 459). This seems likely on the facts as economy and ecology issues would surely be material to the purchaser of a solar heating system, thereby entitling FSL to claim misrepresentation. Note also that if fraud was established, the court would *automatically* assume FSL had been induced into the contract provided those statements were 'actively present' in 'their mind' at the time the contract was formed (see *Ross River Ltd v Cambridge City Football Club Ltd* [2007] EWHC 2115, [2008] 1 All ER 1005).

On the above basis, what type of misrepresentation has occurred? It is most unlikely that FSL could establish a fraudulent misrepresentation unless there was proof that the sales representative intentionally misled FSL (see *Le Lievre v Gould* (1893) 1 QB 491; *Derry v Peek* (1889) 14 App Cas 337). Moreover, in view of the liability imposed by s. 2(1) of the Misrepresentation Act 1967, both an action in deceit and for negligence at common law, under the principles of *Hedley Byrne & Co. Ltd v Heller and Partners Ltd* [1964] AC 465, seem needlessly burdensome for FSL. In effect, s. 2(1) imposes liability for negligent misrepresentations and reverses the normal burden of proof: once the representee proves that there has been a misrepresentation, the burden shifts to the representor to show that he had 'reasonable grounds to believe and did believe up to the time the contract was made that the facts represented were true'. It is clear from *Howard Marine and Dredging Co. Ltd v A Ogden & Sons (Excavations) Ltd* [1978] QB 574 that it is extremely difficult to discharge this burden: honest belief is insufficient as the representor must positively establish the reasonableness of his belief. Consequently, the question is whether S's representative *ought* to have known about the research on cost recoupment and/or the lost ecology rating, with the safest conclusion being that if the information was publicly available before the contract was formed it is unlikely that S will be able to discharge the burden under s. 2(1).

As FSL wishes to return the system and obtain a refund of the price, it would be seeking rescission of the contract. This seems unlikely on the facts. For example, it is arguable that FSL affirmed the contract by continuing with its use for two months (e.g. *Long v Lloyd* [1958] 1 WLR 753) and, more importantly, it seems impossible to restore the parties to their original position as it would require FSL's old heating system to be re-installed and connected, whilst the new system would have significantly depreciated in value through use (but see *Halpern v Halpern (No. 2)* [2006] EWHC 1728, [2006] 3 All ER 1139 which suggests that courts may be more prepared to make 'monetary adjustments', or adopt other measures, in order to circumvent the *impossibility* obstacle).

As regards damages, FSL will presumably pursue its claim under s. 2(1) of the 1967 Act (see above), so damages will be assessed in the tort of deceit (see *Smith New Court Securities Ltd v Scrimgeour Vickers (Asset Management) Ltd* [1996] 4 All ER 769 and its explanation of the direct consequence test). FSL will be entitled to reclaim all those damages which *directly* flow from its reliance upon the misrepresentation such as the failure to recoup its losses within the stipulated time. In the light of *East v Maurer* [1991] 2 QB 297, damages may encompass lost opportunity costs, i.e. the benefits that FSL would have obtained if it had purchased an alternative system (with a Government ecology rating—assuming one was available) capable of meeting the standards originally specified by FSL. Note that this analysis emphasizes the reliance aspect of FSL's losses, but failure to act reasonably once the misrepresentation has been discovered potentially leaves FSL open to a charge of contributory negligence and a consequential reduction in any award of damages (see *Gran Gelato v Richcliff* [1992] 1 All ER 865).

Finally, does the 'entire agreement' clause protect S from any misrepresentation claim? FSL will presumably refer to *Witter (Thomas) Ltd v BTP Industries* [1996] 2 All ER 573 which suggested that a blanket exclusion clause absolving a misrepresentor from liability for all misrepresentations, explicitly or implicitly including fraud, would be automatically deemed unreasonable under s. 8 of the **Unfair Contract Terms Act 1977** (UCTA 1977). On the facts, as the relevant clause refers to 'all previous representations', it would seem to be unenforceable, particularly as the Court of Appeal held in *Stewart Gill Ltd v Horatio Myer & Co. Ltd* [1992] 1 QB 600 that if any part of a non-severable clause was unreasonable the clause would be struck down in its entirety. However, S will counter this argument by referring to *Government of Zanzibar v British Aerospace Ltd* [2000] 1 WLR 2333 in which the High Court appeared to assume that a blanket exclusion clause would not be interpreted as covering fraud unless *explicitly* referred to in the clause (an approach followed in *Granville Oil & Chemicals Ltd v Davis Turner & Co. Ltd* [2003] EWCA 570, [2003] Lloyds 356). Consequently, *assuming* S and FSL are not of unequal bargaining power, it is likely that the court will consider the clause to be 'reasonable' under UCTA 1977, s. 8.

Question 3

Case law suggests that litigants are generally better advised to pursue a claim in misrepresentation rather than for breach of contract.
  Discuss.

Commentary

Although a general comparison of the remedies available for misrepresentation and for breach of contract is called for, the question clearly focuses upon the Court of Appeal decisions in which damages under **s. 2(1)** of the **Misrepresentation Act 1967** have been equated with those available for an action in deceit. Your answer should therefore include a comparison of the following points: (a) the availability of rescission and repudiation; and (b) the basis upon which damages are awarded in misrepresentation and for breach of contract.

Answer plan

- What is the difference between repudiation and rescission?
- How are contract terms classified? Why is this important?
- What is the basis for awarding damages for breach of contract?
- What is the basis for awarding damages for misrepresentation?
- What are the advantages of suing under **s. 2(1)** of the **Misrepresentation Act 1967**?
- What is the relevance of contributory negligence, fraud and direct consequences damages, and loss of opportunity damages?

Suggested answer

The general remedies for breach of contract are repudiation and/or damages, whereas in misrepresentation the remedies are rescission and/or damages. The best means of comparing these remedies is to consider separately (a) the availability of repudiation and rescission, and (b) the basis for awarding damages in each area. One interesting feature will be that, whereas contract remedies will depend primarily upon whether the term which the defendant has broken is a condition or a warranty, in misrepresentation it is the culpability of the defendant which will determine the claimant's remedies.

Rescission v Repudiation

A victim of a breach of contract does not possess an automatic right to repudiate the contract. The right of repudiation generally arises only in two circumstances. First, where it is established that the term which has been broken constitutes either a condition or, following the decision in *Hongkong Fir Shipping Co. Ltd v Kawasaki Kisen Kaisha Ltd* [1962] 2 QB 26, that it is an innominate term breach of which has deprived the victim of a substantial part of the intended benefit under the contract. The second possibility is that the contract-breaker has intimated by words or conduct his refusal to perform outstanding contractual obligations as they fall due (see generally *Woodar Investment Development Ltd v Wimpey Construction (UK) Ltd* [1980] 1 WLR 277). If neither of the above situations applies the victim of a breach will be left with a remedy in damages.

The law on misrepresentation does not consider the relative importance of pre-contractual statements. Provided a false statement of fact has been made, the representee, in principle, will have the right to claim rescission and thereby avoid the contract. The representee need only establish that the statement induced him to enter the contract, i.e. that it was a material factor (see *Edgington v Fitzmaurice* (1885) 29 Ch D 459). This right is available for all types of misrepresentation—innocent, negligent, and fraudulent. However, the right to rescission can be lost on the following grounds:

(a) by affirmation of the contract (see *Long v Lloyd* [1958] 1 WLR 753);

(b) by lapse of time (see *Leaf v International Galleries* [1950] 2 KB 86);

(c) where third parties have acquired rights in the subject matter prior to avoidance of the contract (see *White v Garden* (1851) 10 CB 919); and

(d) where the parties cannot be restored substantially to their original positions (see *Clarke v Dickson* (1858) EB & E 148).

(Note: a good student might make three further points at this juncture.) First, before the passing of the Misrepresentation Act 1967 a representee lost the right to rescind if the representation became part of the contract. In such cases the representee would seek repudiation, provided the term broken was a condition or the representor had shown a clear intention to repudiate the contract. However, s. 1(a) of the 1967 Act provides that the right of rescission remains, notwithstanding that the representation has become a term of the contract. This clearly provides litigants with a powerful weapon when comparing the remedies available in misrepresentation with those for breach of contract. Secondly, under s. 2(2) of the 1967 Act the court is given discretion when dealing with non-fraudulent misrepresentations to declare the contract as subsisting and award damages in lieu of rescission, taking account of the equitable considerations affecting *both* parties. Thirdly, a misrepresentation renders a contract voidable (provided the representee elects to rescind) so the parties are restored to the positions they occupied before the contract was entered into (see *Abram SS Co. v Westville Shipping Co. Ltd* [1923] AC 773). On a superficial level, the right of repudiation is different; i.e. it is prospective in nature, relieving the representee of the *future* performance of obligations. However, this difference often has little meaning in practice as representees may, for example, possess certain restitutionary remedies by which they can (a) recover money transferred under the contract, or (b) claim payment on a *quantum meruit* basis for services rendered.

Damages

In misrepresentation, damages will be assessed on a tortious basis, the general purpose being to place the victim in the position he occupied before the misrepresentation took place. This is often termed 'compensation for reliance losses' as it does not take account of the profit which the victim was expecting to derive from a proper performance of the contract. Conversely, damages for breach of contract often incorporate this wasted expectation loss under the heading of 'loss of bargain'. Here, the purpose of damages is to put the claimant, so far as possible, in the position he would have occupied had the contract been properly performed (see *Robinson v Harman* (1848) 1 Ex 850, 855), although a court, in appropriate circumstances, may protect a victim's reliance or restitution interests (see *Anglia Television Ltd v Reed* [1972] 1 QB 60).

A simple example illustrates the above distinction between contract and tort. X buys a car for £1,000 on the strength of the seller's statement that it is worth £1,200 but later finds out that the car is worth only £500. In contract, the starting point would be the loss of bargain, equivalent to £700, whereas in misrepresentation, the losses associated with X's reliance would suggest an initial figure of £500. Most textbooks consequently assert that damages in contract are normally higher than those in misrepresentation. There are, however, a variety of reasons why this may have changed more recently.

As an introductory remark one might mention that prior to the passing of the Misrepresentation Act 1967 damages were only available for a fraudulent misrepresentation—an allegation of fraud being extremely difficult to substantiate. Damages were based on the tort of deceit, the representor being liable for *all* the losses flowing directly from his fraud even though such losses might not have been reasonably foreseeable (see *Doyle v Olby (Ironmongers) Ltd* [1969] 2 QB 158; *Smith New Court Securities Ltd v Scrimgeour Vickers (Asset Management) Ltd* [1996] 4 All ER 769). Moreover, apart from mere pecuniary loss the courts permitted the recovery of various types of non-pecuniary losses including damages for pain and suffering (see *Burrows v Rhodes* [1899] 1 QB 816), physical inconvenience and discomfort (see *Mafo v Adams* [1970] 1 QB 548), and mental disquiet (see *Archer v Brown* [1985] QB 401; *Kinch v Rosling* [2009] EWHC 286 (QB), [2009] All ER (D) 54). Contrast this with the pre-1967 position for non-fraudulent misrepresentations where rescission was the primary remedy, if available, and damages took the very limited form of an 'indemnity' (see *Whittington v Seale-Hayne* (1900) 82 LT 49). Little wonder that an action for breach of contract contrasted favourably with that in misrepresentation. However, the passing of the Misrepresentation Act 1967 has changed this in at least four ways.

First, damages are now available for all non-innocent misrepresentations, innocence in this context proving difficult to establish (see *Howard Marine & Dredging Co. Ltd v A Ogden & Sons (Excavations) Ltd* [1978] QB 574). In particular, the burden of proof is reversed under s. 2(1) of the 1967 Act, requiring the representor to prove that he had reasonable grounds to believe and did believe up to the time the contract was made, that the facts represented were true.

Secondly, it is currently assumed that the measure of damages under s. 2(1) is based on the tort of deceit. This results from the peculiarity of the wording employed in the subsection (although certain *obiter* comments in *Smith New Court* might suggest a level of disquiet with this conclusion). Specifically, if the representor would have been liable in damages had the misrepresentation been made fraudulently 'that person shall be so liable notwithstanding that the misrepresentation was not made fraudulently' provided objective innocence cannot be proven. Thus, unlike damages for breach of contract which are limited by the reasonable contemplation of the parties (see *Hadley v Baxendale* (1854) 9 Exch 341), damages under s. 2(1) follow the test laid down in *Doyle v Olby (Ironmongers) Ltd* [1969] 2 QB 158. These damages are based on a direct consequence test in which reasonable foreseeability has no application, an approach adopted in such cases as *Naughton v O'Callaghan* [1990] 3 All ER 191, *Royscot Trust Ltd v Rogerson* [1991] 2 QB 297, and *Cemp v Dentsply R&D Corp. (No. 2)* [1991] 34 EG 62.

Thirdly, a further effect of the above is that many types of non-pecuniary loss which are not *normally* available for breach of contract can be recovered in the tort of deceit and also by using s. 2(1) of the 1967 Act (e.g. anxiety and stress).

Fourthly, two Court of Appeal decisions have even blurred the distinction between loss of bargain damages in contract and reliance losses in tort. In *East v Maurer* [1991] 2 QB 297 M owned two successful hairdressing salons. E bought one of them in 1979, being induced by M's representation that M had no intention of working in the other salon. In fact, M continued to work in the other salon, enticing many customers away from E's salon. After several abortive attempts, E sold out several years later at a considerable loss. The court held that a fraudulent misrepresentation had been made and, amongst other things, awarded E a sum of money equivalent to her lost opportunity cost. This sum reflected the profits which E would have derived from the purchase of a different salon if she had not been induced into buying M's salon. This measure seems very similar to awarding damages for loss of bargain (although see *McCullagh v Lane Fox & Partners* [1994] 1 EGLR 48) and reinforces the attraction of bringing an action under s. 2(1) of the Misrepresentation Act 1967, which employs the same measure of damages, as opposed to suing for breach of contract. More recently, in *Clef Aquitaine SARL v Laporte Materials (Barrow) Ltd* [2000] 3 All ER 493, the claimant was allowed to argue that a different and more favourable transaction would have been entered into but for the fraud, with his recoverable loss being measured on that basis (see also *Parabola Investments Ltd v Browallia* [2010] EWCA Civ 486 (unreported); *4 Eng Ltd v Harper* [2009] EWHC 901, [2009] Ch 91).

In conclusion, where a pre-contractual statement constitutes *both* a breach of a contract and a misrepresentation, recent case law has suggested that the representee must think long and hard before choosing which action to pursue. The use of a deceit measure for all non-innocent misrepresentations, with its disregard of any foreseeability criterion, the potentially enhanced recovery of non-pecuniary losses, and even the award of quasi 'loss of bargain' damages, is clearly advantageous in many situations. Against this must be contrasted the problems of recovering any damages for purely innocent misrepresentations, the possible bars to the remedy of rescission, including the exercise of judicial discretion under s. 2(2) of the 1967 Act (see *William Sindall plc v Cambridgeshire County Council* [1994] 1 WLR 1016), and the general emphasis on reliance losses in tort.

Question 4

Edward decides to invest his savings in the purchase of a small post office. He consults 'Postman's Gazette' and is particularly interested in one advertisement which reads: 'Post office to the community—the only life-line for the elderly. Net profits for the current year = £25,000. A steal at £100,000'. Edward speaks to the owner, Cameron, and is offered the opportunity to view the current accounts, which he politely declines. Still uncertain as to whether he should purchase the business, he is convinced when Cameron says: 'I'm finally retiring to sunny Spain'.

Two months after purchasing the post office, Edward discovers that it had only made a profit of £25,000 in the previous year owing to a one-off 'Rural Aid Grant' of £15,000 from the District Council, whilst a nearby grocery store has recently opened up a small post office counter and is proving particularly attractive to the more elderly members of the local community. Finally, Cameron has decided to stay in the village and set up a small corner shop after being informed by his doctor that he is displaying early signs of skin cancer which can only be aggravated by living in a hot climate.

Edward tries to make a success of the post office, even building a small extension so that he could sell local handicrafts. Unfortunately this new sideline turns out to be a disaster and Edward loses all his savings.

Advise Edward whether he can claim misrepresentation and/or breach of contract. If so, what remedies should he be seeking?

Commentary

This is another archetypal problem question on misrepresentation that can be found in many Contract Law LLB examination papers over the years. The same structure should be adopted as per **Question 1**: is there a clear statement of existing fact? Has the representee been induced to enter the contract as a consequence? What type of misrepresentation has been made? What remedies are available? Will rescission of the contract be barred for some reason? What method will be used to assess damages? Finally, is there a possible breach of contract action?

Answer plan

- During the preliminary negotiations, did Cameron make any false statements of fact, or were all his comments mere puffs/opinions?
- Where Cameron remained 'silent' on particular issues is there scope for Edward to claim misrepresentation based on a 'half-truth' or a 'change of circumstances'?
- Were any 'statements of fact' sufficiently material to have induced Edward to enter into the contract?
- What type of misrepresentation, if any, was Cameron guilty of making?
- Is rescission barred for any reason?
- What are the types of losses for which Edward can be compensated?
- Were any of Cameron's pre-contractual statements incorporated into the contract, enabling Edward to sue Cameron for breach of contract?

Suggested answer

Edward's first possible cause of action is to claim that the contract is voidable for misrepresentation. For our purposes, an actionable misrepresentation can be defined as a false statement of fact, made pre-contractually by one party (representor), with a view to inducing the other party (representee) to enter into the contract. The statement must be intended to be acted upon and must actually induce the other party to enter the contract.

In deciding whether any pre-contractual false statements of fact have been made it is probably best to separate out Cameron's comments as follows: 'Post office to the community—the only life-line for the elderly' . . . 'Net profits for the current year = £25,000. A steal at £100,000' . . . 'I'm finally retiring to sunny Spain'. With regard to the first of those comments, how clear is this statement? For example, what is the meaning of 'life-line'? On the one hand it is arguable that the statement is sufficiently vague to make the establishment of an underlying 'fact' problematic (see, for example, *Dimmock v Hallett* (1866) 2 Ch App 21 where use of the words 'fertile' and 'improvable' was considered too vague to constitute 'statements of fact'). On the other hand, Edward might counter this by drawing the court's attention to the post office conversion within the other village shop as this seems to represent an alternative 'life-line'. If the statement was accurate at the time of purchase Edward will fail, whereas if the conversion took place before Edward bought the post office (or Cameron became aware of the planned conversion prior to the sale) Cameron would have a duty to alert Edward to this change of circumstances (see *With v O'Flanagan* [1936] Ch 575). On the facts stated it appears that Edward will struggle to convince a court on this point.

Edward's next argument concerns the profit achieved by the post office in the previous year. Here again the statement appears accurate, but Edward will argue that it constituted a half-truth as it gave the impression that the post office generated that level of profit through normal retailing activity, rather relying on a 'one-off' grant. Reference might be made to *Atlantic Estates plc v Ezekiel* [1991] 35 EG 118 where the impression given in auction particulars was that a wine bar (for sale) was a thriving business whereas its alcohol licence had recently been revoked. On balance, Edward's argument appears reasonably persuasive.

Finally, Cameron informed Edward of his plans to retire to 'sunny Spain'. This represents a statement of future conduct which is rarely actionable unless the representor knew at the time that he had no intention of carrying out his plans (see *Edgington v Fitzmaurice* (1885) 29 Ch D 459). On the facts this is difficult to prove unless Cameron was already aware of his skin cancer before he sold his post office to Edward.

Assuming Edward succeeds in establishing a false statement of fact (e.g. a half-truth regarding last year's profit), he must convince a court that it was a *material* factor in his decision to purchase the post office, a task that should not prove overly taxing. All of Cameron's statements were communicated to Edward, there is no evidence that Edward ignored any of those statements, and each of those statements had the capacity to influence the judgement of a reasonable man when purchasing the business (especially the previous level of profitability and/or existence of local competition). It is true that Edward was given the opportunity to scrutinize the accounts but, as he did not view them, this simply represents *constructive* knowledge of the true position which is insufficient to disprove Edward's reliance on Cameron's statement(s) (see *Redgrave v Hurd* (1881) 20 Ch D 1).

The next question is what type of misrepresentation has Cameron made? Focusing on Cameron's failure to explain fully the constituents of last year's profit figure, Edward would presumably argue that Cameron had been guilty of fraudulent misrepresentation. Fraud was defined in *Derry v Peek* (1889) 14 App Cas 337 as making a 'false statement' (a) knowingly, or (b) without belief in its truth, or (c) recklessly, careless whether it be true or false. The litmus test is that of an absence of honest belief, subjectively assessed (see *Akerheilm v Rolf De Mare* [1959] AC 789). Cameron will presumably plead his innocence by arguing that he had no *intention* to mislead Edward, and that his statement of last year's profit was accurate. The court may need some convincing on this point but, if Cameron was successful, it would simply transfer judicial attention on to s. 2(1) of the Misrepresentation Act 1967. That subsection primarily affords Edward the same level of damages by treating any misrepresentation by Cameron 'as if' it had been made fraudulently, unless the misrepresentor had 'reasonable' grounds for making that statement. Under s. 2(1) the onus of proof rests with Cameron. The Court of Appeal decision in *Howard Marine & Dredging Co. Ltd v Ogden & Sons Ltd* [1978] QB 574 demonstrates the difficulty that Cameron would face in rebutting the statutory presumption as it interpreted s. 2(1) as imposing an 'absolute obligation' on the misrepresentor not to state facts of which he had no reasonable grounds for believing were true. Cameron will struggle on this point. Nor will his task be easier with regard to the other possible misrepresentations; for example, if he knew of local competition then he would have no 'reasonable grounds' for using the words 'only life-line'.

If successful, the remedies available to Edward will be rescission and damages. Dealing with rescission first, we must consider the standard common law bars: lapse of time, affirmation, impossibility to restore the parties to their original positions (i.e. *restitutio in integrum*), and third party rights acquired over the subject matter of the contract prior to any attempted rescission. As Edward continued to run the business after discovering the true state of affairs a court will probably refuse rescission on grounds of affirmation. Failing that, rescission is likely to be refused as it will be difficult to return the parties to their original positions in light of the physical structure of the post office having been altered by the building extension (and presumably the diversification into the sale of local handicraft products). It therefore seems that Edward must settle for damages only.

Damages under s. 2(1) of the 1967 Act are based on those awarded in the tort of deceit. The standard test of 'reasonable foreseeability', as used in the tort of negligence, gives way to the 'direct consequence' test (see *Royscot Trust Ltd v Rogerson* [1991] 2 QB 297) whereby a court awards the claimant all losses *directly* flowing from the misrepresentation, however unforeseeable those losses proved to be. This should result in Edward receiving damages under the following headings: (i) diminution in value (the difference between the contract price and the true value of the business)—whether the true value is estimated at date of purchase or at a later date is subject to the guidance proffered by the House of Lords in *Smith New Court Securities v Scrimgeour Vickers* [1996] 4 All ER 769, and (ii) consequential losses generated by reliance on the misrepresentation (e.g. Edward's loss of personal savings). Moreover, Edward may consider the possibility of claiming 'lost opportunity costs' (see *East v Maurer* [1991] 2 QB 297) as he was deprived of the opportunity to use his original start-up capital to invest in a more profitable business. Indeed, following *4 Eng Ltd v Harper* [2008] EWHC 915, [2009] Ch 91, Edward will not even need to prove that there *was* some other profitable business that he was actively considering purchasing, in substitution for the post office. [Note, always remember that under s. 2(1), as opposed to fraud, there is a possibility that damages can be reduced by the court if it is of the opinion that the claimant had been contributorily negligent—see *Gran Gelato v Richcliff* [1992] 1 All ER 865.]

Edward's alternative course of action is to sue Cameron for breach of contract, requiring proof that one of Cameron's pre-contractual statements constituted a term of the contract that had subsequently been broken. The first obstacle is that the majority of Cameron's statements appear in an advertisement. Following *Partridge v Crittenden* [1968] 1 WLR 1204, these are unlikely to form part of any 'offer' that Edward accepted when agreeing to purchase the post office. However, if these statements were expressly or impliedly repeated during the course of negotiations this problem becomes less relevant. Edward will need to prove that the relevant statements contained a sufficient degree of objective intent to imbue them with a contractual status (see *Heilbut, Symons & Co. v Buckleton* [1913] AC 30). At first glance this seems difficult to argue; for example, what is the meaning of 'a steal' or 'a life-line'? Nevertheless, it seems sensible to refer to the helpful guidelines the courts have produced over the years to help with this process: (i) *specialist knowledge*: Cameron is selling his own business so he has much greater knowledge of its details—this lends greater credence to some, or all, of his pre-contractual statements being part of the final contract (see generally *Oscar Chess Ltd v Williams* [1957] 1 WLR 370); (ii) *importance attached to the statement* (see *Bannerman v White* (1861) 10 CB (NS) 844): if Edward can prove that he attached specific importance to a particular statement, and Cameron was aware of this, it might potentially become a term. On the facts, only Cameron's retirement location stands out as being particularly influential on Edward's decision to buy the post office—and surely it must be doubted whether Cameron intended to bind himself contractually to live in Spain? (iii) *verification*: if the representor advises his counterpart to verify a particular statement, a court is less likely to treat that statement as being contractual in nature (see *Ecay v Godfrey* (1974) 80 Ll LR 286). Here, Cameron did offer Edward the chance to view the 'accounts' so it is unlikely that any profit estimate could form part of the contract; and, finally (iv) *collateral contract*: there is no evidence that Edward identified any of Cameron's statements as being *crucial* to his decision to purchase the post office (compare this to the facts in *City and Westminster Properties (1934) Ltd v Mudd* [1959] Ch 129 where the tenant would *only* sign the new lease agreement if his right to sleep on the premises was guaranteed).

On the above basis, it is unlikely that a court will identify a specific breach of contract. However, if Edward was successful, his primary remedy would lie in damages, their assessment depending on what losses would have been reasonably contemplated by the parties, at the time of contract formation, as liable to result from the relevant breach (see *Hadley v Baxendale* (1854) 9 Exch 341). Repudiation of the contract, assuming the relevant term was viewed as a condition, would be unlikely as Edward continued trading after he had discovered the full extent of his problems and even extended the premises.

[Note, as with **Questions 1 and 2**, it is unlikely that an examiner would expect an extended analysis of damages for breach of contract in a problem question so clearly based on the potential existence of an actionable misrepresentation.]

Further Reading

Case-notes

Gran Gelato Ltd v Richcliff [1992] 1 All ER 865
Chandler & Higgins, 'Contributory Negligence and the Misrepresentation Act 1967, s. 2(1)' [1994] LMCLQ 326

Howard Marine et al v Ogden & Sons [1978] QB 574
Sills, 'Damages for Misrepresentation' (1980) 96 LQR 15

Royscot v Rogerson [1991] 2 QB 297
Hooley, 'Damages and the Misrepresentation Act, 1967' (1991) 107 LQR 547

Smith New Court Securities v Scrimgeour Vickers [1996] 4 All ER 769
Halson, 'Damages for the Tort of Deceit' [1997] LMCLQ 423

Government of Zanzibar v British Aerospace (Lancaster House) Ltd [2000] 1 WLR 2333
Malet, 'Section 2(2) of the Misrepresentation Act' (2001) 117 LQR 524

Articles

Atiyah & Treitel, 'Misrepresentation Act 1967' (1967) 30 MLR 369

Brown & Chandler, 'Deceit, Damages and the Misrepresentation Act 1967 Section 2(1)' [1992] LMCLQ 40

Cartwright, 'Damages for Misrepresentation' [1987] Conv 423

O'Sullivan, 'Rescission as a Self-Help Remedy: A Critical Analysis' (2000) 59 CLJ 509

Poole & Devenney, 'Reforming Damages for Misrepresentation: The Case for Coherent Aims and Principles' [2007] JBL 269

Poole & Keyser, 'Justifying Partial Rescission in English Law' (2005) 121 LQR 273

7

Improper pressure

Introduction

The formation of a contract requires the acceptance of an offer, the requisite degree of contractual intent and the presence of consideration. This 'indivisible trinity' is based on the notion of freedom of contract: parties give their consent to be legally bound. To a layman, freedom and consent would suggest a degree of choice and the exercise of free will, but this is not necessarily true. For example, although a fundamental inequality of consideration might imply that improper pressure had been applied, it was only comparatively recently that courts were prepared to acknowledge this formal link (e.g. *Williams v Roffey Bros & Nicholls (Contractors) Ltd* [1991] 1 QB 1).

The tension in the law is clear. If A signs away his property to B at a gross undervalue, should this suggest a lack of consent, the presence of some impropriety or merely crass stupidity? The basic answer requires one to focus on the relationship between the parties. Commonsense dictates that a court would be more fairly disposed to intervene where the relationship is of a more personal nature, based on confidence and trust, rather than where the parties are businessmen dealing at arm's length. This coincides with the current division in the law as represented by the twin doctrines of undue influence and economic duress.

The doctrine of undue influence covers a variety of personal relationships, fiduciary in nature, where trust is reposed and the possibility of its abuse by the dominant party necessitates adequate protection of the weaker party. Moreover, it is regularly invoked by sureties where their relationship with the creditor is manipulated by the debtor's acting as an intermediary; for example, a husband persuading his wife to guarantee his company's overdraft with a bank. Conversely, in the commercial field, although an emerging doctrine of economic duress has been employed to strike down some of the more morally reprehensible commercial activities, the doctrine is ring-fenced by a variety of restrictive conditions.

Undue Influence

There are two ways that a contract can be avoided for undue influence: (a) affirmative proof of undue influence, or (b) raising the presumption of undue influence which is not rebutted. This chapter adopts the following classification of undue influence (see

Barclays Bank plc v O'Brien [1994] 1 AC 180, as clarified by *Royal Bank of Scotland v Etridge (No. 2)* [2001] UKHL 44, [2001] 4 All ER 449): *Class 1* refers to cases involving affirmative proof of undue influence, *Class 2A* comprises relationships in which it is automatically presumed that the dominant party (B) has influence over the weaker party (A), and *Class 2B*, in which, on the facts, the relationship between the parties (A/B) exhibits a sufficient level of trust and confidence to warrant a presumption of influence. Note that where a presumption of influence has arisen (Class 2A/B) the court will require proof that the transaction/contract is in some way 'wrongful' before it can be presumed that the influence was 'undue'.

Affirmative Proof of Undue Influence (Class 1)

The courts have never attempted to define undue influence with any precision, but it has been described as:

> . . . some unfair and improper conduct, some coercion from outside, some overreaching, some form of cheating and generally, though not always, some personal advantage gained (*Allcard v Skinner* (1887) 36 Ch D 145 *per* Lindley LJ).

The following two factors, therefore, are normally required in order to establish affirmative undue influence:

(a) Evidence of victimization and, inevitably, some personal gain by the dominant party (e.g. *Nottidge v Prince* (1860) 2 Giff 246; *Lyon v Home* (1868) LR 6 Eq 655; *Williams v Bayley* (1866) LR 1 HL 200); and,

(b) Lack of independent advice given to, or voluntary action by, the weaker party (see the comments of Bridge LJ in *Re Brocklehurst's Estate, Hall v Roberts* [1978] Ch 14).

Two further points are worth noting. First, in *CIBC Mortgages plc v Pitt* [1994] 1 AC 200, the House of Lords stated that there was no need for the weaker party (A) to prove, in addition, that the transaction had been manifestly disadvantageous. Secondly, the fact that A would have entered the contract anyway, irrespective of the pressure exerted upon him by the dominant party (B), is irrelevant to a finding of actual undue influence (e.g. *UCB Corporate Services Ltd v Williams* [2002] EWCA Civ 555, [2003] 1 P & CR 12).

Presumption of Undue Influence (Class 2A and 2B)

A contract will be declared voidable for 'presumed undue influence' if the following three conditions are met:

(i) the relationship of the parties gives rise to a presumption of influence,

(ii) the resultant transaction/contract suggests that the dominant party (B) exerted influence of an *undue* nature over the weaker party (A), and

(iii) B is unable to convince the court that A acted voluntarily, free of the potential influence referred to above.

Points (i) and (ii) simply create evidential burdens that B will be required to rebut. The House of Lords' decision in *Royal Bank of Scotland v Etridge (No. 2)* [2001] UKHL 44, [2001] 4 All ER 449, is undoubtedly the most influential case in this area, although divining a clear ratio is particularly challenging given the number of speeches delivered. For this reason, the comments of the Court of Appeal in *Turkey v Awadh* [2005] EWCA Civ 382, [2005] 2 FCR 7 will prove more helpful, providing you with a clearly worked example of how conditions (i) and (ii) will be applied in practice.

(a) *Presumption of influence*: In Class 2A relationships it will be automatically assumed that A reposed trust and confidence in B, potentially giving the latter significant control over the decision-making powers of A and a consequential opportunity to enhance his own position unfairly. Examples of such relationships include: solicitor and client, religious leader and disciple (e.g. *Allcard v Skinner*), and parent and child (e.g. *Lancashire Loans Ltd v Black* [1934] 1 KB 380), but not banker and customer, or husband and wife. If the court decides that it is dealing with a Class 2A relationship the presumption of influence is irrebuttable, although it does not automatically follow that B used *undue* influence to persuade A to enter the transaction.

Alternatively, a Class 2B relationship might exist, requiring demonstrable evidence of B's potential or actual dominance over A (e.g. *O'Sullivan v M.A.M Ltd* [1984] 3 WLR 448—inexperienced songwriter placing all financial matters into the hands of his agent). In particular, did B take on the role of adviser, or encourage A to rely on the advice that was proffered? Alternatively, perhaps B gained some form of personal advantage from A's reliance? An affirmative answer to such questions would suggest that an appropriate level of influence has been identified (i.e. A potentially reposed trust and confidence in B), thereby raising a presumption of influence. In *Lloyds Bank Ltd v Bundy* [1975] QB 326 (at 347), Sachs LJ recognized that if B 'overstepped the boundaries' of a normal confidential relationship, influence would be presumed. In that case the bank manager had taken on the role of adviser to the defendant, thereby converting the normal, arm's length relationship between the bank and its customer into a quasi-fiduciary relationship where the bank was required to put the interests of its customer above its own. As a consequence, a presumption of influence certainly arose.

If the relationship between the parties does not fall within the above two categories (Class 2A/2B) it must be assumed that there is an insufficient level of trust and reliance between A and B to warrant further judicial enquiry; in short, it will be assumed that B had insufficient influence over A's actions.

(b) *Influence that is 'Undue'*: Assuming a presumption has been established (whether for a Class 2A or Class 2B relationship), the court will need to consider whether the resultant transaction/contract is characterizable as 'wrongful'. The House of Lords set out the relevant test in *Etridge (No. 2)*: to an unbiased observer, was the transaction not readily explicable by the relationship of the parties and the circumstances of the case? In applying the '*Etridge* test' the court will look at the nature of the transaction, and the surrounding factual matrix, in order to decide whether A would not *ordinarily* have been expected to enter such a transaction unless his will had been overborne (i.e. the facts raise a suspicion of unfair dealing). Whereas courts had previously emphasized the importance of the transaction being 'manifestly disadvantageous' to A, this factor no longer holds centre stage; rather it remains one of many evidential issues that a court will take into account when deciding whether the relevant transaction was 'wrongful' (see *Macklin v Dowsett* [2004] EWCA Civ 904, [2004] 2 EGLR 75). Finally, if the transaction is considered 'wrongful' a presumption of *undue* influence will be established, requiring evidence of its rebuttal by B.

(c) *Rebutting the presumption:* In *Etridge (No. 2)* it was recognized that the cogency of any explanation proffered by B (for A entering the transaction) needs to increase in line with the degree of perceived wrongfulness. A relatively modest gift by a fiancé to his fiancée excites far less suspicion than the gift of a mansion by a client to his solicitor, so one must assume that B's task of supplying a satisfactory explanation will be easier in the former situation, although by no means straightforward (see *Leeder v Stevens* [2005] EWCA Civ 50, [2005] All ER (D) 40). Traditionally, the most effective way of rebutting a presumption of undue influence was for B to show that A had received independent, expert advice, enabling that person to make a 'full, free and informed estimate' of the expediency of entering the transaction (see *Inche Noriah v Sheik Allie Bin Omar* [1929] AC 127). However, the overriding test remains one of whether A acted voluntarily in the circumstances. Thus, in *R v Attorney-General for England and Wales* [2003] UKPC 22, [2003] EMLR 24, the Judicial Privy Council was prepared to ignore the absence of advice (and the lack of any opportunity to obtain it) where A was fully aware of what he was signing (see also *Re Brocklehurst's Estate, Hall v Roberts, supra*). Conversely, in *Etridge (No. 2)*, it was recognized that there are some circumstances where the wrongfulness of the transaction is so great that it will be almost impossible for B to show that A acted voluntarily (i.e. free of B's continuing influence) even if independent expert advice was received.

Undue Influence and the Intermediary (Indirect Class 2B)

A perennial problem facing banks and other money-lending institutions is the procedures that should be followed when dealing with married couples eager to use their marital homes as security for bank loans. In particular, how far should banks try to protect wives from the unreasonable pressures of their husbands? The heading to this subsection reflects the fact that the relationship between husband and wife, at most, falls within the Class 2B category, but that our real enquiry is directed towards whether the bank/creditor is *tainted* by the improper actions of B (normally the husband).

In order to master this area, it is essential that you are fully conversant with the three pivotal House of Lords' decisions in *Barclays Bank plc v O'Brien* [1994] 1 AC 180, *CIBC Mortgages plc v Pitt* [1994] 1 AC 200, and *Royal Bank of Scotland v Etridge (No. 2)* [2001] UKHL 44, [2001] 4 All ER 449. The legal framework created by the

Law Lords flows from the important distinction that was drawn between wives acting as sureties for their husbands' entrepreneurial activities and those seeking to release the capital tied up within the matrimonial home for purely domestic reasons (e.g. buying a family car). The former increases the possibility that a husband might use 'emotional pressure tactics' in order to gain his wife's approval.

In answering a question in this area the following scheme should be considered (note that 'husband' and 'wife' are interchangeable terms for the purposes of this analysis):

(a) What type of transaction has the wife entered into? Was she (i) acting as surety for her husband's debts (see *O'Brien, Etridge (No. 2)*), or (ii) simply applying jointly with her husband for a straightforward loan (see *CIBC v Pitt*)?

(b) *In (a)(i) transactions* the bank/creditor will automatically be 'put on enquiry', requiring the bank/creditor to take certain steps to avoid being fixed with notice of any undue influence or misrepresentation employed by the husband against his wife (see *Etridge (No. 2)*).

In (a)(ii) transactions a bank/creditor will not be 'put on enquiry' unless it has clear evidence that the transaction appears 'wrongful' (applying the test set out in *Etridge (No. 2)*—as previously explained). Possible examples of a 'wrongful' transaction (i.e. calling for an explanation) might include a 'joint loan' to a husband and wife where the risk/reward ratio is patently unreasonable from the wife's perspective (e.g. a loan to a company, owned by husband and wife, where the wife's shareholding is grossly disproportionate to that of her husband's yet her liability remains the same as his—see *Goode Durrant Administration v Biddulph* **(1994) 26 HLR 625)**, or, generally, where the circumstances are redolent of improper pressure (draw an analogy with *Credit Lyonnais Bank Nederland NV v Burch* [1997] 1 All ER 144—head of company using a very junior employee as surety for his business). In (a)(ii) situations the bank is only 'put on enquiry' if it should have reasonably suspected possible impropriety by the husband.

(c) Assuming that the bank/creditor was 'put on enquiry', it must take reasonable steps to ensure that the nature of the risks arising from the transaction have been brought home to the wife. It is not enough for the bank/creditor to rely upon its knowledge that the wife has spoken to an independent adviser, such as her solicitor (see *First National Bank plc v Achampong* [2003] EWCA 487, [2004] 1 FCR 18). However, the word 'independent' has been a restrictively interpreted, allowing a wife to be advised even by the husband's company solicitor as the latter could be trusted to decide whether any conflict of interest had arisen and act accordingly (see *Banco Exterior Internacional v Mann, Mann and Harris* [1995] 1 All ER 936).

(d) As regards the independent adviser, did that person explain to the wife the nature of the documentation and her possible liability, and ask her whether she wished to proceed? If not, the wife may have an action founded upon negligence. However, the bank/creditor can assume that the adviser has acted properly *provided* it receives confirmation to that effect, though if it withholds material information or knows that the adviser has acted negligently then it proceeds as its own risk (see *Etridge (No. 2)*).

(e) What if the bank has failed to follow the proper procedures? The House of Lords, in *Etridge (No. 2)*, stressed that this does not mean the wife will automatically avoid the transaction as against the bank/creditor. Proof is still required that the husband used improper pressure, or some other form of deception, in order to gain the wife's agreement. In *Etridge (No. 2)* Lord Nicholls stated that a wife's guaranteeing her husband's debts would not normally be considered a 'wrongful transaction' (i.e. one readily explicable only on the basis that it was procured by the exercise of undue influence); thus, the wife will often need to rely on her husband to confess to some form of overt, overbearing conduct or misrepresentation.

(f) What is the effect if the wife succeeds and is allowed to avoid the transaction (see *TSB Bank plc v Camfield* [1995] 1 All ER 951 (CA) and *Dunbar Bank plc v Nadeem* [1998] 3 All ER 876)? The current view is that the *whole* transaction is avoided.

(g) What if the bank/creditor has complied with the procedures set out in *Etridge (No. 2)*, but the transaction replaces/discharges a previous one where the bank/creditor had not complied with these procedures? It now seems that the later transaction will be voidable in such circumstances, provided the bank/creditor remains the same (see *Yorkshire Bank plc v Tinsley* [2004] EWCA Civ 816, [2004] 1 WLR 2380).

(h) Do the above principles apply to any other relationships? In *Etridge (No. 2)* the House of Lords stated that in *all* 'non-commercial' surety arrangements a commercial lender is *automatically* 'put on enquiry' (see (a)(i) and (c) above), thereby including relationships between sureties and debtors based on family links, love, friendship, employment, or simple mutual convenience (e.g. *Avon Finance Co. Ltd v Bridger* [1985] 2 All ER 281—father/son). How one defines a 'non-commercial' arrangement remains a moot point. For example, would it include the use of shares owned by a daughter in her father's company (i.e. commercial context) as security for increasing the available overdraft facility for an old university friend (i.e. personal relationship)?

As regards (a)(ii) situations, primarily involving joint loans, the existing principles are equally applicable to unmarried couples, whether in a heterosexual or homosexual relationship, whether cohabiting or not (see also *Midland Bank plc v Massey* [1995] 1 All ER 929), or to any relationship where a joint debtor occupies a dominant position with regard to the other joint debtor, *provided the bank was aware, or ought to have been aware, of the nature of that relationship* (e.g. *Chater v Mortgage Agency Services Number Two Ltd* [2003] EWCA Civ 940, [2003] HLR 925).

Duress

There are two basic forms of duress: physical and economic. In its original form, the common law normally only recognized violence or its threat as sufficient to avoid a contract. Economic duress, on the other hand, is a very recent innovation, perhaps originating from Lord Denning's theory of inequality of bargaining power and from his judgments in cases such as *D & C Builders Ltd v Rees* [1966] 2 QB 617 and *Arrale v Costain Civil Engineering Ltd* [1976] 1 Lloyd's Rep 98.

Two cases are pivotal in the development of the new doctrine. First, in *The Siboen and The Sibotre* [1976] 1 Lloyd's Rep 293, Kerr J stated, *obiter*, that a court must 'in every case at least be satisfied that the consent of the other party was overborne by compulsion so as to deprive him of any *animus contrahendi*'. Secondly, in *Barton v Armstrong* [1976] AC 104, 121, Lords Wilberforce and Simon (dissenting) stated:

> In life many acts are done under pressure, sometimes overwhelming pressure, so that one can say that the actor had no choice but to act. Absence of choice in this sense does not negate consent in law; for this pressure must be one of a kind which the law does not regard as legitimate.

The link between these two statements was forged by Lord Scarman in *Universe Tank-ships Inc of Monrovia v International Transport Workers' Federation* [1983] 1 AC 366: economic duress required evidence of illegitimate pressure by the dominant party *and* the resultant coercion of the weaker party. The problem is that illegitimate pressure does not necessarily negate consent and lack of consent does not necessarily establish wrongful pressure. For example, if X holds a gun to Y's head and tells him to sign a contract this might appear illegitimate but it hardly constitutes coercion if Y knows that the gun is not loaded. Moreover, as Lord Scarman recognized, pressure which appears legitimate might be illegitimate if applied for the wrong motives.

In deciding whether the pressure exerted on the weaker party was 'illegitimate', the following questions should normally receive affirmative responses:

(a) Was there a calculated threat of unlawful damage to the economic interests of the other party? A mere threat to break an existing contract is not enough (compare *Atlas Express Ltd v Kafco (Importers and Distributors) Ltd* [1989] QB 833 with *Williams v Roffey Bros and Nicholls (Contractors) Ltd* [1991] 1 QB 1).

(b) Was there a lawful excuse for the dominant party to exert pressure on the weaker party, e.g. by enforcing an existing contractual right? However, whilst it had previously been assumed that a party's honest belief (that their pressure was permissible under the terms of the contract) would prevent any finding of illegitimate pressure (compare *CTN Cash and Carry Ltd v Gallaher Ltd* [1994] 4 All ER 715 and *Carillion Construction Ltd v Felix (UK) Ltd* [2001] BLR 1), the more recent case of *Cantor Index Ltd v Shortall* [2002] All ER (D) 161 suggests that even if *both* parties believe, albeit wrongly, that the actions of the dominant party are justified by the terms of the contract this will not necessarily prevent a finding of economic duress.

(c) Were the effects of the pressure upon the weaker party recognized by the stronger party and was the pressure exerted to bring about those effects (see *B & S Contracts and Design Ltd v Victor Green Publications Ltd* [1984] ICR 419)?

If the pressure is illegitimate, the next question is whether the weaker party was thereby coerced into entering the contract. Lord Scarman, in *Pao On v Lau Yiu Long* [1980]

AC 614, identified, *inter alia*, some of the relevant factors: did the party protest, did he possess an adequate alternative course of action, and did he take steps to avoid the contract after entering into it?

Subsequent case law has shown that the absence of effective choice is the cornerstone of coercion, as noted in *Vantage Navigation Corporation v Suhail & Saud Bahwan Building Materials (The Alev)* [1989] 1 Lloyd's Rep 138 and *Adam Opel GmbH v Mitras Automotive UK Ltd* [2007] EWHC 3252, [2007] All ER (D) 272. The other factors merely contribute to this finding but are not essential; for example, lack of protest may simply demonstrate the futility of pursuing any other course of action.

Remedies for Undue Influence and Economic Duress

For the purposes of an examination, a student should know that the main remedy for a successful claimant is rescission of the contract. As with misrepresentation, certain bars operate to prevent rescission. In particular, relief will be refused if (a) the claimant has already affirmed the contract or waited too long before seeking to avoid the contract (note the tighter deadlines in economic duress—*North Ocean Shipping Co. Ltd v Hyundai Construction Co. Ltd* [1979] QB 705), (b) the parties cannot be restored substantially to their previous positions, although judicial *dicta* in *Halpern v Halpern (No. 2)* [2007] EWCA Civ 291, [2007] 3 All ER 478 suggests that if a victim finds it impossible to make counter-restitution a court may, nowadays, be more inclined to identify a 'suitable' solution by, *inter alia*, making appropriate 'monetary adjustments' (see generally *Cheese v Thomas* [1994] 1 All ER 35; *Mahoney v Purnell* [1996] 3 All ER 61), or (c) third parties have acquired rights in the subject matter of the contract prior to its avoidance.

Rescission: In *TSB Bank plc v Camfield* [1995] 1 All ER 951, the Court of Appeal decided that it had no power to impose terms on the defendant when she sought to avoid the contract. Hence, where her husband had innocently represented that their liability would not exceed £15,000 (rather than unlimited liability as was the case) the court would not enforce the agreement against the wife to any extent, rather than limiting her liability to £15,000. However, this 'all or nothing' approach is not absolute. For example, in *Barclays Bank plc v Caplan* [1998] 1 FLR 532, the wife had originally been properly advised of her liability in 1986 when a new mortgage/guarantee had been agreed but, subsequently, when her liability was *extended* no further advice had been proffered. The court held that these subsequent transactions could be severed, limiting the wife's liability to that which had been imposed under the 1986 mortgage.

Question 1

Marjorie, a firm believer in psychic phenomena, was recently devastated by the sudden death of her husband. She was left a sizeable amount of money in her husband's will, as well as his business, Ghosthunters & Co.

She decides to communicate with the spirit of her husband through her long-standing medium, Spook. Spook tells Marjorie that her husband wishes her to donate £25,000 to the Spirit Appreciation Society Ltd (SAS), a company which publishes a journal entitled 'Supernatural Monthly'. Marjorie donates the money by gift under seal.

Meanwhile, Ghosthunters & Co. is facing financial collapse because its main creditor, Banshee, is threatening to call in an overdue loan of £50,000. In return for an extra six weeks to repay the loan, Marjorie agrees to transfer a 33% shareholding in Ghosthunters & Co. to Banshee.

Three months later, Marjorie finds out that Spook is a director of SAS. Moreover, she is becoming worried about the way in which Banshee is using his shareholding to redirect the policy of the business.

Advise Marjorie whether she can avoid either transaction on grounds of unfair pressure.

Commentary

In this problem, the victim of the pressure, Marjorie, is acting in two very different capacities. In her dealings with Spook she is just another private client seeking 'professional' advice. Spook appears to be the dominant party, raising the possibility of undue influence. You should consider whether there is evidence of affirmative proof of undue influence, or whether the relationship between the parties exhibited a level of trust and confidence that either automatically raised a presumption of influence (Class 2A), or did so on the facts (Class 2B). If either of the latter two possibilities emerge, is Marjorie's gift readily explicable by the 'ordinary motives' that govern people acting in such circumstances, or is there an element of suspicious dealing that calls for further explanation (the '*Etridge (No. 2)* test')? Finally, can Spook rebut any resulting presumption of undue influence by arguing that Marjorie acted in a spontaneous manner, free of any improper pressure?

The relationship between Marjorie and Banshee is different. They are acting in their business capacities when arranging the shareholding transfer. The doctrine of economic duress is therefore more relevant. The type of questions which could be posed include: Is Banshee threatening to break an existing contract? Are his actions calculated to cause serious damage to Marjorie's company? Did Marjorie have an alternative course of action?

Answer plan

- Is there any evidence of affirmative undue influence by Spook against Marjorie?

- If not, does the nature of their relationship suggest that the requisite level of trust and confidence existed between them, and that the ensuing transaction was sufficiently suspicious to raise a presumption of undue influence? If so, can Spook effectively rebut that presumption?

- What are the consequences of the contract between Spook and Marjorie being declared voidable?

- Has Banshee acted in an unconscionable manner, suggesting that he is applying some form of illegitimate pressure against Marjorie?

- Did Marjorie have any alternative course of action, as opposed to submitting to Banshee's demands?

Suggested answer

Marjorie v Spook

There are two possible ways in which Marjorie might argue that her donation to SAS is voidable for undue influence: affirmative proof of undue influence (Class 1) or a presumption of undue influence which is not rebutted (Class 2A/B). This distinction emphasizes the shifting onus of proof resulting from the proximity of the parties' relationship.

In establishing affirmative proof the Court of Appeal in *Allcard v Skinner* (1887) 36 Ch D 145 defined undue influence as:

> some unfair and improper conduct, some coercion from outside, some overreaching, some form of cheating and generally, though not always, some personal advantage gained.

In so far as Spook has tricked Marjorie for the purposes of personal gain, it would seem that Spook's conduct is encompassed within the above definition. In particular, Marjorie's recent bereavement and her belief in psychic phenomena are presumably known to Spook. These circumstances will clearly combine to cloud her judgement and make her extremely susceptible to Spook's suggestions. A parallel can be drawn with the cases of *Lyon v Home* (1868) LR 6 Eq 655 and *Nottidge v Prince* (1860) 2 Giff 246 to justify a finding of undue influence. The latter case is especially apposite as the plaintiff had visited the defendant, a spiritualist medium, in order to make contact with her late husband. The defendant's personal gain was more obvious as the plaintiff's late husband apparently advised her to adopt the defendant as her son and ensure his future financial independence.

Furthermore, it is worth emphasizing that it is the 'dominant' party's knowledge of the weaker party's desires and infirmities which is crucial to a finding of undue influence. Thus, if Spook was ignorant of Marjorie's psychic fixation then the difficulty of proof would be increased.

If undue influence is established, the contract is *prima facie* voidable although the right to rescind is lost if the victim waits too long before seeking relief. As fraud is involved, it is generally thought that time runs from discovery of the fraud (e.g. *Leaf v International Galleries* [1950] 2 KB 86) although the alternative opinion is that time runs from when the pressure ceases to operate on the mind of the victim. On the present facts these tests are effectively contemporaneous as both would require Marjorie to unearth Spook's underhand dealing. However, if SAS has spent the donation in the meantime, any ensuing legal victory will be pyrrhic (see *Allcard v Skinner*) as damages are not available in this area. This might suggest that Marjorie should consider framing her action in misrepresentation (e.g. Misrepresentation Act 1967, s. 2(1), or the breach of a duty of care— *Cornish v Midland Bank plc* [1985] 3 All ER 513) but the obvious difficulties of establishing the factual basis of any statement that relied upon the interpretation of psychic phenomena may dissuade Marjorie from this course of action unless she can establish actual fraud.

Marjorie's alternative claim is that a presumption of undue influence has arisen. To succeed Marjorie must explore two possible courses of action. First, that her relationship with Spook fell into the Class 2A category which *automatically* assumes that the requisite degree of trust and confidence existed between the parties to generate a presumption of influence. This argument appears rather tenuous; for example, it is unlikely that in a medium/client relationship the former would be expected to put the interests of his/her client first. Presumably Marjorie's counsel will seek to draw an analogy with *Allcard v Skinner* where the relationship of religious leader and disciple, as interpreted nowadays, fell into Class 2A, but the decision in *Nottidge v Prince* (*supra*) suggests that this argument is unlikely to succeed as regards the relationship of medium and client. Marjorie's second argument is that, *de facto*, the level of trust and confidence that she placed in Spook should raise a presumption of undue influence (Class 2B). On the facts, as Marjorie found herself in a fragile emotional state, and continued to have a firm belief in psychic phenomena, it is not unreasonable to conclude that she would have placed great reliance on the guidance of Spook, her long-standing medium. In short, that Spook occupied a clear position of dominance that would *presumably* enable him to influence the will of his client.

If Marjorie can establish a Class 2A or 2B relationship, the court will apply the test set out by the House of Lords in *Royal Bank of Scotland v Etridge (No. 2)* [2001] UKHL 44, [2001] 4 All ER 449. The court will need to be convinced that the resulting transaction (i.e. the gift of £25,000) was in some way 'wrongful'; that is, not readily explicable by the relationship of the parties. Does the large amount of money transferred raise such suspicions? Alternatively, does Spook's undisclosed directorship at SAS suggest an element of underhand dealing which, if known, *might* have dissuaded Marjorie from making the gift (see *UCB Corporate Services Ltd v Williams* [2002] EWCA Civ 555, [2003] 1 P & CR 12)? It seems very likely that these questions will receive affirmative answers, and that a presumption of undue influence will be levelled against Spook as regards Marjorie's gift to SAS.

To rebut the above presumption Spook must prove that Marjorie's actions were 'voluntary'. This can take two forms: spontaneity of action or proper independent advice. The latter course seems difficult to substantiate as there is no evidence that any independent advice was given. Undoubtedly the concealment of Spook's true role in the transaction would intimate that Marjorie was unable to make a full, free and informed estimate of the expediency of the transaction (see *Inche Noriah v Sheik Allie Bin Omar* [1929] AC 127). Alternatively, Spook might argue that Marjorie acted *spontaneously*, free of any undue pressures at that moment. The majority decision in *Re Brocklehurst's Estate, Hall v Roberts* [1978] Ch 14 supports the view that people should be free to do as they wish with their money and property, that friendship and eccentricity are human characteristics and that, as a result, courts should not interfere with such transactions in the absence of fraud or trickery (see also *R v Attorney-General of England and Wales* [2003] UKPC 22, [2003] EMLR 24). The last point is key to our facts: as Marjorie appears to have been deceived, Spook will struggle to rebut the presumption of undue influence in the absence of proof that Marjorie made the gift with full knowledge of the facts.

If Marjorie successfully establishes undue influence her primary remedy is that of rescission. She must not delay unduly in seeking legal redress. Moreover, the recovery of her donation will be subject to the decision in *Allcard v Skinner*, i.e. if the money has been spent restitution becomes impossible (see, however, the more relaxed approach adopted in *Cheese v Thomas* [1994] 1 All ER 35; *Halpern v Halpern (No. 2)* [2007] EWCA Civ 291, [2007] 3 All ER 478).

Marjorie v Banshee

Marjorie is attempting to avoid the contract in her capacity as proprietor of Ghosthunters Ltd. Thus as the transaction involves arm's length commercial dealing, the doctrine of economic duress is more appropriate.

Courts will not lightly infer economic duress. The *type* of pressure exerted is of paramount importance. Although one may act under overwhelming pressure the absence of choice will not negate consent in law unless it is of a kind that is regarded as illegitimate (see *Barton v Armstrong* [1976] AC 104, 121). Illegitimate pressure generally involves a threat by the dominant party calculated to cause unlawful damage to the economic interests of the other party; for example, a threat to break an *existing* contract which is vital to the economic well-being of the other party. In *Universe Tankships Inc. of Monrovia v ITWF* [1983] AC 366, Lord Scarman identified two aspects of illegitimate pressure: the nature of the pressure and the nature of the demand which the pressure was applied to support. This distinction demonstrates that pressure which appears lawful might still be considered illegitimate if exerted for unconscionable reasons.

On the present facts, one might pose the following questions. Is Banshee trying to hold Marjorie to ransom (e.g. *Atlas Express Ltd v Kafco (Importers and Distributors) Ltd* [1989] QB 833)? Is Banshee threatening to do something which may be construed as unconscionable, knowing the severe consequences which this will visit upon Marjorie's business (e.g. *Universe Tankships Inc. of Monrovia v ITWF* [1983] 1 AC 366)? Is Banshee threatening to break an existing contract (e.g. *North Ocean Shipping Co. Ltd v Hyundai Construction Co. Ltd* [1979] QB 705)? The last question deserves closer attention. There is nothing to suggest that Banshee does not have the right to call in the debt. If so, any advantage which Banshee gains from postponing repayment of the debt would normally be characterized as a simple forbearance. The doctrine of economic duress should not be employed to overturn such a contract *per se*. Conversely, if Banshee is wrongfully calling in the loan (e.g. prematurely) his action may be illegitimate assuming that he knows of Marjorie's plight and that the court is willing to stigmatize his acquisition of a 33% shareholding as being morally reprehensible. (Perhaps one could contrast *D & C Builders v Rees* [1966] 2 QB 617 with *CTN Cash and Carry Ltd v Gallaher Ltd* [1994] 4 All ER 715, the outcome in those cases being determined by the *bona fide* nature of the creditor's claim.)

In conclusion, although exercising an existing contractual right to call in an overdue loan seems perfectly reasonable, Lord Scarman in the *ITWF* case suggested that a lawful demand coupled with an 'illegitimate motive' might be illegitimate. Here, for instance, is Banshee's real motive the procurement of a 33% shareholding or the acquisition of a security to obviate any risks associated with non-payment of the debt at the later date?

Assuming illegitimate pressure has been identified, one must ask whether Marjorie was coerced by this pressure. Did she possess other options that would have avoided the need to transfer her shareholding to Banshee. Could she have considered pursuing an action for breach of contract and would her business have survived in the meantime? Did she enter voluntarily into a compromise agreement, i.e. extending the time for repayment in return for a 33% shareholding? Could she have obtained appropriate refinancing of the debt from another source? If negative replies are forthcoming, it is arguable that the lack of any practicable available alternatives suggests coercion. For example, in *B & S Contracts and Design Ltd v Victor Green Publications Ltd* [1984] ICR 419 and *Carillion Construction Ltd v Felix* (UK) Ltd [2001] BLR 1 the timing of the threatened breach of contract left the plaintiff with no option other than to submit to making the extra payment.

Another factor which has been considered relevant is the lack of any protest by the weaker party at the time the pressure was exerted. Marjorie seems to accept the new arrangement without a murmur. However, as Lord Scarman recognized in *ITWF*, protest is not always relevant if the pressure is so great as to make protest pointless.

Finally, Marjorie has already waited three months before seeking legal advice. The decision in *North Ocean Shipping Co. Ltd v Hyundai Construction Co. Ltd* [1979] QB 705 suggests that time runs quickly against a party seeking rescission on grounds of economic duress. In that case the right to rescission was lost as the plaintiff had waited several months before instituting legal proceedings. In arm's length commercial dealings the defendant is entitled to know reasonably quickly whether his counterpart is considering any legal action. The only *caveat* is that time will probably run from release of the pressure, rather than its exertion. Thus, if Marjorie felt unable to question the shareholding transfer until the existing debt repayment had been resolved her right to rescind would remain intact.

Question 2

Ron is a retired lorry driver who has just set up his own distribution service. His first customer is Cottonvalue PLC, a company with a nationwide network of retail outlets. Cottonvalue wants to use Ron to deliver stationery to all its outlets in the North of England. A contract is signed whereby Ron will deliver a 'minimum 1,000 boxes of stationery' for Cottonvalue over the next twelve months, beginning on 1 January. No maximum figure for deliveries is specified. The stationery will be packed in specially selected boxes, of one size only, incurring a delivery charge of £0.50p per box irrespective of the distance travelled within the designated area. Both parties expect Ron to be called on to deliver far more than the 'minimum' specified in the contract.

Ron relies on the projected profits to take out a bank loan to upgrade his existing fleet of lorries. Unfortunately, midway through the contract, Cottonvalue expresses its wish to renegotiate the delivery charge, threatening immediate withdrawal unless the delivery charge is reduced to £0.40p. Ron agrees as the prospect of losing Cottonvalue's custom is unthinkable.

At the end of the year, Ron asks you for advice as to whether he can reclaim the lost 10p on every delivery he made on the ground that the contractual modification was voidable for improper pressure.

Commentary

This question concerns the limits which courts impose on the principle of freedom of contract as regards arm's length commercial dealings. Nineteenth-century case law extolled the virtues of a *laissez-faire* philosophy refusing to interfere with business contracts unless clear evidence of fraud existed. However, more recently, courts have developed a doctrine of economic duress which limits the morally repugnant excesses of any unbridled freedom of contract principle. In particular, where a dominant party has exerted illegitimate pressure to coerce the other party's will, the ensuing contract may be voidable for economic duress. Thus for Ron to succeed he will need to establish that: (a) Cottonvalue exerted illegitimate pressure, and (b) as a consequence his will was coerced. In this context the good student might identify the factual similarities with *Atlas Express Ltd v Kafco (Importers & Distributors) Ltd* [1989] QB 833.

Answer plan

- Should Cottonvalue's demands be characterized as normal commercial pressure or illegitimate pressure?

- In particular, did Cottonvalue take advantage of its bargaining strength, knowing that Ron would submit because of his precarious financial situation?
- Was Ron coerced by Cottonvalue's request for re-negotiation of the contract?
- In particular, did Ron protest, possess an alternative course of action/legal remedy or demonstrate in some other way total submission to the wishes of Cottonvalue?
- What remedies would Ron possess if successful in his economic duress defence?

Suggested answer

Ron would be best advised to seek avoidance of the modified contract on the ground of economic duress. The doctrine of economic duress is still in its infancy but already it has become clear that a court will not set aside a contract merely because 'normal commercial pressure' has been exerted by the dominant party (*Barton v Armstrong* [1976] AC 104). What is needed is some evidence that the pressure which Cottonvalue exerted was of a type characterizable as 'illegitimate' and that Ron had no alternative but to agree to the new terms (i.e. his will was coerced).

Illegitimate Pressure

In *Universe Tankships Inc. of Monrovia v ITWF* [1983] 1 AC 366, Lord Scarman identified two aspects of illegitimate pressure: the nature of the pressure and the nature of the demand which the pressure was applied to support. This distinction demonstrates that pressure which appears lawful might still be considered illegitimate if exerted for unconscionable reasons. Thus, even if Cottonvalue was contractually entitled to threaten withdrawal, this might not be considered legitimate *per se* (see, however, *CTN Cash and Carry Ltd v Gallaher Ltd* [1994] 4 All ER 715).

More often than not, illegitimate pressure involves a threat by the dominant party calculated to cause unlawful damage to the economic interests of the other party unless some demand is met. One example might be a threatened breach of an *existing* contract. However, additional evidence would be required as such threats are unlikely to be considered illegitimate *per se*. For instance, in *Atlas Express Ltd v Kafco (Importers & Distributors) Ltd* [1989] QB 833, it was the manner in which the plaintiff exerted the pressure which was crucial. In particular, compelling a re-negotiation of an existing contract purely for the plaintiff's benefit, leaving the communication of the threat to an innocent third party, timing its communication to correspond with his own absence, and judging the precise moment when the pressure would be heightened by the defendant's realization that only the plaintiff was in the position to meet his needs (e.g. *Carillion Construction Ltd v Felix (UK) Ltd* [2001] BLR 1). In such situations, it is clear that the dominant party intends to apply the pressure and has sufficient knowledge of the weaker party's predicament to predict the impact of that pressure (e.g. *D & C Builders v Rees* [1966] 2 QB 617).

In the present situation, Cottonvalue has threatened to break an existing contract. Are there any facts which suggest that this threat is illegitimate? Does Cottonvalue recognize that Ron is relying upon the contract to service his existing indebtedness to his bank? Affirmative responses to these questions might suggest that the pressure is illegitimate.

Clearly, hard bargaining is an everyday incident of normal business relationships (see *Barton v Armstrong* [1976] AC 104). For example, Ron was not obliged to upgrade his existing fleet of lorries, i.e. it was not a condition of his contract with Cottonvalue. A predicament of one's own making should not be used to label normal commercial pressure as something which is unconscionable, whereas if Cottonvalue was aware of Ron's financial state, and the serious economic consequences of withdrawing from the contract, this might suggest a contrary finding. As emphasized in *B & S Contracts & Design Ltd v Victor Green Publications Ltd* [1984] ICR 419, the pressure is often illegitimate *because* it represents an intentional threat of unlawful damage to the other party's economic interest. Remove this intent and duress becomes all the harder to establish.

Coercion

The next question is whether Ron has been coerced by the threat. The degree of pressure must be such as to vitiate consent. Various factors have been identified as being of importance: the protest of the weaker party, the unavailability of any other course of action (e.g. legal remedy), the lack of independent advice, and the attempted subsequent avoidance of the contract by the weaker party (see generally *Pao On v Lau Yiu Long* [1980] AC 614, 635). These factors are not of general application. Whereas protest demonstrates the weaker party's explicit reluctance to submit to the pressure, intentional submission (as in Ron's case) manifests an equally strong response, albeit implicitly, if it arises from the realization that there is no practical alternative open to him. Moreover, subsequent steps to avoid the damaging effects of duress may indicate prior submission but such action cannot be expected if the illegitimate pressure has not yet ceased to operate.

The true hallmark of coercion is lack of effective choice: did Ron have an alternative course of action? It is the unavoidable and serious consequence of non-submission which lies at the heart of coercion. For example, in *Vantage Navigation Corporation v Suhail & Saud Bahwan Building Materials, The Alev* [1989] 1 Lloyd's Rep 138, the plaintiffs implicitly threatened non-delivery of the defendants' cargo, perhaps even to jettison or sell it, unless a contribution was made towards paying the increased port and discharge costs. The cargo was aboard ship thousands of miles away. The defendants needed the cargo to be delivered on time. A wait and see approach was not a realistic course of action, especially as other sources of purchase were out of the question. Coercion was thereby established.

What should Ron have done at the time of the threat? Perhaps he should have refused to re-negotiate? The answer, in turn, might depend upon whether Ron had already delivered the 'minimum' quantity of goods specified in the contract. If this had occurred then Cottonvalue would have a contractual right to employ other transport agencies to deliver their goods, leaving Ron with no remedy whatsoever. Conversely, if the 'minimum' had not yet been delivered it would be open to Ron to claim damages if Cottonvalue did not continue to employ his services until the minimum delivery had been fulfilled. But is this practical? The facts suggest that legal action is 'unthinkable'. Cottonvalue are threatening a complete withdrawal, with the clear implication that it might not employ Ron again. This must be preying on Ron's mind when he considers his existing indebtedness to his bank.

Moreover, how would damages have been assessed? Ron would be looking for loss of profits associated with his expected rate of delivery rather than his minimum specified delivery, but this presumably would be too remote in contract law. In truth, an available remedy in damages does not seem to have unduly influenced the courts in duress cases (e.g. *Atlas Express Ltd v Kafco (Importers & Distributors) Ltd*). Perhaps this is because litigation is a protracted affair often requiring considerable financial resources over a long period of time—Ron appears devoid of spare cash and needs to negotiate a solution immediately.

Finally, if Ron can successfully plead economic duress he should be advised to proceed quickly. Economic duress makes a contract voidable, allowing the victim the option of rescission. However, this right can be lost through effluxion of time. The question is whether a court would have expected him to institute legal proceedings against Cottonvalue at an earlier date. The basic principle as applied in *North Ocean Shipping Co. Ltd v Hyundai Construction Co. Ltd* [1979] QB 705 is that a victim of duress must seek rescission as soon as possible after the original pressure has ceased to operate. In *North Ocean*, there was no evidence that, had the plaintiffs sought to reclaim their additional payment immediately, the defendants would have stopped the ship's construction. Equally, in Ron's situation is it reasonable for him to wait until the year has passed before seeking rescission of the modified payment schedule? He might argue that the pressure continued throughout the year as Cottonvalue had the right to redirect their delivery requirements to other firms once Ron had discharged his minimum delivery obligations. Perhaps there was a veiled threat that Cottonvalue might not negotiate with Ron over future delivery contracts? Without such evidence Ron's chances look bleak, as Cottonvalue will presumably contend that *both* parties had a vested interest in ensuring the legality of the contract modification and would therefore welcome a clear ruling as quickly as possible. Whatever else, case law suggests that in business transactions *both* parties must be able to ascertain what their enforceable contractual rights are as quickly as possible so that they can take appropriate contingency measures in their subsequent dealings with each other. In Cottonvalue's situation, if the reduction in delivery charge had been unenforceable, alternative distributors might have been sought *after* Ron had fulfilled his minimum obligations but *before* the year had passed.

(Note: the very good student might also link the absence of consideration and the presence of duress, referring to *Williams v Roffey Bros and Nicholls (Contractors) Ltd* [1991] 1 QB 1: has Ron obtained a 'practical benefit' from the new arrangement or has the reality of intent been compromised by Cottonvalue's unconscionable behaviour? See also *South Caribbean Trading Ltd v Trafigura Beheer BV* [2004] EWHC 2676, [2005] 1 Lloyd's Rep 128 where reference was again made to the nexus between consideration and duress.)

Question 3

Lincoln, who runs his own company, has decided to extend the family home in order to create an office for himself. He recognizes that the best way of raising the necessary finance is to increase his existing mortgage, held with North Bank. He arranges to meet the bank manager, Peter, who is an old school friend.

Peter tells Lincoln that an increased mortgage is only possible if he takes advantage of the 'North Bank House Extension Policy'. This requires the bank, for a moderate fee, to arrange for the production of architect's plans and to apply for all planning consents.

The bank also hires the building sub-contractors, with direct payment from the mortgage advance. Next day, Lincoln persuades his wife, Annabel, who separately owns 5% of the shares in Lincoln's business, to sign the relevant form on the pretext that it is needed as security for the company's existing overdraft. Annabel does not read the form which includes a statement to the effect that all signatories have received independent advice. The bank obtains the necessary planning consent and hires Slapjack & Co. to do the building work, a firm in which Peter is a sleeping partner. The building work commences while Lincoln and Annabel are away on holiday. However, on their return, Annabel is horrified to discover the truth and seeks to avoid the contract. Moreover, Lincoln discovers the connection between Peter and Slapjack & Co.

Advise the parties.

Commentary

This seems like a very straightforward question on undue influence in which the examinee should focus on the relationship between Lincoln and Peter, as representative of the bank. Recourse could be made to *National Westminster Bank plc v Morgan* [1985] AC 686 and *Lloyds Bank Ltd v Bundy* [1975] QB 326 in order to ascertain whether a presumption of undue influence arose or whether Lincoln would need to prove affirmatively the presence of undue influence.

But this is only half the question. Annabel's rights are equally important. The basic question is whether the bank is tainted by any undue influence exerted by Lincoln over his wife, Annabel.

A spate of cases has shown the importance of banks dealing directly with wives and, if possible, either explaining the terms of any mooted agreement or encouraging the wife to obtain independent expert advice. You must consider whether the statement in the mortgage form, advising Annabel to seek independent advice, is sufficient for the bank to avoid liability.

Answer plan

- Can Lincoln establish affirmative proof of undue influence (Class 1), or set up a presumption of undue influence (Class 2A/2B)?
- What type of transaction has Annabel entered into—a surety or joint loan arrangement? Why is this relevant to the application of the *O'Brien* and *Etridge (No. 2)* principles?
- Would the principles set out by the House of Lords in *Etridge (No. 2)* suggest that North Bank was 'put on enquiry'? If so, has North Bank followed the correct procedures?
- If Lincoln and Annabel are successful in their respective actions, what remedies will they possess as against North Bank?

Suggested answer

Lincoln

There are two possible ways in which Lincoln might argue that the mortgage arrangement with the bank is voidable for undue influence: affirmative proof of undue influence (Class 1) or a presumption of undue influence which the Bank fails to rebut (Class 2A/2B). This distinction clearly emphasizes the shifting onus of proof resulting from the closeness of the parties' relationship.

In establishing affirmative proof, the Court of Appeal in *Allcard v Skinner* (1887) 36 Ch D 145 defined undue influence as:

> some unfair and improper conduct, some coercion from outside, some overreaching, some form of cheating and generally, though not always, some personal advantage gained.

Has Peter tricked Lincoln for the purposes of personal gain? Peter is clearly in a dominant position as his bank is holding itself out as possessing some type of specialist skill, i.e. co-ordinating the planning and building of house extensions. But 'dominance' in itself is not sufficient (see *Goldsworthy v Brickell* [1987] Ch 378). Every professional/business relationship involves parties dealing with each other on some unequal footing. As *Allcard v Skinner* (1887) 36 Ch D 145 illustrates, there must be evidence of victimization or improper conduct, generally leading to some personal advantage being gained.

On the one hand, Lincoln is not under pressure from the bank to extend his house. Nor has the bank any specific bargaining leverage, assuming Lincoln can obtain finance from an alternative source. On the other hand, there is a suggestion that Peter has gained from the transaction by using the services of a builder with whom he is financially associated and that by compelling Lincoln to use the bank's home extension service, the bank has also profited. Moreover, this must be viewed in the context of Peter's friendship with Lincoln over many years and Lincoln's desire to use the same bank with which he holds his current mortgage.

In summary, the lack of any overt pressure exerted by the bank should be contrasted with cases such as *Williams v Bayley* (1866) LR 1 HL 200, where success was in part attributable to the 'overbearing' nature of the dominant party and the lack of other choices open to the victim of that pressure. On this basis Lincoln's chances of success are slim.

Lincoln's next course of action is to claim that a presumption of undue influence has arisen between him and Peter (i.e. the bank). This would place the onus upon the bank to show that Lincoln acted voluntarily, after making a 'full, free and informed estimate' of the expediency of the transaction (see *Inche Noriah v Sheik Allie Bin Omar* [1929] AC 127). In *National Westminster Bank plc v Morgan* [1985] AC 686, the House of Lords did not regard a normal bank/customer relationship as falling within Class 2A, whereby the requisite level of trust and confidence automatically raises a presumption of influence. Thus, Lincoln's alternative argument, in line with *Royal Bank of Scotland v Etridge (No. 2)*, is that the nature of his relationship with Peter (Bank) suggested a level of trust and confidence in which Peter occupied a dominant position *vis-à-vis* Lincoln (often referred to as a Class 2B relationship)? If so, proof will be required that the ensuing transaction was 'wrongful', applying the '*Etridge* test'.

On the present facts, the relationship between Lincoln and Peter is not altogether conventional. The bank has 'offered' a home extension service which takes the decisions out of the client's hands. In effect, Lincoln is putting the whole operation in the hands of the bank and is therefore demonstrating a considerable degree of trust. The bank is encouraging, rather than discouraging this reliance, and all in the context of the bank manager, Peter, having formed a friendship with Lincoln over many years. This mixture of friendship, trust, and expertise is a potent cocktail, ripe for exploitation by the dominant party. It is clearly arguable, in these circumstances, that the bank has overstepped the boundaries of an orthodox bank/customer relationship (see *Lloyds Bank Ltd v Bundy* [1975] QB 326) and thereby demonstrated a sufficient level of trust and confidence to raise a presumption of influence. If so, we must ask whether this potential influence resulted in a 'wrongful' transaction; i.e. one that was not readily explicable by the relationship of the parties. Clearly Lincoln offloaded all the difficulties of organizing a home extension on to the bank and stood to gain from owning an extended, more valuable house. Yet Peter's connection with Slapjack & Co. was never revealed, nor the secret profit he stood to gain from the deal. These arguments are finely balanced. For example, in *Turkey v Awadh* [2005] EWCA Civ 382, [2005] 2 FCR 7, although the claimant's purchase of the defendants' property without any thought to its market value appeared 'wrongful', this was counter-balanced by the payment being made well in advance of the transfer of ownership in order to help the defendants 'out of a [financial] hole into which they had dug themselves' (at [41]). The result was that the transaction was not considered to be 'wrongful'. A similar approach might be adopted in our problem as it is Lincoln's wish to extend his home (rather than his bank's wish), although this may be countered by the non-disclosure of Peter's financial interests which may encourage the court to view Lincoln's claim more favourably.

Finally, if a presumption of undue influence is successfully raised the bank will find it almost impossible to rebut this in the light of Peter's deception and the lack of any independent advice being offered to Lincoln.

Annabel

Current case law suggests that banks must take appropriate measures when dealing with wives who wish to act as sureties for their husbands and/or use the jointly-owned matrimonial home as additional security for their husbands' business dealings (see *Royal Bank of Scotland v Etridge (No. 2)*). Failure to do so may mean that North Bank is tainted by any undue influence of Lincoln, leaving it with little chance of enforcing the security against Annabel.

We must first ask whether North Bank was 'put on enquiry'. In considering the nature of the transaction it is apparent that we are not dealing with a 'non-commercial surety' arrangement so Annabel would normally face an uphill task (see generally *Royal Bank of Scotland v Etridge (No. 2)* [2001] UKHL 44). However, the facts suggest that Peter, as manager of North Bank, knew that the purpose of the loan was to benefit Lincoln's business activities. Perhaps one can draw an analogy with *Goode Durrant Administration v Biddulph* (1994) 26 HLR 625 and argue that Annabel's risk/benefit ratio is grossly disproportionate to that of Lincoln's. The Bank would attempt to refute these claims by simply arguing that the transaction appeared on its face to be a secured loan to a married couple for the purposes of extending the marital home. Relying on the earlier House of Lords' decision in *CIBC Mortgages v Pitt* [1994] 1 AC 200, this would suggest that there was no reason for the Bank to enquire further as to whether the wife understood the transaction and her potential liability.

The above arguments are finely balanced but if Annabel successfully persuades the court that North Bank was 'put on enquiry' then the bank will need to demonstrate that it followed the procedures laid down in *Etridge (No. 2)*. What exactly were the actions of North Bank? According to *Etridge (No. 2)*, the bank should have persuaded Annabel to see an independent adviser who would explain the nature of the documentation and her possible liability, and ask her whether she wished to proceed? However, in our scenario, the bank simply relies upon Annabel's signature as evidence that she visited an independent adviser. It makes no attempt to discuss the matter with Annabel, nor does it attempt to discover whether Annabel read the forms, particularly the clause that encourages her to obtain independent advice. This seems to fall well below the standards expected in *Northern Rock Building Society v Archer* (1999) 78 P & CR 65 where the court berated the plaintiff for not informing the solicitor fully of the context in which the transaction was taking place (i.e. the underlying purpose for the loan). More importantly, the guidelines set out in *Etridge (No. 2)* clearly assume that it is the independent adviser who will confirm to the bank that proper advice has been given to the surety (i.e. Annabel), rather than relying upon the surety for such confirmation. This point was reinforced by the Court of Appeal in *First National Bank plc v Achampong* [2003] EWCA 487, [2004] 1 FCR 18.

Finally, if it is found that North Bank has failed to comply with the spirit of *Etridge (No. 2)* Annabel will still need to establish that Lincoln had acted wrongfully towards her. Fortunately for Annabel the facts seem quite clear on this matter. Lincoln deceived her into signing the agreement on the pretext that the security was needed to secure his existing business overdraft, rather than to pay for a house extension. This is a clear misrepresentation, probably fraudulent in nature, which will enable Annabel to claim that the transaction was voidable.

Lincoln and Annabel: Remedies

If Lincoln and Annabel are successful, their primary remedy will be one of rescission. The normal bars will apply, such as lapse of time, affirmation, and *restitutio in integrum*. Damages are not available for undue influence, although if the bank has broken a duty of care to Annabel damages may be available in negligence. The advice to both parties is to act sooner rather than later and notify the bank of their intention to avoid the contract. On the present facts complications might arise as the building work has already commenced. Regarding Lincoln, the Court of Appeal's decisions in *Cheese v Thomas* [1994] 1 All ER 35 and *Halpern v Halpern (No. 2) (Note)* [2007] EWCA Civ 291, [2007] 3 All ER 478 suggest some latitude on this point. However, Annabel could invoke the authority of *TSB Bank plc v Camfield* [1995] 1 All ER 951 to argue that no terms can be attached to the rescission of her contract with the bank. (Note: It is almost inconceivable that a student would be expected to consider this area in any further depth although a comment on the lack of privity between Slapjack & Co. and Lincoln/Annabel might be worth making.)

Question 4

The decisions of the House of Lords in *Barclays Bank plc v O'Brien* [1994] 1 AC 180 and *Royal Bank of Scotland v Etridge (No. 2)* [2001] UKHL 44; [2001] 4 All ER 449, have established a clearer, more coherent set of rules that strike an appropriate balance between the rights of creditors and those of wives who have been unduly influenced by their spouses.

To what extent do you agree with the above statement?

Commentary

One should expect a question on this topic to appear on most Contract examination papers. The House of Lords' landmark decisions proffer important guidance to banks and other financial institutions on how to deal with wives who are acting as sureties for their husbands' debts, as well as those who secure joint advances with their husbands. It is important to note that the House of Lords' decision in *O'Brien* never intended to offer a definitive exposition of the law, applicable in every conceivable situation. Rather, it represented a framework of principle which lower courts would need to adapt and modify, interpret and re-interpret, in accordance with the facts presented to them. Unfortunately, the unpredictability of subsequent case law suggested that greater clarity and specificity was required in this area, culminating in the *Etridge (No. 2)* decision. Interestingly, in both cases, the Law Lords did not merely direct their attention to wives but also to other types of relationship (e.g. unmarried cohabitees) whether heterosexual or homosexual, or any other relationship where the prospect of undue influence by the debtor was foreseeable (e.g. *Avon Finance Co. v Bridger* [1985] 2 All ER 281).

Answer plan

- What was the state of the law prior to the House of Lords' decision in *O'Brien*?
- What policy considerations influenced the House of Lords in *O'Brien*?
- To what extent did subsequent case law depart from the spirit of *O'Brien*?
- To what extent did the House of Lords' decision in *Etridge (No. 2)* clarify any outstanding ambiguities?

Suggested answer

When a bank entrusts certain duties to a debtor-husband who, as intermediary, is capable of exerting undue influence over his wife, the courts have always recognized the possibility that any ensuing transaction entered into between the wife and bank might be voidable for undue influence. Unfortunately, until 1994, there was considerable confusion regarding the specific conditions that were needed to justify judicial intervention on behalf of a wife. In particular, the courts appeared to adopt any one of three possible approaches, making it very difficult to predict the outcome.

Pre-*O'Brien*

First, there was the 'special equity theory', traceable to *Turnbull & Co v Duvall* [1902] AC 429, that seemed to reinforce the patronizing nineteenth-century attitude towards wives and their role and importance in marriage. Its modern reincarnation can be seen in *Yerkey v Jones* (1939) 63 CLR 649 where Dixon J emphasized the importance of the creditor's actually proving that the wife understood the transaction she was entering into, thereby almost placing the bank in *loco parentis* to the wife. The implication was that a wife would be treated more like a child than an independent thinking adult. The second approach was termed the 'agency' theory: a creditor bank that 'left everything to the husband' might be tainted by any undue influence exerted by the husband over his wife (e.g. *Barclays Bank plc v Kennedy* [1989] 1 FLR 356). However, the use of agency principles is both illogical and artificial. It is rare for a bank to appoint a husband formally as its agent. Moreover, once an agency is established, notice by the creditor of an agent's improper conduct is irrelevant as the normal rule is that the principal (creditor) is *automatically* tainted by the actions of his agent. Finally, a line of Court of Appeal decisions from 1985 demonstrated a greater acceptance of notice as being pivotal to the determination of a creditor's liability (e.g. *Coldunell Ltd v Gallon* [1986] QB 1184, and *Midland Bank plc v Shephard* [1988] 3 All ER 17). Briefly, if the circumstances were such that the creditor should have realized the possibility of the husband's using unfair means to procure his wife's signature, the creditor might be tainted by such impropriety. This latter approach was eventually adopted by the House of Lords in *O'Brien*, specifically focusing attention on the *nature* of the transaction between husband and wife, and the consequential probability of influence.

O'Brien and its Aftermath

In *O'Brien* the House of Lords stated that where the creditor had notice, actual or constructive, of some possible impropriety occurring between husband and wife, reasonable steps had to be taken to ensure that the wife's consent had been properly obtained. To that end, the Law Lords distinguished two types of transactions. First, if the wife was acting as surety for her husband's business debts, the creditor would be put on notice if the transaction was financially disadvantageous and there was a substantial risk in such transactions that the wife's signature had been inequitably procured by her husband. Secondly, where the transaction simply involved a joint advance to a husband and wife (e.g. a joint loan to buy a family car) then, unless there were special circumstances known to the creditor, the latter would not be fixed with constructive notice of any impropriety between the married couple. For example, in *CIBC Mortgages PLC v Pitt* [1994] 1 AC 200 the creditor honestly believed that the husband and wife would use the joint advance for the purchase of a holiday home. Separate advice for the wife appeared unnecessary, as both appeared to benefit equally from the transaction.

The House of Lords also recommended that the husband and wife be interviewed separately, circumventing the problem faced by the interviewer in *Bank of Credit and Commerce International SA v Aboody* [1990] 1 QB 923 where the husband's hysterics at a joint meeting clearly affected the wife's will. In particular, it would be sufficient if the creditor insisted that the wife attend a private meeting (in the absence of her husband) with a representative of the creditor at which she was told of the extent of her liability, warned of the risk she was running and urged to take independent advice.

Subsequent case law demonstrated a willingness to embrace the spirit of *O'Brien*, without in any way being restricted by specific rules of interpretation. Thus, in *Goode Durrant Administration v Biddulph* (1994) 26 HLR 625 the creditor was put on notice in a simple joint advance transaction (the loan financing a joint venture) because of the significant disparity between the wife's potential gain and the scale of her liability. As the creditor had done nothing to advise the wife, the transaction was tainted by the husband's undue influence. Unfortunately, this broad approach could be less than beneficial to the wronged wife. For example, in dealing with the actions of the bank, it seemed acceptable for the wife to be advised by the husband's solicitor (e.g. *Bank of Baroda v Rayarel* [1995] 27 HLR 387). To be specific, the bank was entitled to rely on the professional integrity of the solicitor and his/her ability to resolve conflicts of interest properly (e.g. *Banco Exterior Internacional v Mann, Mann and Harris* [1995] 1 All ER 936). Moreover, further cases reinforced the wider view that once advice had been given by a solicitor the bank was relieved of any further responsibilities, irrespective of whether the nature and type of advice that the wife received was appropriate to her needs and circumstances (see *Midland Bank plc v Massey* [1995] 1 All ER 929). It seemed that the best policy for banks to adopt was to leave everything to the solicitor, a state of affairs that was beneficial to the banks as it apparently exonerated them of any culpability in most circumstances.

Etridge (No. 2)

The House of Lords' decision in *Etridge (No. 2)* attempted to address some of the deficiencies in the prevailing case law. It discarded notions of financially disadvantageous transactions, set out much clearer guidelines on the procedures that banks and independent advisers should adopt and, in particular, extended the principles so as to incorporate all 'non-commercial' debtor/surety relationships. Importantly, whilst accepting that the banks could rely upon the good sense and expertise of a solicitor, the Law Lords stressed that if the creditor withheld information from the solicitor or knew that no competent solicitor could ever advise the wife to enter such a transaction, the availability of legal advice would be insufficient for the creditor to avoid being fixed by constructive notice of any legal impropriety perpetrated by the husband debtor upon his wife. Subsequently, the general need for the creditor to take reasonable steps to ensure that the nature of the risks arising from the transaction has been brought home to the wife by the independent adviser was clearly re-emphasized by the Court of Appeal in *First National Bank plc v Achampong* [2003] EWCA 487, [2004] 1 FCR 18, strongly suggesting that the creditor must actually confirm that the independent adviser covered all of the essential points.

A Fair Balance?

The House of Lords has clearly stressed the need to retain a sense of balance in this area. In particular, excess sympathy for wives dealing with powerful banks can be counter-productive: courts need to ensure that the wealth currently tied up in matrimonial homes does not become economically sterile. If financial institutions are too hindered by the law then they will be unwilling to accept such security, thereby reducing the flow of capital to business enterprises.

Moreover, the law cannot operate in a social vacuum. For many years now society has promoted the equality of the sexes, attacking preconceptions that the wife is subservient to her husband in the management of the family's finances. What is important however is that a clear legal safety-net exists which can be used in circumstances where the husband possesses the business acumen and experience and the wife tends to follow her husband's advice in such matters. Courts still recognize that in many marriages the wife places confidence and trust in her husband in relation to their financial affairs, potentially raising the presumption of undue influence between the spouses. Certainly the House of Lords' decisions offer a salutary warning to creditor institutions that, unless they follow the correct procedures in good faith, the ensuing financial transactions may become unenforceable as against wives. However, the *Etridge* decision does have a sting in its tail. Their Lordships made it abundantly clear that the standard surety transaction in which a wife agrees to act as guarantor for her husband's business debts does not necessarily create a presumption of undue influence that would taint the creditor. More evidence will be required to demonstrate that the husband used unfair means to procure his wife's agreement (e.g. some form of misrepresentation). Equally, a court will not be so quick to characterize the ensuing transaction as *wrongful*, and therefore voidable, as a wife's support for her husband's business is perfectly natural, i.e. in the absence of any suspicious facts the bank is not put on enquiry and therefore not expected to ensure that the wife receives independent advice (*per* Lord Nicholls in *Etridge*). This suggests that a wife will struggle unless there is clear evidence that the disparity between the husband's gain and the wife's potential loss is disproportionately large. Some might justifiably argue that this approach tends to swing the pendulum unfairly towards the protection of creditors in such circumstances.

Question 5

The doctrine of economic duress is a formal recognition of Lord Denning's theory of inequality of bargaining power. The latter provides the necessary juristic basis for courts to give relief to a weaker party who has entered into a contract upon terms which are very unfair or in return for a consideration which is grossly inadequate.

Discuss.

Commentary

In answering this question, a simple regurgitation of lecture notes on economic duress, adding a few of Lord Denning's famous judgments to spice up the proceedings, would be unlikely to gain more than a simple pass mark. The central issue raised is the relationship between the very broad brushstroke approach taken by Lord Denning, in his emphasis upon inequality of bargaining power, and the rather more focused doctrine of economic duress. You must therefore set out the constituents of each theory and identify how they overlap.

The suggested answer below provides you with one of many possible approaches. The analysis is slightly unorthodox in that it argues that economic duress and inequality of bargaining power are not as dissimilar as many textbooks would suggest. Two alternative approaches would be: (a) to concentrate on the treatment that Lord Denning's judgments received by other courts, concluding that the development of a doctrine of economic duress rendered Lord Denning's general theory superfluous, or (b) to sidestep economic duress entirely and concentrate on non-commercial transactions where the doctrine of undue influence would be more apposite.

The following is one of many possible answer plans.

Answer plan

- Explain the basic constituents of economic duress.
- Giving examples, explain the meaning of 'inequality of bargaining power'.
- What is the difference between the above two approaches and to what extent can one identify Lord Denning's themes in the area of economic duress?
- Consider the impact of various judicial decisions in the post-*Bundy* era, such as *National Westminster Bank plc v Morgan* [1985] AC 686.

Suggested answer

In *Lloyds Bank Ltd v Bundy* [1975] QB 326, Lord Denning examined the various forms of improper pressure, attempting to identify a single thread which ran through the different categories of duress, undue influence, and general unconscionability. His conclusion was that inequality of bargaining power represented the pervasive theme. The above question paraphrases Lord Denning's judgment but, in so doing, leaves out some important details. In particular, his Lordship stated that the law would give relief to a person who entered a contract:

> . . . on terms which are very unfair or transfers property for a consideration which is grossly inadequate, when his bargaining power is grievously impaired by reason of his own needs or desires, or by his own ignorance or infirmity, coupled with undue influence or pressures brought to bear on him by or for the benefit of the other.

In a series of subsequent decisions, Lord Denning continued to emphasize this aspect of improper pressure (see *Davis (Clifford) Management Ltd v WEA Records Ltd* [1975] 1 WLR 61; *Levison v Patent Steam Cleaning Co. Ltd* [1978] QB 69). It is important to recognize that 'inequality of bargaining power' was not the sole theoretical basis of Lord Denning's principle. Evidence was also required to show that (a) the terms of the contract were unfair, (b) the weaker party's bargaining power was affected by his own 'needs and infirmities', and (c) the stronger party exploited the position to his advantage. Note that this latter point does not require a formal finding of undue influence, duress, or similar wrongdoing—evidence of simple persuasion, explicit or implicit, in all its forms, would probably suffice.

Lord Denning's theory clearly emphasizes the position of the weaker party. The unfairness of the contract is sufficient evidence of unconscionability—judicial intervention merely requires evidence of the weaker party's resultant coercion irrespective of whether the dominant party has acted unlawfully. It is little wonder that the theory was treated with considerable scepticism by subsequent courts. Seldom can one say that the bargaining power is equal in a transaction. Thus, as the resultant terms will reflect this disparity, judicial intervention would be possible in every transaction where the weaker party had been pressured in some way.

In *Pao On v Lau Yiu Long* [1980] AC 614, Lord Scarman preferred to concentrate on a doctrine of duress, opining that a broad theory of inequality of bargaining power would be an 'unhelpful development of law'. Subsequent courts followed this approach (e.g. *Burmah Oil Co. Ltd v Bank of England* [1979] 3 WLR 722). This reticence was best illustrated by Dillon LJ in *Lobb (Alec) (Garages) Ltd v Total Oil (GB) Ltd* [1985] 1 WLR 173 when stating that interference in arm's length commercial dealings was only acceptable where 'as a matter of common fairness it was not right that the strong should be allowed to push the weak to the wall'. Perhaps the death knell for Lord Denning's doctrine was sounded by Lord Scarman in *National Westminster Bank plc v Morgan* [1985] AC 686 when commenting that, in view of the increasing growth of statutory restrictions upon freedom of contract, it was questionable whether there was 'any need in the modern law to erect a general principle of relief against inequality of bargaining power'.

In each of the above cases reference was made to a new doctrine of economic duress. In what ways does this doctrine depart from Lord Denning's general theory of bargaining inequality? First, Lord Denning's judgments inevitably refer to consumer/employment contracts whereas economic duress applies to businesses dealing at arm's length. Bargaining inequality is inevitable in the former situation as it results from lack of access to business/legal expertise and the general status of the parties. Conversely, in the latter circumstances, inequality results from the economic size of the businesses and, in general, the bargaining leverage which this gives the dominant party within an *existing* contractual or pseudo-contractual relationship (e.g. *O'Sullivan v M.A.M Ltd* [1984] 3 WLR 448).

Secondly, Lord Denning concentrated on the *existence* of bargaining inequality and its effect upon the weaker party. Economic duress, on the other hand, is at pains to point out that mere commercial pressure is insufficient to render a contract voidable. What is required is some evidence of illegitimate pressure which results in the coercion of the weaker party. It is the *use* that is made of the bargaining inequality which will determine whether the pressure is illegitimate.

For the above reasons, Lord Denning paid little attention to whether the dominant party had a lawful excuse for his actions whereas this becomes a central issue in present day economic duress. It was this vital omission that persuaded the Court of Appeal in *Lobb (Alec) (Garages) Ltd v Total Oil (GB) Ltd* to reject Lord Denning's theory. But to end here would cause considerable injustice to Lord Denning as, with the benefit of hindsight, many of his judgments could be regarded as laying down markers for a subsequent doctrine of economic duress. For example, in *D & C Builders v Rees* [1966] 2 QB 617 and *Arrale v Costain Civil Engineering Ltd* [1976] 1 Lloyd's Rep 98, Lord Denning set aside the contract on grounds that the weaker parties' consent was 'no true accord', that they had been 'held to ransom', and that no person 'can insist on a settlement procured by intimidation'.

The decision in *D & C Builders* is particularly worthy of consideration. There, the debtor *knew* that the builders were desperate for money and that they would accept part-payment of the existing debt. Refusal would have exacerbated their current liquidity problems and contributed to the firm's premature liquidation. If one were to apply the principles of economic duress to these facts the following remarks could be made. First, the debtor's action was not mere commercial pressure. The pressure was illegitimate because (a) it constituted a threatened breach of an existing contract; (b) the debtor knew that any refusal by the creditor to accept the settlement would have serious and damaging consequences for their business; and (c) the pressure was applied to bring about those effects. These points are ever-present in cases where economic duress has been established (see *Atlas Express Ltd v Kafco (Importers & Distributors) Ltd* [1989] QB 833; *Vantage Navigation Corporation v Suhail & Saud Bahwan Building Materials, The Alev* [1989] 1 Lloyd's Rep 138).

Secondly, the creditor could establish coercion because (a) there was very little alternative but to submit—seeking legal redress was unlikely in view of existing cash-flow problems and the time involved in litigating the issue, (b) it was clear that the creditor was reluctant to agree to the settlement, and (c) the creditor took immediate steps to avoid the transaction after the pressure ceased to exist. Yet again, this is a textbook scenario for coercion.

In conclusion, the basic approach adopted by Lord Denning often contains clear parallels with the developing doctrine of economic duress. The common denominator is that the type of action which encourages judicial intervention in both cases can be characterized as morally unconscionable. Although bargaining inequality and duress start from different positions, it is arguable that Lord Denning's theories provided the necessary stimulus for other courts to develop a more focused, rational and coherent doctrine of economic duress. These cases refined the use that could be made of bargaining inequality and placed it in its proper perspective as a useful contextual factor rather than as a *sine qua non* for judicial intervention.

Further Reading

Case-notes

Atlas Express Ltd v Kafco (Importers & Distributors) Ltd [1989] QB 833 AND *Vantage Navigation Corporation v Suhail & Saud Bahwan Building Materials, The Alev* [1989] 1 Lloyd's Rep 138

Chandler, 'Economic Duress: Confusion or Clarity' [1989] LMCLQ 270

Phang, 'Whither Duress' (1990) 53 MLR 107

Credit Lyonnais Bank Nederland NV v Burch [1997] 1 All ER 144

Chen-Wishart, 'The O'Brien Principle and Substantive Unfairness' (1997) 56 CLJ 60

Hooley & O'Sullivan, 'Undue Influence and Unconscionable Bargains' [1997] LMCLQ 17

Royal Bank of Scotland v Etridge (No. 2) [2001] UKHL 44, [2001] 4 All ER 449

Bigwood, 'Undue Influence in the House of Lords: Principles and Proof' (2002) 65 MLR 435

O'Sullivan, 'Developing *O'Brien*' (2002) 118 LQR 337

Articles

Atiyah, 'Economic Duress and the Overborne Will' (1982) 98 LQR 197

Beatson, 'Duress as a Vitiating Factor in Contract' (1974) 33 CLJ 97

Capper, 'Undue Influence and Unconscionability: A Rationalisation' (1998) 114 LQR 479

Devenney & Chandler, 'Unconscionability and the Taxonomy of Undue Influence' [2007] JBL 541

Reiter, 'The Control of Contract Power' (1981) 1 OJLS 347

Thompson, 'Wives, Sureties and Banks' [2002] Conv 174

Tiplady, 'The Judicial Control of Contractual Unfairness' (1983) 46 MLR 601

8

Mistake

Introduction

The notion of mistake has a severely restricted ambit in the law of contract for several reasons. First, the parties commonly provide expressly for their rights and duties in the contract leading to a clear allocation of risks. Secondly, the notion of *caveat emptor* may apply, placing the risk emphatically on one party. A buyer of goods may thus have made a bad bargain but, in the absence of contract terms describing the goods or some vitiating factor such as misrepresentation, the contract will be binding. Thirdly, the effect of an operative mistake at common law is to render the contract void *ab initio*; thus the contract is a nullity and, for example, no title in goods can be transferred and none acquired by an innocent third party. Consequently, in the interests of commercial certainty, the law has been reluctant to widen the range of operative mistakes that might invalidate a contract. In particular, the modern view is that if the parties have ostensibly agreed in the same terms on the same subject matter the contract should be binding, even if *both* parties are mistaken. Equitable remedies might nevertheless be available to relieve one of the parties from the effects of mistake in three ways: (a) refusal of an order for specific performance, (b) rectification of a written agreement or, until recently (c) rescission of the contract (see later).

Three broad classifications of mistake are widely recognized, viz. common, mutual and unilateral. In common mistake (sometimes confusingly referred to as mutual mistake) both parties share the same mistake about a fundamental fact of the contract, e.g. A and B agree to buy and sell a painting by Picasso which, unknown to both, does not exist. With mutual mistake the parties are at cross-purposes but neither realizes it, e.g. A and B agree to buy and sell a painting, A intending to sell a Picasso and B intending to buy a Constable. In unilateral mistake only one of the parties is mistaken and the other party either knows of the mistake or is deemed to know, e.g. B thinks he is buying a Picasso and thinks that A intends to sell one but A knows that it is a fake and that B is labouring under a misconception. If A does not know of B's mistake, the case would be one of mutual mistake for then A intends to sell a fake whilst B intends to buy a Picasso.

Common Mistake

The instances of *res extincta* (e.g. the sale of goods that neither party realize had already perished) and those of *res sua* (the purchase of goods already owned by the buyer) are regarded as paradigmatic of common mistake in that the shared mistake could not be more fundamental and so the contract should be void *ab initio*. However, as these cases often involve a total failure of consideration (rather than common mistake), whether the contract is valid or void is immaterial as a purchaser cannot be made to pay for that which he has not received (see *Couturier v Hastie* (1856) 5 HL Cas 673) or may, alternatively, recover money so paid (see *Strickland v Turner* (1852) 7 Exch 208).

The leading case is the House of Lords' decision in *Bell v Lever Brothers Ltd* (1932) AC 161 which provides authority for two, separate propositions. First, that the contract must be examined in order to determine whether it allocated the risk of the 'mistake' to one or other parties, or in some other way set out the consequences of the 'mistake' coming to light. This might lead to the following possibilities: the contract remains in force and both parties must perform their obligations (with any failure to do so resulting in a breach of contract), or the contract never came into existence owing to the failure of an implied condition precedent (e.g. *Couturier v Hastie* (1856) 5 HL Cas 673), or the contract stipulates, expressly or impliedly, some other consequence(s) that will flow from the mistake having occurred. Secondly, that an independent doctrine of common mistake exists (that is, independent of the express/implied intentions of the parties), with the contract being declared void if the 'the state of the new facts destroys the identity of the subject matter as it was in the original state of facts?'

The propositions put forward in *Bell v Lever Brothers* raise two important questions: (i) do they represent alternative tests, or should they be applied consecutively? For example, will any independent test of common mistake *only* be applied where the contract has failed to address the possible legal consequences of a mistake (e.g. in terms of risk allocation)? and (ii) can Lord Atkin's test be interpreted as potentially including a fundamental mistake of quality? With regard to point (i), subsequent case law indeed suggests that a court should first employ a construction test in order to discover whether the contract (and surrounding circumstances) can be interpreted as dealing with the consequences of the said mistake. *Only* if the contract is silent on this matter will any independent doctrine of mistake be considered (e.g. *Associated Japanese Bank (International) Ltd v Credit du Nord SA* [1989] 1 WLR 255 and *William Sindall plc v Cambridgeshire County Council* [1994] 1 WLR 1016). For example, there may be an implied condition precedent that if the goods do not exist the contract was never formed (e.g. *Couturier v Hastie* (1856) 5 HL Cas 673), or, alternatively, that the seller is liable in damages for breach of an implied promise that the goods existed at the time of contract formation (see *McRae v Commonwealth Disposals Commission* (1951) 84 CLR 377). Equally, if the parties agree to buy and sell a painting which they both mistakenly believe to be painted by Picasso, one must first consider whether there has been a breach of contract by the seller (owing to the seller guaranteeing the authenticity of the painting), or an assumption of risk by the buyer (i.e. *caveat emptor*), before countenancing the possibility that the contract is void for common mistake.

Regarding point (ii), Lord Atkin seemingly recognized the possibility of a fundamental mistake of quality rendering a contract void when stating that: 'Mistake as to quality . . . will not affect assent unless . . . it is as to the existence of some quality which makes the thing without the quality essentially different from the thing as it was believed to be.' However, in all the hypothetical examples proffered by Lord Atkin the mistake was not found to be sufficiently fundamental, suggesting that any quality test is extraordinarily limited, as borne out by subsequent case law (see *Solle v Butcher* [1950] 1 KB 671, *Leaf v International Galleries* [1950] 2 KB 86, and *Frederick E Rose (London) Ltd v William H Pim Junior & Co. Ltd* [1953] 2 QB 450). Perhaps this explains why Lord Atkin's alternative test ('does the state of the new facts destroy the identity of the subject matter as it was in the original state of facts') is cited more frequently by modern courts (although see *Graves v Graves* [2007] EWCA 660, [2007] 3 FCR 26). Consequently, in our Picasso example, the contract will almost certainly be binding as the state of the new facts do not destroy the identity of the subject matter as it was in the original state of facts (the parties have agreed to buy and sell a painting and both have got what they bargained for), nor do the goods lack the existence of some quality which would make it essentially different (the painting retains all of its physical and aesthetic characteristics). To reach a different conclusion would require the contract to have stipulated expressly, or impliedly, that the seller was guaranteeing the authenticity of the painting, in which case the seller would be liable for breach of contract.

The more recent decision of the Court of Appeal in *Great Peace Shipping Ltd v Tsavliris Salvage (International) Ltd* [2002] EWCA Civ 1407, [2002] 3 WLR 1617, has endorsed the comments made in the above paragraphs, particularly as regards the restrictive view of common mistake emanating from *Bell v Lever Brothers Ltd*. However, as a result of the rather confusing and contradictory *dicta* in Bell, the court took the opportunity to clarify the prevailing mistake test. Instead of asking whether the mistake destroyed the identity of the subject matter, the court's preferred approach was to ask whether the mistake was of sufficient magnitude to render performance of the contract 'impossible'. There was little guidance on the meaning of 'impossible' but the links made with the current test for frustration suggests that the word must refer to something more than physical impossibility. Arguably, impossibility comes in different forms, ranging from physical impossibility (e.g. *Sheikh Bros Ltd v Ochsner* [1957] AC 136—the monthly purchase of 50 tons of sisal fibre grown on a particular field that was incapable of producing that amount), through legal impossibility (see *Cooper v Phibbs* (1867) LR 2 HL 149—the purchase of property already belonging to the buyer), to commercial impossibility (see *Griffith v Brymer* (1903) 19 TLR 434—hire of a balcony to overlook the coronation procession that had already been cancelled). At present, it remains to be seen whether future courts will treat the *Great Peace* test as an alternative way of expressing Lord Atkin's test in *Bell*. For example, in *Brennan v Bolt Burdon* [2004] EWCA Civ 1017, [2005] QB 303, involving the effect of a mistake of law upon a compromise settlement, Sedley LJ questioned whether an 'impossibility' test was appropriate in all factual situations, preferring to ask whether the mistake had rendered the 'service . . . performed something different from the performance that the parties contemplated'. Such sentiments are strongly resonant of Lord Atkin's original test in *Bell* and demonstrate that this area of law continues to undergo an important transformation. Consequently, when answering an examination question in this area it is best to assume that a court may apply either the 'impossibility' test (see *Great Peace*, *supra*) or the 'essentially different' test (see *Bell v Lever Brothers*, *supra*) interchangeably, with the emphasis of the applicable test being dependent upon the nature of the contract and the mistake made (see *Kyle Bay Ltd (Trading as Astons Nightclub) v Underwriters Subscribing Under Policy Number 019057/08/01* [2007] EWCA Civ 57, [2007] 1 CLC 164, esp at [24]–[25]).

Finally, the role performed by equity has, until now, remained suitably ambiguous (compare *Solle v Butcher* [1950] 1 KB 671 and *Bell v Lever Bros Ltd* [1932] AC 161). In *Great Peace Shipping Ltd v Tsavliris Salvage (International) Ltd* [2002] EWCA Civ 1407, [2003] QB 679, the Court of Appeal appeared to resolve this ongoing conflict by stating that where a contract is valid and enforceable on ordinary principles of contract law, there is no equitable jurisdiction to grant rescission of that contract (i.e. declare voidable) on grounds of common mistake. After this decision, the line of cases apparently starting with *Solle v Butcher* must be regarded as of dubious authority.

Mutual and Unilateral Mistake

In common mistake, offer and acceptance coincide and the mistake relates to some underlying fact but in mutual and unilateral mistake there may be no *genuine* agreement. In the latter situations, the general rule is that intention must be construed objectively and if the parties have reached an ostensible agreement the contract may be valid despite the parties' subjective, contrary intentions (see *Smith v Hughes* (1871) LR 6 QB 597; *Wood v Scarth* (1858) 1 F & F 293; *OT Africa Line Ltd v Vickers plc* [1996] 1 Lloyd's Rep 700). Underlying many of these decisions is an assessment of fault: if one party is at fault in making a mistake, yet the negotiations between the parties demonstrate a clear offer and acceptance, the court will ignore the mistake and enforce the apparent contract (see *Tamplin v James* (1880) 15 Ch Dh 215 where the purchaser failed to read the printed 'sale particulars' of the property on offer). Conversely, if the parties are so fundamentally at cross-purposes that offer and acceptance do not correspond the contract will be declared void for mutual mistake (see *Raffles v Wichelhaus* (1864) 2 H & C 906; *Falck v Williams* (1900) AC 176; *Scriven Bros & Co. v Hindley & Co.* (1913) 3 KB 564).

In unilateral mistake, the dominant principle remains *caveat emptor*, supported by the general rule that a party is not under a duty to disclose information to the other or correct obvious errors of judgement. It is therefore very rare for a contract to be declared void on grounds that one party knew the mistake of the other and should not be allowed to take advantage of it. Again it must be a fundamental mistake and it is sometimes said that here it must be a *mistake as to the terms of the contract* or the promise itself, but this is singularly unhelpful in practice (e.g. *Smith v Hughes* (1871) LR 6 QB 597 where the confusion over whether the purchased oats were 'new' or 'old' was not treated as a term of the contract). It is unclear whether the mistake must be known to the other party or whether it is sufficient that it *ought* to be known using an objective test (compare *Centrovincial Estates plc v Merchant Investors Assurance Co. Ltd*

[1983] Com LR 158, where the former view was apparently taken, and *Hartog v Colin and Shields* [1939] 3 All ER 566 where the latter approach was followed).

For cases where there has been equitable relief in mutual mistake, compare *Malins v Freeman* (1837) 2 Keen 25 with *Tamplin v James* (1880) 15 Ch D 215. For unilateral mistake see *Webster v Cecil* (1861) 30 Beav 62; *Garrard v Frankel* (1862) 30 Beav 445; *Torrance v Bolton* (1872) LR 8 Ch App 118.

Unilateral Mistake of Identity

Consider the following possibility: A accepts an offer from B thinking that B is C, intending therefore to contract with C. Until *recently* A was expected to meet four conditions in order to have the contract declared void for mistake: (i) A intended to deal with some person other than B, (ii) B knew of A's mistake, (iii) B's identity was crucial to the contract and, (iv) A took reasonable steps to verify B's identity. A's mistake needed to relate to B's identity, rather than to any attributes that A thought B possessed such as honesty, social status or solvency (see *King's Norton Metal Co. v Edridge, Merrett & Co. Ltd* (1897) 14 TLR 98). The inherent difficulty of this approach lay in drawing the line between a person's attributes and identity, a task of considerable intellectual entertainment for academics but one that offered practitioners little certainty in the application of the law. The House of Lords' decision in *Shogun Finance Ltd v Hudson* [2003] UKHL 62; [2004] 1 All ER 215 sought to resolve these difficulties, although a considerable degree of uncertainty still remains in the aftermath of the decision.

In *Shogun*, all of the Law Lords emphasized the need for an objective appraisal of the facts, adopting the terminology of offer and acceptance in order to resolve the vexed issue of whether A had contracted with B or C. Moreover, all the speeches demonstrated a clear conviction that where A and B contracted with each other face-to-face there was a presumption, bordering on the irrebuttable, that A intended to deal with B whatever the circumstances. Thus the correctness of the decisions in *Phillips v Brooks* [1919] 2 KB 243 and *Lewis v Averay* [1972] 1 QB 198 is confirmed, whilst the Court of Appeal's decision in *Ingram v Little* [1961] 1 QB 31 can now be disregarded.

In relation to written contracts, and those concluded by written correspondence, it becomes much harder to discern any meaningful *ratio* from *Shogun*. A fuller analysis of the Law Lords' various approaches will be considered in the answer to **Question 2** of this chapter. Suffice to say that three different tests emerged: Lord Hobhouse emphasized the parol evidence rule, with its implicit assumption that the names used in a written contract correctly identify the parties; Lords Millett and Nicholls advocated a 'dealing test' which seemed to set up an irrebutable presumption that A intended to deal with the person with whom he physically corresponded, or who physically signed the contract (i.e. B); finally, Lords Phillips and Walker employed an 'intent' test that presumed A intended to direct his offer (or acceptance) to the named individual as stated in the contract or as stated in the written correspondence (i.e. C). Interestingly, it would be wrong to assume that the primary 'dealing' and 'intent' tests lead to different results. For example, in *King's Norton Metal Co. v Edridge Merrett & Co. Ltd* (1897) 14 TLR 98, as C did not exist, both tests would have reached the same conclusion: A *intended* to contract only with B, and *dealt* only with B.

What of the other conditions that A was required to meet in the pre-*Shogun* era? First, it now seems clear that there is no longer any need to ask whether A took reasonable steps to verify the identity of the buyer (previously considered important, e.g. *Phillips v Brooks* [1919] 2 KB 243). Secondly, it is almost inconceivable that any court would depart from the decision in *King's Norton Metal Co. v Edridge, Merrett & Co. Ltd* (1897) 14 TLR 98 which required 'two distinct entities' to exist (i.e. B and C). How can A argue that he made an offer to, or accepted an offer from C, if no such person existed? Thirdly, one point which remains undecided is whether B's knowledge of A's mistake remains important (*The Unique Mariner* [1978] 1 Lloyd's Rep 451). Assuming that *Shogun* has now reclassified such matters as falling exclusively within the domain of offer and acceptance, it is arguable that B's knowledge is of much less significance.

Rectification and *Non Est Factum*

The treatment of mistake would not be complete without at least mentioning two additional points. First, where a mistake has been made by A and B in recording their oral agreement in writing, the relevant document can be rectified if does not accurately represent the *common intentions* of the parties, those intentions *continuing* up to the time of writing (see *Joscelyne v Nissen* [1970] 2 QB 86, *Chartbrook Ltd v Persimmon Homes Ltd* [2009] UKHL 38, [2009] 3 WLR 267). Separately, where the document only fails to reflect accurately the intentions of A, rectification remains possible provided B knew of A's mistake and had acted unconscionably in not drawing A's attention to that matter (see *Commission for the New Towns v Cooper (Great Britain) Ltd* [1995] Ch 259).

Secondly, where a party is able to show they were unaware of the meaning of a written agreement they had signed, that agreement is rendered void (*non est factum* = this is not my deed). However, the mistaken party must prove that the signed agreement was 'essentially different' from the agreement intended to be signed and had not acted carelessly in signing (see *Saunders v Anglia Building Society (formerly Gallie v Lee)* [1971] AC 104).

Question 1

S, an antiques dealer, is negotiating with B the possible sale of a 'nursing chair and an armchair', from the 'mid-Victorian era'. B offers to buy the nursing chair for £3,000, provided it is fully re-upholstered. Moreover, secretly believing the armchair to be a valuable antique from the Jacobean era, he offers S the sum of £25,000 for it. S accepts both offers gladly, particularly as he has been trying, unsuccessfully, to sell the armchair for months at the much lower price of £1,000.

During the re-upholstering of the nursing chair one of S's employees discovers that it is an extremely rare Sheraton chair worth at least £100,000. S decides not to sell the nursing chair to B. A week later B is informed that the armchair is a very good twentieth-century copy worth only £2,500. He decides to return the armchair to S and demand a full refund but S refuses.

Discuss the legal position of S and B in each of the two transactions.

Commentary

In our facts two types of mistakes have potentially occurred. Regarding the nursing chair, both parties appear to have made the same mistake, viz. that it was manufactured in Victorian times, but is this 'common mistake' sufficient to render the contract void? Separately, the sale of the armchair raises issues of mutual and unilateral mistake.

In both parts it is certainly arguable that as the parties were clear about the subject matter of their agreements (and the price to be paid), any potential gains/losses resulting from their deals simply represent the normal risks associated with any commercial transaction. If correct, does the law afford relief in such circumstances?

Answer plan

- How does the law of contract define a 'common mistake'? Does this definition apply to the sale of the nursing chair?
- Outline the two-stage approach courts adopt when dealing with a possible common mistake: (i) identify any term within the contract, express or implied, that sets out who bears the risk of the mistake; and, in the absence of any such term, (ii) distinguish between mistakes of substance and quality as a means of determining whether the contract should be declared void for common mistake.
- On the above basis, as both parties agreed to the sale/purchase of the nursing chair (same terms and subject matter), will the court decide that a binding contract exists or will it be declared void?
- As regards the armchair, only B seems to have made a mistake? Does this mean that we are dealing with a unilateral mistake, or might it be a mutual mistake? Define both types of mistake and apply the definitions to the facts of the problem in order to establish whether there is an operative mistake of either type.

Suggested answer

S and B have clearly entered into a contract for the sale of the two chairs, but one or both of the parties have made certain mistakes regarding the subject matter. Dealing with the nursing chair first, both parties mistakenly believe that it was manufactured in Victorian times, and therefore worth £3,000, whereas it is a rare Sheraton chair worth £100,000. Modern case law (in the shape of *Associated Japanese Bank (International) Ltd v Credit du Nord SA* [1989] 1 WLR 255 and *Great Peace Shipping Ltd v Tsavliris Salvage (International) Ltd* [2002] EWCA Civ 1407, [2003] QB 679) clearly emphasizes that, before any independent notion of mistake can be considered, the court should first seek to identify any existing express or implied terms that might allocate the risk of such a mistake to one or other party. In our facts, the express terms of the contract solely identify the subject matter ('nursing chair'), the period of manufacture ('mid-Victorian period'), and the price ('£3,000'), but do not address the tricky issue of risk allocation. However, perhaps there is an implied term that the contract would be void if the nursing chair was found to be significantly more valuable?

In considering the above issue it is unlikely that cases involving *res extincta* (i.e. where goods have perished at the date of contract or never existed) would prove helpful. Such cases generally involve a total failure of consideration (see *Couturier v Hastie* (1856) 5 HL Cas 673—the buyer did not have to pay for the goods as the seller could not deliver them), but in our facts the nursing chair does exist and does have value. Instead, we must consider whether, in light of the 'business efficacy' and 'officious bystander' tests, the unexpected increase in the value of the chair would put an end to the contract on grounds that this was both *necessary* to the contract and a manifestation of the *common* intention of the parties (see *McRae v Commonwealth Disposals Commission* (1951) 84 CLR 377 and the *Associated Japanese Bank* case). This seems inconceivable as such a term is not *necessary* for the contract's performance (the chair can be physically transferred whatever its value), nor can it represent the parties' *common* intention (all buyers of antiques secretly hope to acquire a 'hidden gem'). In short, any implied term that favoured the seller would undermine the entire notion of a bargain and its attendant risks—the law should not provide a safety net for the consequences of one party's folly. Thus, in line with the principle of *caveat venditor*, it is probable that S will bear the risk of this mistake.

However, if the court remains uncertain as to who *took the risk* of this change in circumstances (i.e. the chair's real value) it might consider the doctrine of common mistake. In *Bell v Lever Brothers Ltd* [1932] AC 161, the House of Lords seemingly admitted the existence of an independent doctrine of mistake, with Lord Atkin proposing at least two tests, predicated on the notion that only a fundamental mistake can invalidate a contract. The first was whether 'the state of the new facts destroy[s] the identity of the subject matter as it was in the original state of facts'. The second test focused on 'the existence of some quality which makes the thing without the quality essentially different from the thing as it was believed to be'. Neither test was applied successfully in *Bell* for whereas both parties considered that Bell deserved £30,000 for loss of office (when in fact previous breaches of duty meant he was entitled to nothing), the resulting mistake of *quality* was insufficient to render the contract void. Indeed, in *Bell*, Lord Atkin suggested, *obiter*, that if A bought a picture from B which was believed by both to be the work of an old master, with a commensurately high purchase price (whereas it was a worthless modern copy), A would have no remedy 'in the absence of representation or warranty'.

In *Great Peace Shipping Ltd v Tsavliris Salvage (International) Ltd* [2002] EWCA Civ 1407, [2003] QB 679, the Court of Appeal acknowledged that, whilst an independent doctrine of common mistake does exist, it has an extremely narrow ambit and the court must ask whether the fundamental, mistaken assumption renders performance of the contract 'impossible'.

If the tests in *Bell* and *Great Peace* are applied to our facts, it is highly unlikely that the contract would be declared void for common mistake. The first test (destruction of the identity of the subject matter), is of little help: the subject matter of the contract is a chair and remains so in light of the new facts. The second test, which relates to the subject matter being essentially different from what it was believed to be, (represented in Lord Atkin's example of the purchase of a valuable painting), is equally fruitless. A chair that is less or more valuable than its contract price does not render that article *essentially* different from what it was believed to be. Finally, the *Great Peace* requirement of 'impossibility' is arguably stricter than either of Lord Atkin's tests. The sale of the nursing chair is obviously capable of literal performance and, even if a wider interpretation of 'impossibility' was adopted and it was asked whether the commercial purpose of the contract had ceased to exist, the answer would remain in the negative. The possibility of immense gain (or loss) *is* the accepted, commercial purpose of this contract and so, rather than ceasing to exist, that purpose has been realized. Almost certainly, the contract in our facts is valid and binding at common law, so S would be in breach of contract if he withdrew from the sale.

Finally, where a contract is declared valid and enforceable under the ordinary principles of common law contract law, it is now clear that rescission cannot be granted in equity on the ground of common mistake (see *Great Peace, supra*).

As regards the sale of the armchair, it must first be decided what category of mistake is applicable to this problem and thereupon ascertain whether it is an operative mistake rendering the contract void. This could be classified as a mutual mistake in that B thinks the armchair heralds from a much earlier era (and therefore commands a higher value) whereas S clearly believes that even the contract price over-values it. Neither realizes the other's error as nothing is said. The facts of the problem resemble those in *Wood v Scarth* (1858) 1 F & F 293 and *Scott v Littledale* (1858) 8 E & B 815. In the latter case, the defendants sold by sample 100 chests of tea but later discovered they had submitted a sample of poorer quality than the bulk. The contract was not declared void, thus allowing the buyer to profit from the transaction. This clearly shows that that if the subject matter of a sale is ascertained precisely, a mistake as to quality is immaterial, otherwise a buyer of goods who has made a bad bargain (as B has done), would be able to re-open contracts at will. In short, this mistake should not render the contract void as objectively there is an agreement in the same terms on the same subject matter: the parties are *ad idem*.

Alternatively, might it be argued that a unilateral mistake has occurred? This would assume that only B made a mistake, with S knowingly taking advantage of the situation. Here, again, objective appearances count and if S has done nothing to mislead B, the dominant principle is *caveat emptor*. Lord Atkin emphasiszed in *Bell* that this was still the position if S *knew* that B was labouring under a mistake. In these situations, B's mistake is one of quality and judgement which is not induced by S: if B has poor judgement he should make provision for it in the terms of the contract. However, this dominant principle does occasionally give way to evidence of subjective mistake. It is usually said that the contract will be void if one party is mistaken as to the *promise itself* and this is known to the other party. In our facts S accepted B's offer but there is no suggestion that he knew of B's mistaken assumption that the chair was worth much more (contrast this with *Hartog v Colin and Shields* [1939] 3 All ER 566, where the contract was declared void as the buyer was assumed to have taken advantage of the seller's confusion as regards whether the contract price referred to 'per piece' or 'per pound'). Moreover, although it appears sufficient that an operative mistake is one that a reasonable man *ought* to have been aware of (see *Centrovincial Estates plc v Merchant Investors Assurance Co. Ltd* [1983] Com LR 158), the decision in *Bank of Credit and Commerce International v Ali* [1999] 4 All ER 83 reminds us that the doctrine of mistake should not be used to extricate parties from 'bad bargains'. Does B's offer of £25,000 for the armchair indicate that he is labouring under some sort of mistake that S ought to have realized? Given that the value of antiques is inherently subjective (it all depends on what the buyer is prepared to pay) and that no two experts would agree on fair value for an item, it is extremely doubtful that a court would depart from the standard principle of *caveat emptor* unless there was clear evidence that S had led B to believe that the armchair was worth a lot more than its true value.

Finally, it is doubtful whether any equitable relief would be forthcoming on the facts. B does acquire the armchair that he bargained for rather than a different one and so there is no material hardship (compare this to *Tamplin v James* (1880) 15 Ch D 215 where, on the facts, specific performance was ordered). Moreover, if B had intended to make a substantial profit on a re-sale, he could scarcely be heard to complain of hardship if the anticipated profits did not materialize. It is often said that 'he who comes to equity must come with clean hands' so the fact that B did not disclose to S the real reason for offering £25,000 (i.e. his anticipated profit on re-sale) would probably persuade a court to refuse equitable relief anyway. Thus, B will be in breach of contract if he seeks to return the chair and demand a full refund.

Question 2

Albert owns three Rolls Royce cars manufactured in 1950, 1960, and 1970 respectively. He wants to sell the 1970 model but ensure that the buyer should be a private car collector. Accordingly, he advertised it for sale in the local newspaper as 'For sale only to a private car collector.' Unfortunately, due to a printing error, the car advertised for sale was the 1960 model. Byron, a car dealer, wished to acquire the 1950 model and was informed incorrectly by a friend that Albert had the 1950 model advertised for sale in the newspaper.

Byron knew that, because he was a car dealer, Albert would not sell the car to him. He therefore telephoned Albert and said 'Hello, I am Mr Jones. I should like to buy the car that you have advertised in the newspaper and will give the full asking price of £80,000 for it.' Albert replied 'I am pleased to sell the car to you Mr Jones and I am glad it will have a good home.' When Albert delivered the 1970 model, he discovered the buyer's identity and refused to complete the sale but Byron wished to enforce the contract even though the car was not the 1950 model.

Discuss the legal position.

Commentary

This is a testing problem which, like the subject of mistake itself, appears easier than it is in reality. The problem involves mutual mistake and unilateral mistake which must be considered separately in the answer. As regards mutual mistake, it must be decided whether the parties are in agreement or sufficiently at cross-purposes to nullify any notion of contract. Does the fact that third parties (the newspaper and B's friend) induce the contracting parties' mistake make any difference? Is there a possibility that the contract is void for unilateral mistake of identity? How has the House of Lords' decision in *Shogun Finance Ltd v Hudson* [2003] UKHL 62; [2004] 1 All ER 215 affected this area? Will the manner in which the pre-contractual negotiations took place (i.e. face-to-face or *inter absentes*) affect this issue? Finally, is B guilty of a misrepresentation and what effect might this have on the contract?

Answer plan

- What is the overall approach of the law when a mistake is made, on entering into a contract, by one or both of the parties? If a mistake is found to be an operative one, what effect does it have on the contract?

- In relation to the first part of the problem, there is a mutual mistake. How does the law evaluate this situation where the parties are at cross-purposes?

- In the second part of the problem, there is a unilateral mistake of identity. How does the law evaluate this situation where only one party is mistaken regarding the identity of the other party?

- If there is no operative mistake of identity in the second part of the problem, might there be an operative unilateral mistake as to the *terms* of the contract, in that A's offer excludes B and B knows that A would not contract with him?

Suggested answer

There are two different types of mistake to consider in this problem. First, the mistake between the parties regarding the year of manufacture of the car and, secondly, Albert's (A) mistake as to the identity of the other contracting party, Byron (B). It should be emphasized at the outset that although mistake permeates this transaction, it does not necessarily follow that the contract will be affected. The law adopts a particularly restricted view of mistake where only the most fundamental errors of substance will render a contract void *ab initio*. In the interests of commercial certainty the courts are thus loath to invalidate contracts without good reason. As a general rule, if the parties agree in the same terms on the same subject matter the contract will be binding even if both parties are mistaken. It remains to be seen which mistakes the law regards as sufficiently fundamental to render a contract void.

There is a mutual mistake in relation to which car is being sold, the parties therefore making different mistakes and being at cross-purposes but neither realizing the other's mistake at the date of contract. Because of confusion caused by third parties, A intends to sell the 1970 model whereas B intends to buy the 1950 model. In order to be operative, a mutual mistake must entail an absence of genuine agreement, offer and acceptance thus failing to coincide. It is tempting to conclude that if the parties are at cross-purposes there can be no agreement but the test is an objective one and so real, subjective intentions may be dominated by ostensible objectivity, meaning that the contract is valid and binding. In *Wood v Scarth* (1858) 1 F & F 293, the defendant offered in writing to let a public house to the plaintiff for £63 per annum. The plaintiff had negotiations with the defendant's clerk and then accepted the offer by letter. The defendant intended that a premium of £500 be payable as well as the rent and assumed that his clerk had made that clear but the plaintiff thought that the only liability was the £63 rent. It was held that the contract was binding. Similarly, in *Scott v Littledale* (1858) 8 E & B 815 the defendants sold by sample to the plaintiff 100 chests of tea then lying in bond but later discovered that the sample was poorer in quality than the bulk. The defendants had made a bad bargain but the contract was held to be valid and the plaintiff's claim for non-delivery upheld. In both these cases the reasonable man would see a coincidence between offer and acceptance but it is equally possible to reach the opposite conclusion where the evidence is ambiguous and conflicting as in *Raffles v Wichelhaus* (1864) 2 H & C 906. There the defendant agreed to buy from the plaintiff a cargo of cotton to arrive 'ex *Peerless* from Bombay'. There were two ships called *Peerless* both sailing from Bombay but the defendant meant a *Peerless* which sailed in October and the plaintiff a *Peerless* which sailed in December. The description of the goods pointed equally to either of the ships' cargoes. The court did not in fact decide whether there was a contract or not but upheld the defendant's refusal to accept the goods from the

December shipment on the basis that he could show that the contract was ambiguous and that he intended the October ship. The buyer and seller were similarly at cross-purposes in *Scriven Bros & Co. v Hindley & Co.* (1913) 3 KB 564 where the plaintiff intended to sell a quantity of tow and the defendant to buy hemp, the court holding that there was such ambiguity that the subject matter of the contract could not be established with certainty. The same result was reached in *Falck v Williams* (1900) AC 176, and *Henkel v Pape* (1870) LR 6 Ex 7 illustrates that no contract will exist if the parties arrive at fundamental cross-purposes because of the act of a third party—there a telegram clerk who transmitted the wrong message.

It is arguable that these cases are not based upon an independent concept of mistake but, instead, are illustrations of lack of concurrence between offer and acceptance. In the problem, the parties are not *ad idem* and, moreover, there is nothing in the contract which could clarify the ambiguity. Indeed, the advertisement to which the parties refer advertises the 1960 model for sale and *neither* party wants to make that car the subject of a contract. That there is no contract on the facts of the problem may be tested by postulating facts which would point to an objective agreement. This would occur if A wished to sell the 1970 model but B wished to buy the 1950 model and the 1950 model was advertised for sale, the parties then referring to 'the car advertised in the paper'. It is suggested that the contract would be binding on those facts as A's mistake would not be apparent as in *Wood v Scarth*.

There are further difficulties if A attempts to prove that he did not intend to contract with B. Until recently, if A appeared to contract with B yet alleged mistaken identity, he needed to meet four requirements, viz. A intended to contract with some person other than B, identity was fundamental and material, B knew of A's mistake and A took reasonable steps to verify B's identity. The heart of these requirements was that the mistake needed to be a fundamental mistake of substance, meaning in this context a mistake of identity rather than one relating to the attributes or qualities of a person; see, for example, the different outcomes reached in *Cundy v Lindsay* (1878) 3 App Cas 459 and *King's Norton Metal Co. Ltd v Edridge, Merrett & Co. Ltd* (1897) 14 TLR 98. However, the House of Lords' decision in *Shogun Finance Ltd v Hudson* [2003] UKHL 62, [2004] 1 All ER 215 has fundamentally altered the existing common law. The facts involved a rogue who sought to purchase a car on hire-purchase terms, pretending to be a Mr Durlabh Patel. The rogue had stolen Mr Patel's driving licence and other personal documents. The car dealer faxed the information to the claimant, Shogun Finance, who carried out a full credit check on Mr Patel. Satisfied with the result, the claimant agreed to finance the purchase of the car by the rogue on standard hire-purchase terms, signed by both parties. The rogue took possession of the car and wrongfully sold it to the defendant. The House of Lords, by a simple majority, concluded that the parties to the hire-purchase contract could only be

Mr Patel, as named in the contract, and the claimant finance company. The contract stated the name and address of Mr Patel and made no reference whatsoever to the rogue. Thus, as no offer and acceptance had taken place between the two parties, no contract could come into existence and no title to the car could be transferred to the defendant. It remains unclear whether this was an alternative way of saying that the contract had become 'void for mistake of identity'.

The facts in our problem are slightly different as they involve an apparent exchange of offer and acceptance by telephone rather than in writing. How do the speeches in *Shogun* help us resolve this difficulty? Does the instant problem involve face-to-face dealings, or those conducted *inter absentes*? Assuming the former, and in line with *Shogun*, there is an almost irrebuttable presumption that Albert intended to reach an agreement with Byron. In *Shogun* the Law Lords considered the extent and meaning of 'face-to-face'. Lords Millett and Nicholls thought there was no logic in excluding televisual links and telephone conversations from any definition of the term. Lord Walker accepted that the face-to-face presumption might be extended to cover telephone conversations, although any presumption might be more easily rebutted. Finally, Lord Phillips saw no reason to depart from the standard meaning of face-to-face. On our facts these arguments are finely balanced as Lord Hobhouse, the fifth Law Lord in *Shogun*, offered no view on the matter. Clearly it is open to a future court to view A and B's telephone call as falling within the definition of face-to-face, in which case it would presumably conclude that A intended to deal with B and that, as a consequence, the ensuing contract was enforceable.

Conversely, if a telephone conversation is not an example of face-to-face dealings (that is, the dealings are considered to be *inter absentes*) then it is difficult to find any clear test in *Shogun* that would resolve the matter. The intent test advocated by Lords Phillips and Walker suggests that A did not intend to contract with B or, put another way, he did not intend to accept the offer from B. Traditionally, this would not have supported a claim of mistake of identity unless A could also establish the existence of another, identifiable party, with whom he *did* intend to deal (see *King's Norton Metal Co. Ltd v Edridge, Merrett & Co. Ltd* (1897) 14 TLR 98). However, this requirement is less important after *Shogun* as the Law Lords moved away from comparing the differences between B and C (as proof of A's intentions) and, instead, emphasized the presence of offer and acceptance. Is there some scope for A to argue that his advertisement clearly evidenced a desire to receive offers only from private car collectors and therefore explicitly or implicitly excluded B? Perhaps this is one possible explanation of *Said v Butt* [1920] 3 KB 497 as B knew from A's previous refusals that A would not contract with him and so could not circumvent this by employing an agent to act on his behalf. If correct, A could successfully argue that he had not displayed any objectively verifiable intention of accepting an offer from B and, thus, no contract could arise. There is even the possibility of using *Hartog v Colin and*

Shields [1939] 3 All ER 566 on the basis that there has been a fundamental, unilateral mistake of the *terms* of the contract or the promise itself: B knows of his express exclusion from the relevant class of car collectors and his consequent inability to contract with A.

The alternative dealing test proposed by Lords Nicholls and Millett in *Shogun* would reach a more definite, albeit different, conclusion: A spoke to the physical person at the other end of the telephone line and therefore an exchange of offer and acceptance occurred between those persons. The known intention of A would have no bearing on this issue. Interestingly, in *Shogun*, Lord Millett had occasion to comment on *Said v Butt*, preferring to interpret the decision as one which recognized that an undisclosed principal (B) cannot intervene where the nature of the contract shows that it was intended to be concluded with the agent personally. Clearly the arguments as to whether we are dealing with a contract concluded face-to-face or *inter absentes*, and whether an 'intent' or 'dealing' test should be employed, are finely balanced. However, whatever the outcome, one should note that in the light of *Shogun* the failure of A to take reasonable steps to verify B's identity no longer appears fatal to his claim that the contract is void (a condition that was previously considered to be important, e.g. *Phillips v Brooks* [1919] 2 KB 243).

Finally, there is always the possibility that B is guilty of misrepresentation which would render his contract with A voidable at A's option. For example, B does specifically state that he is 'Mr Jones'. Assuming this to be false, it appears that he has made a false statement of fact capable of representing an actionable misrepresentation. A will also presumably argue that he was induced into the contract by the fraud-induced assumption that he was not dealing with a car dealer. Finally, none of the normal bars to rescission seem applicable on the facts (e.g. B has not sold the car to a third party) so A should be able to avoid the contract.

In conclusion, there is probably a sufficient mutual mistake regarding the age of the car to render the contract void. There also remains the possibility that A could successfully assert that he was mistaken as to B's true identity, rendering the contract void, or, alternatively, that B misrepresented his identity in pre-contractual negotiations, rendering the contract voidable.

Question 3

The single thread of principle running through all types of mistake is that, no matter how serious, the courts will not relieve mistakes of quality.
   Discuss.

Commentary

This essay title demands a critical analysis of common, mutual and unilateral mistakes and an investigation of whether operative mistakes relate to substance or quality. Moreover, it should be asked if a meaningful distinction can be made between substance and quality in reality. A close knowledge of the cases is required coupled with an ability to compare and contrast the decisions and evaluate the rationale of the mistake doctrine.

Answer plan

- Explain why the law considers that the notion of mistake must be confined narrowly.
- Outline the principal theories underlying the decisions concerning mistake: (i) an analysis of the formation and construction of the contract, and (ii) an independent doctrine of mistake based upon the distinction between a mistake of substance and a mistake of quality.
- How can the distinction be made between substance and quality in the three recognized categories of mistake?
- Should a mistake as to quality be sufficient to render a contract void?

Suggested answer

At common law, the notion of mistake is confined within narrow limits but if it is operative its effect is to render a contract void *ab initio*. By placing mistake in a strait-jacket, both freedom of contract and certainty of contract are preserved. A man may make a very bad bargain due to his own error and thereby receive something of inferior quality in comparison with his expectations but the courts are not prepared to grant relief on that ground alone, for, otherwise, the very essence of bargain and *caveat emptor* would disappear. Accordingly, if the parties agree in the same terms on the same subject matter, the general rule is that they are bound and should look to the stipulations of the contract for 'protection from the effects of facts unknown to them' (*Bell v Lever Brothers Ltd* [1932] AC 161, *per* Lord Atkin).

It is arguable that the so-called mistake cases really turn on questions of formation, contract interpretation, and risk allocation, rather than representing an independent theory of mistake. If so, cases of common mistake may be resolved by asking whether the contract terms put the risk on one or other of the parties or whether a term can be implied regarding the presence or absence of the fact at issue (see, for example, *McRae v Commonwealth Disposals Commission* (1951) 84 CLR 377). Similarly, the cases on mutual mistake where the parties are at cross-purposes and unilateral mistake where only one party is mistaken arguably involve nothing more than contract formation in terms of offer and acceptance. Nevertheless, in *Bell v Lever Brothers*, the House of Lords appeared to acknowledge an independent doctrine of mistake based upon the distinction between *substance* on the one hand and *quality/attributes* on the other. Subsequently, in *Associated Japanese Bank (International) Ltd v Credit du Nord SA* [1989] 1 WLR 255 and *Great Peace Shipping Ltd v Tsavliris Salvage (International) Ltd* [2002] EWCA Civ 1407, [2003] QB 679, it was held that the question of whether the contract allocated the risks to either party should be considered first and separately from mistake, thereby acknowledging the existence of independent rules of mistake.

In *Bell v Lever Brothers* the plaintiff had been compensated by the defendant company for the premature termination of his contract of service, both parties assuming the contract to be valid when, in fact, Bell could have been dismissed summarily without compensation because of previous breaches of duty. Lever Brothers sought recovery of the money. In terms of quality, both parties thought that Bell was 'worth' £30,000 whereas he was worth nothing. The House of Lords held the contract to be valid and binding as the substance of the contract was a compensation agreement which remained unchanged by the mistake. Peculiarly, Lord Atkin appeared to accept the possibility of a contract being declared void for mistake of quality if the contract was 'essentially different' from that which the parties agreed upon. However, as the mistake in *Bell* could surely not have been any worse (i.e. payment for no reason), this has led some commentators to argue that a contract will only be void for common mistake when the contract has no subject matter (i.e. cases of *res extincta* and *res sua*), thereby supporting the contention in the question that quality will never be a ground of relief. This may be an overly narrow interpretation of Lord Atkin's approach, but it raises the question of how one applies the test of 'essentially different' to mistakes of quality. Might a thing be so deficient in quality that it becomes a different thing? This seems difficult to prove.

In *Solle v Butcher* [1950] 1 KB 671, a mistake as to whether the lease agreement was subject to the Rent Restriction Acts was not considered sufficient to invalidate the contract at common law. The same result was reached in *Leaf v International Galleries* [1950] 2 KB 86 where the parties entered into a contract to sell a painting which both erroneously believed to be painted by Constable. It is arguable that, for an operative mistake on the facts of *Leaf*, a sculpture would have to be tendered instead of a painting. It follows that *defects* in the subject matter of the contract, no matter how serious, are not a ground of relief and that the threshold of operative common mistake for quality is reached only in the most extreme cases.

The decision in *Great Peace Shipping Ltd v Tsavliris Salvage (International) Ltd* [2002] EWCA Civ 1407, [2003] QB 679, also sanctions a very restricted view of common mistake. In that case, the *Great Peace* (GP) was chartered for five days to offer assistance to a stricken vessel, the *Cape Providence* (CP). The parties never discussed the exact location of GP, but cancellation of this contract required payment of the minimum hire charge. The defendant was then informed that GP would take 39 hours to reach CP. Accordingly, the defendants procured the services of another, more proximate vessel and cancelled the contract with the claimants, refusing to pay the cancellation charge. The defendant argued that the contract had been entered into on the basis of a common, fundamental, mistaken belief that GP was 'in close proximity' to CP and that, consequently, the contract was either void at common law or voidable in equity.

The Court of Appeal found for the claimant on the following grounds. First, GP was still able to perform its stand-by function for part of the five-day charter period (i.e. this was not a total failure of consideration). Secondly, no term could be implied that GP should be closer to CP as this would contradict the pre-contract negotiations where the precise location of GP had not been mentioned—the defendants must bear the risk of their own lack of prudence. Finally, the requirements of the common law doctrine of common mistake had not been met. In reaching this conclusion the Court of Appeal made several important observations, aimed at clarifying the law relating to common mistake. If no express or implied risk allocation can be discerned from an examination of the contract, it will be necessary to decide whether the mistake was of sufficient magnitude to render performance of the contract *impossible,* and therefore void. This is a particularly strict test which follows the confined view of mistake emanating from *Bell v Lever Brothers Ltd* and appears to rule out a mistake of quality. Nor could a court circumvent this conclusion by drawing on its equitable jurisdiction to declare the contract voidable (e.g. for a fundamental mistake of quality—see *Solle v Butcher*) as this would be inconsistent with *Bell v Lever Brothers Ltd.*

The restrictive approach to mistake is also present in mutual mistake where the definition of an operative mistake means that the parties must be at fundamental cross-purposes such that it is impossible to construe an agreement between them. If the parties are crossed on the question of quality alone this will not render the contract void, one party thus profiting at the expense of the other. In *Scott v Littledale* (1858) 8 E & B 815, the defendants sold by sample to the plaintiff 100 chests of tea then lying in bond but later discovered that the sample was poorer in quality than the bulk. The defendants had made a bad bargain but the contract was held to be valid and the plaintiff's claim for non-delivery upheld. Similarly, in unilateral mistake where only one party is mistaken as to quality and the other party knows it, the contract is still binding on the basis of *caveat emptor*. If S sells a painting to B knowing that it is not a Constable yet knowing that B thinks it is a Constable, the contract is valid provided that S has not misled B. Here B's mistake simply relates to quality or his motive for entering into the contract. It is only if B is mistaken as to the *promise itself* and S knows it, that S cannot take advantage of B, the contract then being void. Thus if S intends to sell a painting but B thinks S intends to sell a Constable and S knows of B's mistake, the contract is void for B is in error regarding the nature of S's promise. This is perhaps a fine distinction but it is supported by *Hartog v Colin and Shields* [1939] 3 All ER 566 and certainly points up the substance/quality divide.

In unilateral mistakes of identity, until the House of Lords' decision in *Shogun Finance Ltd v Hudson* [2003] UKHL 62; [2004] 1 All ER 215, we could see the concept of 'identity/substance' being replicated in the terminology of 'attributes/ quality'. For example, in *Boulton v Jones* (1857) 2 H & N 564, as the defendant had wanted to deal only with the former owner of a shop with whom he had an enforceable set-off, his apparent contract with the new owner of the shop, against whom the set-off was unenforceable, was declared void as the mistake destroyed the whole purpose of dealing with the seller (i.e. the contract had no substance). However, if A's mistake related simply to the other party's honesty and creditworthiness then, as these were mere qualities/attributes, it could not lead to the ensuing contract being declared void for mistake (*King's Norton Metal Co. Ltd v Edridge, Merrett & Co. Ltd* (1897) 14 TLR 98). In *Shogun*, the House of Lords ignored such fine distinctions, reinterpreting the jurisprudence of mistaken identity as being a matter of offer and acceptance. Henceforth the courts will not be required to delve into the metaphysical distinctions of identity and attributes, a clear improvement when one recognizes that a person's identity is merely an amalgamation of their various attributes. Perhaps Lord Denning MR was correct when, in *Lewis v Averay* [1972] 1 QB 198, he concluded that the separation of identity from attributes was a 'distinction without a difference'.

As a general rule, equity follows the law in not relieving a bad bargain simply on grounds of a mistake of quality. In *Tamplin v James* (1880) 15 Ch D 215, the defendant made a mistake of quality in buying a public house at auction thinking that a piece of land was included. As there was no ambiguity or misrepresentation in the sale particulars, specific performance of the contract was decreed. In contrast, the defendant in *Malins v Freeman* (1837) 2 Keen 25 successfully bid for one piece of land believing he was buying an entirely different lot and, although it was his own fault, specific performance was refused. The two decisions can be reconciled by arguing that *Malins* was a mistake as to substance, not quality.

In conclusion, it is tempting to argue that a mistake as to quality which goes to the root of the undertaking should render a contract void. If, for example, the parties agree to buy and sell a painting which they both mistakenly believe to be painted by Picasso, it is surely the identity of the artist which lies at the root of the contract and it is unacceptable to assert that the subject matter of the contract is 'a painting' with the artist's identity being merely an attractive attribute relating to the painting's value rather than its substance. However, it is equally inviting to conclude that, if there are no express or implied terms of the contract to the effect that the painting is by Picasso, the parties have agreed merely to buy and sell 'a painting' and the law should not be concerned with the inherent, obvious risks, of such a speculative transaction. Whilst the decision in *Great Peace Shipping Ltd v Tsavliris Salvage (International) Ltd* (*supra*) recognized an independent doctrine of mistake, this doctrine was not based on the distinction between substance and quality but, instead, upon whether the performance of the undertaking became 'impossible'. In the example above, where the parties agree to buy and sell a painting which they both mistakenly believe to be painted by Picasso, it seems clear that the impossibility test postulated by *Great Peace Shipping* would result in the contract being binding: performance of the contract is not rendered impossible as the unaltered painting exists and it is, indisputably, the correct subject matter of the contract. If a broader test of commercial sterility/impossibility were to be applied, along the lines used in frustration cases, the outcome would arguably be the same: although the buyer may have paid far too much for his painting, the commercial purpose of the contract of sale remains intact in that speculative profit and loss are inherent aspects of the bargain.

The distinction between substance and quality is criticizable as being elusive and metaphysical but it does provide a basis for distinguishing acceptable from unacceptable contractual risks. Whilst the approach in *Great Peace Shipping* eschews the terminology of substance and quality, it is arguable that one set of epithets has been supplanted by another concerned with the ramifications of 'impossibility'. Regrettably, the difficulty which the terminology attempts to resolve remains as intractable as ever.

Question 4

Pike buys and sells paintings and antiques. He sees that Shark, an art dealer, has a Renoir for sale but he knows that Shark would never sell the painting to him as he (Pike) still owes a debt to Shark from a previous contract. Pike therefore emails Shark in the following way: 'Hello, I am Lord Chub. I am staying at the Grand Hotel. I should like to acquire the Renoir that you have advertised for sale as it fits into my personal collection perfectly.' Shark has to bribe the porter at the Grand Hotel in order to discover whether Lord Chub is staying there but when he discovers that Lord Chub is registered at the Hotel he is pleased to have attracted a prestigious customer. In fact, Pike is staying at the Grand Hotel in the name of Lord Chub having stolen the latter's driving licence and cheque book.

The next day, Pike faxes Shark a copy of his driving licence as proof of identity and tells Shark that he will arrange for a courier to visit his premises with a cheque for the correct amount. Shark is agreeable to this proposal and when the courier arrives with the cheque Shark allows him to take the Renoir away. Pike displays the painting in his shop and sells it almost immediately to Rudd, a private collector, who pays in cash. Shark has now discovered that the cheque has been dishonoured and that Rudd is in possession of the Renoir.

Advise Shark, paying special attention to how the decision of the House of Lords in *Shogun Finance Ltd v Hudson* [2003] UKHL 62, [2004] 1 All ER 215 might have affected his rights.

Would your advice differ in any way if Pike had visited Shark's premises, heavily disguised as Lord Chub, and had been allowed to take away the Renoir on handing over his cheque?

Commentary

This problem concerns an area commonly known as unilateral mistake of identity. Students will need to possess a comprehensive knowledge of the House of Lords' decision in **Shogun Finance Ltd v Hudson [2003] UKHL 62, [2004] 1 All ER 215,** as well as a general understanding of the case law that preceded that decision, recognizing the changing significance of applicable presumptions relevant to dealings concluded between the parties *inter absentes* and *inter praesentes*. The basic question that must be considered is whether Shark accepted an 'offer' from Pike or from Lord Chub? Separately, the contract may also be voidable if Pike is guilty of making a misrepresentation, in which case one must decide what effect this has on the third party, Rudd. The question also calls for a knowledge of rescission and the ways in which rescission can be communicated.

Answer plan

- Can Shark establish that no contract came into existence between him and Pike as, objectively speaking, any exchange of offer and acceptance appeared to occur between Shark and Lord Chub? If so, what effect would this have on his contract with Pike?

- What are the different tests that Shark may be required to consider when arguing that he was fundamentally mistaken as to Pike's identity?

- Is Pike guilty of fraudulent misrepresentation ? What effect does this have on the contract?

- Has Shark made any attempt to rescind the contract for fraudulent misrepresentation? What does rescission entail in this context?

- Is Pike a buyer in possession of the goods within the **Sale of Goods Act 1979, s. 25(1)** and the **Factors Act 1889, s. 9**? Does Rudd acquire title to the painting under the contract with Pike?

Suggested answer

Shark (S) has two possible remedies in this situation. First, he can try to establish a unilateral mistake of identity which, if operative, would render the contract with Pike (P) void. If successful, no title in the painting would transfer to P and, consequently, none to Rudd (R) who would be liable in conversion to S. Secondly, P is almost certainly guilty of fraudulent misrepresentation which would render his contract with S voidable at the latter's option. S could rescind the contract with P and, if communicated in time, the rescission would mean that no title could transfer to R. There are obvious difficulties here as to which of two innocent parties should suffer for the act of a swindler who probably cannot be traced. Consequently, there are conflicting judicial *dicta* favouring either the owner or the bona fide, third party. This tends to distort the clarity of the law.

Traditionally, in order to establish an operative mistake of identity, S had to show that (a) he intended to deal with Lord Chub, (b) P was aware of this intention,

(c) P's identity was crucial in the circumstances, and (d) S took reasonable steps to verify P's identity. The first requirement is easy to prove and therefore allows a court to ignore the decision in *King's Norton Metal Co. Ltd v Edridge, Merrett & Co. Ltd* (1897) 14 TLR 98 where the swindler concocted a fictitious company with credentials intended to attract the interest of the plaintiff. The court held that as this company did not exist the plaintiffs must have intended to deal with the swindler (compare this with *Cundy v Lindsay* (1878) 3 App Cas 459 where a separate, reputable company with whom the plaintiffs intended to deal did exist and so the contract with the swindler was held to be void). Equally, requirement (b) is self-evident as the facts demonstrate P's fraudulent mind, whilst requirement (d) might be established by proof of the porter's bribe (an analogy could be drawn with *Ingram v Little* [1961] 1 QB 31, where the plaintiffs' cursory examination of the telephone directory was treated as a reasonable method for verifying the fact that the reputable third party lived at the address provided by the swindler).

Unfortunately, the conditions for establishing requirement (c) were particularly opaque under the old law. S was required to establish that he intended to contract positively with Lord Chub. Objective appearances were crucial in this regard. For example, in *Phillips v Brooks Ltd* [1919] 2 KB 243, a swindler named North entered the plaintiff's shop and selected some jewellery. He wrote a cheque for £3,000 saying that he was Sir George Bullough and giving an address in St James's Square which the plaintiff verified by consulting a directory. North was allowed to take a ring away with him which he pledged with the bona fide defendant. It was held that the contract was not void for mistake as the plaintiff intended to deal with the person in front of him and was simply impressed that he had secured a reputable customer. However, the contract was voidable for misrepresentation but had not been avoided, so the defendant acquired a good title. The decision was seemingly ignored in the later Court of Appeal decision in *Ingram v Little*, but thankfully re-affirmed in *Lewis v Averay* [1972] 1 QB 198. The facts of *Lewis v Averay* bear repetition. A swindler posed as the actor Richard Greene and showed an admission pass to Pinewood studios bearing a photograph of the swindler. It was held that the plaintiff intended to contract with the person in front of him, especially as the negotiations had been conducted face-to-face. The plaintiff's mistake was only one of attributes (e.g. creditworthiness) rather than identity and therefore the defendant acquired a good title as the initial contract was voidable for fraud but had not been avoided by the plaintiff. These facts appear very similar to those in the problem except that here Shark (S) never meets P (Pike) in person. Older case law certainly manifested a greater inclination to declare a contract void for mistake where the parties dealt with each other at a distance (e.g. *Cundy v Lindsay* (1878) 3 App Cas 459 and *Boulton v Jones* (1857) 2 H & N 564) but S would still be required to prove that there was a fundamental difference between the person he dealt with and the person he intended to deal with; put another way, his mistake was one of *substance* rather than *attributes*. On the facts, and applying the old law, S would presumably argue that if he had known P was an unpaid debtor he would not have dealt with him (i.e. the contract is void) but a court might equally conclude that this was simply a mistake of P's creditworthiness and no more (i.e. the contract might be voidable for fraud but not void for mistake). The latter reasoning would accord with the recommendations of the 1966 Law Reform Committee (Cmnd 2958) that in cases of mistaken identity the contract should be voidable so far as the acquisition of title by third parties is concerned, thereby clarifying the state of the, then, confused body of decisions.

How does the House of Lords' decision in *Shogun Finance Ltd v Hudson* [2003] UKHL 62, [2004] 1 All ER 215 affect the above analysis (see the analysis in **Question 2**)? The first point to note, in the problem, is that the parties never dealt with each other face-to-face, nor did they sign a written contract. On this basis Lord Hobhouse's approach in *Shogun*, which relied on the application of the parol evidence rule to a written contract, is irrelevant to these facts. The remaining Law Lords divided equally on the correct approach. Lords Millett and Nicholls advocated a *dealing test* which, in essence, sets up an irrebutable presumption that the seller (S) intends to deal with the person with whom he physically corresponds (P), or who physically signs the contract. Their Lordships used an identical test for contracts involving face-to-face dealings, viz. you intend to deal with the person standing in front of you. If correct, this would lead to the previous decision of the House in *Cundy v Lindsay* (1878) 3 App Cas 459 being overruled and, as applied to our facts, the contract between S and P would not be declared void, thereby allowing P to pass good title to R provided S had not rescinded in the meantime. Conversely, Lords Phillips and Walker employed an *intent test,* thereby supporting the final outcome in *Cundy*. The application of the 'intent' test pre-supposed that A intended to direct his offer (or acceptance) to the named individual as stated in the contract or as stated in the written correspondence (i.e. B). On this basis, as P pretended to be Lord Chub when emailing S with his offer (and faxed a copy of Lord Chub's driving licence), it is clearly arguable that no exchange of offer and acceptance took place between S and P; hence, P cannot pass good title to R.

It is unfortunate that there was no clear majority in *Shogun* regarding the issue of contracts being concluded *inter absentes* without any formal written instrument. Certainly it would be dangerous to extrapolate any meaningful guidance from Lord Hobhouse's speech on this issue as he concentrated his attention exclusively on written contracts. Perhaps a future court, faced with the obvious tension between the 'dealing' and 'intent' tests, will be swayed by the respective conduct of the two innocent parties, S and R. Whereas R appears to have acted in good faith and would have legitimately assumed that P was the owner of the painting, S, in his dealings with P, seems to have taken too much on trust and should therefore suffer the consequences. This would, in effect, support the recommendations of the 1966 Law Reform Committee (Cmnd 2958).

Assuming that the contract between Pike and Shark is not void for mistake, it will still be voidable for misrepresentation. Pike has clearly misrepresented his identity, which constitutes a false statement of fact, and this deception must have been a material factor in inducing Shark to sell the painting to Pike. Does this mean Shark can rescind his contract with Pike and recover the painting from Rudd? It seems not. R has acquired a valid title and S has made no attempt to rescind. If S had discovered the fraud before the sale to R the possibility of rescission must be considered. The general rule is that rescission must be communicated to the other party who has the voidable title but in *Car & Universal Finance Co. Ltd v Caldwell* [1965] 1 QB 525 it was recognized that a public act (there informing the police and Automobile Association) could suffice if the swindler was deliberately evading the plaintiff. Such would be the position in the problem where S would not appear to know that P perpetrated the fraud. This rule is very protective of ownership and the Law Reform Committee recommended that it be abrogated but it is of limited application. P is clearly a buyer in possession of the goods by virtue of the Factors Act 1889, s. 9, and the Sale of Goods Act 1979, s. 25(1) and the decision in *Newtons of Wembley Ltd v Williams* [1965] 1 QB 560 establishes that the provisions of these statutes override an attempted rescission of the *Caldwell* variety meaning that the third party will normally acquire title. As P sells the painting to R in his (P's) shop and R appears to be bona fide, the other requirements of the statutes would seem to be satisfied meaning that R should acquire a valid title in the painting.

Finally, what if Pike had visited Shark's premises? Prior to the *Shogun* decision there was a strong presumption of a binding contract when formed *inter praesentes* (face-to-face) and, consequently, it was difficult to establish a *valid reason* for contracting with some other party (i.e. Lord Chub) other than that he had the attributes of good reputation and creditworthiness. This would inevitably lead to the conclusion that S intended to deal with P, following a similar approach to that adopted in *Lewis v Averay*. The difficulty here is that P is said to be 'heavily disguised'. If this means disguised so that *his* identity is hidden, it adds nothing to the above conclusion but if it means disguised so as to resemble Lord Chub there is perhaps a greater chance that S could prove that he wanted to deal only with the latter. Has *Shogun* affected this aspect of mistake? It appears not, as all of the Law Lords clearly supported the operation of the face-to-face presumption. However, when considering possible ways in which the presumption might be rebutted, Lord Walker cited the example of the Tichborne claimant who attempted to impersonate a member of the relevant family, presumably via effective character mimicry and the aid of a suitable physical disguise. Lord Walker wondered whether this might provide an appropriate example where the face-to-face presumption might be rebutted. Our facts do not appear to require such a complicated subterfuge and so it would seem more reasonable to conclude that the contract between S and P is voidable for fraudulent misrepresentation but not void for mistake of identity.

Further Reading

Case-notes

Associated Japanese v Credit du Nord [1989] 1 WLR 225

Brown, 'Contractual Conditions and Common Mistake' (1989) 40 NILQ 268

Cartwright, '*Associated Japanese Bank v Credit du Nord*' [1988] LMCLQ 300

Treitel, 'Mistake in Contract' (1988) 104 LQR 501

Shogun Finance Ltd v Hudson [2003] UKHL 62, [2004] 1 AC 919

Chandler & Devenney, 'Mistake of Identity: Threads of Objectivity' [2004] Journal of Obligations and Remedies 7

Hare, 'Identity Mistakes: A Missed Opportunity' (2004) 67 MLR 993

Macmillan, 'Mistake as to Identity Clarified?' (2004) 120 LQR 369

Scott, 'Mistaken Identity, Contract Formation and Cutting the Gordian Knot' [2004] LMCLQ 292

Articles

Atiyah, '*Couturier v Hastie* and the Sale of Non-existent Goods' (1957) 73 LQR 340

Chandler, Devenney & Poole, 'Common Mistake: Theoretical Justification and Remedial Inflexibility' [2004] JBL 34

Goodhart, 'Mistake as to Identity in the Law of Contract' (1941) 57 LQR 228

MacMillan, 'Rogues, Swindlers and Cheats' (2005) 64 CLJ 711

Phang, 'Common Mistake in English Law: The Proposed Merger of Common Law and Equity' (1989) 9 LS 291

Smith, 'Contracts—Mistake, Frustration and Implied Terms' (1994) 110 LQR 400

Steyn, 'Contract Law: Fulfilling the Reasonable Expectations of Honest Men' (1997) 113 LQR 433

9

Illegality and restraint of trade

Introduction

The fundamental principle is that courts will not enforce an illegal contract. The most obvious example would be an agreement to commit a crime, e.g. A pays B £1,000 to shoot C. One can hardly imagine a court viewing with sympathy B's claim to payment after execution of the deed. Unfortunately, the simplicity of this example is rarely emulated in the field of illegality. For instance, few textbook writers agree on any appropriate classification. Should statutory and common law illegality be treated differently? What is the overlap between contracts which break the law and those which are contrary to public policy? Are uniform standards of unenforceability applied to all forms of illegal activity? Probably the best treatment of this area can be found in the current edition of *Cheshire, Fifoot & Furmston's Law of Contract*.

It is undoubtedly true that illegality is the most confusing area within the law of contract, not least with regard to its lack of structure. For the sake of brevity the following comments classify the law into three parts: contracts contrary to law, contracts contrary to public policy and contracts in restraint of trade. The third category will be dealt with separately later in this chapter.

Contracts Contrary to Law

Obvious examples in this area include agreements to commit a crime (see *Bigos v Bousted* [1951] 1 All ER 92) or a civil wrong (see *Begbie v Phosphate Sewage Co. Ltd* (1875) LR 10 QB 491) or those which contravene an express statutory prohibition (*Harse v Pearl Life Assurance Co.* [1904] 1 KB 558). However, there are many other examples which fall into this category:

(a) A contract which has as its object something contrary to the law. Here, the state of the parties' minds can be crucial (see *Adamson v Jarvis* (1827) Bing 66); for example, a seller who knows that the buyer intends to put the goods to an unlawful use may not be allowed to recover the contract price (see *Pellecat v Angell* (1835) 2 Cr M & R 311).

(b) A contract which is performed in an illegal manner. Contracts can often be performed in several ways, some of which are perfectly lawful and others which are not (see *Cope v Rowlands* (1836) 2 M & W 149). If the method of performance is regulated by statute, the court will need to consider whether the statute penalizes a particular method of performance or prohibits the contract *in toto* (see *St John Shipping Corp. v Joseph Rank Ltd* [1957] 1 QB 267).

(c) A contract contingent on the commission of an unlawful act. This would include an agreement to indemnify a party who commits a crime unless, in general terms, liability has been innocently or negligently incurred (see *Beresford v Royal Insurance Co. Ltd* [1938] AC 586 and *Osman v Ralph (J) Moss Ltd* [1970] 1 Lloyd's Rep 313).

(d) A contract contingent on the commission of a civil wrong. Thus, an agreement to indemnify a person against deceit would be illegal as deceit requires proof of *intent* (see *Brown Jenkinson & Co. Ltd v Percy Dalton (London) Ltd* [1972] 2 QB 621). However, an indemnity against civil liability which has been innocently or negligently incurred would be valid (see *Betts v Gibbins* (1834) 2 A & E 57).

Contracts Contrary to Public Policy

Contracts are said to be contrary to public policy when they have a clear tendency to bring about a state of affairs which the law regards as harmful or *contra bonos mores*. Obviously the courts will adapt to changes in social attitudes and economic conditions (compare *Cowan v Milbourn* (1867) LR 2 Ex 230 with *Bowman v Secular Society Ltd* [1917] AC 406).

The main categories of such contracts are:

(a) Contracts which promote immoral conduct. For example, the hire of a carriage to a known prostitute so that she could ply her trade more effectively was considered illegal unless the hirer was ignorant of the intended use (see *Pearce v Brooks* (1866) LR 1 Ex 213). However, case law now suggests that courts have adopted a more flexible approach to contracts promoting extra-marital sexual intercourse (see *Horrocks v Foray* [1976] 1 WLR 230) or to contracts for the placing of advertisements in certain magazines advertising the defendant's pre-recorded sex messages and one-to-one conversations (see *Armhouse Lee Ltd v Chappell* (1996) The Times, 7 August).

(b) Contracts prejudicing the public service. This would include bribes for the acquisition of honours or contracts for the sale of public offices (see *Parkinson v Royal College of Ambulance* [1925] 2 KB 1).

(c) Contracts tending to pervert the course of justice. For example, criminal charges should not be compromised by private agreement between criminal and victim, unless there is no strong public interest in prosecuting the offender (see *Fisher & Co. v Apolinaris Co.* (1875) LR 10 Ch App 297; *Elliot v Richardson* (1870) LR

5 CP 744). Other examples would include bribing a prosecution witness (see *R v Panayiotou* [1973] 3 All ER 112).

(d) Contracts prejudicial to public safety. This category covers agreements tending to benefit a country with which the UK is at war, or to disturb the good relations of the UK with a friendly country (see *Foster v Driscoll* [1929] 1 KB 470; *De Witz v Hendricks* (1824) Bing 314).

There are many other examples of contracts which would offend public policy such as unduly restricting personal liberty (see *King v Michael Faraday & Partners Ltd* [1939] 3 KB 753) and contracts to defraud the Inland Revenue (*Miller v Karlinski* (1945) 62 TLR 85). (Note: In applying public policy considerations the courts regard contracts that are in restraint of trade as being void rather than illegal—these contracts will thus be dealt with separately later in this chapter.)

Effects of Illegality

The most common effect of illegality, whether through being contrary to the law or as against public policy, is to prevent enforcement of the contract, either wholly or in part. It may even prevent a party who has transferred property or money from recovering it under the contract. In considering this area students are best advised to pose two questions:

(a) Was the contract (i) illegal at its inception, or (ii) only illegal in the manner of its performance? Category (i) includes contracts in which *both* parties intend, from the outset, to perform the contract in an illegal manner.

(b) If (ii) applies, is one of the parties innocent of any guilty intent? It will be seen that an innocent party often possesses the normal contractual remedies.

Illegal at Inception

In general the contract is void: there is no remedy of enforcement and no recovery of property transferred or money paid, although enforceable rights in the property may pass to a buyer *as against* a third party (see *Bel voir Finance Co. Ltd v Stapleton* [1971] 1 QB 210). Thus in an illegal sale of goods contract, the buyer who has paid the price cannot recover his money from the seller on grounds of non-delivery. Ignorance of the law is no excuse in this area (see *Nash v Stevenson Transport Ltd* [1936] 2 KB 128), although there is a suggestion that if performance of the illegal contract has some moral justification a court might adopt a more lenient attitude (see *Howard v Shirlstar Container Transport Ltd* [1990] 3 All ER 366).

However, there are some important exceptions to the general rule in which a court may permit the recovery of property or money. Thus, always consider the following questions:

(a) Is the disclosure of illegality essential to the claimant's cause of action? For example, in *Amar Singh v Kulubya* [1964] AC 142 the claimant recovered his property as he possessed an independent cause of action (see also *Bowmakers Ltd v Barnet Instruments Ltd* [1945] KB 65 and *Tinsley v Milligan* [1994] 1 AC 340).

(b) Are the parties *in pari delicto*? If parties have been pressured into contracts by misrepresentation, fraud, duress or oppression by others, they may recover property from, or money transferred to, those other persons (see *Hughes v Liverpool Victoria Legal Friendly Society* [1916] 2 KB 482). This principle has also been extended to cover parties who are protected by statute from the illegal activities of their contractual counterparts (see *Kiriri Cotton Co. Ltd v Dewani* [1960] AC 192).

(c) Did one of the parties 'repent' before performance of the illegal contract had begun (see generally *Kearley v Thomson* (1890) 24 QBD 742)? Note: (i) that the act of repentance must represent a *voluntary* abandonment of the contract (see *Bigos v Bousted* [1951] 1 All ER 92) or (ii) if the illegal transaction has not yet been performed, wholly or in part, then voluntary withdrawal will normally lead to the recovery of money or property already transferred (e.g. *Tribe v Tribe* [1995] 4 All ER 236).

Contracts Illegal as Performed

The general rule is that only parties to an agreement who possessed an unlawful intention are precluded from suing upon it. Thus, an objectively innocent party possesses all the normal contractual remedies available, e.g. recovery of property and damages for breach (see *Marles v Philip Trant & Sons Ltd* [1954] 1 QB 29 and *Ashmore, Benson, Pease & Co. Ltd v AV Dawson Ltd* [1973] 1 WLR 828). However, where the connection between the criminal intention of a party and the contract's performance is *remote*, a court may allow an innocent representative of that party to enforce the contract, or, at the very least, obtain payment for services already rendered (see *21st Century Logistic Solutions Ltd v Madysen Ltd* [2004] EWHC 231, [2004] 2 Lloyd's Rep 92).

Statutory illegality generates its own problems. First, if the contract is absolutely prohibited then talk of rights and remedies is irrelevant (i.e. the contract is illegal at inception). Secondly, the statute might strike at the manner in which performance takes place, in which case any innocent party may possess the normal contractual remedies. Thirdly, the statute might provide certain classes of people with the normal contractual remedies even though they are aware of the illegal performance. Finally, the statute may contain its own regulatory sanctions (e.g. imposition of a fine) leaving the parties with their normal contractual remedies, irrespective of their state of knowledge (see *Hughes v Asset Managers plc* [1995] 3 All ER 669).

Thus, apart from innocence, there are two questions worthy of consideration:

(a) If illegality is imposed by statute, what is the purpose of the statute? For example, is it to protect a class of persons, regulate the manner in which a certain type of contract is performed, or simply to prohibit any such contract being formed? The answer will determine the remedies of the parties (see *Shaw v Groom* [1970] 2 QB 504).

(b) Is there a collateral warranty which stipulates that the defendant must perform the contract legally? Here, the claimant might be treated as if he were innocent (see *Strongman (1945) Ltd v Sincock* [1955] 2 QB 525).

Severance

An act of severance involves the court in removing the objectionable parts of a contract whilst enforcing the remainder (see *Storer v Gordon* (1814) 3 M & S 308). This power is seldom used by the courts as it is tantamount to condoning unlawful activities (see *Bennett v Bennett* [1952] 1 KB 249), although contracts in restraint of trade provide a marked exception to this policy (see below).

Question 1

Arnold, a professional burglar, plans a major robbery of the National Bank and enters into the following transactions in order to further his objective:

(a) Arnold agrees to use Buster's services as a 'safe-breaker' provided Buster pays him £500 immediately. Arnold promises to refund this payment after the robbery.

(b) Arnold purchases 50 kilos of dynamite from Crackit Ltd, the payment to be made in six one-monthly instalments of £500. The sales person fails to ask Arnold to produce a licence verifying his right to use dynamite.

(c) Arnold pressures Desmond into selling him a rifle. Desmond, the owner of a rifle range, obtains the appropriate statutory licence and agrees to deliver to Arnold, within the month, certain personal documents establishing his ownership of the rifle. Payment is delayed for one week, by which time Arnold hopes he will be in possession of the proceeds of the planned robbery.

Buster never arrives at the bank to help Arnold but the robbery nevertheless goes ahead as planned. However, there is much less in the safe than Arnold expected. He therefore refuses to pay the outstanding instalments on the dynamite and, in fact, sells some of it to Edward. Moreover, he refuses to pay Desmond for the rifle or return the £500 to Buster.

Discuss the legal position of all the parties.

 Commentary

It is undoubtedly true that there is no easy problem question in the field of illegality. There are five parties involved and their rights will be determined by their state of knowledge, the purposes underlying existing statutory regulations and their comparative blameworthiness. However, as the facts are suitably ambiguous, you will need to consider how the addition of various hypothetical facts will affect your ultimate conclusions.

Clearly, the best approach is to look at each party individually, identifying the nature of the illegality, e.g. is the contract *ex facie* unlawful or unlawful as performed? This will ensure that you can identify more accurately the respective rights of the parties *vis-à-vis* the possible enforcement of the contract, the recovery of monies paid under the contract, and the recovery of property transferred.

Answer plan

- Which of the contracts that Arnold entered into are potentially illegal at inception?
- Which of the contracts that Arnold entered into are potentially illegal only as performed?
- Does the licensing law regarding the use of dynamite completely forbid Arnold's contract, or merely render it illegal as performed?
- Has Buster repented in time and, if so, what are the consequences for Arnold?
- In what circumstances would a court allow Crackit Ltd or Desmond to recover their property?
- With regard to Desmond's contract, what is the effect if one of the parties is deemed 'innocent', or perhaps less blameworthy?

Suggested answer

Arnold v Buster

In his contract with Arnold, Buster is clearly agreeing to aid the commission of a crime. As the contract is *ex facie* illegal, it will be declared void. This should mean that neither party will acquire any rights under the contract nor will a court permit the recovery of property or money transferred under the contract. If so, Arnold will be entitled to hide behind the illegality of the contract in order to retain the £500 payment (see *Re Mahmoud and Ispahani* [1921] 2 KB 716). But there is an alternative answer. The facts state that Buster did not arrive to help Arnold. Does this suggest that he 'repented'?

At present, the law on this point is in an extremely muddled state. However, two points seem reasonably clear. First, the act of repentance must represent a *voluntary* abandonment of the contract (see *Bigos v Bousted* [1951] 1 All ER 92). Thus, a plea of repentance would fail if Buster was prevented by external forces from helping Arnold (e.g. he crashed his car on the way to the bank, was incapacitated by illness, or was aiding the commission of a different crime). Secondly, repentance is impossible after the contract has been substantially performed (see *Kearley v Thomson* (1890) 24 QBD 742). However, provided Buster can argue that his failure to arrive before the robbery took place, constituted a genuine repentance, this should suffice. If Buster succeeds on both these points the court will allow him to recover his £500.

Crackit Ltd v Arnold

The facts are slightly more ambiguous on this point. For example, does Crackit know about Arnold's intended use of the dynamite? If this knowledge is established, the contract is unlawful from its inception (as with *Arnold v Buster*). Reference could be made to the case of *Pearce v Brooks* (1866) LR 1 Exch 213 in which the plaintiff's constructive knowledge of events was sufficient to defeat his claim of innocence. On the present facts, should Crackit Ltd be put on guard? Does the purchase of dynamite require some discussion with the customer regarding its intended use? This might be unnecessary if Arnold owned a quarrying business but would clearly be important if Arnold was a stranger purchasing the dynamite in a personal capacity.

This emphasizes a more important point. The purchase of dynamite is clearly regulated by some form of statutory regulation. It is unlikely that a sale of dynamite over the counter is permissible without compliance with some further bureaucratic procedures. The vital issue for the court to resolve will be whether the relevant statute completely prohibits the type of contract under consideration (i.e. *ex facie* unlawful) or merely renders it illegal as performed.

If the statute expressly prohibited the sale of dynamite to unlicensed individuals under any circumstances, Crackit Ltd would have no right to sue Arnold for breach of contract or seek recovery of the unused dynamite (see generally *Cope v Rowlands* (1836) 2 M & W 149). Conversely, if the statute merely imposed conditions on the formation and execution of a dynamite sale, a different result might apply. For example, in *Shaw v Groom* [1970] 2 QB 504 the plaintiff landlord successfully sued the defendant tenant for rent arrears even though the former was liable to a fine for issuing the rent-book in contravention of the Landlord and Tenant Act 1962. The court held that the statute did not invalidate the tenancy agreement but merely regulated its circumvention through the imposition of fines. On our facts, this raises two possibilities. First, if Crackit Ltd is merely liable to a fine for selling to an unlicensed buyer, the company may still possess the normal contractual remedies, enabling it to recover the unused dynamite on learning of Arnold's repudiatory conduct and/or seek enforcement of outstanding contractual sums. Alternatively, if the statute prohibits the manner of performance, with no intention to substitute its own sanctions for those of the common law, Crackit Ltd's remedies will depend upon proof of innocence. This would be difficult to establish as the test is objective, preventing Crackit Ltd from arguing that it *honestly* thought that Arnold's intentions were lawful. The strictness of this objective test can be seen in *Ashmore, Benson, Pease & Co. Ltd v AV Dawson Ltd* [1973] 1 WLR 828.

Crackit Ltd v Edward

Even if the contract between Arnold and Crackit Ltd is illegal, the case of *Belvoir Finance Co. Ltd v Stapleton* [1971] 1 QB 210 may yet allow Crackit Ltd to recover the dynamite still in Edward's possession. In *Belvoir Finance* the plaintiffs bought various cars from dealers and sold them on hire purchase terms to X, all parties recognizing that the transactions were illegal. In breach of contract, X's employee, the defendant, sold one of the cars to an innocent purchaser. It was held that the plaintiffs could successfully maintain an action in conversion against the defendant as they still enjoyed the 'general property' in the car. A similar finding was made in *Bowmakers Ltd v Barnet Instruments Ltd* [1945] KB 65, the Court of Appeal pointing out that as the illegal sub-sale constituted a fundamental breach of contract by the defendant, the plaintiffs could reassert their original title to the goods. On our facts, Crackit Ltd would argue that in selling the dynamite to Edward, Arnold had committed a fundamental breach of contract, allowing Crackit Ltd to reassert its title against Edward, irrespective of the latter's innocence.

Desmond v Arnold

Three questions could be posed here. What is Desmond's state of knowledge? What is the effect of Arnold's pressure tactics? What is the relevance of Desmond retaining the documents of title? Regarding the first point, if Desmond can establish his innocence he may be entitled to reclaim the contract price, subject to the comments below. Innocence in this context is objectively defined and is best illustrated by the case of *Pearce v Brooks* in which the plaintiff hired to the defendant an unusually designed carriage. It was held that the plaintiff's realization that the defendant was a prostitute, who intended to use the carriage as a means of attracting customers, prevented him from recovering the outstanding hire fee. Note that an objective test of innocence entitled the jury to conclude that a reasonable person would make a connection between the defendant's calling and the peculiar design of the carriage. Does Desmond know the purpose for which Arnold intends to use the rifle? If he was aware of Arnold's criminal proclivities or Arnold had told him that the rifle would be useful in the planned robbery, the contract would be *ex facie* unlawful. On this basis, Desmond would have no right to enforce the contract (subject to the comments below). Alternatively, if Desmond is totally innocent he will possess all the normal contractual remedies available, e.g. recovery of property and/or damages for breach (see *Marles v Philip Trant & Sons Ltd* [1954] 1 QB 29).

However, there is evidence that Desmond was forced into the contract with Arnold. Even if Desmond knows of Arnold's intentions the question arises as to whether the parties were *in pari delicto*? If the court is convinced Arnold exerted sufficient pressure to break down the physical and emotional reserves of a reasonable person, Desmond may be allowed to recover his rifle. The principle being applied in this context is that the parties can never be considered equally blameworthy when 'one has the power to dictate, the other no alternative but to submit' (*Atkinson v Denby* (1862) 7 H & N 934, 936 *per* Cockburn CJ). Desmond's remedy would be the recovery of the rifle, not the right to enforce contractual payment.

Finally, even if the contract between Arnold and Desmond is *ex facie* unlawful, Desmond may still be entitled to recover his rifle if he can frame his cause of action entirely independently of the contract (see *Tinsley v Milligan* [1994] 1 AC 340 and, for a recent example, *Q v Q* [2008] EWHC 1874 (Fam), [2009] 1 FLR

935). In *Amar Singh v Kulubya* [1964] AC 142, Ugandan law prohibited the lease of 'Mailo' land to a non-African without the permission of the Governor. The plaintiff leased his land to the defendant without obtaining the necessary consent. Several years later the plaintiff gave the defendant notice to quit under the lease agreement. It was held that although the lease was void for illegality, the plaintiff's claim to possession would be upheld as it was not based upon the agreement but, rather, upon his independent and untainted ground of freehold ownership. On our facts, Arnold is now in possession of the rifle but Desmond has retained certain documents which would suggest that he is the rightful owner. It is submitted that Desmond has a stronger case as he can assert ownership on independent grounds which Arnold would be unable to rebut as their original agreement is void for illegality.

Question 2

In English law only the innocent have rights under an illegal contract.
Discuss.

Commentary

This type of question does not simply require a summary of the law. Marks will be earned for a coherent structure, evaluation and analysis of existing precedent and, in particular, an ability to concentrate on those aspects of illegality relevant to the question.

In particular, your answer should focus on three issues. First, in dealing with a contract illegal at its inception, when will the innocence of either party be relevant to the determination of their rights under that contract? Secondly, is there a difference if the contract is only illegal as performed? Thirdly, are there any circumstances where a guilty party would possess rights under an illegal contract?

Answer plan

- What is the difference between a contract *ex facie* unlawful and one that is only illegal as performed?
- When can a party reclaim property transferred under an illegal contract?
- In what circumstances will innocence entitle one party to enforce the contract?
- In what circumstances will a 'guilty' party retain the right to enforce the contract?

Suggested answer

The general approach of the courts to illegal contracts is neatly summarized by the maxim *ex turpi causa non oritur actio* (no right of action arises from a base cause). On this basis, neither party would acquire enforceable rights under an illegal contract nor would they be entitled to sue on the contract for the return of any money or property transferred. But the *ex turpi* rule is subject to a variety of exceptions. In particular, a vital distinction must be drawn between contracts illegal at their inception and contracts which are only illegal because of the manner in which they have been performed. Judicial attitudes are far stricter when dealing with the first category, irrespective of the innocence of one or other party.

Contracts Illegal at Inception

In general, an agreement to do something which is expressly or impliedly prohibited by the law is unenforceable and property or money transferred under the contract cannot be recovered: *in pari delicto potior est conditio defendentis* (where both parties are equally at fault the position of the possessor is better). Neither party can assert that they had no intention of breaking the law, nor will any allowance be made for either party's ignorance of the law.

Notwithstanding the above, the courts will permit the recovery of property or money transferred under the contract where the *comparative innocence* of one party is established. Thus, if the parties are not *in pari delicto*, a court may allow the less blameworthy to recover money or property transferred under the contract. Available precedent suggests that there must be some evidence of oppression or misrepresentation by the defendant, or that the statute which prohibits the contract is aimed at protecting one of the parties. For example, in *Hughes v Liverpool Victoria Legal Friendly Society* [1916] 2 KB 482 the plaintiff was allowed to recover premiums paid under an illegal life insurance policy as he was induced to enter into the contract by the defendant's fraudulent misrepresentation that the policy was valid. However, a claimant's innocence is insufficient without evidence that the defendant acted in some unconscionable manner. Thus, in *Edler v Auerbach* [1950] 1 KB 359 the plaintiff lessee could not recover premiums, paid under an illegal lease, from the defendant lessor, as there was no evidence that the latter had been fraudulent. Regarding class-protecting statutes, in *Kiriri Cotton Co. Ltd v Dewani* [1960] AC 192, the landlord charged the tenant an illegal premium which the tenant then sought to recover. It was held that as the relevant statute placed the obligation firmly on the landlord, the tenant could recover the rent on the grounds that he was not *in pari delicto*.

One further example of 'comparative innocence' is provided by the principle of repentance. Specifically, the recovery of property and money will be permitted if the claimant repents by discontinuing his illegal activities before the contract has been substantially performed (see *Kearley v Thomson* (1890) 24 QBD 742). Moreover, repentance must be voluntary, the defendant thereby demonstrating that he has seen 'the error of his ways'. For example, in *Bigos v Bousted* [1951] 1 All ER 92 the plaintiff agreed to purchase Italian lire from the defendant. Payment was to be made in sterling, which contravened existing exchange control regulations. When the defendant failed to deliver the lire, the plaintiff claimed back his money, arguing that he had repented. The claim failed as there was no evidence that the claimant would have withdrawn from the contract if the defendant had supplied the lire.

Contracts Illegal as Performed

In this area an innocent party possesses all the normal contractual remedies available, e.g. recovery of property and/or damages for breach of contract (see *Marles v Philip Trant & Sons Ltd* [1954] 1 QB 29). Here again the test of innocence is objectively applied. Thus, in *Ashmore, Benson, Pease & Co. Ltd v AV Dawson Ltd* [1973] 1 WLR 828 the contract involved the transportation of a load in excess of the legal limit for the lorries used. The claim by the plaintiff's transport manager, who supervised the loading of the lorries, that he had not noticed the error, was rejected by the court.

The same principles apply to contracts which are performed in ways prohibited by statute: the innocent party will possess all the normal remedies whilst the guilty party will have none (see *Anderson Ltd v Daniel* [1924] 1 KB 138). Naturally, if the claimant's 'innocence' is compromised then he may forfeit his rights, e.g. perhaps the innocent party ought to have recognized that the contract could only be performed in an illegal manner, though this seems less important if the statute is there to protect him in the first place (see *Shaw v Groom* [1970] 2 QB 504). This general objective test has been applied, in a different context, to a collateral contract which stipulated that the defendant would obtain the required statutory licence before commencing work. The defendant failed to do so. Nevertheless, the 'innocence' of the plaintiff persuaded the court to afford him an independent cause of action based on the collateral contract (see *Strongman (1945) Ltd v Sincock* [1955] 2 QB 525).

So far we have seen that an innocent party possesses better remedies in comparison with his guilty counterpart. But the latter is not completely denuded of rights.

Rights of a Guilty Party

The general rule that no rights emerge from a contract illegal at inception can often be successfully utilized by the defendant as an effective defence against a claimant who seeks enforcement, damages or recovery of property (see *Re Mahmoud and Ispahani, Re* [1921] 2 KB 716). For example, in *Pearce v Brooks* (1866) LR 1 Ex 213, although the prostitute used the carriage, she could successfully rely on the illegality of the contract when the plaintiff sued for the hire-charge. Moreover, there is a suggestion that although a claimant cannot generally rely upon the contract to recover goods transferred to the defendant, the defendant can use the contract as a means of protecting himself against third parties who claim to have acquired rights in the subject matter (see *Belvoir Finance Co. Ltd v Stapleton* [1971] 1 QB 210).

Other than this, a guilty party can seek recovery of property under an illegal contract provided disclosure of the illegality is not essential to his cause of action. For example, in *Amar Singh v Kulubya* [1964] AC 142 the plaintiff was the owner of land leased unlawfully to the defendant. It was held that he could recover his land on the basis of his untainted, independent title of freehold ownership. Naturally, if the illegality is apparent from the evidence brought before the court, it is questionable that the guilty party will be entitled to recover his property (see *Snell v Unity Finance Co. Ltd* [1964] 2 QB 203), although in *Tinsley v Milligan*, the House of Lords allowed the defendant's counterclaim on the ground that evidence of illegality only emerged in cross-examination rather than in her original pleadings. More recently, in *21st Century Logistic Solutions Ltd v Madysen Ltd* [2004] EWHC 231, [2004] 2 Lloyd's Rep 92, this approach appears to have been extended even further. The claimants sold computers to the defendants before going into liquidation. The liquidators thereupon sought to enforce payment. From the outset, 21st Century had intended to defraud HM Revenue and Customs (HMRC) of the VAT payable on the transaction. The defendants therefore argued that this guilty intent deprived the liquidators of any right to recover the contract price. It was held that the original contract was legally performed and any future illegal intent to evade payment of VAT was too remote, so the liquidators could enforce payment. Clearly not every contract entered into with the intention of committing an illegal act is illegal and unenforceable, especially where the innocent party appears to take advantage of the other's fraudulent intent in order to secure a windfall (i.e. retaining possession of unpaid property and thereby depriving the HMRC of legitimate revenue).

Finally, there has been a suggestion that if the guilt of one party does not amount to an affront to public conscience, the courts may be more lenient. For example, in *Howard v Shirlstar Container Transport Ltd* [1990] 3 All ER 366, the plaintiff, who was a pilot, agreed to recover a plane that was being held by the Nigerian authorities. Although clearly illegal, the Court of Appeal upheld his claim to the agreed payment. If this approach is followed, the effects of illegality may reflect more accurately the relative fault and guilty intentions of the parties. Admittedly, the House of Lords, in *Tinsley v Milligan* refused to accept a test based on public conscience: although recognizing the deficiencies in the present law, Lord Goff considered that parliamentary intervention was required if 200 years of precedent was to be swept aside. Nevertheless, more recent case law has again highlighted the importance of the parties' respective blameworthiness (e.g. *Mohamed v Alaga & Co.* [2000] 1 WLR 1815).

Contracts in Restraint of Trade

Many employment contracts possess the customary restraint clause directed towards restricting employees' activities during the course of employment and after its termination. Restraint clauses are traditionally drafted in terms of restricting activities within a certain geographical area and for a certain time; for example, the employer might wish to prevent departing employees from working for any competing firm within a two-mile radius and for six months thereafter. Restraint clauses can also appear in commercial dealings between businesses such as where the purchaser of a business wishes to protect its goodwill.

The common starting point is that all restraints of trade are presumed void unless shown to be reasonable as between the parties and to be in the public interest, the latter point rarely proving critical as a distinct feature. The test for reasonableness is seen at its most stringent when dealing with employment contracts because restricting employees' freedom of operations may deny them the opportunity to earn a living.

Employees

The enforceability of restraint clauses in employment contracts is dependent upon the employer establishing two things: that a legitimate proprietary interest is being protected, and that the restraint is not unreasonably wide in terms of protecting those interests.

The following questions should therefore be considered in answering any question on this topic:

(a) Is the employer protecting a legitimate proprietary interest? The most common example involves the protection of confidential information (e.g. trade secrets) or trade connections (see generally *Thomas Marshall (Exports) Ltd v Guinle* [1979] 1 WLR 251).

(b) Is the clause unreasonably wide in terms of the *type* of activities which it restricts? A general non-competition clause may be too wide (see *GW Plowman and Son Ltd v Ash* [1964] 1 WLR 568) whereas a clause which only prevents soliciting of former customers will be viewed more favourably.

(c) Is the clause unreasonably wide in terms of the employer's activities and what the employee was employed to do? For example, there must be a functional correspondence between the area circumscribed by the clause (e.g. not to work within five miles) and the area particularly associated with the employee's place of work (see *Spencer v Marchington* [1988] IRLR 392).

(d) Is the clause unreasonably wide in terms of the *type* of employee involved and the influence that he could exert over the employer's customers? For example, a non-solicitation clause for employees who have little personal contact with their employers' customers may be unreasonable (see *SW Strange Ltd v Mann* [1965] 1 WLR 629).

(e) Is the clause unreasonably wide in terms of the time and area restraints that it imposes? For instance, a time constraint should not last longer than the projected useful life of the information it is attempting to protect (see *Little-woods Organisation v Harris* [1977] 1 WLR 1472).

As mentioned above, the whole doctrine of restraint of trade is based on the concept of public interest; the balancing of an individual's liberty with principles of freedom of contract. Courts can therefore 'fall back' on pronouncements of public interest or public policy in order to strike out clauses which, though reasonable perhaps as between the parties, offend some vague judgement as to what is acceptable. For example, in *Panayiotou v Sony Music Entertainment (UK) Ltd* [1994] EMLR 229 the court held it would be against public policy to allow the plaintiff singer/songwriter to question the enforceability of a previous bona fide compromise settlement which he had later affirmed voluntarily.

This brings us to one final point: the doctrine of restraint of trade has developed rapidly in the post-war years and has been used successfully in quasi-employment situations. For example, in the music industry, although the plaintiff failed in *Panayiotou*, others have met with greater success (e.g. *ZTT v Holly Johnson* [1993] EMLR 61, *Silverstone Records Ltd v Mountfield* [1993] EMLR 152, *Schroeder (A) Music Publishing Co Ltd v Macaulay* [1974] 1 WLR 1308).

Moreover, current litigation demonstrates the link between this area, undue influence, and the wider notions of inequality of bargaining power (e.g. *O'Sullivan v M.A.M. Ltd* [1984] 3 WLR 448, *John v James* [1991] FSR 397). Students would therefore be well advised to recognize that cases of this nature can be of use in answering questions on improper pressure (e.g. **Chapter 7, Question 5**).

Sale of a Business

Clearly the purchaser of a business does not wish to see its assets diminished by the vendor's post-completion activities. If the vendor was able to entice all his old clients away from the purchaser then the latter would be left with a worthless asset. A purchaser will therefore consider the insertion of restraint clauses which consolidate the business's commercial assets. Are such clauses enforceable? As with employment contracts, the basic test is whether the clause is reasonably protecting the legitimate proprietary interests of the purchaser, the courts striking a balance between the public policy implications of anti-competitive behaviour and the contractual freedom of commercial parties who are often of equal bargaining strengths. For example, in *Nordenfelt v Maxim Nordenfelt Guns and Ammunition Co.* [1894] AC 535, the plaintiff sold his armaments business to the defendant and undertook not to carry on such a business for 25 years, except on behalf of the company, anywhere in the world. It was held that this condition was valid and enforceable given the plaintiff's reputation and the global nature of the armaments trade.

In dealing with this area the following questions seem the most appropriate to ask:

(a) Is the purchaser protecting a legitimate proprietary interest? The customer-base and goodwill of the business are invariably the most important protectable interests.

(b) Is the clause unreasonably wide in terms of the *type* of activities which it restricts? A clause should not restrict competition *per se* as this would be unduly wide in terms of the protectable interest (see *British Reinforced Concrete Engineering Co. Ltd v Schelff* [1921] 2 Ch 563 where the restraint was more subtly framed).

(c) Is the clause unreasonably wide in terms of the time and area restraints that it imposes? The *Nordenfelt* decision clearly demonstrates that the clause must reflect the extent of the vendor's sphere of influence, his geographically located client base, and the period of time over which both would evaporate.

(d) Can the restraint doctrine apply to contracts other than sales of businesses? The doctrine has been used to control the growth of solus agreements, i.e. those which restrict a retailer's distribution network, pricing policies, or chain of supply (see *Esso Petroleum Co. Ltd v Harper's Garage (Stourport) Ltd* [1967] 1 All ER 699, *Alec Lobb (Garages) Ltd v Total Oil Great Britain Ltd* [1983] 1 WLR 87). In this area, the public interest assumes greater importance as a restraint clause might affect the public in terms of prices charged or the choice of goods available for purchase (see generally *Schroeder (A) Music Publishing Co. Ltd v Macaulay* [1974] 1 WLR 1308).

Severance

Generally, a contract will not be nullified simply because it is found that one of its clauses constitutes an unreasonable restraint of trade. Rather, the objectionable clause will, if possible, be severed completely or reduced in its effect.

The complete elimination of a clause will only be allowed if it forms a subsidiary rather than a substantial part of the consideration, otherwise the contract becomes totally unenforceable (see *Goodinson v Goodinson* [1954] 2 QB 118). Alternatively, it may be possible to sever specific parts of a clause by employing the 'blue pencil' test. This test provides that the objectionable part of a clause will only be severed if it leaves the remainder in a grammatically correct and understandable form (see *Goldsoll v Goldman* [1915] 1 Ch 292). The only precondition is that the clause itself is divisible in nature; that is, that the clause is not a single covenant but is in effect a combination of several distinct covenants (see *Attwood v Lamont* [1920] 3 KB 571). Interestingly, where the covenant is inserted in a contract for sale of a business the courts have recently shown a preparedness to ignore the 'blue pencil' test and simply alter the clause in order to give effect to the parties' original intentions (see *Chips-Away International Ltd v Kerr* [2009] EWCA Civ 320, [2009] All ER (D) 180).

Question 3

(a) Sam is employed as Deputy Accountant by Albright Ltd, a firm of financial analysts located in Cardiff, Wales. Most of Sam's work involves sitting in front of a computer predicting the future profit expectations of Albright's clients located in Wales. His work has always greatly impressed these clients. Recently, Sam resigned from his job and joined a similar firm located in Swansea. A number of Albright's clients heard about this move and transferred their allegiance to the Swansea firm. Albright Ltd has now written to Sam pointing out that there was a clause in his original contract which stated that on termination of employment he must not 'for a period of two years solicit custom from any Albright client with whom the employee has had contact in the year prior to termination of the contract, or join any firm of financial analysts located in Wales'.

Discuss. (66%)

(b) John owns a very profitable business, Wacko Enterprises Leeds, a firm specializing in the provision of professional entertainment for birthday parties, e.g. magicians and musician bands. He decides to sell this firm to Mary with an undertaking that he will not 'start up any new firm within five miles of Leeds which specializes in any form of adult entertainment'. John now wants to start up a travel agency in Leeds, specializing in adult adventure holidays.

Discuss. (34%)

Commentary

The question clearly weights the different parts unequally. Your answer must reflect this disparity in the length of treatment accorded to each part. The basic issue in part (a) will be resolved by posing the following questions: What is Albright's protectable proprietary interest? Is the clause unduly wide in protecting this interest? Can the offending portions be severed whilst allowing the remainder to remain enforceable?

Similar considerations apply in part (b). Mary has the right to prevent John from unfairly competing with her after the purchase has been completed; otherwise John could entice his old customers away. The issue is whether the clause reflects this in a reasonable manner. In particular, if the clause restricts John's subsequent commercial aspirations in areas that have no connection with Wacko Enterprises then, unless severance is possible, the clause may fail in its entirety.

Answer plan

- What proprietary interests is Albright attempting to protect?
- Is the clause used by Albright unreasonably wide, in terms of Sam's existing duties and his degree of influence over Albright's clients?
- Is the clause used by Albright unreasonably wide, in terms of Albright's geographical area of influence and the commercial duration of any trade secrets?

- Has Mary drawn her net too widely in terms of protecting her existing client base?
- Are Sam's legitimate career aspirations being unreasonably constrained?
- In either contract, what scope is there to sever the offending parts of the clauses?

Suggested answer

(a) The simple issue is whether the restraint clause is enforceable by Albright Ltd. The presumption with all restraint clauses is that they are void unless shown to be reasonable. 'Reasonableness' depends upon whether Albright Ltd can establish that it has a legitimate proprietary interest to protect and that the clause is not drafted in unreasonably wide terms for the protection of those interests.

Does Albright Ltd possess such legitimate interests? This is debatable as regards the protection of business connections because Sam seems to have little personal contact with Albright's clients. If he does have the opportunity to exert personal influence over the clients, or possibly if his reputation is such that clients might move their accounts when he leaves Albright, such an interest will exist. After all, Albright is attempting to prevent departing employees from poaching their existing clients: an important asset within any firm (see *Plowman (GW) and Son Ltd v Ash* [1964] 1 WLR 568). Moreover, Sam has access to a considerable amount of confidential information which could be used unfairly in this context and will, therefore, constitute a proprietary interest (see *Roger Bullivant Ltd v Ellis* [1987] ICR 464).

Assuming a protectable interest, is the clause unreasonably wide in terms of the *type* of activities which it restricts? Insofar as the clause prevents the solicitation of clients this is likely to be reasonable if the two-year period accurately reflects how long it would take the employer to reinstate *influence* over the clients; and should receive a more sympathetic hearing from a court because it is limited in the scope and range of clients affected (see *Plowman (GW) and Son Ltd v Ash*, *supra*). However, the clause also prevents Sam from joining a competing firm. This is much more difficult to defend. Reasonableness here will depend upon: (a) Sam's duties and his degree of influence over Albright's clients and, (b) the area and time limits imposed within the clause.

First, as noted above, Sam was employed as a back-room expert with little personal contact with clients. This would suggest that the clause is unreasonable (see *Strange (SW) Ltd v Mann* [1965] 1 WLR 629) because the clause does not reflect the employee's job. However, Sam did occupy a senior position within the firm and his work impressed the clients for whom he worked. This may represent an effective substitute for personal contact as clients are often more interested in ability and results, rather than general personality traits. As these positive factors induce reliance and some degree of attachment, a properly-drawn restraint might be considered reasonable (see *Marley Tile Co. Ltd v Johnson* [1982] IRLR 75).

The actual wording of the clause imposes a blanket prohibition on working for another firm of 'financial analysts'. There is no mention in what capacity Sam would seek employment, e.g. as a clerk, an auditor, or an accountant. As such, the clause may appear too widely drawn insofar as it prevents Sam from diversifying into other types of employment. The question notes that the clients have moved their business. It is irrelevant here whether they would or would not wish to continue dealing with Albright in any event.

On the second point, there must be a functional correspondence between the area circumscribed by the clause (i.e. not to work in Wales) and the area particularly associated with the employee's place of work (see *Spencer v Marchington* [1988] IRLR 392). The guiding principle is that the wider the geographical area of restraint, the more likely that it is unreasonable, although density of population should be taken into account (see *Mason v Provident Clothing and Supply Co. Ltd* [1913] AC 724). In Sam's position we do not know whether his clients are located throughout Wales or are limited to a narrower area. If the clients are widely dispersed, the clause seems more reasonable, whereas if they are all situated within a few miles of Cardiff, a court might reach a different conclusion.

Regarding the time constraint, this period must not be longer than the projected useful life of any trade secrets which Albright Ltd is attempting to protect (see *Faccenda Chicken v Fowler* [1986] ICR 297). Nor must any restraint regarding trade connections be longer than it would take Albright to recruit a replacement and for that employee to gain the same status and contacts as Sam possessed. Both these points are questions of fact, although current precedent suggests that one year is often a generally accepted norm for protecting trade connections.

Finally, can any reasonable portions of the clause be enforced? The principle of severance does not countenance the rewriting of contracts by the courts. The 'blue pencil' test, as far as employee-focused restraint of trade clauses, ensures that an objectionable part of a clause can only be severed if it leaves the remainder in a grammatically correct and understandable form and does not radically alter the original agreement (see *Goldsoll v Goldman* [1915] 1 Ch 292). On our facts, it would be possible to delete the words 'or join any firm of financial analysts located in Wales', leaving the non-solicitation clause intact. However, it would not be possible to substitute a different length of time for the restraint, so if the existing period was unreasonable the clause would fail in its entirety. Equally, if the court decided that the clause was not a combination of two undertakings but, rather, an indivisible covenant, the clause would again fail completely (see *Attwood v Lamont* [1920] 3 KB 571).

(b) The starting point is that the clause will be presumed void unless reasonable as between the parties and in the public interest. The clause is clearly attempting to protect Mary's legitimate proprietary interests by conserving the existing client base of Wacko Enterprises. However, is it framed too widely in terms of the *type* of activities which it restricts? For example, in *British Reinforced Concrete*

Engineering Co. Ltd v Schelff [1921] 2 Ch 563, it was held unreasonable for the defendant to be precluded from engaging in the manufacture or sale of road-reinforcements generally, as the business that he sold was concerned with the manufacture of a specialized road improvement product.

On our facts Wacko deals with a very limited type of entertainment, providing services for birthday parties. However, the clause restricts John's activities far beyond such provision, employing the words 'any form of adult entertainment'. On the one hand the parties were presumably of equal bargaining strength when they entered into the contract—the freedom of contract principle is influential in this area. On the other hand, John's subsequent entrepreneurial flair is being subdued thereby depriving the public of his talents in his newly discovered 'vocation' of adult adventure holidays. It is submitted that the latter argument is stronger as (a) Mary has no legitimate interest in preventing John from taking up his new business activity as there appears to be very little overlap with Wacko, and (b) even if a substantial overlap existed, a non-solicitation clause would seem more appropriate in the circumstances. This analysis is reinforced by the fact that the clause includes no time restraint, thereby restricting John's business aspirations for the whole of his life. Is this not unduly onerous? Existing precedent would certainly agree (see *Pellow v Ivey* (1933) 49 TLR 422) except in very exceptional circumstances (e.g. the enforceable 25-year restraint in *Nordenfelt v Maxim Nordenfelt Guns and Ammunition Co.* [1894] AC 535).

Finally, severance of the objectionable part seems at first glance inappropriate. Traditionally, the courts have refused to rewrite such clauses (e.g. add a reasonable time constraint), whilst use of the 'blue pencil' test produces grammatical nonsense, so the restraint appears completely unenforceable. Mary may therefore argue that the remainder of the contract has suffered from a substantial failure of consideration (see *Goodinson v Goodinson* [1954] 2 QB 118 and *Stenhouse Australia Ltd v Phillips* [1974] AC 391), as it is arguable that goodwill and existing trade connections are the only important assets for which the contract price is paid to purchase a small business. If successful, the contract will be void and Mary will receive back her purchase monies. However, more recently, the courts have shown a preparedness to rewrite restraint clauses in business sale contracts. In *ChipsAway International Ltd v Kerr* [2009] EWCA Civ 320, [2009] All ER (D) the Court of Appeal stated that as the restraint of trade clause was incomprehensible, it required an amendment that 'involved the minimum changes necessary to achieve a sensible meaning and which gave effect to the commercial purpose of the clause' (*per* Dyson LJ). Consequently, the court might simply incorporate a reasonable time constraint clause; although if there is no evidence that this was discussed in pre-sale negotiations it is difficult to see on what basis a court could identify a specific length of time.

Further Reading

Case-notes

Tinsley v Milligan [1994] 1 AC 340

Berg, 'Illegality and Equitable Interests' (1993) JBL 513

Cohen, 'The Quiet Revolution in the Enforcement of Illegal Contracts' [1994] LMCLQ 163

Bowmakers Ltd v Barnet Instruments Ltd [1945] KB 65

Coote, 'Another Look at *Bowmakers Ltd v Barnet Instruments*' (1972) 35 MLR 38

Illegal Transactions: The Effect of Illegality on Contracts and Torts (Law Com. Consultation Paper No. 154, 199)

The Illegality Defence (Law Com. Consultation Paper No. 189)

Articles

Buckley, 'Implied Statutory Prohibition of Contracts' (1975) 38 MLR 535

Creighton, 'The Recovery of Property Transferred for Illegal Purposes' (1997) 60 MLR 102

Rose, 'Reconsidering Illegality' (1996) 10 JCL 271

Virgo, 'Withdrawal from Illegal Transactions—A Matter for Consideration' 96 CLJ 23

Smith, 'Reconstructing Restraint of Trade' (1995) 15 OJLS 565

Woodley & Wilson, 'Restraint, Drafting and the Rule in *General Billposting*' [1998] JBL 272

10

Frustration

Introduction

The doctrine of frustration evolved during the mid-nineteenth century to moderate the common law's uncompromising insistence on the literal performance of absolute contractual obligations (e.g. *Paradine v Jane* (1647) Aleyn 26). The hallmark of frustration is that it refers to a supervening event not reasonably contemplated by the parties at the time of contracting which radically alters the foundation of the contract or renders it physically or legally impossible to perform (e.g. *Taylor v Caldwell* (1863) 3 B & S 826— the hiring of a music hall was held to be frustrated when the hall burned down). The event, however, must have a fundamental impact on performance of the contract; thus, disappointed expectations, hardship, or mere inconvenience, do not in themselves give rise to frustrated contracts (e.g. *Davis Contractors Ltd v Fareham Urban District Council* [1956] AC 696). Note that frustration refers to events that take place *after* the contract was made, whereas if the change of circumstances was *pre-contractual,* recourse should be made to the law of mistake and the presumed allocation of risks between the parties.

In addressing issues of possible frustration three questions will need to be posed, as outlined below.

Is there a Radical Change in Circumstances?

Perhaps the event has made the contract physically incapable to perform, or a change in the law has had the same effect? Alternatively, performance remains possible but would bear no relation to what was intended. In these circumstances it is often said that the contract has been struck by commercial sterility. In order to identify whether a *potentially* frustrating event has occurred, consider the following:

(a) Is the contract physically incapable of performance in the business sense (e.g. *Taylor v Caldwell* (1863) 3 B & S 826 a music hall that was hired burned down)? If incapability results from personal, physical incapacity a court may take a broader, commercial view, e.g. *Condor v Barron Knights Ltd* [1966] 1 WLR 87— the limited appearances by a key member of a musical group, owing to long-term ill health, was held to be a frustrating event;

(b) Did an unexpected interruption in performance delay, to an unacceptable degree, the eventual completion of the contract? This will depend on how long the interruption is expected to last in comparison with the originally anticipated date of completion (e.g. *Metropolitan Water Board v Dick, Kerr & Co.* [1918] AC 119; *Finelvet AG v Vinaya Shipping Co. Ltd, The Chrysalis* [1983] 2 All ER 658), or, where the interruption occurs during a fixed-term contract, it will depend on whether the interruption took up a disproportionate period of time (e.g. *Tamplin (FA) Steamship Co. Ltd v Anglo-Mexican Petroleum Products Co. Ltd* [1916] 2 AC 397). As regards the specific problem of employees being temporarily unavailable for work, see *Chakki v United Yeast Co. Ltd* [1982] 2 All ER 446 and *Gryf-Lowczowski v Hinchingbrooke Healthcare NHS Trust* [2005] EWHC 2407, [2006] ICR 425);

(c) Did the supervening event *fundamentally* alter the obligations of the parties, or simply increase the costs of performance and/or cause some other type of inconvenience (e.g. *Davis Contractors Ltd v Fareham UDC* [1956] AC 696; *Tsakiroglou & Co. Ltd v Noblee Thorl GmbH* [1962] AC 93; *Thames Valley Power Ltd v Total Gas & Power Ltd* [2005] EWHC 2208 (Comm), [2006] 1 Lloyd's Rep 441—increased gas prices making contract uneconomic to perform did not frustrate the contract)? and,

(d) Did the non-occurrence of a specified event fundamentally undermine the performance of the contract (e.g. *Krell v Henry* [1903] 2 KB 740)—often referred to as the frustration of a 'common purpose'?

In answering question (d) it will be necessary to identify the 'object' of the contract. This requires a separation of the parties' motives in entering into the contract from the object of the contract itself. For example, X purchases a train ticket (Crewe to St Andrews, weekend return) in order to take him to the venue of the British Open Golf Championship in Scotland. The Open is cancelled owing to appalling weather conditions. In these circumstances, although the train journey is now pointless (the *motive* for going no longer exists), the object of the contract is still performable, i.e. to take X to St Andrews and back. Thus, the contract would not be frustrated. However, X's motive and the contract's object could become inseparable if, for example, the railway company had advertised in the following way: 'Travel in style to the British Open. First class seats at second class prices.' This might suggest that fare payers were travelling for the express purpose of seeing the Open, i.e. the object of the contract was to facilitate the viewing of the Golf Open rather than to transport a passenger from A to B (see *Krell v Henry* [1903] 2 KB 740).

Finally, some understanding of the underlying juristic basis of frustration is important. Two tests have been adopted over the years with varying degrees of success: implied terms and construction. The implied terms theory was pre-eminent at the turn of the century, necessitating an *objective* assessment of the hypothetical reactions of a party to an unforeseen event (e.g. *Tamplin (FA) Steamship Co. Ltd v Anglo-Mexican Petroleum Products Co. Ltd* [1916] 2 AC 397, 404). The question, put simply, was whether a term covering the frustrating event could be implied into the contract on the basis that it was so obvious and necessary that it went without saying that both parties would have assumed its inclusion when the contract was made. The weakness of the test is that as the supervening event is supposedly unforeseen, the idea that either party would have considered the automatic inclusion of a term to cover the event at the time of the contract is patently contradictory. Nowadays, the 'construction' test has supplanted the implied term theory. This test requires a court to examine the terms of the contract in order to construe the intentions of the parties at the time the contract was made and, in that context, impose upon the parties a *just and reasonable* solution which the new circumstances demand.

> The event is something which happens in the world of fact, and has to be found as a fact by the judge. Its effect on the contract depends on the meaning of the contract, which is a matter of law. Whether there is frustration or not in any case depends on the view taken of the event and of its relation to the express contract by 'informed and experienced minds' (*Denny, Mott and Dickson Ltd v James Fraser & Co. Ltd* [1944] AC 265, at 276 *per* Lord Wright).

Does any Rule of Law Render Frustration Inoperative?

The central question here is whether the supervening event was foreseen by either party and, in particular, whether either could be assumed to take the risk that such an event might occur. For example, if parties accept the risk of a particular event occurring then it ill behoves them to claim frustration when that event materializes. In these circumstances a court would only reluctantly discharge the parties. Why? Because it is reasonable to assume that they would have sought adequate insurance cover against such contingencies or, if that was not possible, that the terms of the contract would have counterbalanced the risk in some other way (see *Bank Line Ltd v Arthur Capel & Co.* [1919] AC 435). Equally, if an agreement trades certainty for the risks of the uncertain, or achieves finality where rights are subject to protracted negotiations, courts will be extremely unwilling to embrace the doctrine of frustration (e.g. *Amey v Amey* [1992] 2 FLR 89).

The element of risk, in many ways, lies at the heart of frustration. The following examples illustrate this point: (a) neither party is assumed to take the risk of subsequent illegality unless there is an express clause to the contrary; (b) destruction of the subject matter will frustrate the contract unless, for example, one party is expected to take out appropriate insurance against such an event, insurance in this context intimating an acceptance of risk; (c) if the event is foreseen, but the contract makes no provision for it, it is unlikely that a plea of frustration will succeed as the *normal* assumption is that the parties have accepted the risk of that event occurring. These points clearly show that any discussion of frustration must consider if and how risks have been apportioned between the parties.

Other than foreseeability and risk it may be necessary to consider the potential applicability of the following rules: neither party can take advantage of their own fault/breach where this has created a potentially frustrating event (often referred to as a 'self-induced frustration—see *Maritime National Fish Ltd v Ocean Trawlers Ltd* [1935] AC 524 and *Lauritzen (J) A/S v Wijsmuller BV, The Super Servant Two* [1990]

1 Lloyd's Rep 1); clauses which purport to cover frustrating events must do so unequiv-ocally and unambiguously (see *Metropolitan Water Board v Dick, Kerr & Co.* [1918] AC 119); and, a contract of lease can hardly ever be frustrated (*National Carriers Ltd v Panalpina (Northern) Ltd* [1981] 1 All ER 161).

What are the Effects of Frustration?

Generally the parties are discharged from the performance of any future obligations. Moreover, the **Law Reform (Frustrated Contracts) Act 1943** states that any money paid or payable before the frustrating event ceases to be payable or is recoverable by the payee. This rule is subject to two exceptions: (a) any advance payment (paid or pay-able) may be retained in full or in part by the *payee* (subject to the discretion of the

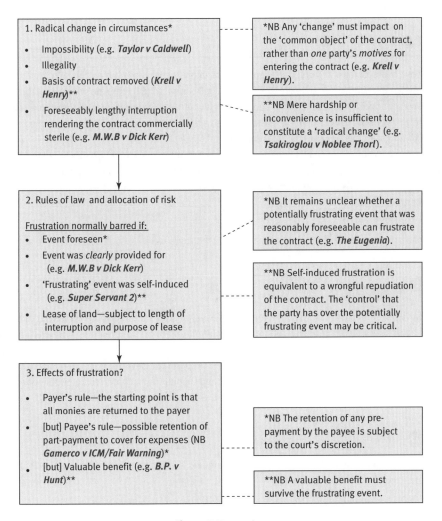

1. Radical change in circumstances*

- Impossibility (e.g. *Taylor v Caldwell*)
- Illegality
- Basis of contract removed (*Krell v Henry*)**
- Foreseeably lengthy interruption rendering the contract commercially sterile (e.g. *M.W.B v Dick Kerr*)

*NB Any 'change' must impact on the 'common object' of the contract, rather than *one* party's *motives* for entering the contract (e.g. *Krell v Henry*).

**NB Mere hardship or inconvenience is insufficient to constitute a 'radical change' (e.g. *Tsakiroglou v Noblee Thorl*).

2. Rules of law and allocation of risk

Frustration normally barred if:
- Event foreseen*
- Event was *clearly* provided for (e.g. *M.W.B v Dick Kerr*)
- 'Frustrating' event was self-induced (e.g. *Super Servant 2*)**
- Lease of land—subject to length of interruption and purpose of lease

*NB It remains unclear whether a potentially frustrating event that was reasonably foreseeable can frustrate the contract (e.g. *The Eugenia*).

**NB Self-induced frustration is equivalent to a wrongful repudiation of the contract. The 'control' that the party has over the potentially frustrating event may be critical.

3. Effects of frustration?

- Payer's rule—the starting point is that all monies are returned to the payer
- [but] Payee's rule—possible retention of part-payment to cover for expenses (NB *Gamerco v ICM/Fair Warning*)*
- [but] Valuable benefit (e.g. *B.P. v Hunt*)**

*NB The retention of any pre-payment by the payee is subject to the court's discretion.

**NB A valuable benefit must survive the frustrating event.

Figure 5 Frustration

court) in order to reimburse the payee for specific expenses incurred in performing the contract (see the interesting exercise of discretion in *Gamerco SA v ICM/Fair Warning Ltd* [1995] 1 WLR 1226); and (b) if either party obtains a valuable benefit a court may require the recipient to pay for it (see *BP Exploration Co. (Libya) Ltd v Hunt (No. 2)* [1979] 1 WLR 783).

In conclusion, as with previous areas, there are no definite answers in a problem question on frustration. Try to consider both sides of the argument. For example, if there are strong arguments for saying that the supervening event will not radically affect the performance of the contract, do not stop there. Consider whether a court might decide otherwise. If there are *any* reasons then proceed to questions two and three (i.e. consider rules of law and effects).

Question 1

IMC own a piece of land in Dorset, 80 square miles in area, with planning permission to mine for tungsten ore. IMC agree to lease this land to Dig Deeper Ltd (DD Ltd) who will extract the ore. The contract provides that DD Ltd will supply all relevant plant, machinery, and technology for the extraction of the tungsten ore and that the lease rental will become payable when the first tonne of tungsten has been extracted from the land.

A year later, when the site has been developed and mining operations are due to commence, local pressure groups force a public inquiry. As a result of the inquiry, planning permission for mining operations is restricted to an area of 20 square miles. DD Ltd claims that the contract has been frustrated.

Advise the parties.

 Commentary

The above problem covers all the main areas of frustration. You should consider: whether the mining of 20 square miles is radically different from the mining of 80 square miles or does it merely cause additional hardship and a consequential reduction in profitability, whether the object of the contract is to lease land or extract ore, whether either party foresaw the possibility of the public inquiry and, if the contract is frustrated, has a valuable benefit been conferred on either party? The following answer adopts the structure outlined in the introduction to this chapter.

 Answer plan

- Does the reduction in planning permission represent a sufficiently radical change in circumstances to frustrate the contract?
- What is the common objective of the contract and how has this been affected?
- Was it reasonably foreseeable/foreseen that a subsequent planning inquiry might be set up that would lead to the current planning permission being scaled down?

- Is a specialist mining lease capable of being frustrated?
- As there is no pre-payment, can DD Ltd claim any wasted expenditure?
- Has either side received a valuable benefit and, if so, how will this be valued?

Suggested answer

Is the Event Capable of Frustrating the Contract?

The doctrine of frustration applies when a change of circumstances renders a contract physically or legally impossible to perform or the changed circumstances transform the expected contract performance into something which is radically different from that which the parties intended when they entered into the contract. On the present facts the mining of tungsten ore is still physically possible, albeit restricted to only 20 square miles. The same considerations apply to legal possibility. Two questions arise in this context: first, what is the object of the contract and, secondly, in the light of this object, has the contract become commercially sterile?

How clear is the object of the contract? For example, it might be: (a) to lease land; or (b) to lease land for the purpose of mining tungsten ore; or (c) to mine the land for tungsten ore. This is particularly important, for if object (a) was correct, frustration would be difficult to argue as the actual lease would remain unaffected by the changed circumstances. Although the problems of leases will be considered later, it would seem appropriate to state that claim (a) is the least likely to succeed. First, IMC are not just leasing land and washing their hands of it; rather, IMC's future profits are linked inextricably with DD Ltd's effective use of the land. Secondly, the pre-contractual negotiations between IMC and DD Ltd must have focused on DD Ltd's intended use of the land. One can hardly imagine IMC advertising the availability of a lease without a clear and specific reference to the presence of tungsten deposits. Clear parallels could be drawn with *Krell v Henry* [1903] 2 KB 740 where the initial advertisement stated the intended use to which the room and balcony would be put, that use eventually constituting the object of the contract. If claim (b) or (c) is correct the next question is whether the planning limitations constitute a sufficiently radical change in circumstances to warrant a finding of frustration.

On a purely mathematical basis, the 75% restriction in the mining area appears fundamental. But what if the ore is primarily located in the specified area? If so, the public inquiry has made little difference to the expectations of the parties. Note that an event that reduces profitability (or makes a contract loss-making), increases logistical hardship or simply causes inconvenience, is not *per se* sufficient to frustrate the contract (see *Tsakiroglou & Co. Ltd v Noblee Thorl GmbH* [1962] AC 93, involving a carriage of goods by sea contract that was rendered unprofitable by the closure of the Suez Canal, or *Thames Valley Power Ltd v Total Gas & Power Ltd* [2005] EWHC 2208 (Comm), [2006] 1 Lloyd's Rep 441, where increased energy costs made the contract uneconomic to perform).

Conversely, if the ore is distributed evenly across the whole 80 square miles and the initial site development costs remain the same, it is more arguable that there has been a radical change in circumstances. Reference to a case such as *Herne Bay Steamboat Co. v Hutton* [1903] 2 KB 683 might be appropriate. There, as the defendant could attain one of the two primary objectives from performance of the contract, his plea of frustration failed. However, on the present facts, a 75% reduction appears rather more drastic.

Will any Rule of Law Render Frustration Inoperative?

There are two important questions here: (a) was the decision of the public inquiry foreseen by either party and/or did either party take the risk of such an event's occurring and, (b) can the mining lease be frustrated?

Generally, where land is intended to be redeveloped it is the buyer who is assumed to take the risk that planning permission will be refused unless the contract states otherwise. For example, in *Amalgamated Investment and Property Co. Ltd v John Walker & Sons Ltd* [1956] 3 All ER 509, the buyer purchased a warehouse for business redevelopment purposes. The building was worth over £1.7 million with planning permission, without which it was worth only £200,000. Subsequent to the sale the warehouse was legally designated as a building of historic importance, making the intended redevelopment all but impossible. The court concluded that in such circumstances the buyer was taken to have accepted the risk of such an event. But the present facts are slightly different. When IMC and DD Ltd entered into the contract, planning permission had already been successfully obtained. In these circumstances it might be difficult to place the risk on DD Ltd unless, for example, it was clear at the time of contracting that local pressure was mounting for a public inquiry. Equally, in a more environmentally friendly society it might indeed be reasonably foreseeable that large-scale projects might attract unfavourable media comment but unless the contract specifically allocates this risk to one or other of the parties, there is nothing to prevent a court from discharging them. For example, in *Ocean Tramp Tankers Corporation v VO Sovfracht, The Eugenia* [1964] 2 QB 226, involving carriage of goods via the Suez Canal, Lord Denning MR recognized that *both* parties had foreseen the possible closure of the canal. However, as they had been unable to reach agreement on any provision to meet this contingency, Lord Denning was quite prepared to make a finding of frustration when the relevant vessel became trapped in the canal. In the present case, there is nothing to suggest that the parties turned their minds to the possibility of a planning limitation so frustration seems possible.

The second point concerns leases of land. Traditionally it has been argued that a lease cannot be frustrated as it not only creates a contract but also an estate in land. If land is requisitioned by the government, for instance, the lessee would still be expected to pay the rent as the act of requisition has not affected the ownership of the estate (e.g. *Whitehall Court Ltd v Ettlinger* [1920] 1 KB 680).

But there are two cases of more recent origin which have doubted that, *as a matter of law*, leases are incapable of being frustrated. First, in *Cricklewood Property and Investment Trust Ltd v Leighton's Investment Trust Ltd* [1945] AC 221, the Law Lords were divided equally on the matter (Lord Porter expressing no view). Lords Simon and Wright argued persuasively that a special purpose lease (e.g. a building lease), in which that purpose could not be performed, might be capable of being frustrated. Secondly, in *National Carriers Ltd v Panalpina (Northern) Ltd* [1981] 1 All ER 161, the House of Lords expressed the opinion that frustration should 'hardly ever' apply to leases rather than discounting the possibility entirely. For our purposes, as DD Ltd have taken a lease exclusively for the mining of ore (i.e. a special purpose lease), which may now be commercially redundant, it is arguable that the lease has been frustrated (see also *BP Exploration Co. (Libya) Ltd v Hunt (No. 2)* [1979] 1 WLR 783, affirmed [1983] 2 AC 352, where an oil concession, similar in many ways to a mining lease, was held capable of being frustrated).

Effects

If a contract is frustrated it is discharged from the date of the frustrating event and thereafter both parties are excused further performance. However, the position at common law has been qualified, to some extent, by the **Law Reform (Frustrated Contracts) Act 1943**.

Under the **1943 Act**, the general rule is that any money paid or payable before the frustrating event ceases to be payable or is recoverable by the payee. There is no evidence of such a payment so the general rule is inapplicable. Moreover, as the lease rental was only payable when mining had actually commenced, this liability is extinguished under the normal common law rules (e.g. *Fibrosa Spolka Akcyjna v Fairburn Lawson Combe Barbour Ltd* [1943] AC 32). Finally, insofar as s. 1(2) offers the possibility of wasted expenses being recovered, this again has no application in the absence of any obligation to make payments *before* the frustrating event.

However, under s. 1(3) of the **1943 Act**, the court may award a 'just sum' where one party has obtained a 'valuable benefit' before discharge of the contract. Can DD Ltd claim that IMC has retained the benefit of land which has been suitably adapted to mineral extraction? Recourse should be made to the judgment of Goff J in *BP Exploration Co. (Libya) Ltd v Hunt (No. 2)* on this point. The learned judge stressed that the value of any benefit must be equated with the end product of services not their cost of provision. This causes DD Ltd some difficulty as much of the site development may be worthless to IMC in the light of planning restrictions. In particular, Goff J commented that the effect of the frustrating event might be to reduce, or even extinguish, the value of the benefit received. If DD Ltd has built roads on IMC land which are now unusable, there appears to be little benefit to IMC.

Question 2

Victor, as Secretary of a local tennis club, hires a bus from the Rambler Bus Company (RBC) to take 45 members of the club to see the Final of the Men's Singles Championships, held at Wimbledon. A term of the contract provides: 'This contract may be cancelled provided that notice of 3 working days is given to the company, otherwise the full hire charge is payable.'

RBC charges £1,500 for fares and Victor pays a deposit of £250 in advance. As RBC guarantees the roadworthiness of all of its buses, the designated bus is properly serviced the day before its intended use. However, on the morning of the trip it is announced that none of the tennis matches will be played as political demonstrators have dug holes in the tennis courts. Victor immediately claims that the contract has been frustrated and demands the return of the £250 deposit.

Advise the parties.

Commentary

Here again it is useful to begin by identifying the 'object of the contract'. Is it to hire a bus or to facilitate the viewing of the sporting event? If the former, a plea of frustration will almost certainly fail. Beyond this the following questions may be considered: is there a radical change in circumstances, what is the effect of the cancellation clause, was the event foreseen or foreseeable, can RBC recover its servicing costs, and has any valuable benefit been conferred on either party?

What is important, especially in frustration, is that you try to look at the potential arguments of *both* sides. Thus, a student who recognizes all the points but whose analysis is superficial will often do worse than a student who concentrates in-depth on a few selected issues.

Answer plan

- What is the common object of the contract and has it been radically changed by the subsequent events?
- Was the cancellation of the tennis tournament a reasonably foreseeable event?
- Can the cancellation clause be used by RBC to prevent Victor from claiming frustration?
- As Victor paid a deposit of £250, can this money be claimed by RBC to cover for any expenses incurred in performing the contract?
- Has either party received a valuable benefit?

Suggested answer

Is the Event Capable of Frustrating the Contract?

A contract will be discharged by frustration where unforeseen events render performance of the contract radically different from that which was originally intended by the parties: *Non haec in foedera veni*. 'It was not this that I promised to do' (*Davis Contractors Ltd v Fareham UDC* [1956] AC 696 at 729 *per* Lord Radcliffe).

On the present facts, the contract to hire the bus can still be performed, as RBC would readily argue. However, from Victor's viewpoint, performance would be pointless as the *motive* for hiring the bus has disappeared. How would a court decide this issue? Clearly one must identify the *object* of the contract. Have the changed circumstances made performance of this object radically different from the original intentions of the parties? The starting point is *Krell v Henry* [1903] 2 KB 740 which considered the hypothetical example of a contract for the hire of a cab to go to Epsom on Derby day. The races were subsequently cancelled. The court felt that the contract would not be frustrated as it would be viewed as one in which the passenger was transported to Epsom, his motive of seeing the Derby being irrelevant to the cabby. This argument would be used by RBC, contending that the contract was merely to transport Victor and his passengers rather than to facilitate the viewing of Wimbledon tennis matches.

Conversely, Victor would rely on the actual decision in *Krell v Henry* where the contract was frustrated as the court considered that the basis of the contract was to afford a private view of the coronation procession rather than the simple hire of a room.

Which argument is stronger? Although both are possible, it is submitted that the court's decision will be determined by the manner in which RBC advertised its services and the general intentions of the parties. In *Krell*, for example, the plaintiff advertised the room specifically for the purpose of viewing the coronation—the room hire and its intended use became inseparable. If the facts show that RBC advertised their services in this way (e.g. 'hire our bus and see Wimbledon tennis') Victor may be successful on this point. If not, RBC will be entitled to claim that the contract remains in force and that, consequently, the cancellation fee is payable.

If Victor's arguments prevail it is clear that the cancellation of Wimbledon will be of sufficient magnitude to frustrate the contract. Whether it will be on the grounds of physical impossibility (e.g. *Taylor v Caldwell* (1863) 3 B & S 826) or that non-occurrence of the event would render performance of the contract pointless (e.g. *Krell v Henry*) is not especially relevant in this context. It is proposed to proceed on the basis that Victor succeeds on this first point.

Will any Rule of Law Render Frustration Inoperative?

A party is rarely able to rely on an event which he has foreseen in order to claim frustration (e.g. *Walton Harvey Ltd v Walker & Homfrays Ltd* [1931] 1 Ch 274). The rationale is that if an event has been foreseen, then in the absence of an express provision covering that event, one or other of the parties must be taken to have accepted the risk of its occurring. In short, the element of foreseeability often determines the allocation of risk.

In considering this issue courts have, on occasion, distinguished between events that were foreseen by the parties (or one of them) and events which were foreseeable at the time of the contract. In the first situation if the event and its magnitude have been foreseen then a plea of frustration will fail except, perhaps, where there is evidence that the parties intended 'to leave the lawyers to sort it out' (see *The Eugenia* [1964] 2 QB 226, *per* Lord Denning MR). On the present facts, there is nothing to intimate that the parties foresaw that a political demonstration would lead to the event's cancellation. (Note: in this context, see below for the possible effect of the cancellation clause.)

If the event was foreseeable at the time of the contract it becomes a question of construction as to whether the contract allocates the risk of the event to one or other of the parties (e.g. *Larraga & Co. v Societe Franco-Americaine des Phosphates de Medulla* (1923) 92 LJKB 455). On the present facts, it is arguable that in the modern age of violent political demonstration, the possibility that people will resort to such activity in order to enhance the publicity of a particular campaign cannot be discounted. If so, the disruption of a major event is foreseeable. The question then becomes: have the parties made provision for this eventuality by incorporating a clause which restricts the effects of the potentially frustrating event? In particular, what is the effect of the cancellation clause?

Victor appears to have accepted responsibility for any cancellation which takes place *within* three days of the anticipated performance. However, in this area, courts apply a very strict test: as the frustrating event, by definition, is unforeseen (though not unforeseeable) clear evidence is required that the parties intended the clause to cover the said event (e.g. *Metropolitan Water Board v Dick, Kerr & Co.* [1918] AC 119).

On the present facts, it is arguable that the parties merely intended the clause to cover a situation where, for example, Victor was unable to find enough passengers to make the trip cost-effective. Moreover, if the object of the contract is to arrange transport to a sporting event, it is arguable that Victor does not so much 'cancel' the contract as that the political demonstrators 'frustrate' it; i.e. Victor does not notify a desire to cancel as the events have already brought the contract to an end. On this basis it might be justifiably concluded that as the cancellation clause does not cover political demonstration, there is no other evidence from which one could deduce that the parties had allocated that particular risk in a certain way. Hence, although the event might be foreseeable, the contract is still capable of being frustrated.

Effects

Under the **Law Reform (Frustrated Contracts) Act 1943** the general rule is that any money paid or payable before the frustrating event ceases to be payable or is recoverable by the payer. However, if the payee incurred expenses in performance of the contract, a court has discretion to allow that party to retain some or all of the specified pre-payment. On the present facts, Victor will be claiming a refund on his £250 deposit whereas RBC will argue that it should retain some part of the deposit as compensation for its servicing costs. It is submitted that RBC's claim is unlikely to attract judicial sympathy as RBC presumably services its buses at periodic intervals anyway, making it unfair to saddle Victor with the ensuing costs. Support for this can be found in *Gamerco SA v ICM/Fair Warning Ltd* [1995] 1 WLR 1226 where the court refused to deduct an amount from the pre-paid sum to cover the defendants' expenses as the plaintiff's loss had been so much greater. However, an alternative argument might be that servicing only takes place because the buses are actually hired for future use, i.e. without use, the need to service disappears.

Has any valuable benefit been conferred on either party? Technically speaking RBC is now in possession of a 'recently serviced' bus but there are two reasons why the court would probably ignore this: under s. 1(3) the valuable benefit must be conferred by the other party, whereas here RBC does its own servicing; as this benefit is paid for by RBC, s. 1(3)(a) would expect the court to take account of the servicing costs when determining the real benefit received.

Question 3

When comparing the common law with the **Law Reform (Frustrated Contracts) Act 1943**, it becomes clear that the latter is more clearly directed towards equitably apportioning the loss between the parties.

Discuss.

Commentary

There are few hidden depths to this question. The answer divides itself broadly into two parts. First, a brief description of the common law and an assessment of its advantages and disadvantages is required, setting this in the context of the House of Lords' decision in *Fibrosa Spolka Akcyjna v Fairburn Lawson Combe Barbour Ltd* [1943] AC 32. Secondly, the changes brought about by the **1943 Act** and whether they improved the situation, focusing especially upon the analysis adopted in *BP Exploration Co. (Libya) Ltd v Hunt (No. 2)* [1979] 1 WLR 783. The better students will try to answer the question by including their own evaluation of whether the **1943 Act** ensures a more equitable apportionment of loss.

Answer plan

- What was the approach of the common law prior to the passing of the **Law Reform (Frustrated Contracts) Act 1943**?
- What inadequacies remained after the House of Lords' decision in *Fibrosa*?
- How did the **1943 Act** change the law?
- What discretion does a court have under the **1943 Act** to compensate either party for wasted expenditure, or even to apportion losses?
- How have the courts interpreted and applied the 'valuable benefit' rule?
- What weaknesses remain under the present system?

Suggested answer

When a contract is frustrated the parties are excused from the performance of any future obligations. This is because at the date of discharge further performance has become impossible in circumstances which involve no liability in damages for the failure of either party (see *Fibrosa Spolka Akcyjna v Fairburn Lawson Combe Barbour Ltd* [1943] AC 32 *per* Lord Wright).

At common law the logical corollary was that any obligation that had accrued before the frustrating event still had to be performed. This could cause considerable injustice as illustrated in *Chandler v Webster* [1904] 1 KB 493 where the plaintiff hired a room for the purpose of overlooking the coronation procession but the coronation was subsequently cancelled. The price exceeded £140 and was payable in advance. Although the plaintiff actually paid £100 he was still held liable for the balance. The Court of Appeal rejected counsel's submission that there had been a total failure of consideration. As the doctrine of frustration only released the parties from *future* performance, as opposed to past and future obligations, the absence of consideration was irrelevant.

In *Fibrosa*, the House of Lords mitigated the harshness of the common law by ruling that a total failure of consideration, in terms of non-performance, released the parties from the performance of existing obligations and allowed either to recover payments already made. The actual facts bear repetition. The respondents agreed to make and deliver machinery according to the appellant's specifications. The contract price was £4,800, £1,600 payable in advance of which only £1,000 had been paid at the time of the frustrating event. As no machinery had been delivered, the House of Lords held that the appellants need not pay the outstanding £600 and were entitled to recover their £1,000.

At first glance the *Fibrosa* decision appears perfectly logical: the appellants did not receive any benefit so they were not expected to pay any money. However, closer examination reveals certain flaws. First, the respondents were merely performing their contractual obligations by manufacturing machinery in accordance with the appellant's specifications. Why should the respondents bear the whole loss when their performance was stipulated by the appellants? Secondly, the machinery was almost complete when the contract was frustrated; on the facts, it seems that it could have been sold without loss. But what if the machinery had been 'custom-built' and was only saleable at a loss? Would it be just and equitable for the respondents to receive no recompense for work done? On these hypothetical facts, the respondents' prudence in stipulating for a pre-payment would be accentuated, especially in view of their blameless conduct. Yet the common law would still place the whole loss on their shoulders. Thirdly, consider a variation on the above facts in which the appellants received a very small part of the anticipated delivery of machinery. Insofar as this represented only a partial failure of consideration, the appellants would forfeit their £1,000 and be liable for the balance of £600, even if the delivery had been unusable without the remainder of the consignment.

The above points demonstrate the inadequacies of the common law even after *Fibrosa*. Moreover, that decision was limited to the recovery of money payments and did not offer any general restitutionary relief for the conferment of non-monetary benefits.

The Law Reform (Frustrated Contracts) Act 1943 implicitly addressed some of these issues. It introduced a general principle that all money paid or payable before the frustrating event was recoverable or ceased to be payable, irrespective of whether there had been a total failure of consideration. However, this rule was subject to two exceptions.

First, under s. 1(2) a court could disregard this general rule by allowing the payee to retain the whole or part of any advance payment (paid or payable before the frustrating event) in order to compensate for expenses incurred in performance of the contract. Applied to the facts of *Fibrosa*, this might have allowed the respondents, subject to the court's discretion, to retain and/or claim a part of the £1,600 advance payment as recompense for their manufacturing expenses. However, this exception only applies if the contract provides for an advance payment prior to the frustrating event (or an actual payment *is* made), otherwise compensation for expenses is unavailable. Equally, if expenses exceed the advance payment, a court is powerless to award the excess under this provision, emphasizing another deficiency in the 1943 Act. The moral is to negotiate for payment of the entire contract price in advance. These two points, taken together, suggest that the 1943 Act was never intended to apportion losses equitably as, otherwise, the expenses rule would operate without the need for an advance payment.

Secondly, under s. 1(3) of the 1943 Act the court may award a 'just sum' where one party has obtained a 'valuable benefit' before discharge of the contract. Recourse should be had to the judgment of Goff J in *BP Exploration Co. (Libya) Ltd v Hunt (No. 2)* [1979] 1 WLR 783 (affirmed [1983] 2 AC 352) in which a number of useful observations were made. Most importantly, the value of any benefit was to be equated with the end product of services, not the cost of their provision. Perhaps for this reason Goff J emphasized that the 1943 Act was more concerned with preventing unjust enrichment rather than providing for an equitable apportionment of loss. For example, if the benefit conferred was destroyed by the frustrating event no sum would be payable except, possibly, where one party had benefited from insurance cover. This confirms that a valuable benefit must be conferred, rather than payment made for *work done*. Thus, if the facts of *Fibrosa* were to be repeated, there would be no valuable benefit as no machinery had been delivered.

Goff J's interpretation has been criticized by many commentators. It is true that under s. 1(3)(b) the court must take account of the effect of the frustrating event upon the said benefit, thereby suggesting that destruction of the benefit will render it valueless. However, s. 1(3) expects a court to value the benefit *before* the time of discharge and then have 'regard to all the circumstances', including the effect of the frustrating event. This implies that a court could value a benefit before discharge and only *partially* reduce its value in the event of its subsequent destruction. The decision in *BP v Hunt* ignores this potential flexibility, thereby emphasizing the role of undue enrichment at the expense of an equitable apportionment of loss. As the law stands, the effect of Goff J's judgment would be that if the facts of *Appleby v Myers* (1867) LR 2 CP 651 were to be repeated, the claimants would still bear the whole loss as the frustrating event destroyed the machinery.

Goff J's judgment also considered that, although the Act was silent on the matter, the best guide to valuing a benefit was the contract price. Thus if a party's expenditure exceeded the contract price, conferring a benefit which also exceeded the contract price, the party would be unlikely to recover all his expenses under s. 1(3).

The above points, taken together, establish clear limits on a court's flexibility to apportion losses fairly. Nevertheless, there are exceptions.

First, s. 1(3) requires a court to take into account any advance payment made which the court has allowed the payee to retain under s. 1(2), thereby preventing a double payment for the same benefit. In the same context, any expenses incurred by the benefited party have to be deducted from the benefit received rather than the 'just sum' which is eventually awarded by the court. Secondly, the Act can apportion benefits, i.e. if both parties confer benefits on each other a court would be entitled to award the balance to the less favoured party. Thirdly, s. 1(3) can include 'benefits' of a more intangible nature, such as the knowledge and experience gained from pre-frustration contractual performance (e.g. *BP v Hunt*). This might allow the provider of specialist advice to be paid a reasonable sum of money for its potential post-frustration use by the recipient.

In summary, the 1943 Act offers considerable advantages over the common law by allowing courts greater flexibility in the awards that can be made. However, the scheme is not perfect. Expenses cannot be recovered in the absence of a provision for pre-payment or actual payment and compensation for benefits conferred is dependent upon those benefits surviving the frustrating event. This clearly falls short of any scheme aimed at apportioning losses equitably between the parties.

Question 4

The Marine Biology Unit (MBU) at Poppleton University has received a six-month government grant to study the effects of oil pollution off the coast of England. MBU approach Cumbrian Trawlers & Co. (CTC) to negotiate a six-month charter of an appropriate vessel to perform daily off-shore pollution checks. CTC, which owns a fleet of five 'B51' trawlers, allocates one of these trawlers to the MBU charterparty. The final contract states that: (a) MBU will take possession of the designated trawler from 1 June, (b) one-half of the charter rates (£5,000) is payable in advance, and (c) the trawler will be returned for servicing at the end of each month.

At the end of the first month's charter MBU sends back the trawler for its routine servicing. However, a fire in CTC's dry dock badly damages the trawler. CTC refuses to allocate another B51 trawler to MBU, claiming that all other trawlers are fully utilized. CTC adds that if specialist parts are available the trawler will be ready 'in the not too distant future'. As pollution testing is at a critical stage, MBU has entered into negotiations with another company to hire a substitute trawler.

Advise the parties.

Commentary

The main questions raised by the facts are: what is the effect of the interruption upon the contract, who takes the risk of the fire, what is the effect of CTC refusing to allocate one of its remaining trawlers to the contract with MBU, what if CTC was responsible for the fire, what are the effects if the contract has been frustrated, what if MBU was found to have acted prematurely in breaking the link with CTC?

Permeating your answer must be a consideration of what happens if the contract is not frustrated. For example, would MBU's hire of an alternative trawler constitute repudiatory conduct entitling CTC to sue for breach of contract? Can MBU sue CTC for failure to provide a trawler?

Answer plan

- Did the interruption to the performance of the contract radically change the nature of that contract?
- Did the contract allocate the risk of the fire to either party?
- In the light of *Lauritzen (J) A/S v Wijsmuller BV, The Super Servant Two* [1990] 1 Lloyd's Rep 1, is there any evidence that CTC might have induced the frustrating event (note: this could be dealt with earlier as it raises the question of whether it is the fire or the refusal by CTC to allocate another trawler that 'potentially frustrated' the contract)?
- In the light of the stipulated pre-payment, can CTC claim for all its expenses?
- Has a valuable benefit been conferred on either party?

Suggested answer

Radical Change in Circumstances

Frustration occurs whenever a court recognizes that, without default of either party, the contract has become incapable of further performance because a super-vening event has rendered it radically different from that which was originally undertaken by the parties (see *Davis Contractors Ltd v Fareham UDC* [1956] AC 696). The present facts require the court to consider whether the anticipated delay in repair of the trawler was of sufficient duration to render further performance commercially impracticable. This question must be considered in the light of the circumstances existing at the moment when the fire occurred. What view would a reasonable person have formed at that moment, without regard to the fuller information available to the court at the time of the trial? One month of the contract has already been performed so five months remain. At what point will the *predicted* delay make complete nonsense of the contract?

Part of the answer lies in identifying the object of the contract. MBU had very specific reasons for chartering a trawler. Conversely, provided the trawler's use was not illegal or dangerous, CTC would not be particularly concerned with the purpose for which MBU chartered it. In short, as MBU's *motive* for using the trawler would not represent the object of the contract the court would probably ignore the reasons for MBU's requiring immediate access to another trawler. If so, there is a need to establish whether the predicted delay, on a purely mathematical basis (e.g. 2, 3, or 4 months' use out of 6), was of a sufficient extent to frustrate the contract. In *Tamplin (FA) SS Co. Ltd v Anglo-Mexican Petroleum Products Ltd* [1916] 2 AC 397, a five-year charter agreement, of which just over two years had elapsed, was held not to be frustrated by requisitioning of the vessel by the Government. However, this decision was influenced by the fact that the vessel might still be usable by the charterer for certain periods during the remainder of the charterparty. (Note: recourse might also be had to the decisions in *Morgan v Manser* [1948] 1 KB 184 and *Metropolitan Water Board v Dick, Kerr & Co.* [1918] AC 119.)

In the end it becomes a matter of fact for the judge to decide. It may be that the fire does not automatically frustrate the contract but, rather, the subsequently predicted length of delay in relation to the intended duration of the contract (e.g. *Pioneer Shipping Ltd v Btp Tioxide Ltd, The Nema* [1981] 2 All ER 1030, 1047. Perhaps the reasonable person would have postponed any decision until the duration of the repairs had been more accurately gauged (e.g. *Finelvet AG v Vinaya Shipping Co. Ltd, The Chrysalis* [1983] 2 All ER 658). If a 'wait and see' policy was expected, any premature withdrawal would constitute repudiatory conduct entitling the other side to damages for breach of contract. In summary, the longer the predicted delay the more likely that there has been a radical change in circumstances—the shorter the delay the more likely this will be a case of mere hardship and inconvenience insufficient to frustrate the contract.

Will any Rule of Law Render Frustration Inoperative?

Two issues might be considered in this context: (a) who took the risk of the fire's occurring and was CTC in any way responsible? and (b) was CTC's decision to refuse the allocation of another trawler tantamount to inducing the frustrating event?

The first question concerns the cause of the frustrating event. Must the party seeking discharge of the contract be free of any blame or fault? This issue has generated considerable debate. In *Bank Line Ltd v Arthur Capel & Co.* [1919] AC 435, 452, Lord Sumner asserted that frustration 'arises without blame or fault on either side'. This definition was confined by an *obiter dictum* of Lord Wright in *Joseph Constantine Steamship Ltd v Imperial Smelting Corporation Ltd* [1942] AC 154 to positive acts against the faith of the contract which amounted to repudiatory conduct and would therefore justify rescission. Furthermore, doubt was expressed over whether 'mere negligence' would render an event 'self-induced'.

However, more recently, in *Lauritzen (J) A/S v Wijsmuller BV, The Super Servant Two* [1990] 1 Lloyd's Rep 1, Bingham LJ regarded responsibility for and control over the event as the key issues (see also *The Hannah Blumenthal* [1983] 1 AC 854, 882 *per* Griffiths LJ). CTC clearly possessed the requisite degree of control over their servicing operations. Thus, if CTC claimed frustration it would need to show that the fire precautions were adequate, that the fire was not caused by the negligence of any of its employees or that in some other way it was responsible. Failure to achieve these standards might allow MBU to claim that the resultant non-availability of a trawler constituted a breach of contract by CTC.

An additional argument would be that the risk of fire in a boatyard is always foreseeable and that one normally expects the owner (CTC) to insure against any ensuing losses. Thus, unless MBU had agreed to take out appropriate insurance cover for the six-month period, the risk seems to lie squarely with CTC, i.e. CTC cannot claim frustration. If so, the remaining arguments on self-induced frustration are academic insofar as they relate to CTC claiming frustration.

In refusing to allocate another trawler to MBU, has CTC induced the frustrating event? Two cases are clearly relevant in this context. First, in *Maritime National Fish Ltd v Ocean Trawlers Ltd* [1935] AC 524 the defendants allocated government licences to their fleet of trawlers in such a way that their contract with the plaintiffs became illegal to perform. The Privy Council concluded that the defendants had *elected* not to supply the necessary licence and, therefore, could not rely upon frustration. Speculation as to why the defendants preferred to allocate the licences to other trawlers was considered irrelevant. Equally, in *The Super Servant Two*, Bingham LJ stated that the doctrine of frustration could not depend on 'any decision, however reasonable and commercial, of the party seeking to rely on it'. The court did not accept the argument that conscious election was irrelevant when the only choice was which contract to frustrate.

Both cases emphasize the 'election' of the defendants as corroborative proof of self-induced frustration. Investigation as to what constraints operated on the minds of the defendants in cancelling the contracts appears superfluous. This leaves CTC in a particularly unenviable position. Whatever decision CTC made they would open themselves to a breach of contract action from a disgruntled client. The only defence on the present facts is for CTC to argue that from the start only one trawler was designated for performance of the contract and that there was no suggestion that a substitute would be found if the designated trawler became unusable. This would distinguish the facts from those of the above two cases. Put simply, in *Maritime National Fish* no trawlers had been designated with an appropriate licence at the time of contract formation, whilst in *The Super Servant Two* the defendants did not nominate a specific vessel for the towing contract. Thus, in both those cases election took place *after* the supposed frustrating event.

Effects

Under the Law Reform (Frustrated Contracts) Act 1943 the general rule is that any money paid or payable before the frustrating event ceases to be payable or is recoverable by the payee. However, if the payee incurred expenses in performance of the contract, a court has discretion to allow that party to retain some or all of the specified pre-payment. On the present facts, if the contract is discharged by frustration, MBU will claim a refund of its initial £5,000 payment whereas CTC will argue for its partial retention as compensation for its costs.

Presumably CTC may have spent money in preparing the trawler for use from 1 June. However, such a claim is unlikely to attract judicial sympathy for two reasons. First, CTC have guaranteed the trawler's seaworthiness. If a court allowed CTC to recover expenses for its servicing costs it would be tantamount to making MBU pay for this guarantee. Secondly, although MBU cannot be classified as a 'payee' it would not weigh heavily on the scales of justice if CTC recovered expenses for the type of activity which MBU had also performed; that is, MBU must also have incurred expenses in preparing for the charter of the trawler but would be unable to use s. 1(2) for its benefit—a point which clearly influenced the decision in *Gamerco SA v ICM/Fair Warning Ltd* [1995] 1 WLR 1226.

Finally, has any valuable benefit been conferred on either party? MBU have certainly obtained one month's use of the trawler. The question must be whether this has benefited MBU. For instance, will an interruption at this stage put paid to the experiments already carried out? Is six months use of the trawler a minimum requirement for the pollution survey? Negative responses might suggest that no benefit has been conferred. Moreover, s. 1(3)(a) would require a court to take account of any expenses recoverable by CTC under s. 1(2) before awarding a 'just sum' for the benefit conferred on MBU.

Further Reading

Case-notes

BP Exploration Co. (Libya) Ltd v Hunt (No.2) [1979] 1 WLR 783
Baker, 'Frustration and Unjust Enrichment' (1979) 38 CLJ 266
Haycroft & Waksman, 'Frustration and Restitution' [1984] JBL 207

Gamerco S.A. v ICM/Fair Warning (Agency) Ltd [1995] 1 WLR 1226
Clark, 'Frustration, Restitution and The Law Reform (Frustrated Contracts) Act 1943' [1996] LMCLQ 170

Krell v Henry [1903] 2 KB 740
McElroy & Williams, 'The Coronation Cases' (1941) 4 MLR 241 and 5 MLR 1

Lauritzen AS (J) v Wijsmuller BV, The Super Servant Two [1990] 1 Lloyd's Rep 1
Chandler, 'Self-Induced Frustration: Foreseeability and Risk' (1990) 41 NILQ 362
McKendrick, 'The Construction of *Force Majeure* Clauses and Self-Induced Frustration' [1990] LMCLQ 153

Articles

Hall, 'Frustration and the Question of Foresight' (1984) 4 Legal Studies 300

Stewart & Carter, 'Frustrated Contracts and Statutory Adjustment: The Case for a Reappraisal' (1992) 51 CLJ 66

Swanton, 'The Concept of Self-Induced Frustration' (1990) 2 JCL 206

11

Damages

Add to Cart

Introduction

The common law places great emphasis on damages as the primary remedy for breach of contract, reinforced by the fact that although a victim of a breach may seek specific performance or an injunction, such orders are equitable in nature and therefore discretionary. Thus, unlike our European neighbours, contractual rights are perceived more in terms of their breach than in terms of their performance.

Damages: Basis for Award

Damages for breach of contract are available as of right even if no loss has been suffered. In such cases damages are said to be nominal. The purpose of awarding damages is to *compensate* the victim for the loss caused by the defendant's breach of contract, rather than to punish the wrongdoer (see *Surrey County Council v Bredero Homes* [1993] 3 All ER 705). For example, if A, in breach of contract, fails to deliver goods to B, damages will primarily reflect the difference between the original contract price and the price which B has to pay for identical goods from an alternative supplier. A court will not penalize the contract-breaker by arbitrarily increasing the damages payable to the victim, nor will the court be swayed by evidence that A had no legitimate excuse for non-delivery. Moreover, as compensation is the overriding principle, if B is able to purchase the goods at a lower price elsewhere no damages will be payable, subject to such matters as the additional expense of arranging alternative supplies.

In claiming damages, the victim of a breach will need to establish that:

(i)   The claimed method for assessing damages is appropriate (*Measure*)

(ii) The damages are not too remote (*Remoteness*)

(iii) If relevant, non-pecuniary losses are recoverable (*Non-Pecuniary*)

(iv) The losses could not have been reasonably mitigated (*Mitigation*)

(v)   The recoverable losses have been properly quantified (*Quantification*)

(vi) Any agreed damages clause is, or is not, valid (*Agreed Damages*)

In point (i) you will need to consider the appropriate basis for awarding damages (e.g. loss of bargain or reliance) and the means used to identify the claimant's losses (see *Ruxley Electronics and Construction Ltd v Forsyth* [1996] AC 344). In point (ii), the victim of a breach may need to establish that his counterpart possessed specific knowledge which would allow the latter to predict more accurately the loss caused to the victim by a particular breach. In point (iii), the fact that the victim suffered considerable distress and disappointment may prove irrelevant if the contract was not of a kind which offered protection against such losses. In point (iv), the victim whose tender of performance has been rejected, for example, is not expected to sit back and claim the full contract price. Where reasonable he must consider making alternative arrangements with potential clients, in order to alleviate his current losses. Point (v) refers to the various mechanisms devised by the courts for quantifying recoverable losses. Finally, in point (vi), if the contract contains an agreed damages clause one must ask whether it is a liquidated damages clause or a penalty clause [note: you might wish to pose this question first as an enforceable liquidated damages clause supersedes any assessment of damages derived from an application of points (i)–(v)].

(i) Measure

Traditionally, damages are intended to place the victim, so far as money can do so, in the position he would have occupied if the contract had been properly performed, i.e. *loss of bargain* is the main yardstick for awarding damages (see *Robinson v Harman* (1848) 1 Ex 850). However, this principle should be treated with a certain degree of caution. Alternative bases for awarding damages include the recovery of pre-contract wasted expenditure (e.g. *Anglia Television Ltd v Reed* [1972] 1 QB 60), the costs incurred by the claimant in relying upon the contract (e.g. *McRae v Commonwealth Disposals Commission* [1951] 84 CLR 377), the release of the defendant from a hypothetical order of specific performance or injunction (e.g. *Wrotham Park Estate Co. Ltd v Parkside Homes Ltd* [1974] 1 WLR 798), or even an account of profits, colloquially known as 'restitutionary damages' (e.g. *Attorney-General v Blake* [2001] 1 AC 268).

The real difficulty lies in identifying precisely what loss the claimant has incurred. For example, in *Ruxley Electronics*, involving the construction of a swimming pool with a specific depth, what loss resulted from the pool being slightly less deep? Was it the cost of re-building the pool to the required depth (such cost would have exceeded the original contract price) or the difference in value between the pool as constructed and the pool as specified in the contract (there was no difference in value) or the reduced utility that the plaintiff would acquire from using the swimming pool (characterizable as either a lack of pleasurable amenity or the lack of a subjective preference, often referred to in terms of a 'consumer surplus')? Interestingly, although the House of Lords recognized that defective construction normally required the court to choose between the first and second options, the actual circumstances necessitated use of the third option. More importantly, the speeches contain useful guidance on the purpose of awarding damages and the choice of the appropriate *measure*.

(ii) Remoteness

The claimant must next establish that a sufficiently strong causal connection exists between the breach of contract and the loss claimed. See, for example, *Galoo Ltd v Bright Grahame Murray* [1995] 1 All ER 16 and *Beco Ltd v Alfa Laval Co. Ltd* [1994] 4 All ER 464 which clearly state that the breach must be the dominant or effective cause of the loss. Once causation has been established the claimant must address the general issue of remoteness. Adopting the principle first enunciated by Alderson B in *Hadley v Baxendale* (1854) 9 Exch 341, damages are only recoverable if:

(a) they were fairly and reasonably considered to arise naturally from the breach, *or*

(b) they were in the reasonable contemplation of the parties as liable to result from the breach.

This offers a single test for awarding damages for breach of contract based on the 'reasonable contemplation' of the parties, the level of liability depending upon the degree of knowledge possessed by the contract-breaker. Put another way, the greater knowledge that the contract-breaker possesses, the greater his horizon of contemplation when predicting the consequences of his breach.

In considering the issue of remoteness within an examination context you will be expected to consider the following types of question:

(a) What was the actual knowledge of the parties? For example, in *Hadley v Baxendale* the carrier had no reason to believe that the mill owner did not possess a spare shaft and, therefore, was not liable for the delay in returning the repaired shaft. Note that the House of Lords, in *Jackson v Royal Bank of Scotland* [2005] UKHL 3, [2005] 2 All ER 71, has again emphasized that the reasonable contemplation of the parties is assessed at *the time of formation*, rather than at the time when the breach of contract actually occurred;

(b) What type of loss might the breach have been expected to produce in the ordinary course of events (see *Victoria Laundry (Windsor) Ltd v Newman Industries Ltd* [1949] 2 KB 528 which distinguished the foreseeability of normal and exceptional profits)? *Moreover*, did the contract-breaker implicitly or explicitly assume responsibility for the resulting loss (see *Transfield Shipping Inc. v Mercator Shipping Inc., The Achilleas* [2008] UKHL 48, [2008] 4 All ER 159), although this is unlikely to form the basis of any future reformulation of the remoteness test (see *ASM Shipping Ltd of India v TTMI Ltd of England, The Amer Energy* [2007] EWHC 927, [2009] 1 Lloyd's Rep 293, *Classic Maritime Inc. v Lion Diversified Holdings Berhad* [2009] EWHC 1142, [2010] 1 Lloyd's Rep 59).

(c) Did the contract-breaker possess any special expertise that would have enabled him to contemplate additional loss? In *Koufos v Czarnikow (C) Ltd, The Heron II* [1969] 1 AC 350 the shipowner's *general* knowledge of price fluctuations in commodity markets was crucial in assessing their liability for late delivery of the cargo; and,

(d) Was the contract-breaker informed at the time of contract formation, or before, of specific circumstances that might lead to the reasonable contemplation of 'unusual losses' (see, *Cottrill v Steyning & Littlehampton Building Society* [1966] 1 WLR 753, where the vendor of a hotel knew that the purchaser intended to convert the premises into flats. On refusal to complete, the former was held liable for damages based on the latter's loss of redevelopment profits).

(iii) Non-Pecuniary Losses

In light of *Addis v Gramophone Co. Ltd* [1909] AC 488 the recovery of damages in a contractual action for injured feelings is rare. Thus, when the defendant company dismissed the plaintiff employee in a most humiliating manner, his claim, insofar as it related to injured feelings, failed. However, there are a number of exceptions.

It is important to identify the type of contract which has been broken. In particular, is *one* of the main objects of the contract to guarantee peace of mind, freedom from distress or the provision of pleasure and enjoyment (see *Farley v Skinner* [2001] UKHL 49, [2002] 2 AC 732)? If so, a claim to damages for disappointment, injured feelings and/or inconvenience may be successful. Within this category the following have been included: a holiday that falls short of the standard promised (see *Jarvis v Swan Tours Ltd* [1973] 1 QB 233), a breach of contract regarding the taking of wedding photographs (see *Diesen v Samson* 1971 SLT (Sh Ct) 49), physical inconvenience associated with a solicitor's negligent handling of a conveyancing transaction (see *Bailey v Bullock* (1950) 66 TLR (Pt 2) 791), distress caused to a client because a solicitor negligently fails to take necessary steps in non-molestation proceedings (see *Heywood v Wellers* [1976] 1 QB 446), loss of a pleasurable amenity (see *Ruxley Electronics and Construction Ltd v Forsyth* [1995] 3 All ER 268), sensory inconvenience caused by unexpectedly high levels of aircraft noise (see *Farley v Skinner* [2001] UKHL 49), and negligent storage of frozen sperm leading to subsequently infertile husbands being unable to become natural fathers (such storage being referred to as a 'peace of mind' bailment contract—see *Yearworth and others v North Bristol NHS Trust* [2009] EWCA Civ 37, [2010] QB 1).

However, if the avowed aims of a contract do not correspond with the above situations, damages for such non-pecuniary losses will not be awarded (see *Bliss v SE Thames Regional Health Authority* [1987] ICR 700). Arguably, the underlying reason for this is that in most arm's length commercial contracts neither party would reasonably contemplate specific psychological suffering or disappointment resulting from a breach.

[NB a claimant cannot recover more than once for the same loss (see *Cullinane v British 'Rema' Manufacturing Co.* [1954] 1 QB 292). For example, the *sensory inconvenience* caused by unexpectedly high levels of aircraft noise may simply be another way of defining the disappointment resulting from experiencing that noise (see *Farley v Skinner*).]

Injured Reputation

Damages for injured reputation are difficult to recover, especially as the law of tort offers remedies in defamation and malicious falsehood. Exceptions include: injury to business reputation from the wrongful dishonour of a cheque (see *Gibbons v Westminster Bank Ltd* [1939] 2 KB 882), loss of customer goodwill (see *Anglo-Continental Holidays Ltd v Typaldos Lines (London) Ltd* [1967] 2 Lloyd's Rep 61), wrongful expulsion from a trade union (see *Edwards v SOGAT* [1971] Ch 354, 378–9), and wrongful conviction owing to a solicitor's negligence (see *McLeish v Amoo-Gottfried* (1993) The Times, 13 October). Moreover, in *Malik v Bank of Credit and Commerce International SA* [1998] AC 20 the House of Lords accepted the theoretical recovery of damages for injured reputation where the employer had carried on its business in such a way as to besmirch the professional reputations of all its employees (but see the practical limits of this approach in *Johnson v Unisys Ltd* [2001] UKHL 13, [2001] 2 WLR 1076).

Speculative Damages

In all of the above cases it is clear that the quantification of loss is at best speculative. This will not deter a court from awarding damages. For example, in *Chaplin v Hicks* [1911] 2 KB 786 the claimant was awarded damages for the loss of a right to belong to a limited class of competitors.

(iv) Mitigation

The victim of a breach must minimize any loss suffered, not act unreasonably so as to increase that loss, and account for any benefits received. A court will not expect the claimant to take the *most* reasonable course of action or explore *every* avenue in order to minimize his losses. For example, if a buyer refuses to take delivery of goods one would reasonably expect the seller to find an alternative buyer. Equally, if the seller refuses to deliver, the buyer should find an alternative supplier. As to whether the buyer would be expected to find the *best* price, this requires a court to balance the inconvenience of attempting to find the most competitive source against the unfairness to the seller if the buyer takes the first offer that comes along, however high the price.

In dealing with the issue of mitigation, consider the following questions:

(a) In an effort to mitigate losses, what courses of action would it be reasonable for the victim to take? If an employee is wrongfully dismissed it may be reasonable to accept an offer of re-engagement from his previous employer, or refuse the offer and seek employment elsewhere, but it would not be reasonable to sit at home and watch the television (see generally *Yetton v Eastwood Froy Ltd* [1967] 1 WLR 104).

(b) Is there any particular course of mitigation which it would be unreasonable for the victim to take? Consider *Pilkington v Wood* [1953] Ch 770 in which the plaintiff was not expected to take steps that would involve him in complicated litigation against a third party.

(c) When can a victim recover additional losses *caused* by the process of mitigation? See *Banco de Portugal v Waterlow & Sons* [1932] AC 452 and *Hoffberger v Ascot Bloodstock Bureau Ltd* (1976) 120 SJ 130 which illustrate the leniency of the courts in this respect.

(d) Has the victim obtained any additional benefits in the course of mitigation? A court will normally expect the victim to account for this benefit (see *British Westinghouse v Underground Electric Railways Co. of London* [1912] AC 673) although this is not necessarily the case if the claimant, as a result, is unfairly penalized (see *Bacon v Cooper (Metals) Ltd* [1982] 1 All ER 397).

Note that the claimant is not compelled to accept an anticipatory breach even if, by continuing with the contract, he increases the defendant's loss (see *White & Carter (Councils) Ltd v McGregor* [1962] AC 413), although in *Clea Shipping Corporation v Bulk Oil International Ltd* [1984] 1 All ER 129 the court stipulated that the plaintiff must possess a 'legitimate interest' before refusing the defendant's repudiatory conduct and continuing with the contract. More recently, in *Golden Strait Corporation v Nippon Yusen Kubishika Kaisha ('The Golden Victory')* [2007] UKHL 12, [2007] 3 All ER 1, the House of Lords stated that in assessing damages where an anticipatory breach has been accepted, the standard common law rules should apply; namely, that the victim of the breach should be placed, so far as damages can do this, in the position he would have occupied had the contract been performed (see *Robinson v Harman*). However, where a contract has been terminated by repudiatory conduct, but subsequent events might have led to termination of the contract anyway (e.g. by *force majeure*), the damages awarded can be reduced in accordance with the probability of that subsequent event occurring.

Finally, recent case law has questioned whether the Law Reform (Contributory Negligence) Act 1945 applies to breach of contract actions. The 1945 Act affords courts discretionary powers to apportion liability on the basis of the respective parties' fault. This generally refers to an assessment of who contributed to the initial loss, rather than how the parties reacted thereafter. Although normally applicable to actions in tort it has been held that the 1945 Act is relevant where the contractual duty (which has been broken) is co-extensive with such a duty in tort (see generally *Barclays Bank plc v Fairclough Building Ltd* [1995] 1 All ER 289).

(v) Quantification

This is an extremely wide-ranging area. Your knowledge will be determined by the particular emphasis which your lecturer places on selected aspects of quantification. However, there are several general rules which will be covered within most contract law syllabi. These normally relate to the non-delivery or non-acceptance of goods and can be summarized generally in the following ways:

(a) If a seller fails to deliver goods the buyer is entitled *prima facie* to claim the loss which he sustains in buying identical goods at a higher price from an alternative source (see **Sale of Goods Act 1979, s. 51(3)**). A subsale by the buyer is generally disregarded unless contemplated by the seller at the time of the original contract (compare *William Bros v ET Agius Ltd* [1914] AC 510 with *Williams v Reynolds* (1865) 6 B & S 495).

(b) If a buyer refuses to accept delivery, the seller's recoverable loss will consist *prima facie* of the difference between the contract price and the market value (see *Kwei*

Tek Chao v British Traders Ltd [1954] 2 QB 459). This is subject to a variety of exceptions discussed in **Question 3** of this chapter.

(c) If a seller delivers defective goods the normal measure of damages will be the difference between the value of the goods as warranted and the value of the goods actually delivered (see also **Sale of Goods Act 1979, s. 53(3)**). However, this presumption can be displaced, for example, if the seller knows that the buyer intends to sell the goods onwards to another person. In such circumstances, damages may be based on the loss that the buyer sustains from an abortive or defective sub-sale (see *Bence Graphics International Ltd v Fasson UK Ltd* [1998] QB 87).

(d) In general terms, if the claimant is claiming reliance losses, as opposed to loss of bargain/expectation losses, damages must return him to the position he occupied before he entered into the contract.

(vi) Agreed Damages Clauses

It is the inherent difficulty of estimating the likely recoverable damages flowing from a breach that encourages so many businesses to consider the insertion of a 'damages' clause. This clause is supposedly designed as an alternative to litigation, offering a sum of money by way of compensation to the victim of a specified breach of contract.

However, the potential for abuse is clear. An agreed damages clause can be used as a threat, compelling performance of a contract as the consequences of any breach are too disastrous to contemplate; for example, specifying the payment of £1,000,000 in damages if a builder is one day late in completing the construction of a £200,000 house. Courts have therefore attempted to distinguish between legitimate clauses aimed at avoiding the vagaries of litigation and those clauses which are merely inserted by a dominant party to compel performance. If the agreed sum is a *genuine pre-estimate of likely loss* it will be classified as a liquidated damages clause and will be enforceable irrespective of the loss actually suffered (i.e. the normal rules of remoteness, mitigation, etc. do not apply). Conversely, if the agreed sum is inserted *to exert pressure on one party to perform*, it will be considered a penalty clause and therefore invalid. Here, a court will disregard the clause in its entirety and, instead, have recourse to the normal common law principles regarding the recovery of damages (e.g. remoteness). The basic rules for distinguishing such clauses are helpfully contained in *Dunlop Pneumatic Tyre Co. Ltd v New Garage and Motor Co. Ltd* [1915] AC 79.

The current law can be distilled into the following propositions

(a) It is a penalty clause if the sum stipulated is extravagant or unconscionable in comparison with the greatest conceivable loss (e.g. *Jeancharm Ltd v Barnet Football Club Ltd* [2003] EWCA Civ 58, [2003] 92 Con LR 26, where interest was chargeable at 260% per annum). See, however, *Murray v Leisureplay plc* [2005] EWCA Civ 963, [2005] IRLR 946 which recognized that this test was overly simplistic and did not require a detailed analysis of the contractual background.

Thus, a 'generous' sum should still be acceptable if justified by the need to create the desired certainty of legal rights;

(b) The finding of a penalty clause in commercial arm's length dealings, on grounds that the stipulated sum is unconscionable, should not rest solely on a consideration of remote, *hypothetical* breaches (e.g. *Philips Hong Kong Ltd v AG of Hong Kong* (1993) 61 BLR 41, (1993) 9 Const LJ 202);

(c) It is a penalty clause if the breach involves non-payment and the agreed figure is greater than the price due;

(d) The clause is one of liquidated damages if the consequences of the breach are such as to make precise pre-estimate impossible and the actual amount specified bears a *reasonable relation* to the probable consequences of the breach (e.g. *Dunlop Ltd v New Garage* [1915] AC 79). In *Alfred McAlpine Capital Projects Ltd v Tilebox Ltd* [2005] EWHC 281 (TCC), 104 Con LR 39, the court emphasized that 'reasonableness' was not judged by the accuracy of the pre-estimate *per se* but, rather, by whether there was a 'substantial discrepancy' between the pre-estimated and the likely loss. In this context, the genuineness or honesty of those making the estimate was not especially relevant as the test was primarily objective; and,

(e) Where the sum is payable for more than one type of breach, necessarily causing different amounts of loss, the presumption is that it is a penalty clause (e.g. *Ford Motor Co v Armstrong* (1915) 31 TLR 267). However, in *Cenargo Ltd v Izar Construcciones Navales SA* [2002] EWCA Civ 524, [2002] CLC 1151 it was held that, in such circumstances, a court should interpret this type of clause as applying only to major breaches of the contract (for which it may be a valid pre-estimate) and not for insignificant breaches.

Question 1

Jack is a manufacturer and seller of frozen food. Botchit & Co agree to lay the floor in Jack's newly constructed factory, the work to be completed on 1 April, at a cost of £25,000. Clause 12 of the contract provides: 'If Botchit & Co fail to complete the contract within the stipulated time, we undertake to pay, by way of penalty, a sum of £10,000 in full satisfaction of our liability.'

Jack also enters into a contract with Marko & Co to install machinery in his factory (5 to 14 April), for the purposes of converting fresh food into frozen, at a cost of £750,000. Botchit & Co is informed of Jack's contract with Marko & Co.

Jack intends to commence production of frozen food on 15 April, and, in consequence, he enters into a contract with Fatts Ltd for fresh food to the value of £200,000 to be delivered to the factory on 14 April.

Botchit & Co only complete the floor on 8 April. As a result, Jack decides to pay Marko & Co an extra £50,000. This sum of money is intended to cover overtime payments for Marko's employees caused by the shortened time for completion, thus enabling the machinery to be installed by 14 April. Whether Marko & Co was contractually entitled to any compensation remains unclear. Jack finally commences frozen food production on 18 April. Unfortunately, the fresh food that had been delivered by Fatts Ltd on 14 April had to be sold off by Jack for £10,000 to local pig farmers.

Advise the parties.

 ## Commentary

This represents the archetypal damages question. It contains the main ingredients of the law relating to damages: remoteness, mitigation, and agreed damages clauses. Note that if clause 12 is a liquidated damages clause Jack would receive £10,000 in full and final settlement of his claim, no more and no less.

 ## Answer plan

- Is the agreed damages clause a penalty clause or an enforceable liquidated damages clause; e.g. was it a genuine pre-estimate of likely loss or simply inserted in order to exert pressure on one party to perform the contract?
- Do the additional overtime payments to Marko & Co represent a 'natural' or 'special' loss resulting from Botchit & Co's delay?
- What 'special knowledge' did Botchit & Co possess regarding Jack's business plans (e.g. the intended date for manufacturing operations to begin)?
- Can Jack claim damages for loss of reputation?
- Did Jack take reasonable steps to minimize his losses and avoid taking any unreasonable steps that might result in his losses being increased?

Suggested answer

The difficulty in predicting the damages recoverable for a breach of contract often encourages the parties to insert an agreed damages clause, thereby obviating the need to seek legal redress. However, a court will intervene if it believes that the clause is not truly an expression of the freedom of contract principle but rather an attempt by a dominant party to exert unfair pressure on the weaker party. Does this happen here?

Agreed Damages Clause

The general principle is that any damages clause which makes a genuine attempt at pre-estimating likely loss will be enforceable, whatever the actual loss suffered. As the common law rules (e.g. remoteness) are disregarded by the courts, the parties can rely on specific sums being paid in the event of specified breaches and order their affairs accordingly. Conversely, if the underlying purpose of a damages clause is to exert pressure on one party to perform his contractual obligations then it will be labelled as a penalty clause. In effect, the clause shows that the parties have not made a genuine attempt to pre-estimate the likely loss resulting from a particular breach. Such a clause is void, allowing the court to award damages in accordance with the normal rules of contract. Into which category does this clause fit?

In *Dunlop Pneumatic Tyre Co. v New Garage and Motor Co. Ltd* [1915] AC 79 the following guidelines were formulated by the House of Lords. First, the clause will be considered penal if the sum stipulated is extravagant or unconscionable in comparison with the greatest conceivable loss which could arise. Consequently, as recognized in *Murray v Leisureplay plc* [2005] EWCA Civ 963, [2005] IRLR 946, the recovery of a sum greater than the actual loss suffered does not inevitably lead to the clause being deemed penal in nature. In *Murray* a director was entitled to one year's salary on dismissal, without any concomitant duty to give a full year's notice of resignation. Nevertheless, it was held that the clause was not penal as the company was perfectly entitled to include in the director's remuneration package a 'generous reassurance' against the eventuality of his dismissal. On the facts, Botchit is expected to pay Jack £10,000 for the delay. It is arguable that this is not an exorbitant sum bearing in mind the expected loss of production and the dislocation of other arrangements caused by a two-week delay.

Secondly, the clause is one of liquidated damages if the consequences of the breach are such as to make precise pre-estimate impossible and the actual amount specified bears a reasonable relation to the probable consequences of the breach (see the facts of *Dunlop v New Garage*). Superficially, it would appear difficult to estimate the real loss resulting from delay but this argument would be found lacking. The specified sum is not graduated in accordance with the severity of the breach. For example, the loss sustained by Jack might be minimal if Botchit delayed by only one day, but it might be considerable if the delay exceeded two months. Thus, it is difficult to argue that the sum bears a reasonable relation to the probable consequences of the breach. Put another way, the clause is not making a genuine attempt to pre-estimate the likely loss and so should be considered a penalty clause.

(Note: for the sake of completeness, one might mention the third rule, although this would seem unnecessary in an examination: there is a presumption of a penalty clause where the sum is payable on one or more of several breaches which must cause different amounts of loss (see *Ford Motor Co. (England) Ltd v Armstrong* (1915) 31 TLR 267). Here the clause covers only one type of breach, namely delay, so it would seem irrelevant.)

On the basis that the damages clause is penal, the court will have to assess Jack's actual losses under the normal common law rules of recovery. Particular emphasis will be placed on remoteness and mitigation.

Measure

This poses no real problems. Clearly Jack will be claiming damages equivalent to being put in the position he should have occupied if the contracts had been properly performed (see *Robinson v Harman* (1848) 1 Ex 850). If successful, Jack would be entitled to claim any lost profits resulting from the delay in commencing production, the loss incurred in selling off the fresh food consignment as pig food, as well as the additional payment of £50,000 to Marko & Co. The first question, therefore, is whether these losses are too remote? (NB the very good student *might* also consider the loss to Jack's reputation—see below.)

Remoteness

The basic principle is contained in *Hadley v Baxendale* (1854) 9 Exch 341 which can be distilled in the following way. Losses are too remote if, at the time of the contract, they were not in the reasonable contemplation of the parties as liable to result from the particular breach. This requires the court to consider the actual knowledge of the parties, eliciting responses to the following types of question: in the ordinary course of events would one expect a customer such as Jack to adopt such a tight schedule for the completion of all the desired works? Was Botchit & Co expected to know, or were they informed, of the consequences of a delay in completion? Is Botchit's trade experience a relevant consideration? What if Jack had no contractual requirement to compensate Marko for the additional overtime payments?

The answers to the above questions will form the basis of the court's decision. For example, as Botchit knew about the anticipated installation of machinery by 14 April, a court might conclude that Botchit had implicitly accepted liability for any production delays suffered by Jack as a consequence of the late completion of the factory floor (see generally *Transfield Shipping Inc. v Mercator Shipping Inc., The Achilleas* [2008] UKHL 48, [2008] 4 All ER 159). Conversely, if Botchit was not aware that Jack was intending to start production from 15 April, would any loss of profits resulting from the delay have been reasonably contemplated? In this context, the decision in *Hadley v Baxendale* may prove helpful: the carrier was not expected to foresee the consequences of his delay as the mill owner failed to inform him of the absence of any spare shaft.

Moreover, the ability of the defendant to foresee possible losses may arise from his special calling or the capacity in which he contracted. For example, in *Heron II* the shipowners were expected to know of the fluctuating prices on the commodity markets. It was therefore within their reasonable contemplation that a delay might cause loss to their clients if the market price moved against them. Equally, as Botchit are assumed to be experienced builders they might be expected to predict more accurately the consequences of their actions. As a factory floor is often laid as a precursor to the installation of machinery, any delay in completion of the floor might foreseeably cause a consequential delay to that installation.

As all these issues raise questions of fact, it is difficult to come to a specific conclusion. However, in practice, it is likely that of the three potential losses outlined above, the first (delay in commencing production) seems the most foreseeable as Botchit must realize that Jack is a frozen food manufacturer who wishes to utilize his assets (factory) as quickly as possible. The second claim (overtime payments) is potentially dependent upon the success of the first claim: if the delay in frozen food production was too remote, surely an additional payment to a third party to ensure timely installation of the production machinery would be equally remote? However, Jack's counsel will refer to *John Hunt Demolition Ltd v ASME Engineering Ltd* [2007] EWHC 1507, [2008] 1 All ER 180 which suggests that the payment to Marko will be recoverable from Botchit provided it is viewed as a 'reasonable settlement' by the court—such reasonableness potentially being established even though the legal enforceability of that payment was questionable. As Botchit was aware of the tight deadline for installation of the machinery by Marko, a court would presumably conclude that the overtime payments that were made, so as to ensure compliance with that newly prescribed schedule, were reasonably foreseeable under the second branch of the *Hadley v Baxendale* remoteness principle. Finally, the third item (sale of the fresh food) seems the most remote as it requires Botchit to foresee the possibility of Jack organizing a consignment of food before the works had definitely been completed and the potential consequences of food storage facilities being unavailable.

Non-Pecuniary Losses

This seems a long shot but one might consider the possible impact of delay on Jack's reputation. Generally, damages for injured reputation are difficult to recover, especially as the law of tort offers remedies in defamation and malicious falsehood. But there are exceptions. In particular, it may be possible to claim damages for injury to commercial reputation. In *Anglo-Continental Holidays Ltd v Typaldos Lines (London) Ltd* [1967] 2 Lloyd's Rep 61, for example, a travel agent recovered such damages from the defendant shipowner who was in breach of contract in failing to provide passengers with accommodation on a pleasure cruise. Jack's reputation might also suffer if he has entered into contracts to supply frozen food to certain customers by a particular date. However, it is submitted that Jack would fail in such a claim as these losses would be considered too remote by a court.

Mitigation

Jack has a 'duty' to mitigate any loss. A court will not expect him to take the *most* reasonable course of action or explore every avenue in order to minimize his losses. Rather, he must adopt a reasonable course of action. What options were available to Jack? Was the course that he pursued reasonable? Presumably, Jack must have known by 2 April that Botchit would not be completing on time. Should he have contacted Fatts Ltd and delayed delivery until he was confident that his processing plant would be operational by a specific date? Ought he to have considered the temporary storage of the fresh food, assuming that such facilities were available? Could he have obtained a better price for the food? If an affirmative answer to *any* of these questions is forthcoming, it will raise serious doubts as to whether Jack's course of action could be regarded as 'reasonable'. Alternatively, if the court decided that delaying delivery, and/or securing alternative, temporary storage facilities, and/or securing a more profitable re-sale, involved too much practical inconvenience for Jack, then such possible courses of action would be ignored (see generally *Pilkington v Wood* [1953] Ch 770).

Question 2

Deco Ltd purchased an eighteenth century property to be used as its new business premises from 19 April. The property needed to be completely repainted and a central heating system to be installed. Deco Ltd hired Jerry for the sum of £1,000 to do the painting, all work to be completed by 18 April, otherwise a deduction of 5% in the contract price would be made for each day that completion was delayed. Deco Ltd also purchased a new heating system from Warmwall & Sons. The contract stipulated that the system needed to be installed by 18 April, with Warmwall being required 'to pay £100 by way of penalty to Deco Ltd for any late completion of the work'.

Jerry did not complete the work until 28 April (ten days late). This meant that Deco Ltd was unable to operate normally from its new premises until 29 April, causing an approximate loss of profits in the region of £500 per day (from 18 April).

Coincidentally, the heating system was not fully installed until 28 April, so Deco Ltd was required to hire six portable electric heaters as the house was cold and damp—total hire charge and electricity was approximately £150 per day, for ten days. Moreover, two days later, owing to a gas leak, the heating system exploded causing severe structural damage to the property and ruining an antique tapestry which had recently been acquired by Deco Ltd for hanging within its client reception area.

Advise Deco Ltd.

 Commentary

As mentioned in the introduction to this chapter, consider adopting a simple structure to your answer: remoteness, special types of damages, mitigation, and agreed damages clauses. Clearly one cannot predict the decision of the court on any issues involving a question of fact. What is important is that you state the law accurately, identify any specific problems and make several remarks on how the law might sensibly be applied to the facts.

Answer plan

- Did Deco Ltd sustain its losses in the normal course of events?
- What special knowledge did Jerry and/or Warmwall possess that might suggest either could have reasonably contemplated some or all of Deco Ltd's losses?
- Can a court award damages for any non-pecuniary losses that Deco Ltd might have suffered, such as inconvenience or loss of reputation?
- Did Deco Ltd act reasonably in order to mitigate its losses?
- Are the agreed damages clauses penal in nature or genuine attempts to pre-estimate likely losses?

Suggested answer

Deco must first establish that the damages it has suffered are not too remote from Jerry or Warmwall's breaches of contract; i.e. that there is a sufficiently strong causal connection between the breach of contract and the claimed loss. Adopting the principle first stated by Alderson B in *Hadley v Baxendale* (1854) 9 Exch 341, damages are only recoverable if: (a) they were fairly and reasonably considered to arise naturally from the breach, or (b) they were in the reasonable contemplation of the parties as liable to result from the breach. This offers a single test for awarding damages for breach of contract based on the 'reasonable contemplation' of the parties, the level of liability depending upon the degree of knowledge possessed by the contract-breaker. If the remoteness test is successfully negotiated, Deco will need to show that the losses were of a type that are recoverable for breach of contract and that it had not acted unreasonably in failing to mitigate any of those losses.

Remoteness

Clearly Jerry and Warmwall have been asked to complete their respective contractual duties by the 18 April. As traders they must encounter many situations where time limits are imposed and, consequently, late completions will inevitably cause their customers some inconvenience. However, Deco's losses generally result from the need to occupy and operate from their premises from 19 April. Was this fact known to Jerry and Warmwall, and that delays in completion might prevent Deco opening for business? Perhaps Deco can rely on the first branch of the remoteness principle set out in *Hadley v Baxendale* (1854) 9 Exch 341; namely, that the losses were fairly and reasonably considered to arise naturally from the breach (i.e. delayed completion prevented occupation of the premises for business purposes)? However, in *Hadley* the court decided that the mill owner's failure to inform the carrier of the absence of a spare shaft prevented him from claiming any loss of profits resulting from the delayed return of the repaired shaft. Surely any failure by Deco to inform either party of its intention to use the offices from 19 April would be treated similarly? Moreover, there is no evidence that either set of builders *assumed responsibility* for such an unquantifiable loss (see *Transfield Shipping Inc. v Mercator Shipping Inc., The Achilleas* [2008] UKHL 48, [2008] 4 All ER 159—although it is unlikely that this 'assumption' test would determine the remoteness issue anyway, given subsequent case law; e.g. *Classic Maritime Inc. v Lion Diversified Holdings Berhad* [2009] EWHC 1142, [2010] 1 Lloyd's Rep 59). Alternatively, what if Jerry and/or Warmwall had been notified of the consequences of late completion? Applying the second branch of the rule in *Hadley*, this would prove that the consequences of late completion were reasonably contemplated, although this would not necessarily prove that either of the builders had accepted liability for such losses (consider the various speeches in *Transfield* which attribute differing levels of importance to this matter).

The damage caused by the gas leak offers interesting possibilities. Assuming that Warmwall caused the leak, and that Deco was not expected to have been checking for such problems (compare this with *Beco Ltd v Alfa Laval Co. Ltd* [1994] 4 All ER 464), it would seem that the two rules in *Hadley v Baxendale* would cover the situation. The only issue would be whether the purchase of the antique tapestry, *after* the contract with Warmwall had been entered into, was a relevant consideration. Is it likely that gas leaks will cause damage to any artefacts stored on premises and that Deco, as a company, might well have expensive ornaments in order to impress its clients? Arguing that Warmwall should have been told the value of the precise items on the premises as a pre-condition of liability would appear needlessly burdensome for Deco.

Non-Pecuniary Losses

Apart from the normal pecuniary loss, it seems unlikely that Deco could recover any other special damages. The main objects of the contract are all business related. It may well be that the owners of Deco will be 'disappointed' by the delays but that is insufficient. In *Bliss v SE Thames Regional Health Authority* [1987] ICR 700 it was clearly stated that such damages were irrecoverable in an arm's length commercial contract, although certain *obiter* comments in *Farley v Skinner* [2001] UKHL 49 would suggest that the distinction between 'business' and 'non-business' contracts should not be the critical determinant in such circumstances. Similar reasoning could be used as regards any physical inconvenience suffered by Deco employees. Presumably, the purpose of the contract is primarily to enhance the earnings potential of Deco, not to improve the working environment of its employees.

Mitigation

To what extent would Deco be expected to mitigate its losses? It will only be expected to act reasonably, rather than taking the *most* reasonable course of action. Could Deco have stayed at its old premises for another few days, or was the move irreversible? Was alternative accommodation available or would the inconvenience and disruption caused to Deco make that option unreasonable? Finally, the hire of portable heaters at that cost seems extravagant. What other options did Deco consider and with which other suppliers did it communicate? (Note that the purpose of posing such questions, although unanswerable on the paucity of facts given, demonstrates to the examiner an understanding of how the rules of mitigation would be theoretically applied by a court. On this basis, reference to cases such as *Banco de Portugal v Waterlow & Sons Ltd* [1932] AC 452 and *Hoffberger v Ascot Bloodstock Bureau* (1976) 120 SJ 130 might be helpful as it demonstrates the latitude that the courts afford to innocent parties when responding to a breach of contract.)

Agreed Damages Clauses

A fuller discussion of this topic can be seen in **Question 1**. The overall purpose of the rules expressed in *Dunlop v New Garage and Motor Co. Ltd* [1915] AC 79 is to distinguish clauses which legitimately attempt to pre-estimate likely loss resulting from a breach and those which penalize one of the parties for a breach of the contract. At first glance the sums of money mentioned in either clause do not appear to be unduly extravagant. However, Jerry might be deprived of any payment if he is more than 20 days late. Is this a genuine pre-estimate of likely loss? If not, then it is a penalty clause and void—requiring the court to apply the normal common law rules regarding the recovery of damages.

Secondly, although both sums of money are payable for one particular type of breach, the clause in Warmwall's contract does not appear to graduate its liability. Whether Warmwall completes one hour late or one year late seems to make no difference: the same amount of money is payable. Thus, under the second rule in *Dunlop*, it might be difficult to argue that the sum of £100 bears a reasonable relation to the probable consequences of the breach. As above, this would make the clause penal in nature, again requiring the court to resort to the normal common law rules on recovery.

Question 3

(a) Estelle Restaurant contracts with Janice to provide a buffet lunch for her wedding celebrations. Estelle is paid on the basis that sufficient food will be supplied for 50 guests and the resident photographer will be engaged to take appropriate photographs of wedding guests and the happy couple. On the day of the wedding, Janice is informed that, owing to a clerical oversight, the buffet room has been double-booked. As a result, a smaller room has been allocated for the buffet. Janice has the embarrassing task of turning away half of the wedding guests. Moreover, the photographer fails to arrive and no other substitute can be found in the time available.

Advise Janice.

(b) John owns a garage which specializes in the sale of Bentley cars. James agrees to purchase one of the Bentleys for £40,000. At this price, John would expect to make a profit of £5,000. Unfortunately, James later decides that the price is too high and refuses to take delivery of the Bentley.

Advise John.

Commentary

This is a popular type of question in certain institutions, especially where damages are concerned. The question comprises two completely separate short problems. Unless otherwise stated, both parts are equally weighted so it is important that your treatment is similarly apportioned. In particular, the fact that the length of the questions varies does not mean that the length of each of your answers should be similarly different. Rather, it suggests that the shorter of the two questions is more general in nature, encouraging you to speculate on other possible factual variations which might lead to different responses.

Answer plan

- What exactly are Janice's losses and are they too remote?
- Is this the type of contract where courts will award damages for non-pecuniary losses (e.g. disappointment and inconvenience)?
- Has Janice acted reasonably in attempting to mitigate her losses?
- What is the normal measure for awarding damages in breach of contract actions?
- Identify the precise losses that John has sustained?
- What reasonable steps should John take to mitigate his losses?

Suggested answer

(a) The main thrust of Janice's claim to damages for breach of contract will be that she has suffered two forms of non-pecuniary loss: (i) she has been deprived of photographs of her wedding buffet and, (ii) she has suffered personal humiliation in having to turn away half of the wedding guests. Presumably she will also be successful in reclaiming part of the contract price on grounds of the reduced value of the services supplied, i.e. a smaller room and a buffet for only 25 guests. Will her two-part claim also succeed?

The question of remoteness and mitigation hardly arises. It must clearly have been in the reasonable contemplation of the parties that a smaller room would take fewer guests, necessitating some form of rationing of places (see, generally, the test laid down in *Hadley v Baxendale*). Equally, as the acquisition of a substitute professional photographer at such short notice would be unlikely (i.e. mitigation impossible), Janice would be permanently deprived of a photographic souvenir of her wedding day. We should therefore co   on the issue of the recovery of non-pecuniary loss.

In general, courts limit the recovery of damages fo   intment and injured feelings to those contracts where *one* of the main obj   provide for pleasure and/or peace of mind (e.g. *Jarvis v Swan Tours Ltd*   QB 233 and *Farley v Skinner* [2001] UKHL 49). This must be contraste   e normal commercial contract where courts have restricted the recovery   amages (see *Bliss v SE Thames Regional Health Authority* [1987] ICR 7   s v James and Charles Dodd* [1990] 2 All ER 815).

One must therefore identify the main objects   tract. Presumably they must be to provide peace of mind (stress-free   on of buffet) and some sentimental benefit (photographs). As such, it   sonable to award damages for injured feelings and inconvenience a   party who defeats that object. In *Diesen v Samson* 1971 SLT (Sh Ct) 4   r arranged for a photographer to attend his daughter's wedding. The   pher failed to arrive. The father was awarded substantial damages for   manently deprived of the pleasure that he would obtain 'in years ahead   he recollection of a happy occasion'. Equally, in *Hotson & Hotson v P*   8 CLY 1047, a father was awarded damages when buffet arrangements   ry. There, as the father had to organize a buffet at another location, usin   r room, he was left with the humiliating task of deflecting a large propor   he invited guests.

The above analysis clearly supports Jan   claim to the recovery of non-pecuniary losses. But there *may* be one par   r limitation. In awarding Janice damages for the inconvenience of re-arrang   he buffet guest list one must be careful that any award of damages is not se   compensation for loss of reputation. This head *may* apply only to loss of c   ercial reputation, as evidenced in *Rae v Yorkshire Bank* [1988] FLR 1. How   in *Kpoharor v Woolwich Building Society* [1996] 4 All ER 119, the court ref   to award damages for loss of reputation to a private individual whose cheq   ad been wrongfully dishonoured by his bank (compare this with the rights of   ommercial customer—*Rolin v Stew-ard* (1854) 14 CB 595). Whether the d   ions in *McLeish v Amoo-Gottfried*, (1993) The Times, 13 October and *Farl   Skinner* [2001] UKHL 49, will affect these issues may depend upon how broa   one can define the words 'reputation' and 'inconvenience'.

(b) The general principle of awarding damages in a breach of contract action is that the victim of the breach must be placed in the position he would have occupied had the contract been properly performed. In assessing John's recoverable loss one must first consider the principle of remoteness as outlined in *Hadley v Baxendale*. Briefly, damages are recoverable provided (i) they were fairly and reasonably considered to arise naturally from the breach, or (ii) they were in the reasonable contemplation of the parties as liable to result from the breach.

On this basis, it is clear that John has been deprived of a sale and will be claiming the resultant loss of profit. But the issue is not that clear-cut. In circumstances where a seller has been deprived of a sale, the law distinguishes between sellers who are private individuals and those who are dealers. In the former case, for example, s. 50 of the Sale of Goods Act 1979 provides that where there is an 'available market' for the goods in question the measure of damages will be the difference between the contract price and the market price. However, John is a dealer, so separate considerations apply.

As a dealer, John is entitled *prima facie* to recover his lost profit. The case of *WL Thompson Ltd v Robinson (Gunmakers) Ltd* [1955] Ch 177 suggests that James will be unable to claim that John could have sold the Bentley to another customer as, in these circumstances, if he successfully arranges a substitute sale he will only have profited from one, not two sales. In particular, Upjohn J, commenting on s. 50 of the Sale of Goods Act 1979, stated that the phrase 'available market' referred to conditions in a particular trade in which goods could be readily and freely resold in the event of the buyer's default. On the facts in *WL Thompson*, as the supply of particular cars exceeded demand, the dealer's loss was clearly a loss of profit on the sale of the car.

Hence, if excess demand for Bentley cars applies in John's situation, it would appear that a claim to lost profits will succeed. But what if demand exceeds supply? In this case John's claim will fail as the number of car sales that he can successfully negotiate will depend upon the supply of cars rather than the supply of buyers (see *Charter v Sullivan* [1957] 2 QB 117). In short, in refusing to accept delivery, James has not reduced the number of sales that John could conclude, assuming an excess demand.

Finally, the above analysis is based on the assumption that James is buying a new Bentley car. What if the car is second-hand? If so, different considerations apply. In *Lazenby Garages Ltd v Wright* [1976] 1 WLR 459 it was held that a second-hand car was a 'unique' object, presumably because each such car is different in terms of its mileage, condition of its bodywork, and so forth. As such, if the car was resold for a higher price to another customer then the original customer would not be liable for loss of profit. Moreover, the possibility that the dealer might have sold a different, second-hand car to the second customer was dismissed as being too remote. On our facts, there is no evidence that John has found another customer although a court would expect him to mitigate his losses by attempting to do so. But even if this occurs, James will still be liable for any expenses incurred by John in negotiating a second sale of the Bentley and, in addition, any loss of profits sustained from selling the car at a lower price (i.e. below £40,000).

Question 4

The overriding principle in the award of damages for breach of contract is that the victim should be fully compensated for all the losses which flow from that breach.
  Discuss.

Commentary

In many ways, the rules regarding the recovery of damages for breach of contract represent a process of elimination. A court will identify the actual damage caused by the breach and then scale down these damages, where appropriate, on grounds that they are (a) too remote, or (b) not of a type that are recoverable, or (c) should have been mitigated by the claimant. The net result is that a claimant may not recover *all* the losses directly caused by the breach of contract.

  Good students will not merely regurgitate their lecture notes but will try to identify particular situations where the claimant's actual losses are not fully recoverable. The answer below adopts one of many possible structures. As an alternative, one might consider other aspects such as the basis upon which damages are awarded (e.g. compare reliance and expectation losses), or the quantification of loss (e.g. non-delivery of goods which thwarts a profitable sub-sale by the buyer), or the enforceability of agreed damages clauses which often do not fully compensate the victim of a breach.

Answer plan

- What is the meaning of causation?
- How will the contract-breaker's knowledge at the time of contracting affect the application of the remoteness test?
- Contrast direct consequence and reasonably contemplated losses.
- What limitations are imposed on the recovery of non-pecuniary losses?
- What steps should the victim take in order to minimize his losses?
- Give examples throughout your answer that illustrate how the victim's damages do not fully compensate him for all the losses resulting from the breach.

Suggested answer

Few would question that the purpose of awarding damages for breach of contract is to compensate the claimant rather than punish the defendant, thereby excluding the award of exemplary damages. Thus, although damages can be claimed as of right by the victim of a breach, such damages will only be nominal, substantial damages requiring proof that actual losses were sustained as a result of the breach. The claimant will fail even if there is proof that the defendant's breach was committed deliberately and with a view to profit, unless the court is prepared to disguise such an award under the general heading of injury to the claimant's feelings (e.g. *Cox v Phillips Industries Ltd* [1976] 1 WLR 638).

However, three questions emerge from the quotation. How does one assess whether the loss suffered is actually *caused* by the breach? Is the recovery of damages based upon an assessment of the direct consequences of the breach or is it limited by a test of foreseeability? Finally, will the victim be fully compensated for *all* the losses suffered?

Causation

It is often said that there must be a sufficiently strong causal connection between the loss suffered and the actual breach. In this context, causation is not exclusively subsumed within the remoteness principle. For example, if the breach of contract is one of two causes for the loss suffered, both causes acting concurrently, then a court will still award normal damages (see *Heskell v Continental Express Ltd* [1950] 1 All ER 1033). Thus, in *Smith, Hogg & Co. v Black Sea Insurance Co. Ltd* [1940] AC 997, the cargo was lost because of bad weather and also because, in breach of contract, the ship did not fulfil the seaworthiness criterion. It was held that the breach was sufficient to support a claim for damages. However, if the bad weather had been so extreme that no ship would have survived, then damages might not have been recoverable (see generally *Monarch SS Co. v Karlshamns Oljefabriker (A/B)* [1949] AC 196). In this way, the principle of causation ensures that the claimant does not recover for losses under the notional pretext that a breach has occurred.

Remoteness

The principle of remoteness clearly limits the recovery of losses directly caused by the breach. The courts have adopted a test which limits recoverable loss to that which was in the reasonable contemplation of the parties as liable to result from the particular breach (see *The Heron II*).

The knowledge of the parties is the determining factor and can be illustrated by a comparison of the following two cases. In *Diamond v Campbell-Jones* [1961]

Ch 22 the defendant, in breach of contract, refused to sell a house to the plaintiff. The defendant knew that the plaintiff was a dealer in real property but not that he intended to redevelop the premises, converting them into offices and flats. It was held that, as the defendant did not possess any knowledge of the plaintiff's specific intentions, he was not liable for the loss of redevelopment profits. Conversely, in *Cottrill v Steyning & Littlehampton Building Society* [1966] 1 WLR 753, the vendor of a hotel knew that the purchaser intended to convert the premises into flats, as well as erecting a further six houses on the land. It was held that in refusing to sell the hotel, in breach of contract, the vendor was liable to pay damages assessed upon the lost redevelopment potential. It can be seen that in both cases the defendant *caused* the plaintiff's losses, but that the defendants' state of knowledge was crucial in determining whether the court would award their full recovery (see also *Seven Seas Properties Ltd v Al-Essa (No. 2)* [1993] 3 All ER 577). (Note: a comparison of any two cases would have sufficed in this context, e.g. *Horne v Midland Railway* (1873) LR 8 CP 131 versus *Simpson v L & NW Railway* (1876) 1 QBD 274.)

Recovery of Losses

There are three general issues which arise under this heading: the recovery of non-pecuniary loss, the general duty imposed on the claimant to mitigate his losses, and the recent developments in the way loss is calculated.

With regard to the first aspect, there are clear limitations on the recovery of such losses. In the seminal case of *Addis v Gramophone Co. Ltd* [1909] AC 488, the House of Lords stated in general terms that damages for injured feelings were not recoverable in a pure contract action. This blanket prohibition was eventually questioned, with the current position being that non-pecuniary losses (e.g. disappointment) are recoverable provided only that *one* of the main objects of the contract is the provision of enjoyment, peace of mind or freedom of distress, such as occurs with a standard holiday contract (e.g. *Jarvis v Swan Tours Ltd* [1973] 1 QB 233). Nevertheless, these types of damages are exceptional as illustrated by the position in most commercial contracts where even the clearest indication that the claimant will suffer psychological trauma as a consequence of the breach will not be compensated (see *Bliss v SE Thames Regional Health Authority* [1987] ICR 700; *Hayes v James and Charles Dodd* [1990] 2 All ER 815). The *Bliss* decision demonstrates that the current limitations that are being imposed are not explicable by recourse to the principle of remoteness (i.e. the defendant could easily have been expected to contemplate such losses) but are referable to wider policy considerations. However, the more relaxed approach of the House of Lords in *Farley v Skinner* [2001] UKHL 49 and the recovery of damages for mental distress in *Hamilton Jones v*

David & Snape [2003] EWHC 3147, [2004] 1 All ER 657, may presage some changes in this area.

(Note: the good student might also consider the difficulties of recovering damages for injured reputation, that being the basis for an action in tort. A summary of the general principle linked to a couple of exceptions might demonstrate to the examiner a useful breadth of knowledge, e.g. the dishonour of cheques and *Gibbons v Westminster Bank Ltd* [1939] 2 KB 882; *Kpoharor v Woolwich Building Society* [1996] 4 All ER 119; damage to reputation and *Anglo-Continental Holidays Ltd v Typaldos Lines* (London) Ltd [1967] 2 Lloyd's Rep 61; or even damage to personal reputation and *McLeish v Amoo-Gottfried*, above.)

Secondly, even if the loss which the claimant has suffered is recoverable in principle, damages will be reduced on evidence that the victim failed to mitigate his loss properly. This duty requires the claimant to act reasonably in trying to minimize his loss and not to act unreasonably in increasing his loss. Available precedent suggests that the claimant need only adopt a reasonable course of action rather than the *most* reasonable course of action. Thus, an employee who is wrongfully dismissed must take reasonable steps to find another, hopefully comparable, position. But he would not be expected to accept an offer of re-engagement from his original employer where his original dismissal occurred in particularly humiliating circumstances (compare *Payzu v Saunders* [1919] 2 KB 581 with *Brace v Calder* [1895] 2 KB 253). One can justify this rule of mitigation on the following grounds: either that a claimant's inaction causes the loss to occur rather than the defendant's being in breach, or that the defendant reasonably contemplated that the claimant would wish to minimize his loss rather than seek redress through the courts (but see *White & Carter (Councils) Ltd v McGregor* [1962] AC 413). Either way, the effect is seemingly that the defendant should not be liable for losses which are not of his own making.

Finally, current case law demonstrates that courts are willing to devise novel mechanisms for compensating a claimant where the traditional methods of calculating damages might lead to injustice. For example, in *Attorney-General v Blake* [2001] 1 AC 268 damages were awarded against the defendant equivalent to the profits which the defendant had secured in publishing his memoirs as an ex-employee of the UK Secret Intelligence Service in breach of his undertaking of confidentiality, even though the information no longer remained confidential. The normal rules for the award of damages suggested that the claimant had not suffered a pecuniary loss, but the House of Lords held that the claimant possessed a *legitimate interest* in preventing publication of the said memoirs for reasons of staff morale and the need to discourage revelations from other employees, the account of profits securing those twin aims. Similar innovations can be observed in the line of cases stemming from *Wrotham Park Estate Co. Ltd v Parkside Homes Ltd* [1974] 2 All ER 321 where courts have been prepared to award damages based on the release of a hypothetical order for specific performance, or a hypothetically negotiated payment for the relaxation of an existing covenant within a contract (e.g. *Lane v O'Brien Homes Ltd* [2004] EWHC 303, [2004] All ER (D) 61 and *WWF-World Wide Fund for Nature v World Wrestling Federation Entertainment Inc.* [2006] EWHC 184 (Ch), [2006] All ER (D) 212).

Conclusion

The foregoing analysis demonstrates the limits on the recovery of loss caused by the defendant's breach. In a commercial sense it seems fair that the defendant should not be liable for losses which he could never have contemplated. Both parties take risks when entering into a contract and part of the allocation of those risks is that non-recoverable loss might be suffered by the victim of a breach. Conversely, recent case law, such as *Blake*, has demonstrated that courts are prepared to bend those rules where a purposeful breach of contract leaves the claimant without any damages under traditional principles. In so doing, the law continues to reflect the ever present tension between the layman's assumption that all losses flowing from a breach of contract should be compensated and the economist's view that a contract represents a man-made instrument of risk allocation in which the precise reimbursement of loss for breach is often of secondary importance to the strategic commercial imperatives governing the original process of contract formation.

Further Reading

Case-notes

Farley v Skinner [2001] UKHL 49, [2002] 2 AC 732
Capper, 'Damages for Distress and Disappointment—Problem Solved' (2002) 118 LQR 193

Transfield Shipping Inc. v Mercator Shipping Inc., The Achilleas [2008] UKHL 48, [2008] 4 All ER 159
O'Sullivan, 'Damages for Lost Profits for Late Redelivery: How Remote is Remote?' (2009) 68 CLJ 34
Kramer, 'The New Test of Remoteness in Contract' [2009] 125 LQR 408

Ruxley Electronics and Construction Ltd v Forsyth [1996] 1 AC 34
Coote, 'Contract Damages, Ruxley and the Performance Interest' (1997) 56 CLJ 537
Poole, 'Damages for Breach of Contract—Compensation and "Personal Preferences"' (1996) 59 MLR 272

Articles (see also *Chapter 12: additional remedies*)

Cartwright, 'Remoteness of Damage in Contract and Tort: A Reconsideration' (1996) 55 CLJ 488
Chandler & Devenney, 'Breach of Contract and the Expectation Deficit: Inconvenience and Disappointment' [2007] LS 126

Friedmann, 'The Performance Interest in Contract Damages' (1995) 111 LQR 628

Harris, Ogus & Phillips, 'Contract Remedies and the Consumer Surplus' (1979) 95 LQR 581

McKendrick, 'Breach of Contract and the Meaning of Loss' [1999] Current Legal Problems 53

Tettenborn, 'Hadley v Baxendale Foreseeability: a Principle Beyond Its Sell-By Date?' (2007) 23 JCL 120

12

Additional remedies

Introduction

The standard common law remedy of damages will not always prove adequate for the victim of a breach of contract; for example, how can a court estimate the damages payable to the buyer of a unique artefact, unavailable elsewhere, when the seller refuses to part with its possession (see *Falcke v Gray* (1859) 4 Drew 651—the sale of two china jars)? Equity therefore developed a number of additional remedies, discretionary in nature, aimed at ensuring that a claimant was not unreasonably confined to an award of damages; in particular, specific performance and injunctions.

In addition, the fast-developing law of restitution offers remedies which can prove even more attractive to claimants. Traditionally the courts have allowed for the recovery of money paid on grounds of failure of consideration, as well as the provision of a *quantum meruit* for work carried out and services rendered, as the acquisition of a benefit at the expense of the other contracting party potentially represents a form of 'unjust enrichment'. More recently, courts have been prepared to consider the award of 'restitutionary damages', *seemingly* based on the recovery of gains secured by the defendant as opposed to, or in excess of, any loss suffered by the claimant. Controversy surrounds whether this remedy should be viewed as simply another form of damages, governed by the overriding principle of reasonable compensation for foreseeable loss. For the present, the topic will be located in this chapter as the underlying remedy is more akin to a claimant seeking *restitution* of the defendant's 'profit' rather than *compensation* for his own loss.

Specific Performance

An order for specific performance will compel the addressee to fulfil the terms of a contract. These terms must be positive in nature (e.g. to deliver goods), whereas negative stipulations are normally enforced by an injunction (e.g. a restraint of trade clause).

Any question concerning specific performance inevitably requires a consideration of three issues. First, where damages are an adequate remedy, an order for specific performance will rarely be granted, such as the claimant being able to acquire an equivalent performance from a third party (e.g. obtaining substitute goods from another source—see *Societe des Industries Metallurgiques SA v The Bronx Engineering Co. Ltd* [1975] 1 Lloyd's Rep 465). Conversely, if the quantum of damages is difficult to assess or, as occurred in *Beswick v Beswick* [1968] AC 58, the award of damages would be unfair to the claimant, specific relief will be granted. Courts have even awarded specific performance where there was a serious doubt over whether the defendant would have sufficient funds to pay any damages awarded (e.g. *Evans Marshall & Co. Ltd v Bertola SA* [1973] 1 All ER 992).

Secondly, there are many reasons why the court might refuse an order in the exercise of its equitable discretion, such as if there is a lack of mutuality (see *Sutton v Sutton* [1984] 1 All ER 168) or the claimant has acted unfairly (see *Walters v Morgan* (1861) 3 DF & J 718).

Finally, there are certain types of contracts where an order would normally be refused; for example, personal service contracts and building contracts. The former is generally justifiable on the grounds that the mutual trust and confidence that exists between the parties has irretrievably broken down (especially in employment contracts). As for the latter, it results from the difficulty of continually supervising the building work (i.e. enforcing the order) and often because damages provide an adequate remedy.

Injunctions

An injunction seeks to restrain the defendant from committing a breach of contract, and is therefore framed as a negative stipulation (e.g. preventing a departing employee from breaching a restraint of trade clause in the original employment contract—see **Chapter 9**). If the injunction is prohibitive in nature (restraining a *future* breach) a court, in the exercise of its discretion, will not be influenced by the fact that the defendant's compliance with the injunction would be unduly onerous or that the breach would cause the claimant little prejudice (see *Marco Productions Ltd v Pagola* [1945] KB 111). However, if the injunction is mandatory in nature, requiring the defendant to reverse the effects of an *existing* breach, a court will apply the 'balance of convenience test', refusing relief if the hardship caused to the defendant by compliance with the order outweighs the consequential advantages to the claimant and/or damages would prove to be an adequate remedy in the circumstances.

The basic rule is that an injunction will not be awarded if it would compel the defendant to perform acts which in themselves cannot form the basis of an order for specific performance, such as an employer seeking to enforce a restraint clause in such a way that the employee's only option is to work for the employer (see *Ehrman v Bartholomew* [1898] 1 Ch 671). However, there are exceptions to this basic rule as will be outlined in **Question 1** of this chapter.

Damages in Equity

Under s. 2 of the **Chancery Amendment Act 1858** (**Lord Cairns Act—LCA**), a Court of Chancery has a discretion to award damages in lieu of, or in addition to specific performance (or injunction) provided the contract is of a type that is specifically enforceable (see now s. 50 **Supreme Court Act 1981**). Moreover, under s. 49 of the **Supreme**

Court Act, 1981, a claim to specific performance (or injunction) can be combined with claims for damages, thereby rendering it unnecessary to resort to those special powers originally contained in the LCA. Finally, the assessment of damages under the LCA or under the common law is identical (see *Johnson v Agnew* [1979] 2 WLR 487), although this cannot apply where there is no *existing* common law action such as where specific relief is sought to prevent *future* breaches (e.g. *Jaggard v Sawyer* [1995] 1 WLR 269).

Restitution

The modern law of restitution is primarily rooted in the notion of unjust enrichment (see generally *Lipkin Gorman v Karpnale Ltd* [1991] 2 AC 548). Traditionally, restitutionary relief has been linked to those situations where the defendant has secured a gain/benefit from his breach of contract (almost certainly *at the expense* of the claimant) and its retention would be unjust in the circumstances, there being no defence or bar to the claim (e.g. such as it being a gift). Three of the more common examples of permitted restitution are:

- the recovery of the contract price on grounds of total failure of consideration, such as in *Fibrosa Spolka Akcyjna v Fairburn Lawson Combe Barbour Ltd* [1943] AC 32 where the contract was frustrated before any goods had been delivered, or *Guinness Mahon & Co. Ltd v Kensington & Chelsea RLBC* [1999] QB 215 where the contract was void for illegality. In this context, the term 'failure of consideration' refers to a failure to perform the actual promise(s), rather than the existence of consideration at the moment of contract formation. Naturally, faced with a total failure of consideration, the claimant may prefer to sue for breach of contract (if available) rather than seek reimbursement of the contract price. The ultimate decision will depend on the predicted benefits of either action (e.g. if the contract would have turned out to be loss-making for the claimant, securing restitution of the original contract price would appear to be more advantageous);

- the award of a *quantum meruit,* representing the value of services rendered or goods supplied in circumstances where insufficient payment has been received or incomplete performance was tendered. This remedy is now embodied in such statutes as the **Sale of Goods Act 1979** (s. 8) and the **Supply of Goods and Services Act 1982** (s. 15) but has its origin in situations where one of the parties had abandoned performance of the contract prior to completion, yet a benefit had already been transferred (via partial performance). The recipient of this benefit (whether the innocent party, or the party in breach) may be required to pay a fair price for this benefit. Use of *quantum meruit* even extends to situations where no valid contract ever existed; for example, in *British Steel Corporation v Cleveland Bridge & Engineering Co. Ltd* [1948] 1 ALL ER 504 the absence of a clear offer and acceptance prevented a contract coming into being but still enabled the plaintiff to secure a *quantum meruit* for work already carried out *at the request of* the defendant; and,

- payment made under a mistake whereby recovery is permissible provided it was the 'mistake' that caused the original payment to have been made and the payment would not have been made if the payer had known the true position at the time. In *Kleinwort Benson Ltd v Lincoln* CC [1999] 2 AC 349, the House of Lords went further by allowing for recovery irrespective of whether the mistake was one of law or fact (see also *Deutsche Morgan Grenfell Group plc v Inland Revenue Commissioners* [2006] UKHL 49, [2007] 1 AC 558).

More recently, the development of 'restitutionary damages' (perhaps erroneously referred to as an 'account of profits') has added a potent weapon to the court's armoury, with damages being awarded where the defendant, in breach of contract, has been unjustly enriched yet the claimant has suffered no measurable loss. Previously, this type of claim had received short shrift from the courts, best exemplified in *Surrey County Council v Bredero Homes Ltd* [1993] 3 All ER 705 where the Court of Appeal refused to order the disgorgement of profits (secured by the defendant in breach of its contract with the plaintiff) on grounds that the plaintiff found itself in the same position as if the contract had been properly performed. Admittedly, exceptions already existed where a form of restitutionary damages had been awarded on grounds that the defendant had secured an unjust gain, predominantly at the expense of the claimant; for example, the retention of goods or buildings beyond the period of their hire/letting (e.g. *Swordheath Properties Ltd v Tabet* [1979] 1 WLR 285), the receipt of a bribe by an agent, an employee's gain resulting from the misuse of his employer's confidential information (e.g. *Robb v Green* [1895] 2 QB 315), or the defendant's gain secured by wrongly ignoring the legitimate property interests of the claimant (e.g. *Wrotham Park Estate Co. Ltd v Parkside Homes Ltd* [1974] 1 WLR 798). However, to this list we must now add the decision of the House of Lords in *Attorney-General v Blake* [2001] 1 AC 268 which seemingly extended the principles established in *Wrotham Park* to a much wider category of cases.

So what is the present state of the law on 'restitutionary damages'? First, a court may order a partial disgorgement of profits which has resulted from a breach of contract. The actual sum payable will represent what the claimant would have charged the defendant in order for the latter to be released from an existing contractual undertaking (e.g. *Experience Hendrix LLC v PPX Enterprises Inc. and Edward Chaplin* [2003] EWCA Civ 323, [2003] EMLR 25). Secondly, the decision in *Blake* recognizes that damages can be measured by the benefit the defendant has secured from a breach of contract, with disgorgement of *all* profits being possible in *exceptional* cases. This principle is not apparently limited to a defendant's interference with the claimant's property interests, nor is it predicated on some type of fiduciary or quasi-fiduciary relationship existing between the parties. Rather, the relevant considerations for this award include the availability/adequacy of other remedies, the level of intent displayed by the defendant (e.g. was it a purposeful breach in order to secure a profit?), and the 'legitimate interest' of the claimant in preventing the defendant from profiting from the deliberate breach—such considerations surely being too broad, as yet, to allow for the accurate prediction of future case law developments.

Finally, the most up-to-date analysis of this confusing body of case law is provided by Chadwick LJ in *WWF-World Wide Fund for Nature (formerly World Wildlife Fund) and another v World Wrestling Federation Entertainment Inc.* [2007] EWCA Civ 286,

[2007] 1 All ER 74. This case (considered in greater depth in **Question 2** of this chapter) raises two interesting points. First, that damages which are intended to reflect either the disgorgement of some/all of any breach-induced profits (*Blake*), or what the claimant might have charged for releasing the defendant from an existing contractual undertaking (*Wrotham Park*), are considered to be 'juridically highly similar'. Secondly, that the damages awarded in both *Blake* and *Wrotham Park* are compensatory rather than restitutionary in nature, although whether the recovery of all profits in *Blake* can truly be considered compensatory remains a moot point. If the analysis adopted in *WWF* proves correct in the long term, an examination of the above cases will need to be reserved solely for the previous chapter, but this area is fast-moving and to predicate the categorization of such 'damages' on a single Court of Appeal decision remains highly problematic at present.

Question 1

The circumstances in which a court may be prepared to order specific performance or grant an injunction are so limited as to make such remedies almost superfluous nowadays.
  Discuss.

Commentary

Never be fooled by a question that is seemingly encouraging you to adopt a particular stance. Essay questions certainly give you an opportunity to reveal the extent of your knowledge, but their primary purpose is to see how you can use that knowledge to produce a well thought-out argument that is directed towards defending or attacking a particular proposition. It is probably worth noting that it is very unlikely a question would be set exclusively on equitable remedies. Rather, some aspect may arise in a damages question. For an example, see **Chapter 14** in which equitable remedies form *part* of a mixed question.

Answer plan

- What factors influence a court in making an order of specific performance?
- Give examples where a court would refuse to make such an order based on the adequacy of damages or the problems of enforcing specific types of contracts. Have there been any recent changes in judicial outlook?
- Why is injunctive relief more likely where the breach refers to a negative stipulation within the contract? Have there been any recent developments?
- What other options are available to a court, such as the **Chancery Amendment Act 1858 (Lord Cairns Act)**?

Suggested answer

Specific Performance

An order of specific performance is perceived by courts as a drastic remedy. For example, in many instances it will involve some form of personal constraint over the defendant. The courts are therefore cautious in granting such an order: 'The court gives specific performance instead of damages, only when it can by that means do more perfect and complete justice' (*Wilson v Northampton and Banbury Junction Ry Co.* (1874) 9 Ch App 279 at 284 *per* Lord Selborne). In particular, a court will pose the following questions: Are damages an adequate remedy? How should the court use its discretion? Is the contract of a type that is specifically enforceable?

Damages are an Adequate Remedy

The critical first stage is to persuade a court that damages are not a reasonable substitute for specific performance. A court would normally prefer the claimant to go through the standard route of mitigation in order to minimize the loss arising from a breach rather than hide behind an enforcement order and do nothing. Consequently, specific performance of contracts of sale are rarely ordered where they involve goods that are readily available in the market. In the face of non-delivery, a purchaser will be expected to purchase the required goods elsewhere, and if the alternative source charges a higher price, or the purchaser is put to costly inconvenience, the court can award damages to cover these items. In short, damages would be considered an adequate remedy. Conversely, if the purchaser finds that he cannot obtain a satisfactory substitute elsewhere, damages will be viewed as inadequate (see *Phillips v Lamdin* [1949] 2 KB 33, at 41, involving the wrongful removal of an Adam door). Other examples of inadequacy potentially include the speculative nature of the claimed damages, the difficulty of proving loss, or the irrecoverability of the claimed loss in law (see generally *Decro-Wall International SA v Practitioners in Marketing Ltd SA* [1971] 1 WLR 361).

However, more recent case authority suggests a relaxation in this approach, presaging a greater use of enforcement orders. In *Laemthong Lines Co. Ltd v Artis (The Laemthong Glory) (No. 2)* [2005] EWCA 519, [2005] 1 Lloyd's Rep 632, specific performance was ordered as the assessment of damages in similar circumstances had not been 'an entirely straightforward matter'. More importantly, in *Thames Valley Power Tool Ltd v Total Gas and Power Ltd* [2005] EWHC 2208, [2006] 1 Lloyd's Rep 441 the defendant sought to be released from an obligation to supply gas to the claimant for 15 years, at a rate that was subject to a complicated formula, on grounds of *force majeure*. This argument was rejected and, seemingly, the obligation to supply the gas was specifically enforced as the original contract had been based on the claimant's need to receive gas from a first-rate supplier for a minimum period of time. Put another way, as the claimant would not have been able to secure supply from an equivalent, substitute source, damages were an inadequate remedy. A separate justification revolved around the difficulty of calculating future losses and the delay that might be encountered in obtaining payment of any damages.

Judicial Discretion

A court also possesses a broad discretion when deciding whether or not to order specific performance: 'Equity will only grant specific performance if, under all the circumstances, it is just and equitable to do so' (see *Stickney v Keeble* [1915] AC 386 at 419). Nevertheless, an order will only be made if: (i) the contract could also be enforced by the defendant, at the time of the hearing (see *Sutton v Sutton* [1984] 1 All ER 168); (ii) the defendant can comply with the order (see *Watts v Spence* [1976] Ch 165—sale of land not owned by the vendor; *The Sea Hawk* [1986] 1 WLR 657—defendant owned no assets within the court's jurisdiction); (iii) the claimant has not taken unfair advantage of the defendant or has acted dishonestly (e.g. negotiating with a drunkard) or in some other unconscionable way (compare *Watkin v Watson-Smith* (1986) CLY 424 with *Shell UK Ltd v Lostock Garages Ltd* [1976] 1 WLR 1187); and (iv) it will not cause the defendant *severe* hardship (see *Patel v Ali* [1984] Ch 283), or the costs of performance are not wholly disproportionate to the benefit conferred on the claimant (see *Tito v Waddell (No. 2)* [1977] Ch 106 at 326). On a general note the claimant who seeks specific relief must not delay too long as the doctrine of *laches* may operate to bar his claim. The above cases and examples demonstrate the overarching fairness of the existing judicial approach to specific performance of a contract. The possibilities of enforcement are wide-ranging, but their use is significantly influenced by the individual circumstances of both parties. Recent cases have not undermined that approach.

Specific Types of Contracts

Finally, there are certain types of contracts that courts prefer not to enforce, such as a contract of personal service. Thus employees cannot be forced to work for their employer and an employer who is found to have unfairly dismissed an employee cannot be compelled to reinstate or re-engage him—as shown by part X of the Employment Rights Act 1996 which assumes that a recalcitrant employer will simply be ordered to pay damages for failure to re-instate (notwithstanding ss. 69–71 of the Employment Protection (Consolidation) Act 1978, as amended by the Employment Act 1980, s. 5 and Sch. 1). Indeed, this exception encompasses other types of personal service contracts such as partnerships. The courts are also wary of enforcing contractual performance where constant supervision would be required. For example, in *Ryan v Mutual Tontine Association* [1893] 1 Ch 116 the lease of a service flat gave the tenant a right to have a porter 'constantly in attendance'. The court was not prepared to supervise such activities on a daily basis and therefore refused to grant an enforcement order. Similar considerations apply to cases involving building contracts, particularly as supervision is rendered more difficult as a result of general imprecision in most building specifications. Yet here again, the courts have shown greater flexibility in this regard. In *Co-operative Insurance Society Ltd v Argyll Stores (Holdings) Ltd* [1998] AC 1 the House of Lords stated its disquiet with any refusal of an enforcement order based *solely* on the need for constant supervision, helpfully highlighting the difference between supervision of an ongoing 'activity' and a 'result', the latter being far easier to execute. Since then, courts have been prepared to enforce building/repair obligations where the required work could be described with greater certainty (e.g. *Rainbow Estates Ltd v Tokenhold Ltd* [1999] Ch 64), whilst in *Thames Valley Power* (see above) the potential problems of supervising the maintenance of a gas supply contract that still had five years to run were seemingly ignored by the court.

The above comments potentially augur a subtle adjustment in the mindset of judges, suggesting at the very least that orders of specific performance remain an important remedy for dealing with contract breaches. Can the same be said for the use of injunctions?

Injunctions

Traditionally, an injunction will be refused if it would compel the defendant to perform acts which could not form the basis of a decree of specific performance (e.g. a contract of personal service—see *Chappell v Times Newspapers Ltd* [1975] 1 WLR 482). There are some important exceptions to the general rule, although no recent case developments would suggest any significant expansion of this list.

First, if the contract contains a negative stipulation it may be possible for the injunction to be framed in such a way as to enforce this negative aspect without compelling positive performance of the whole contract. For example, consider what happens when an existing employee resigns in order to take up employment with another firm. The ex-employer now wishes to enforce an existing restraint clause which prevents ex-employees working for competing firms within a specified area. A properly framed injunction could enforce this negative obligation without forcing the employee to work for his old employer; for example, he could find work outside the specified area or join a non-competing firm (see *Fitch v Dewes* [1921] 2 AC 158; *Littlewoods Organisation Ltd v Harris* [1977] 1 WLR 1472). However, the employee must possess a reasonable, alternative way of earning his living otherwise an injunction serves as a disguised form of specific performance (see generally *Page One Records v Britton* [1968] 1 WLR 157).

Secondly, except in contracts of personal service, courts have been prepared to *imply* negative stipulations even though the contract as a whole may not be specifically enforceable. Thus in *Associated Portland Cement Manufacturers Ltd v Teigland Shipping A/S* [1975] 1 Lloyd's Rep 581, an injunction was granted to prevent a shipowner from employing a ship under charter in ways that were inconsistent with the charterparty.

Thirdly, a negative stipulation which is too wide can be severed and enforced in part. For example, in *Warner Bros Pictures Inc. v Nelson* [1937] 1 KB 209, the defendant undertook not to act for third parties without the plaintiff's consent nor to 'engage in any other occupation' without requisite permission. The latter undertaking was considered unenforceable as it would force the defendant, an actress, to work for her existing employer, but an injunction was awarded to enforce the former obligation.

Naturally, the courts are not compelled to adopt an 'either/or' approach to the award of damages or specific performance/injunction. Although s. 50 of the Supreme Court Act 1981 (SCA 1981) allows courts to award damages in lieu of, or in substitution for specific performance and injunction (see previously s. 2 of the Chancery Amendment Act 1858—known as Lord Cairns Act), s. 49 of the SCA 1981 also continues to permit courts to entertain a *combined* claim to damages and specific performance or injunction. Consequently, a court can prevent future breaches via the grant of an injunction whilst compensating a claimant for past breaches via the award of damages (see *Experience Hendrix LLC v PPX Enterprises Inc. and Edward Chaplin* [2003] EWCA Civ 323, [2003] EMLR 25).

In conclusion, the above comments clearly suggest that specific performance and injunctions perform an important role in policing breaches of contract, even if damages remains the judicial remedy of choice in breach of contract actions, their adequacy being the critical issue. In particular, the decisions in *Laemthong* and *Thames Valley Power* emphasize the continuing importance of specific performance, perhaps reflecting the fact that our European civil law neighbours consider this remedy to be the *starting point* for relief, rather than at common law where damages remains the primary remedy for dealing with breaches of contract.

Question 2

The concept of 'restitutionary damages', as exemplified in *Attorney-General v Blake* [2001] 1 AC 268, displaces the standard rules for assessing recoverable loss in a breach of contract action in favour of measuring the claimant's loss by the value of the defendant's unjust enrichment. Discuss.

Commentary

The concept of 'restitutionary' damages is a relatively new innovation in contract law jurisprudence. It represents an interesting addition to the judicial armoury as it focuses more on the potential gains that a contract-breaker secures from his actions, rather than the losses (expectation or reliance) sustained by the victim. For the present, it is extremely difficult to predict how this area of law will develop, but one can assume that it will surface in many Contract Law examination papers, or coursework, over the next few years. The most important thing to remember is that the use of the word 'restitutionary' in this context remains a hotly contested topic of debate in the academic fraternity as it is unclear whether the defendant is being asked to:

(i) restore unjustly acquired profits to the victim; or

(ii) reimburse the victim for the latter's reliance losses (i.e. return the victim to his original position); or

(iii) pay a sum of money equivalent to that which the victim would have charged the defendant for release from an existing legal/contractual duty.

The phrase 'there is never one answer' is never more apposite than in this area.

 ## Answer plan

- What is meant by the phrase 'standard rules for assessing recoverable loss in a breach of contract action'?

- What were the facts of *Attorney-General v Blake* and what decision did the House of Lords reach?

- Have subsequent decisions interpreted *Attorney-General v Blake* expansively or sought to limit its application?

- Did *Blake* represent a fundamental departure from existing precedent in that the damages were restitutionary, rather than compensatory, in nature?

- What is the future for 'restitutionary damages'? Will it prove irrelevant to mainstream litigation?

Suggested answer

The primary purpose of awarding damages for breach of contract is to ensure that the victim is compensated for his or her losses, provided those losses would have been reasonably contemplated as liable to result from that breach (at the time of contract formation). The court will seek to place the victim, so far as money can do this, in the position he should have occupied if the contract had been properly performed (*Robinson v Harman* (1848) 1 Ex 850). Such damages therefore compensate the victim for lost expectations although, where such expectations are difficult to value, the courts have been prepared to award reliance damages as a substitute (e.g. *McRae v Commonwealth Disposals Commission* (1951) 84 CLR 377). In either situation, as damages are intended to offset the victim's loss, rather than punish the defendant for his breach, damages will be purely nominal if the claimant has suffered no loss. Nor does the award of damages predicated on the claimant's lost consumer 'surplus' (e.g. *Jarvis v Swan Tours Ltd* [1973] 1 QB 233) change the above approach as this perceived loss simply represents the value that a court would have attributed to the claimant's known, subjective expectation (e.g. the level of enjoyment anticipated from going on a pre-booked holiday). This last point is perhaps best illustrated by *Ruxley Electronics v Forsyth* [1996] AC 344 (HL) where the plaintiff was awarded damages for loss of an 'enjoyable amenity' arising from the installation of a swimming pool that failed to conform to the original contract specification in terms of its required depth, the consequent restriction on diving into the pool thereby potentially limiting the plaintiff's level of enjoyment from its use.

Clearly the historical focus of the courts on compensating the claimant for actual losses necessarily diverts attention from those circumstances where the defendant has purposely breached the contract in order to secure an additional benefit or profit, yet the claimant has apparently suffered no financial loss. It is arguable that in *Attorney-General v Blake* [2001] 1 AC 268 the House of Lords sought to address this omission. The facts were that the defendant, a former member of MI5, had defected to the Soviet Union where he had written his autobiography. Publication of this book in England was a breach of the defendant's former employment contract. The Law Lords held that, in exceptional circumstances, where the normal basis for damages provided inadequate compensation, and particularly where the discretionary remedies of specific performance and injunctions were unavailable (the autobiography had already been published), the defendant could be compelled to account to the victim for any benefits secured from the breach. Such damages would protect the claimant's 'interest in performance' and was analogous to previous case law where damages had been awarded for invasion of another's property rights (but without any correlative diminution in the value of those rights), or where the contract-breaker had been forced to account for secret profits acquired during the performance of fiduciary duties (e.g. *Mahesan v Malaysia Government Officers' Co-op Housing Society Ltd* [1979] AC 374).

At first glance the approach adopted in *Blake* seems to follow the earlier decision in *Wrotham Park Estate Co Ltd v Parkside Homes Ltd* [1974] 1 WLR 798 where a form of 'gains-based' damages had been awarded for the breach of contract (albeit the breach was inextricably linked to the plaintiffs underlying *property* rights—see above). Specifically, the defendant builders in *Wrotham* were ordered to pay the plaintiffs 5% of the anticipated profits resulting from their intentional breach of a restrictive covenant, such damages representing the sum of money which the plaintiffs could have reasonably demanded for relaxation of the covenant (see also *Bracewell v Appleby* [1975] 1 Ch 408). However, *Blake* appeared to go much further, as the Crown successfully recovered *all* of the defendant's profits. How could this be justified? Lord Nicholls, representing the majority view, appeared to emphasize the quasi-fiduciary nature of the parties' employment relationship: the defendant's breach of confidentiality fundamentally undermined the morale and trust of existing MI5 personnel and their informers, and, more importantly, the general operational effectiveness of the intelligence services. Beyond that, Lord Nicholl's speech was rather short on detail, although one can draw a number of very general conclusions. First, this type of award could only be justified in *exceptional* circumstances. Secondly, a claimant would need to establish the existence of a *legitimate interest* that enabled the prevention of the defendant's profit-making activity. Finally, evidence of 'skimped perform-ance', or proof that the defendant had profited by doing the very thing he had contracted not to do, was insufficient *per se* to be considered 'exceptional'.

Although *Blake* was initially viewed as a 'one-off' decision, it was followed soon after by *Esso Petroleum Co. Ltd v Niad Ltd* [2001] EWHC 6, [2001] All ER (D) 324. Here, the parties had entered into a petrol solus agreement, with the claimant also providing a monetary inducement to each of its tied custom-ers, including the defendants, to charge specified (and lower) petrol prices to its forecourt customers. On proof that the defendants had failed to discount the forecourt price, the court awarded 'restitutionary damages', following *Blake*, compelling the defendant to reimburse the claimants for all previous monetary inducements received as part of the original scheme. No attempt was made to jus-tify this award on grounds that it represented the price for which the defendants would have paid for being released from an existing contractual commitment (i.e. adoption of a *Wrotham Park* analysis). Undoubtedly *Niad* prompts some obvious questions; in particular, whether the circumstances were sufficiently 'exceptional' (as *per Blake*) to enable a court to award restitutionary damages. However, what remains clear is that the court's assessment of damages was predicated on the defendant's gain rather than the claimant's financial loss. Nor does the subsequent decision in *Experience Hendrix LLC v PPX Enterprises Inc.* [2003] EWCA Civ 323, [2003] EMLR 515, affect this interpretation as, on the facts, the court's refusal in that case to order an account of the defendant's profits (secured from a breach of an existing copyright licence agreement between the parties) followed on from its conclusion that the facts were not sufficiently *exceptional* to warrant such an award. In particular, there was no existing fiduciary relationship between the parties, the intentional breaches took place in an ordinary commercial con-text, and alternative remedies were available; consequently, damages represented no more than the sum that might reasonably have been demanded by the claimant for releasing the defendant from its relevant contractual restrictions.

We are therefore left with the problem of identifying the basis upon which damages were awarded in *Blake*. Clearly any suggestion that the damages were punitive in nature should be dismissed outright—the defendant had been compelled to give up all profits received or expected, but there was never any question of an additional financial penalty being imposed. Consequently, in the aftermath of *Blake*, only two possible interpretations have emerged:

(i) the decision was simply a logical extension of *Wrotham Park* and therefore represented a new method of *compensating* the claimant for a breach of contract which nevertheless complied with the overriding approach advocated in *Robinson v Harman*; or

(ii) the decision represented a form of restitutionary relief (akin to an account of profits) in which the level of damages was determined by the size of the defendant's gains rather than the hypothetical amount the claimant might have charged for releasing the defendant from an existing contractual commitment.

As a starting point, the current weight of authority clearly favours the view that compensatory damages were awarded in *Wrotham Park*—an important conclusion because so much of the analysis contained in *Blake* relies upon this case. These damages seemingly reflected the plaintiff's loss rather than the defendant's gain. Indeed, in *Jaggard v Sawyer* [1994] EWCA Civ 1, [1995] 1 WLR 269, Sir Thomas Bingham pointed out that the court in *Wrotham Park* had been influenced by the level of the defendants' profits *not* for the purposes of stripping them of *those* profits but, rather, because it provided a suitable context within which to identify the amount they would have been willing to pay to secure a release from the relevant contractual commitment (see also *Gafford v Graham* [1998] EWCA Civ 666, (1998) 77 P & CR 73). Interestingly, this approach conflicts with the Law Commission's own conclusions (Report No. 247, 1997, *Aggravated, Exemplary and Restitutionary Damages*) in which *Wrotham Park* was viewed as an example of an award of 'restitutionary damages reversing the defendants' unjust enrichment' (at para. 1.36). However, the more important question is whether one can extrapolate from *Jaggard* that the damages awarded in *Blake* were *also* compensatory? Clearly the result achieved in *Niad* suggested otherwise, whilst the court in *Harris v Wynne* [2005] EWHC 151, [2006] 2 P & CR 595 again adopted the label of 'restitutionary damages' as applied to *Blake* (at para. 34) and treated the defendant's 'underhand dealings' as the *sine qua non* for making such an award.

This ongoing debate was most recently visited by the Court of Appeal in *WWF-World Wide Fund for Nature (formerly World Wildlife Fund) v World Wrestling Federation Entertainment Inc.* [2007] EWCA Civ 286, [2007] 1 All ER 74. Here, Chadwick LJ (delivering the main judgment) found 'puzzling' any suggestion that restitutionary damages had been awarded in *Wrotham Park*. His Lordship considered the remedy adopted in *Wrotham Park*, and the account of profits in *Blake*, as being 'juridically highly similar', especially as their common underlying feature was the need to compensate in circumstances where the claimant could not establish an identifiable loss. The implication of these statements is that the dividing line between restitutionary damages and an account of profits is becoming blurred, even if the future direction of judicial pronouncements is, as yet, difficult to predict.

It would therefore seem safer to conclude that *Blake* represents a judicial preparedness to award gains-based damages in exceptional circumstances where the defendant has calculated that a breach of contract will prove beneficial (i.e. the gains will outweigh the probable damages awarded), the claimant suffers no apparent loss (as calculated on conventional grounds), and there is no other remedy available (e.g. specific performance). Whilst *Niad* appears to go much further, it is unlikely to be followed, with the *Blake* principle primarily operating where the parties have an existing fiduciary or quasi-fiduciary relationship, as this will magnify the responsibilities of the defendant in terms of not taking advantage of a dominant position. Notwithstanding the above, a court will always have the power to compensate the victim of a breach of contract in the most effective way possible, said compensation including either the award of damages predicated on the claimant's lost expectation (*Robinson v Harman*), or the costs of his reliance (*McRae v Commonwealth Disposals Commission*), or the deprivation of a financial interest which, on occasion, is best measured by the gains secured by the defendant (*Wrotham Park*). Consequently, the original question is only partly correct. It is true that the damages awarded in *Blake* were measured by the defendant's gain, but this approach can also be adopted in calculating compensatory damages (*Wrotham Park*). In short, the prevailing case law demonstrates that use of the term 'restitutionary damages' is inaccurate because damages measured by the defendant's gain (*Wrotham Park*) is not the same as damages specifically intended to restore *that* gain to the claimant (*Blake*). The former is primarily compensatory whereas the latter is most certainly restitutionary. This analysis is reinforced by posing one simple question. How can damages in *Blake* be viewed as *compensatory* when the parties never concluded a bargain and in no circumstances would have done so (i.e. compensation for loss of bargain was never possible)?

Further Reading

Case-notes

Attorney-General v Blake [2001] 1 AC 268
Fox, 'Restitutionary Damages to Deter Breach of Contract' (2001) 60 CLJ 33

Co-operative Insurance Society Ltd v Argyll Stores (Holdings) Ltd [1998] AC 1
Phang, 'Specific Performance—Exploring the Roots of "Settled Doctrine"' (1998) 61 MLR 421

Jones, 'Specific Performance: A Lessee's Covenant to Keep Open a Retail Store' (1997) 56 CLJ 488

Surrey County Council v Bredero Homes [1993] 3 All ER 705
Birks, 'Profits of Breach of Contract' (1993) 109 LQR 518
Burrows, 'No Restitutionary Damages for Breach of Contract' [1993] LMCLQ 453

Experience Hendrix LLC v PPX Enterprises Inc. and Edward Chaplin [2003] EWCA Civ 323, [2003] EMLR 25
Campbell & Wylie, 'Ain't No Telling (Which Circumstances Are Exceptional)' (2003) 62 CLJ 605

Articles

Cunnington, 'The Assessment of Gains-based Damages for Breach of Contract' (2008) 71 MLR 559

Schwartz, 'The Case for Specific Performance' (1979) 89 Yale LJ 271

Smith, 'Disgorgement of the Profits of Breach of Contract: Property, Contract and "Efficient Breach"' (1995) 24 Can Bar LJ 121

13

Privity of contract

Introduction

The doctrine of privity of contract, which only became entrenched in the latter half of the nineteenth century, is the mechanism by which contractual rights and liabilities are limited to the parties to the contract. The theory is simple: contract is based upon agreement and therefore only the parties to that agreement have consented to contractual responsibility. The common law reasoned that, first, only a promisee may enforce the promise, meaning that if the third party is not a promisee he is not privy to the contract. Thus if A promises B that, in return for a consideration provided by B, A will do something for C, C is not a promisee and is unable to enforce the promise. Secondly, there is the principle that consideration must move from the promisee. Thus A may make a promise to both B and C, with a consideration provided by B, that he will do something for C's benefit. Here C is clearly a promisee but no consideration has moved from him, meaning that he is unable to enforce the promise. The two principles of privity and consideration have become entwined, but the Law Commission has suggested (Privity of Contract: Contracts for the Benefit of Third Parties, Consultation Paper No. 121, 1991) that two separate policy issues can be identified, viz. privity relates to those *who* can enforce a contract whilst consideration concerns the *types* of promise that can be enforced. The leading decisions which should be read are *Tweddle v Atkinson* (1861) 1 B & S 393; *Dunlop Pneumatic Tyre Co. Ltd v Selfridge & Co. Ltd* [1915] AC 847; *Midland Silicones Ltd v Scruttons Ltd* [1962] AC 446.

The Law Commission's provisional suggestions (Consultation Paper No. 121, 1991) were, for the most part, subsequently enacted in the Contracts (**Rights of Third Parties**) **Act 1999**.

Common Law Limitations to the Doctrine of Privity

Where A/B have a contract which seeks to confer a benefit upon C, are there any ways of ensuring that C will secure proper performance of the A/B contract or, alternatively, receive compensation for any losses caused by A or B's breach of the primary contract? The following possibilities currently exist (A being the party in breach):

(a) B may obtain a decree of specific performance against A thereby compelling him to confer the benefit upon C (see *Beswick v Beswick* [1968] AC 58);

(b) B may claim damages from A for any breach of contract that fails to confer the intended benefit upon C. The problem here is to ascertain the measure of damages, one view being that B may only obtain nominal damages as he has suffered no loss (e.g. *West v Houghton* (1879) 4 CPD 197; *Beswick v Beswick, supra*). In *Jackson v Horizon Holidays Ltd* [1975] 1 WLR 1468, the Court of Appeal broke with tradition and allowed a father, who had booked a skiing holiday for his family, to claim damages for the disappointment that the whole family suffered as a consequence of the holiday provider's breach. Subsequently, in *Woodar Investment Development Ltd v Wimpey Construction UK Ltd* [1980] 1 WLR 277 the House of Lords questioned the award in *Jackson*, except insofar as the damages reflected the father's disappointment at his family being disappointed (note that the Package Travel, Package Holidays and Package Tours Regulations 1992, SI No. 3288, reg. 2(2) now state that all named persons in a package holiday contract can sue directly for any breach of contract);

(c) in a commercial contract concerning goods or property, if A/B contemplate that B may transfer the goods/property to a third party (e.g. C), and such transfer occurs prior to any breach by A (or even before A/B entered their contract), B may be treated as if he entered the contract on behalf of C (and subsequent transferees), thereby entitling him to claim damages on behalf of C, calculated on the basis of the latter's actual losses (e.g. *The Albazero* [1977] AC 774; *Linden Gardens Ltd v Lenesta Sludge Disposals Ltd* [1993] 3 All ER 417; and *Darlington BC v Wiltshier Northern Ltd* [1995] 3 All ER 895). Note, however, that this principle presupposes that C has no separate contractual right to sue A for any breach (e.g. *Alfred McAlpine Construction Limited v Panatown Ltd* [2001] AC 518); and,

(d) if A seeks to avoid the consequences of his contract with B by suing C, B may be entitled to obtain an injunction to restrain A. For example, in *Snelling v John G Snelling Ltd* [1973] 1 QB 87 the directors of a company agreed to forfeit any loan that they had made to their company on resigning their posts. The plaintiff director resigned and sought recovery of his loan direct from the company, rather than the directors, but the court awarded a stay of proceedings on application by the remaining directors.

Common Law Attempts to Evade Privity

Trusts

Privity applies only to contracts whereas a trust can attach to property of any kind including choses in action, e.g. rights under contracts. It follows that where A makes a promise to B for the benefit of C, C can enforce the promise if B has constituted himself as trustee of A's promise for C (see *Affréteurs (Les) Réunis SA v Leopold Walford (London) Ltd* [1919] AC 801). However, this exception fell by the wayside because of the strict requirements of constituting a trust; for example, the need for a specific intention on the part of the person declaring the trust that it should be a trust, which the courts are unwilling to imply without clear expression (see *Vandepitte v Preferred Accident Insurance Corp.* [1933] AC 70; *Re Schebsman* [1944] Ch 83).

Restrictive Covenants

In land law a vendor of property may impose restrictive covenants which 'run with the land' and restrict its future use. This was carried over into the law of contract by the Privy Council in *Lord Strathcona SS Co. v Dominion Coal Co.* [1926] AC 108, but the notion has little scope for extension after Diplock J's refusal to follow the decision in *Port Line Ltd v Ben Line Steamers Ltd* [1958] 2 QB 146. Subsequently, in *Law Debenture Trust Corp. plc v Ural Caspian Oil Corp. Ltd* [1993] 2 All ER 355, Hoffmann J held that this concept did not provide 'a panacea for outflanking the doctrine of privity of contract'. Moreover, the principle solely permits the grant of a negative injunction to restrain the person acquiring the property from doing acts which would be inconsistent with the performance of the contract by his predecessor and has never been used to impose upon a purchaser a positive duty to perform the covenants of his predecessor.

Collateral Contracts

A contract between A and B may be accompanied by a collateral contract between B and C relating to the same subject matter and is a very effective means by which to avoid privity (see *Shanklin Pier v Detel Products Ltd* [1951] 2 KB 854; *Charnock v Liverpool Corporation* [1968] 1 WLR 1498).

Liability in Tort to Third Parties

Where A and B have a contract it may impose upon A a duty of care which is owed to C, and C may be able to sue A in the tort of negligence if the duty is breached. The most controversial extension of tortious liability was made in *Junior Books Ltd v Veitchi Co. Ltd* [1983] 1 AC 520 where B and C had a contract whereby B agreed to build a factory for C, C having the right to nominate sub-contractors. C nominated A and a contract was formed between A and B, but there was no contract between A and C. It was held that A was liable in tort to C for the financial loss caused by a defective floor which had to be re-laid. Later cases have virtually interpreted *Junior Books* out of existence and, whilst it is clear that a manufacturer may be liable in tort for injury to persons or damage to property caused by a defective chattel, he will not be liable in tort to persons who suffer economic loss simply because the chattel is defective in quality. Such claims are properly the province of the law of contract. (See *D & F Estates Ltd v Church Commissioners for England* [1989] AC 177; *Simaan General Contracting Co. v Pilkington Glass Ltd (No. 2)* [1988] QB 758; *Murphy v Brentwood District Council* [1991] 1 AC 398.)

Agency

The concept of agency is an exception to the doctrine of privity in that an agent may contract on behalf of his principal with a third party and form a binding contract between principal and third party. Agency has also provided a fertile ground for evading privity in relation to exclusion clauses. A third party may be able to take the benefit of an exclusion clause by proving that the party imposing the clause was acting as the agent of the third party, thereby bringing the third party into a direct contractual relationship with the claimant (see *Elder, Dempster & Co. Ltd v Paterson, Zochonis & Co. Ltd* [1924] AC 446; *New Zealand Shipping Co. Ltd v AM Satterthwaite & Co. Ltd (The Eurymedon)* [1975] AC 154).

Statutory Developments

Contracts (Rights of Third Parties) Act 1999

The **Contracts (Rights of Third Parties) Act 1999** fundamentally modifies the doctrine of privity. Section 1 provides third parties with the right to enforce a term contained within a contract if the contract expressly so provides or the term purports to confer a benefit on the third party (see, generally, *Nisshin Shipping Co. Ltd v Cleaves & Co. Ltd* [2003] EWHC 2602, [2004] 1 Lloyd's Rep 38). The latter possibility depends on whether, in construing the contract, the contracting parties intended the particular term to be enforceable by the third party. In exercising this right the third party will possess any remedy that would have been available to him in an action for breach of contract if he had been a party to the contract (e.g. damages injunctive relief). Moreover, s. 1(6) makes it clear that a third party should have the benefit of any exclusion clause, provided that the third party is referred to in the clause, thereby circumventing the rather artificial analysis employed by the common law to secure this result (e.g. *New Zealand Shipping Co. Ltd v AM Satterthwaite & Co. Ltd (The Eurymedon)* [1975] AC 154).

Section 2 limits the power of the contracting parties to vary the terms of the contract unless such power has been expressly included in the contract. Any alteration of a term covered by s. 1 requires the consent of the third party if that person has already communicated his assent to the term, or it is known that the third party has relied upon the term, or it is reasonably foreseeable that such reliance would, and in fact did, take place. Further sections address the availability of defences (s. 3), double liability (s. 4), exempted contracts (s. 6), and the compatibility of other legislation (s. 7).

Overall, the 1999 Act will have important consequences for common law precedent. Under the Act cases such as *Beswick v Beswick* [1966] Ch 538 will no longer be good law—clearly the parties intended Mrs Beswick to have a legally enforceable right to claim payment from her nephew. However, the Act gives freedom to the contracting parties to exclude expressly the provisions of the Act or to set out procedures for post-contractual variation of arrangements that avoid the need to obtain the third party's consent. On this basis, any suggestion that common law precedent is rendered redundant by the 1999 Act is indeed premature (see *Nisshin Shipping Co Ltd v Cleaves & Co. Ltd* [2003] EWHC 2602, [2004] 1 Lloyd's Rep 38, which dealt with the interplay between s. 1 of the 1999 Act and an express trust in favour of the 'third party', the latter representing one of the common law exceptions to privity).

Question 1

It is clearly desirable to amend the rule that a third party may not sue on a contract which is made for his benefit.
  Discuss.

Commentary

This essay question requires an understanding and evaluation of the traditional rules of privity regarding contracts which are made for the benefit of third parties. A critical examination should also be made of whether the law was ripe for reform in 1999 and, consequently, students should be acquainted with the Law Commission's provisional recommendations regarding contracts made for the benefit of third parties (Consultation Paper No. 121, 1991) and the **Contracts (Rights of Third Parties) Act 1999**.

Answer plan

- What purpose did the courts originally intend the doctrine of privity to serve?
- How does this rule interrelate with the modern doctrine of consideration?
- Why did so many exceptions develop to the privity rule?
- What are the guiding principles of the **Contracts (Rights of Third Parties) Act 1999**?
- What limits are imposed on those contracting parties who wish to amend their existing contractual arrangements?

Suggested answer

Before the passing of the Contracts (Rights of Third Parties) Act 1999 it was clear that a third party could not sue on a contract to which he was not privy, even if the sole purpose of the contract was to benefit the third party. This rule is relatively modern and only became entrenched in the nineteenth century. For example, in *Tweddle v Atkinson* (1861) 1 B & S 393 the fathers of a husband and wife agreed in writing that both should pay money to the husband, adding that the husband should have the power to sue them for the respective sums. The husband's claim against his wife's father was dismissed, the court justifying the decision largely because no consideration moved from the promisee i.e. the husband. Since *Tweddle*, the House of Lords has steadfastly continued to enforce the privity rule, albeit subjecting it to trenchant criticism (compare *Dunlop Pneumatic Tyre Co. Ltd v*

Selfridge & Co. Ltd [1915] AC 847 and *Midland Silicones Ltd v Scruttons Ltd* [1962] AC 446, with *Beswick v Beswick* [1968] AC 58 and *Woodar Investment Development Ltd v Wimpey Construction UK Ltd* [1980] 1 WLR 277).

The injustice of the doctrine of privity was further reinforced by the rules relating to damages. In *Jackson v Horizon Holidays Ltd* [1975] 1 WLR 1468, the defendants contracted with the plaintiff to provide holiday accommodation for the plaintiff, his wife, and their two children. The accommodation was totally inadequate and the plaintiff recovered damages including £500 for 'mental distress'. Lord Denning MR considered that £500 would have been an excessive amount for the plaintiff's own distress but regarded the award as adequate on the basis that the plaintiff had made a contract for the benefit of himself and his family and that he could recover in respect of their loss. This approach was strongly disapproved by the House of Lords in *Woodar* but the promisee's inability to recover damages in respect of loss suffered by the third party was described as 'most unsatisfactory' and in need of re-evaluation by the legislature or by the House itself (although the Package Tours Regulations 1992, SI No. 3288, reg. 2(2), now allows all named parties in a package holiday contract to sue the operator directly for any breach of contract). Moreover, in *Forster v Silvermere Golf and Equestrian Centre* (1981) 125 SJ 397, Dillon J described the position as 'a blot on our law and most unjust'. There the plaintiff transferred land to the defendant who agreed to build a house on it and to allow the plaintiff and her children to live in it rent-free for life. It was held that the plaintiff could recover damages in respect of her own loss but not in relation to any rights of occupation which the children might have enjoyed after her death. It is scarcely surprising that this arbitrary rule engendered attempts at its circumvention in the guise of trusts (*Affréteurs (Les) Réunis SA v Leopold Walford (London) Ltd* [1919] AC 801) and restrictive covenants (*Lord Strathcona SS Co. v Dominion Coal Co.* [1926] AC 108), but no single attack by the common law courts successfully abrogated it. Moreover, the inroads upon the rule were created on an *ad hoc* basis and were both artificial and over-complicated (e.g. *New Zealand Shipping Co. Ltd v AM Satterthwaite & Co. Ltd (The Eurymedon)* [1975] AC 154). One might therefore question whether the doctrine of privity was ever justifiable and, if not, whether its fundamental modification by the Contracts (Rights of Third Parties) Act 1999 was the most appropriate way forward.

Several justifications have been advanced in denial of rights to third parties under the privity rule. First, it is argued that rights and duties remain the personal domain of those who create them and, as the third party has played no part in the technical formation of the contract, he should obtain no contractual rights. In particular, the Law Commission (Consultation Paper No. 121, 1991) emphasized that the purpose of requiring consent in contracts is to protect personal autonomy but that allowing third parties to obtain *benefits* under a contract would not undermine such autonomy. Indeed, where both parties have agreed to benefit the third party, his right of enforcement gives effect to their intention and promotes the essence of agreement. Secondly, the third party's failure to furnish any consideration is often thought to be fatal to his having any rights under the contract, a point which is reinforced by asserting that the third party beneficiary should not be better off than a gratuitous promisee who has provided no consideration. Again, the Law Commission pointed to the fact that consideration was provided by the promisee meaning that the promisor's promise had been paid for, albeit not by the third party; the gratuitous third party thus has rights under a valid contract whereas in the case of a gratuitous promisee there is no valid contract to enforce. Thirdly, it is suggested that it is unjust that a person should be treated as a party to a contract for the purpose of suing on it when he could not be sued. It is clear, however, that the promisor's interests are protected by his having a claim against the promisee whereas the third party has no such security under the existing rule of privity. Fourthly, there is the argument that the promisor could be liable to two actions from both the promisee and the third party but, as the Law Commission suggested, one answer is to say that there is only one promise giving rise to one cause of action and, once the promise is enforced it is extinguished, the promisor then ceasing to be liable. Fifthly, there is the assertion that, whilst privity does not permit the creation of contractual rights in third parties, it does not prohibit the achievement of the same result in practice provided that the appropriate drafting is used, e.g. collateral contracts. But the Law Commission emphasized that laymen will often fail to draft around the rule and that problems are still engendered where the parties have taken legal advice (e.g. *Beswick v Beswick*, above). Finally, it is argued that the ability of third parties to sue on the contract made for their benefit would detract from the rights of the contracting parties to rescind or vary their contract and would expose the promisor to a potentially wide range of possible third party claimants. The Law Commission acknowledged that reform would need to safeguard the rights of the parties and that provision should be made for a circumscribed definition of third parties in order to prevent a flood of litigation.

The Law Commission's proposals for reform were that nothing short of a 'detailed legislative scheme' would suffice to guarantee the rights of third parties. In this regard the 1999 Act appears to have fulfilled the Law Commission's plea. On the central issue of the test of an enforceable benefit, s. 1 provides that a third party will be entitled to enforce a contractual term in his own right if either the contract 'expressly' so provides (s. 1(1)(a)), or the term '*purports* to confer a benefit' on the third party (s. 1(1)(b)). As regards the latter possibility, the Act, in effect, sets up a rebuttable presumption that if the parties confer a benefit on a third party, they intend that the third party is empowered to enforce the term that creates the benefit (see s. 1(2)).

Use of the word 'purports' suggests scope for litigious dispute. For example, if the primary contractors simply *wished* to benefit a third party, or their agreement *appeared* to benefit a third party, would this fall within the meaning of 'purport to confer'? Initially it was assumed that such intentions would not easily be inferred and that, before any rebuttable presumption could be established, the necessary objective legal intent needed to have been ascertained. However, recent case law suggests that courts are prepared to find the requisite intent via a process of implication. For example, in *Nisshin Shipping Co. Ltd v Cleaves & Co. Ltd* [2003] EWHC 2602, [2004] 1 Lloyd's Rep 38, the third party had previously been required to enforce any right to unpaid commission from the shipowner by joining in the charteree to any action. The court held that the *purported* intent to allow the shipowner to be sued directly by the third party was established as the parties had seemingly chosen not to amend the relevant clause, in the light of the passing of the 1999 Act, in order to prevent third party from suing the shipowner directly. Similar *default* reasoning was adopted by the Court of Appeal in *Laemthong International Lines Co. Ltd v Artis* [2005] EWCA Civ 519, [2005] 1 Lloyd's Rep 688.

Nevertheless, the unintended consequences of interpreting s. 1(1) too widely is somewhat mitigated by s. 1(3), which requires any third party to be expressly identified in the contract by name, or as a member of a class, or as answering a particular description (s. 1(3)). On this basis, if the facts of *Jackson v Horizon Holidays* were to be repeated one assumes that as the family members had all been referred to in the contract (i.e. satisfying s. 1(3)), all members were travelling together, all arrangements concerned a 'family trip', and the cost clearly encompassed all the family, a court would conclude that the contract had purported to confer the benefit of the contract terms on all of the claimant's family. However, where the contract does not specify the names of third parties but prefers, instead, to refer to categories or classes of people, matters become more problematic. In *Avraamides v Colwill* [2006] EWCA Civ 1533 the respondents sought to hold the appellants personally liable for failures in refurbishing two bathrooms, even though the respondents had actually contracted with the Bathroom Trading Company (BTC). The argument put forward was that the appellants had taken over the assets of the BTC and had agreed to 'settle the current liabilities of [BTC]' (Clause 2) and 'complete outstanding customer orders' (Clause 3). The Court held that the word 'expressly' did not permit a 'process of implication or construction' and that, as Clause 2's potential benefit (viz. to pay liabilities) was directed towards a wide range of unidentified persons (e.g. customers, suppliers, utility companies), it could not be said that the respondents had been 'expressly' identified for the purposes of s. 1(3).

Section 2 concerns the difficult issue of variation and rescission. In general it recognizes that where a third party has a right under s. 1 to enforce a term of the contract, the parties to the contract cannot, by agreement, rescind the contract, or vary it in such a way as to alter that right without prior permission from the third party. This restriction pre-supposes that the third party has communicated to the promisor his assent to the term, or the promisor is aware that the third party has relied upon the term, or the promisor could reasonably foresee reliance by the third party on the term and such reliance has in fact occurred. In so doing, the Act seems to uphold the right to vary subject only to express intervention by the third party. In practice, the power to vary will be much weaker. As it will often be reasonably foreseeable that the third party might rely on the term in question, the parties will be best advised to contact the third party before any agreed variation has occurred in order to check whether such reliance had indeed taken place.

Finally, the 1999 Act makes no mention of consideration. Are we to infer that the decision in *Tweddle v Atkinson* is preserved, thereby representing a major loophole to the Act? It would appear not, because the Law Commission seemingly re-interpreted *Tweddle* by distinguishing promises that are supported by consideration (albeit enforced by a third party) and promises that are wholly gratuitous. The resultant interpretation of the 1999 Act will therefore focus on the right to enforce a promise supported by consideration, even though the third party conferred no benefit.

In conclusion, many of the artificial and often questionable exemptions that the common law created to circumvent the unfairness of the privity rule can now be laid to rest. Attention has moved away from the direct contractual relationship embodied in the bargained-for exchange of promises. Instead, the 1999 Act gives effect to the intentions of the contracting parties and the legitimate expectations of named third parties, raising a different set of complex legal issues. Indeed, the skeletal nature of the statutory provisions will require future explanation and elaboration. First, ascertaining the precise circumstances in which the contracting parties intended the third party to benefit from the contract. Secondly, the limits imposed on the parties' freedom to vary their contract where the third party's views are unknown. Nevertheless, legislation openly acknowledging the third party's rights is long overdue and removes the need for the common law to construct artificial and elaborate mechanisms in order to confer benefits upon third parties.

Further Reading

Case-notes

Nisshin Shipping Co Ltd v Cleaves & Co Ltd [2003] EWHC (Comm), [2004] 1 Lloyd's Rep 38

Parker, 'Shipbrokers' Commission and Arbitration Clauses' [2004] LMCLQ 445

Articles

Adams, Beyleveld, & Brownsword, 'Privity of Contract—The Benefits and the Burdens of Law Reform' (1997) 60 MLR 238

Andrews, 'Strangers to Justice No Longer—The Reversal of the Privity Rule under the Contracts (Rights of Third Parties) Act 1999' [2001] 60 CLJ 353

Burrows, 'The Contracts (Rights of Third Parties) Act and its Implications for Commercial Contracts' [2000] LMCLQ 540

Macmillan, 'A Birthday Present for Lord Denning: The Contracts (Rights of Third Parties) Act 1999' (2000) 63 MLR 721

Roe, 'Contractual Intention under Section 1(1)(b) and 1(2) of the Contracts (Rights of Third Parties) Act 1999' (2000) 63 MLR 887

Law Commission Report: Privity of Contract: Contracts for the Benefit of Third Parties, Law Com. No. 242, Cm 3329, 1996.

14

Mixed questions

Introduction

This final chapter introduces students to those examination questions which contain overlapping topics. For example, a contract question might include aspects of mistake, undue influence and misrepresentation. Clearly, if students identify all the relevant areas then they will have established a firm base from which a good answer can be developed.

As the main purpose of reading this chapter is to test your ability to identify different topics contained within one question, the suggested answers offer a *broad outline* of the issues raised rather than a more detailed analysis of relevant points which would be required by an examiner.

Question 1

The NSC is a Government body which arranges for the salvaging of shipwrecks lying within the coastal waters of the UK. Recently, the *Hesperus* was reported as having been damaged in heavy seas and that its captain had run the ship aground on a remote Scottish island. The NSC invites salvage operators to bid for the salvage rights of the *Hesperus* in the following terms: 'We imagine great interest in the ship as its cargo includes a quantity of Roman coins. Bidding is by sealed competitive tender. Only one bid will be accepted from any one company. All bids will remain confidential. We bind ourselves to accept the highest bid.'

Scrappit Ltd and Junkit Ltd both bid for the salvage rights. Scrappit Ltd bids £100,000 whilst Junkit Ltd bids '£90,000 or £10,000 more than the next highest bid, whichever is the greater'. NSC assumes that Junkit Ltd's bid is the highest (i.e. £110,000) and therefore accepts it. Scrappit Ltd now claims that its bid is the highest and that NSC is in breach of contract in accepting Junkit Ltd's bid.

Discuss the legal position of the parties.

Would your answer differ in each of the following separate situations:

(a) *Hesperus* is found to have survived the heavy storms and is sailing off the coast of South America.

(b) The 'Rare Coins and Antiquities Act 1964' prevents the sale of Roman coins without the prior permission of the Department of the Environment, with an unlimited maximum fine being payable for any transgression.

Suggested answer

This question deals with offer and acceptance, terms, mistake and illegality.

Regarding the formation of a contract four questions arise: was the invitation to bid an offer; if so, did it form a unilateral contract; if so, was it the intention that referential bids would be excluded; if so, does Scrappit Ltd have an enforceable contract with NSC? The starting point would be to define an offer as opposed to an invitation to treat: it must be specific, certain and display sufficient legal intent to be bound. Although the facts appear similar to an auction, in which it is the bidder who makes the offer, there are some important differences. NSC's invitation clearly demonstrates an intention to be bound as NSC is willing to 'bind itself' to accept the highest bid. The words are very clear and unambiguous. Moreover, although the invitation is directed to the world at large this might not detract from its being an offer (see *Carlill v Carbolic Smoke Ball Co.* [1893] 1 QB 256). Parallels could also be drawn with the *obiter* statements in *Warlow v Harrison* (1859) 1 E & E 309 in which it was stated that advertising an auction without reserve constituted an offer to sell to the highest bidder (see also *Barry v Heathcote Ball & Co. (Commercial Auctions) Ltd* [2000] 1 WLR 1962). Is not NSC offering to do exactly that? Finally, the House of Lords' decision in *Harvela Investments Ltd v Royal Trust Co. of Canada (CI) Ltd* [1986] AC 207 should be mentioned in which, on similar facts, the invitation was treated as an offer to accept the highest bid. Lord Diplock went so far as to say that the offer constituted a unilateral contract which would be followed by a bilateral contract with the person who made the highest valid bid.

So far this would suggest that Junkit Ltd should succeed. However, the *Harvela* decision also dealt with the problems of referential bids. The House held that on the facts referential bids were invalid, thereby leaving the only other remaining valid bid as representing the highest bid submitted. This conclusion was reached because referential bids would undermine the purpose of sealed confidential bids which was to obtain the maximum bid that any bidder was prepared to make. On our facts, if the same result followed, Scrappit Ltd would have submitted the only valid bid and would thus have a legally binding contract with NSC.

(Note: the very good student who has read the *Harvela* decision might recognize that Lord Diplock, in particular, placed emphasis on the defendant's inviting bids from two specified individuals. There was an implication that an invitation to a random number of individuals would have been treated differently.)

(a) The altered facts are reminiscent of those in *McRae v Commonwealth Disposals Commission* (1951) 84 CLR 377, except that unlike *McRae*, the tanker does exist, albeit in an unsolvable form! If a contract has been formed between the parties it becomes a question of construction whether: (i) NSC should accept the risk of the vessel not being shipwrecked off Scotland—following the *McRae* decision, or (ii) that there is an implied condition precedent that the specified vessel exists and is subject to salvage rights—if this fails the contract would be void (see *Couturier v Hastie* (1856) 5 HL Cas 673). Under point (ii) you would probably mention the doctrine of common mistake, drawing appropriate support for your arguments from *Bell v Lever Bros* [1932] AC 161; *Associated Japanese Bank (International) Ltd v Credit du Nord SA* [1989] 1 WLR 255; and *Great Peace Shipping Ltd v Tsavliris Salvage (International) Ltd* [2002] EWCA Civ 1407; [2002] 3 WLR 1617.

(b) This deals with illegality. Is the contract illegal as formed or as performed? Although ignorance of the law is no excuse it would seem that the relevant statute does not prohibit the sale of Roman coins but merely imposes a condition upon NSC to obtain prior Government approval, on pain of an unlimited fine. Thus two questions arise: how does one interpret the underlying purpose of the statute, and what is the effect of the illegality? Cases such as *Hughes v Asset Managers plc* [1995] 3 All ER 669 and *Shaw v Groom* [1970] 2 QB 504 could be used in the analysis of the first point, one possible conclusion being that the statute merely represents a bureaucratic procedure by which sales of Roman coins are monitored. Consider also the importance of whether the statute places the burden on NSC's shoulders to obtain approval. If, in these circumstances, the buyer is considered innocent then all the normal remedies for breach of contract will be available. Alternatively, if the contract is completely prohibited, there may have been an implied collateral warranty that NSC would obtain a licence (see *Strongman (1945) Ltd v Sincock* [1955] 2 QB 525) or that for public policy reasons the innocent party should be allowed some form of restitutionary relief anyway (see *Phoenix General Insurance Co. of Greece SA v Administratia Asigurairilor de Stat* [1988] QB 216).

Question 2

For the past five years Fastbuild Ltd, a company that specializes in the building of housing estates, has entered into one-yearly contracts with Bricklast Ltd for the supply of house bricks. Each of these contracts has been preceded by protracted negotiations in which new terms and conditions have been agreed between the parties. In the most recent set of negotiations, for a proposed contract in 2008, the parties had agreed the type and quantity of bricks to be supplied, the specified quantity easily exceeding Bricklast Ltd's expectations bearing in mind previous contracts. Fastbuild Ltd thereupon sends Bricklast Ltd a letter of intent which includes the following statement: 'As per negotiations we intend to contract with you, purchasing 2.5 million bricks (type agreed) for the year 2008 at a price to be confirmed.' Bricklast Ltd purchases additional machinery in order to manufacture the increased quantity of bricks and goes into immediate production.

Consider the legal position of the parties if negotiations between them break down and Fastbuild Ltd refuse to purchase any bricks from Bricklast Ltd.

Suggested answer

This question deals with formation of contracts and involves a consideration of offer and acceptance, certainty, intent, and consideration.

First, does the letter of intent constitute an offer? An offer has to be certain, specific and demonstrate an intention to be bound. Leaving aside the particular problems associated with letters of intent, Fastbuild Ltd's communication does contain specific terms (quantity and period of delivery) but two problems remain: use of the word 'intend' and omission of an agreed price. The word 'intend' imports some degree of reticence and might be referring merely to *future* intentions. For example, in *Clifton v Palumbo* [1944] 2 All ER 497 the claimant's statement that he was 'prepared to offer' was held to constitute a mere invitation to treat (see also *Gibson v Manchester City Council* [1979] 1 All ER 972). Equally, omission of an agreed price should detract from the letter's certainty although use of the word 'confirmed' might suggest that the parties have already reached a definite agreement elsewhere. Contrast the cases of *Hillas & Co. Ltd v Arcos Ltd* (1932) 147 LT 503 and *Scammell (G) and Nephew Ltd v Ouston* [1941] AC 251, the first case showing that the omission of a price might not affect contractual validity if viewed in the light of the parties' previous course of dealing. Note the general policy that courts will always seek to implement rather than defeat the reasonable expectations of the parties. It might also be relevant to consider the impact of *Blackpool & Fylde Aero Club Ltd v Blackpool Borough Council* [1990] 1 WLR 1195 in that the clear intentions of the parties might override the technical requirements of offer and acceptance. Finally, lack of certainty might be argued with reference to *Walford v Miles* [1992] 2 AC 128—even if the letter implies an undertaking not to contract with anyone else this does not establish an enforceable, positive contract to negotiate in good faith as it is too uncertain. (Note: many of the issues concerning the certainty of an offer would be equally applicable to the certainty of the final contract, assuming an offer and acceptance had actually taken place, e.g. *Foley v Classique Coaches Ltd* [1934] 2 KB 1.)

Regarding the issue of letters of intent, the decision in *Kleinwort Benson Ltd v Malaysia Mining Corporation Bhd* [1989] 1 WLR 379 shows that the courts have no preconceived notion as to the enforceability of letters of comfort. Rather, the enforceability of such letters will depend upon the precise wording used. In *Kleinwort*, the words 'it is our policy' were not considered to be promissory in nature. On the present facts the word 'intend' might be considered to import an unacceptable degree of uncertainty, although contrast this with the decision in *Wilson Smithett & Cape (Sugar) Ltd v Bangladesh Sugar and Food Industries Corporation* [1986] 1 Lloyd's Rep 378.

Secondly, if an offer has been made, has there been an acceptance? Acceptance can take many forms: written, spoken, or conduct. Although there is no suggestion that Bricklast has responded formally to Fastbuild's letter, there is clear evidence of reliance. At first glance, *Brogden v Metropolitan Railway Co.* (1877) 2 App Cas 666 seems applicable but in that case *both* parties acted on the strength of the new agreement (see also *Wettern Electric Ltd v Welsh Development Agency* [1983] QB 796). This is important as, in general, acceptance is ineffective until it has been communicated (see *Powell v Lee* (1908) 99 LT 284). Thus, no contract will have come into existence unless Bricklast Ltd can argue that starting work is sufficient in itself to create a contract. Consider the effect of *Trollope & Colls Ltd v Atomic Power Constructions Ltd* [1963] 1 WLR 333 and, in particular, *British Steel Corporation v Cleveland Bridge and Engineering Co. Ltd* [1984] 1 All ER 504 which concerned the twin impact of an existing letter of intent and reliance by the recipient that a contract would be finalized. An alternative approach would be to consider cases where courts have been prepared to adapt, if not modify, the orthodox rules of offer and acceptance (e.g. *Blackpool*; *Kleinwort, supra*, [1988] 1 WLR 799 (High Court); *Evans (J) & Son (Portsmouth) Ltd v Andrea Merzario* [1976] 1 WLR 1078). Naturally it would help if the parties, during their negotiations, had set up independent machinery (e.g. arbitration) for determining the meaning of uncertain terms (see *Sudbrook Trading Estate Ltd v Eggleton* [1983] 1 AC 444).

Finally, even if a court is prepared to find an offer that has been accepted, is there consideration for this agreement? Briefly, as there has been no exchange of promises a court would find great difficulty in identifying valid consideration (see *Combe v Combe* [1951] 2 KB 215). Traditionally, reliance would be considered too uncertain in English law to constitute consideration. But we are dealing here with a specific promise rather than one which is random. Perhaps one could circumvent this problem by arguing that the original letter sent by Fastbuild Ltd constituted an offer leading to a unilateral contract and that Bricklast Ltd's reliance demonstrated that they had embarked upon a course of performance leading to acceptance, thereby making the offer irrevocable (see *Daulia Ltd v Four Millbank Nominees Ltd* [1978] Ch 231).

Question 3

Alicia, who is the niece of Gilbert, had an £8,000 overdraft with North Bank. Gilbert wrote to North Bank, enclosing a cheque for £5,000 with the following message: 'Please accept this payment in full satisfaction of my niece's debt. If you refuse I will transfer my company's existing account to another bank.' North Bank, which has lost a large number of high-profile customers over the past year, decided to cash the cheque rather than challenge Gilbert.

Gilbert was also keen on persuading Alicia to become a sales representative for his company. On 2 April, Gilbert offered to pay the weekly rent of £120 on Alicia's current flat for the next six months if she joined his company. Alicia was reluctant to give up her existing well-paid job but capitulated when Gilbert threatened to tell her mother of her current drug habits. On 1 June Gilbert promised to extend his payment of Alicia's current rent to a full year as a 'reward' for all her 'hard work in May'.

One month later Gilbert informed Alicia that he had stopped paying her rent. Alicia immediately started looking for a better-paid job elsewhere but was horrified to discover that her existing contract of employment required her to give six months' notice. To compound her misery, Alicia discovered that North Bank was taking measures to recover the remaining £3,000 on her overdraft.

Advise Alicia.

Suggested answer

This answer deals with consideration, promissory estoppel, intent to create legal relations, undue influence, and economic duress.

Gilbert v North Bank

The general rule is that part-payment of a debt is insufficient to release the debtor (see *Foakes v Beer* (1884) 9 App Cas 605). However, part-payment from a third party which has been accepted by the creditor constitutes one of the exceptions to this rule as otherwise a fraud would have been perpetrated on the former (see *Welby v Drake* (1825) 1 C & P 557). It is clearly arguable that North Bank's cashing of the cheque constitutes a voluntary acceptance of the new arrangement, although the decision in *Ferguson v Davies* [1997] 1 All ER 315 suggests that a court might require further evidence of the creditor's acceptance. Of equal importance is whether Gilbert is holding the Bank to ransom, thereby undermining reliance upon the third party part-payment exception? Undoubtedly this would prove more compelling if Gilbert knew that the Bank was encountering difficulties in maintaining its customer base (draw an analogy with *D & C Builders Ltd v Rees* [1966] 2 QB 617). However, as the principle of economic duress becomes ever more relevant to the application of the rules of consideration, proof that the dominant party acted in an *illegitimate* manner becomes more crucial (see *Universe Tankships Inc. of Monrovia v International Transport Workers' Federation* [1983] 1 AC 366). On the facts, the accusation of 'illegitimate pressure' may prove difficult to sustain as customers will normally have the right to move their accounts to other banks whenever they choose.

Gilbert v Alicia

With regard to the payment of six months rent by Gilbert, is there an intention to create legal relations? In family arrangements, the presumption is against such intent being apparent (*Balfour v Balfour* [1919] 2 KB 571), although Alicia's reliance in giving up her existing job might prove useful (see the *obiter* comments in *Jones v Padavatton* [1969] 1 WLR 328). Alternatively, if the purpose of this arrangement is to secure Alicia's services as a sales representative, it is equally arguable that we are dealing with a commercial arrangement, in which case there is a strong presumption that the parties did intend legal relations. Consideration is presumably present as Gilbert is paying Alicia's rent while Alicia is to give up her current job and work for Gilbert, although a court may require proof that Alicia's actions were tied to Gilbert's promise (see *Combe v Combe* [1951] 2 KB 215 which stressed that the provision of consideration must be *in return for*, rather than *as a result of*, the other's promise). Finally, do not consider promissory estoppel as the principle refers to the modification of an *existing* contract (Gilbert and Alicia did not have one), rather than the creation of a contract based on one person's promise.

As for the contract of employment and its lengthy notice period, the best advice would be for Alicia to argue that the whole contract is voidable for undue influence. This seems likely as Gilbert's threat to inform on her drug habits is akin to blackmail and, consequently, would normally constitute affirmative proof of such influence being exerted (see *Lyon v Home* (1868) LR 6 Eq 655 and the wider implications of *Credit Lyonnais Bank Nederland NV v Burch* [1997] 1 All ER 144).

Finally, any argument that Gilbert is bound contractually by his subsequent promise to pay a full year's rent is liable to fail as Alicia's consideration is in the past (the extension was for work Alicia had already carried out), unless it can be argued that Gilbert derived some continuing practical benefit from the arrangement in terms of maintaining Alicia's loyalty (see generally *Williams v Roffey & Nicholls (Contractors) Ltd* [1990] 1 All ER 512). Alternatively, Alicia might rely upon the doctrine of promissory estoppel to delay Gilbert's abrupt withdrawal of his promise until he has given reasonable notice. This would require proof that she had relied upon Gilbert's promise in the first place.

Question 4

S & M Ltd agree to purchase 100,000 towels, of specified dimensions, over the next year from TT Ltd. The contract is signed on 1 January.

Six months later S & M Ltd tell TT Ltd that they are so impressed by the quality of the towels supplied that, as a goodwill gesture, an extra payment of £1 would be made at the end of the year for the delivery of every towel outstanding under the existing agreement. S & M Ltd add that they 'hope to negotiate a new contract for further supplies on similar terms for the next year'. With this in mind, TT Ltd purchase additional factory machinery.

On 1 December, S & M Ltd tell TT Ltd that they have no intention of paying the additional £1 per towel. Moreover, although TT Ltd is expecting to deliver the remainder of the towels in December (approximately 10,000 towels) S & M Ltd refuse to accept any more unless TT Ltd deliver the remainder at a 50% discount. S & M Ltd's manager adds: 'I hope that you adopt a constructive attitude or this will jeopardise our future relations.' TT Ltd agree to deliver the remaining 10,000 towels at the required discount as the loss of future contracts with S & M Ltd would probably lead to the company's going into liquidation.

Subsequently, negotiations between S & M Ltd and TT Ltd regarding a new contract, are terminated. TT Ltd now seeks your advice as to the possibility of recovering the 50% discount as well as enforcing the July promise to pay an extra £1 per towel.

Suggested answer

This question primarily involves an analysis of economic duress and promissory estoppel, perhaps brought together within the wider context of consideration.

The additional payment is linked to promissory estoppel. TT Ltd provide no consideration for the additional payment. The promise is gratuitous, modifies an existing contract, and is equitably created. The only two question marks concern (a) S & M Ltd's intent, and (b) TT Ltd's reliance. On point (a) the promise appears specific and certain. But was it made in circumstances which would suggest an intention to be bound? The evidence suggests that it is a gesture of goodwill which might militate against an affirmative answer (but see the useful comments in *Scandinavian Trading Tanker Co. v Flota Petrolera Ecuatoriana, The Scaptrade* [1983] QB 529). On point (b) has TT Ltd acted upon the promise or, as some judges have stated, altered their position on the faith of the promise? Probably no. The towels had to be delivered anyway—although it might be arguable that TT Ltd purchased additional machinery not just because of future potential contracts with S & M Ltd but also because of the additional payment for 1992. If an estoppel is established one would probably follow *Central London Property Trust Ltd v High Trees House Ltd* [1947] KB 130, arguing that it would be inequitable to revert to the original position as TT Ltd has relied upon the extra payment. Moreover, as the year has already passed, there is no scope for S & M Ltd to give reasonable notice to return to its original position.

On the face of it, the December re-negotiation should fail for lack of consideration, i.e. TT Ltd do not derive any benefit from the change. However, reference should be made to *Williams v Roffey & Nicholls (Contractors) Ltd* [1991] 1 QB 1 in which the Court of Appeal appears to have extended the definition of consideration so as to include 'practical benefits'. Does TT Ltd receive any benefit? Possibly, in that there is an enhanced possibility of forging future, profitable links with S & M Ltd. Whether a practical benefit can include a future potential benefit is as yet a moot point. One might also mention Russell LJ's famous *dictum* in *Williams v Roffey* in which courts were encouraged to identify consideration if the parties clearly intended to be bound by new contractual arrangements. However, this approach emphasizes the importance of the doctrine of economic duress as a means of policing the possible abuse arising from a marked inequality in bargaining powers between the parties.

The facts incorporate all the hallmarks of economic duress: a threatened breach of an existing contract (*North Ocean Shipping Co. Ltd v Hyundai Construction Co. Ltd* [1979] QB 705), disastrous consequences of non-compliance with this threat (*B & S Contracts and Design Ltd v Victor Green Publications Ltd* [1984] ICR 419), and perfect timing of the threat (*Atlas Express Ltd v Kafco (Importers and Distributors) Ltd* [1989] QB 833). But this is not enough. TT Ltd must establish that the pressure exerted by S & M Ltd was illegitimate and that TT Ltd's will was resultingly coerced. The above points would be helpful in demonstrating the first point, especially if linked with the comments of Lord Scarman in *Universe Tankships Inc. of Monrovia v International Transport Workers' Federation* [1983] 1 AC 366. Regarding the issue of coercion, the litmus test appears to be whether the victim had an alternative course of action. This is assessed objectively, irrespective of the pressure which the victim *feels* is being exerted. Could TT Ltd have found other customers? All this should be seen in the context of TT Ltd's reliance on future links with S & M Ltd which, even if encouraged, should not be taken too seriously in a commercial world. Support for this might be gained from *Lobb (Alec) (Garages) Ltd v Total Oil (GB) Ltd* [1985] 1 WLR 173 where the court was not impressed by the plaintiff's argument that the defendant offered the only source of financial backing.

Question 5

The principle of freedom of contract has allowed courts to elevate the needs of certainty and predictability above those of reasonableness and fairness.

In the light of modern case law, to what extent do you agree with this statement?

Suggested answer

There are innumerable ways in which you can answer this question. This is because you can draw upon most topics within a law of contract syllabus to support your arguments. Thus, the suggested outline merely gives you three possible structures for your answer. Option 1 offers the most restrictive treatment of the question, concentrating on the more obviously relevant features of a contract law syllabus. Option 2 builds on this base by adding aspects of statutory regulation. Option 3 provides the most expansive treatment, drawing together the effect of case law across the whole range of contract law.

Whichever option is selected, a student would be expected to provide a brief introduction to the principle of freedom of contract: nineteenth century principles of *laissez-faire*, the need to ensure predictability and certainty when dealing with arm's length commercial dealings, and the growing preparedness of courts in the twentieth century to intervene in consumer/business transactions. Following from this:

Option 1

This would restrict attention to the more obvious areas, dealing with developments in undue influence and economic duress as well as the decline in Lord Denning's theory of bargaining inequality. Undue influence could be considered in the context of judicial intervention where trust which has been reposed by a weaker party is abused by the dominant party. The increased tendency for courts to intervene was perhaps illustrated, at its extreme, in *Lloyds Bank Ltd v Bundy* [1975] QB 326, with clear limits being subsequently imposed by the House of Lords in *National Westminster Bank v Morgan* [1985] AC 686. The most recent developments in this area centre upon the rights of wives who act as sureties for their husbands' debts, or elderly parents who finance their offspring's entrepreneurial activities (see for example *Barclays Bank plc v O'Brien* [1994] 1 AC 180; *Royal Bank of Scotland v Etridge (No. 2)* [2001] UKHL 44, [2001] 4 All ER 449; *Yorkshire Bank plc v Tinsley* [2004] EWCA Civ 816, [2004] 1 WLR 2380). Compare this with the more restricted approach shown in commercial transactions where the doctrine of economic duress has been used sparingly (see *Lobb (Alec) (Garages) Ltd v Total Oil (GB) Ltd* [1985] 1 WLR 173). The clear conclusion is that courts prefer to encourage predictability and certainty in commercial transactions but place concepts such as fairness and reasonableness on a higher plane when dealing with personal, and especially fiduciary, relationships.

Option 2

This would draw on the above comments whilst emphasizing the limits of judicial intervention. For example, in dealing with unconscionable exclusion clauses the common law has imposed restrictions upon the incorporation of such clauses, requiring reasonable notice to be given of these clauses (see *Parker v South Eastern Railway* (1877) 2 CPD 416) and the special highlighting of onerous clauses (see *Interfoto Picture Library Ltd v Stiletto Visual Programmes Ltd* [1989] QB 433). A more concerted and successful effort to curb the excesses of exclusion clauses materialized with the rule that the consequences of a fundamental breach could not be excluded (see *Karsales (Harrow) Ltd v Wallis* [1956] 1 WLR 936). However, the courts recognized that the common law had almost abrogated freedom of contract/intent and consequently restored these notions in such cases as *Photo Production Ltd v Securicor Transport Ltd* [1980] AC 827. You might therefore focus on statutory intervention as represented by the Unfair Contract Terms Act 1977 (UCTA 1977) and the Sale of Goods Act 1979 (SGA 1979). UCTA 1977 applies a reasonableness test to certain types of exclusion clauses, with a complete prohibition of clauses which seek to exclude liability for negligence causing death or personal injury. The Act polices specific types of clauses such as those excluding liability for breach of the implied terms contained in ss. 13–15 of the SGA 1979. In such cases, these clauses are prohibited in consumer sales but are subjected to a reasonableness test in commercial transactions. Yet again there is a clear link between the hands-off, non-interventionist approach to commercial parties (subject to economic duress and so forth) and the interventionist stance adopted with regard to consumers (see also the protection of consumers in the Unsolicited Goods and Services Act 1971).

Option 3

This would draw upon a number of disparate points within a contract syllabus ranging from economic duress/undue influence, as well as statutory intervention, through to offer and acceptance, intent, frustration, damages, and illegality. Options 1 and 2 cover a number of these points but the following additional aspects could be considered:

(a) the possible modification of offer and acceptance rules in the interests of fair dealing and the reliance of the parties (see *Blackpool & Fylde Aero Club Ltd v Blackpool Borough Council* [1990] 1 WLR 1195; *British Steel Corporation v Cleveland Bridge and Engineering Co. Ltd* [1984] 1 All ER 504);

(b) the growing emphasis upon the role of intent in contract formation in order to support the legitimate expectations of commercial parties and, in particular, their post-contractual re-allocation of risk (see *Williams v Roffey & Nicholls (Contractors) Ltd* [1991] 1 QB 1);

(c) the greater flexibility that the Law Reform (Frustrated Contracts) Act 1943 offers courts in terms of the equitable apportionment of loss where a contract has been discharged on grounds of frustration;

(d) the distinction which courts make between liquidated damages and penalty clauses, thereby preventing the abuse of a dominant position (see *Dunlop Pneumatic Tyre Co. Ltd v New Garage and Motor Co. Ltd* [1915] AC 79); and

(e) the compromises which courts have reached in assessing the rights of innocent parties under illegal contracts, or the rights of employees under contracts in restraint of trade (see *Strongman (1945) Ltd v Sincock* [1955] 2 QB 525; *Phoenix General Insurance Co. of Greece SA v Administratia Asigurairilor de Stat* [1988] QB 216; *Plowman (GW) and Son Ltd v Ash* [1964] 1 WLR 568).

Question 6

Dick has inherited a substantial amount of money and seeks advice regarding its investment. He approaches Stirling, a 'financial consultant' who, for a fixed fee, advises him on the investment potential of paintings and antiques. Stirling suggests that Dick should visit Cheetham & Co., fine art dealers of Bond Street, as 'they have always given sound advice to my clients in the past'.

Dick studies the soaring prices fetched at auction by the French Impressionists and, desirous of buying a painting from this school, he visits Cheetham & Co. He is introduced to Fortescue, who has recently bought the gallery from Cheetham but carries on the business in the former trade name for the purposes of business goodwill. After two hours perusing the paintings, Dick is particularly taken with a painting described in the gallery's catalogue as painted by Renoir. Fortescue informs Dick that 'the French Impressionists continue to rocket in price and these type of lake scenes by artists such as Renoir are particularly in vogue'. Accordingly, Dick buys the Renoir for £850,000.

Six months later, Dick has the painting valued for insurance purposes and is told that it is definitely not by Renoir but that it is nevertheless an important picture and thus worth £200,000. Dick has discovered that Stirling and Fortescue are both directors of a separate company which specializes in the renovation of dilapidated Georgian mansions. Moreover, in their dealings with Dick they both disclaimed liability in writing in the following terms: 'No liability can be accepted for loss arising from advice given or statements made to clients who should verify the accuracy of statements for themselves.'

Advise Dick.

Suggested answer

Dick v Stirling

Breach of contract:

(a) Implied term by statute—Dick (D) has contracted for the supply of advice on the 'investment potential of paintings and antiques' which is a contract for the supply of a service. In these circumstances it is an implied term that the service will be provided with reasonable care and skill (Supply of Goods and Services Act 1982, s. 13). Liability is based on fault; can D prove that Stirling (S) was negligent?

(b) Express term—was the statement by S intended to be a contractual promise (*Heilbut, Symons & Co. v Buckleton* [1913] AC 30)? What about the parol evidence rule?

Negligent misstatement: can D show a special relationship (*Hedley Byrne & Co. Ltd v Heller & Partners Ltd* [1964] AC 465)? If so, can D prove a breach of duty and that loss was foreseeable (note s. 2(1) of the Misrepresentation Act 1967 is not applicable as D is induced to enter into a contract with Fortescue (F) not S).

Disclaimer: subject to the clause being validly incorporated, ss. 2(2) and 3 of the Unfair Contract Terms Act 1977 (UCTA 1977) subjects the disclaimer to the reasonableness test (s. 11 and Sch. 2). As the clause potentially excludes liability for fraud it is probably unreasonable (see *Stewart Gill Ltd v Horatio Myer & Co. Ltd* [1992] 1 QB 600; *Thomas Witter Ltd v TBP Industries* [1996] 2 All ER 573).

Dick v Cheetham

Misrepresentation:

(a) '... described in the gallery's catalogue as painted by Renoir'. This is clearly a statement of fact (e.g. *Atlantic Estates plc v Ezekiel* [1991] 2 EGLR 202).

(b) '... the French Impressionists continue to rocket in price and these type of lake scenes by artists such as Renoir are particularly in vogue'. This might be an opinion (*Bisset v Wilkinson* [1927] AC 177), but what of F's purported expertise (*Smith v Land & House Property Corp.* (1884) 28 Ch D 7)?

Inducement and reliance: has D relied upon any representation in entering the contract, rather than his own judgement (*Attwood v Small* (1838) 6 CL & F 232)? Type of misrepresentation? Any evidence of fraud (*Derry v Peek* (1889) 14 App Cas 337)? Is there a special relationship between C and D (see, for example, *Hedley Byrne*; *Esso Petroleum Co. Ltd v Mardon* [1976] QB 801). Section 2(1) of the Misrepresentation Act 1967—can C discharge the burden of proof (see *Howard Marine & Dredging Co. Ltd v A Ogden & Sons (Excavations) Ltd* [1978] QB 574)?

Remedies for misrepresentation: has any right to rescind been lost through time (*Leaf v International Galleries* [1950] 2 KB 86)?

Damages: available for fraudulent, s. 2(1) and negligent misrepresentations. Under s. 2(1) (Misrepresentation Act 1967), D can recover damages which are assessed as if the misrepresentation had been made fraudulently. What about lost opportunity costs in not having a Renoir which may have '... rocketed in price ...' (*East v Maurer* [1991] 2 QB 297)?

Breach of contract: is there an express term that the painting is a Renoir? Note the difficulties in proving objective contractual intent (*Heilbut*). Apply general guidelines: has C suggested that D should verify the statements (*Ecay v Godfrey* [1974] 80 Ll LR 286) or is it normal practice in this area not to rely on such statements of attribution (*Harlingdon & Leinster Enterprises Ltd v Christopher Hull Fine Art Ltd* [1991] 1 QB 564)? Implied term? Consider the relevance of the Sale of Goods Act 1979 (SGA 1979) to this transaction. Is there a *sale by description*, i.e. has the buyer relied on the description (e.g. *Harlingdon*)? Is there a breach of the implied term relating to *satisfactory quality* (s. 14 of the SGA 1979) although in the light of *Harlingdon* this is unlikely as s. 14 probably does not apply to non-physical defects.

Disclaimer: has the clause been incorporated at common law? Does s. 3 of the UCTA 1977 apply or is the clause merely defining liability rather than excluding it? (Note also that as regards any breach of contract exclusion, if there has been a breach of an implied term—e.g. s. 13 of the SGA 1979—then the disclaimer will be subject to s. 6 of the UCTA 1977 and consequently void.)

Other Issues

Undue influence (*Dick v Stirling*): this is not an obvious category of a Class 2A relationship in which a presumption of influence would automatically arise (see *Royal Bank of Scotland v Etridge (No. 2)* [2001] UKHL 44, [2001] 4 All ER 449 HL). But is it arguable that a relationship of trust and confidence exists between the parties: S is a paid professional adviser, D is relying upon the advice, S is cheating by not disclosing his alliance with F? This seems very unlikely: we are simply dealing with an arm's length seller/buyer relationship in which the principle of *caveat emptor* holds centre stage.

Breach of a collateral contract (*D v S*): this would be relevant only if it is objectively established that the statement was intended to be a contractual term of a collateral contract (e.g. *Heilbut*) *and* the statement is supported by separate consideration. In these circumstances it would be difficult to prove that the statement was intended to *guarantee (promise)* the soundness of Cheetham's advice (see *Esso Petroleum Co. Ltd v Mardon and Kleinwort Benson Ltd v Malaysia Mining Corp. Bhd* [1989] 1 All ER 785—statement of present intention) and to find separate consideration. Further, this situation differs from other collateral contract cases in that the statement concerns the advice of a third party and not the properties of a product (e.g. *Andrews v Hopkinson* [1956] 3 All ER 422) or the terms of another contract between the parties (e.g. *City & Westminster Properties v Mudd* [1959] Ch 129).

Mistake (*D v C*): common mistake—it would be difficult to establish a fundamental mistake here since it is likely to be treated as a mistake of quality rather than an example of impossibility (see *Bell v Lever Brothers*; *Great Peace Shipping Ltd v Tsavliris Salvage (International) Ltd* [2002] EWCA Civ 1407, [2002] 3 WLR 1617).

Unilateral mistake—this is unlikely as it is not clear that F is aware of D's mistake, unlike in *Boulton v Jones* (1857) 27 LJ Ex 117 where the innocent party specifically addressed his purchase order to the previous proprietor of the shop; moreover, in the light of *Shogun Finance Ltd v Hudson* [2003] UKHL 62, [2004] 1 All ER 215, as the dealings were conducted face-to-face, there is an almost irrebuttable presumption that D intended to deal with F.

Third party undue influence: this would be relevant only if it could be established that S had made a misrepresentation which induced D to enter the contract with F, who had actual or constructive knowledge of S's wrongdoing; if this was established, D may be able to avoid the contract with F (see *Barclays Bank v O'Brien* [1994] 1 AC 180 and *Royal Bank of Scotland v Etridge (No. 2)* [2001] UKHL 44, [2001] 4 All ER 449).

Question 7

Rex entered a jeweller's shop and asked Barker, the proprietor, 'How much is that gold necklace in the window?' Barker replied, '£1,250 to you, Sir.' Rex said: 'Good, I'll take it then.'
Consider the contractual position in EACH of the following circumstances:

(a) Rex thinks that the necklace is pure gold, and so worth £1,250, whereas in reality it is only gold-plated.

(b) There are two necklaces in the window, one worth £500 and the other worth £1,250. Rex intends to buy the valuable necklace whilst Barker intends to sell the cheaper one.

(c) Rex purports to be Rover, an accounts' customer of Barker's, signing the proffered credit slip and showing identification stolen from Rover's wallet. Rex sells the necklace to Setter.

(d) Having concluded the sale, Barker's shop window is smashed by a gang of robbers who steal all the items on display, including the necklace. Rex demands another, identical necklace. Rex replies that it was unique and, therefore, an irreplaceable piece of jewellery.

Suggested answer

This question deals with misrepresentation, all forms of mistake, breach of contract and frustration. A small point on specific performance might also be considered.

(a) Misrepresentation: Does Barker make a false statement of fact? For example, Barker's initial response implies a confirmation that the necklace is gold—is this a half-truth? Inducement and reliance present no problems, assuming Rex did not attempt to verify that the necklace was pure gold before purchase. In considering the type of misrepresentation, it is unlikely that Barker could establish innocence—fraud and s. 2(1) of the Misrepresentation Act 1967 seem more relevant. Rescission seems possible in which case damages would appear unlikely. Alternatively, Rex may wish to keep the necklace provided he is awarded appropriate damages.

Mistake: The principle of *caveat emptor* suggests that Rex bears the risk that the necklace might not be solid gold. Alternatively, does Rex's initial enquiry imply that it is an implied condition precedent that the necklace is solid gold. If the parties' intentions cannot be gauged (which is very doubtful) the doctrine of common mistake might be applied (*Associated Japanese Bank (International) Ltd v Credit du Nord SA* [1989] 1 WLR 255). The goods are still in existence but does the common law recognize mistake as to quality (see *Leaf v International Galleries* [1950] 2 KB 86)? One might use Lord Atkin's test in *Bell v Lever Bros* [1932] AC 161 (does the state of the new facts destroy the original identity of the subject matter); or, consider whether the contract is now impossible to perform—again very unlikely (see *Great Peace Shipping Ltd v Tsavliris Salvage (International) Ltd* [2002] EWCA Civ 1407, [2002] 3 WLR 1617). Moreover, in light of *Great Peace*, there is no scope for equity to declare the contract *voidable* on grounds of mistake as to quality.

(Note: *common* mistake may be difficult to establish as there is no evidence that Barker believed the necklace to be solid gold. Unilateral mistake would require proof of Barker's fraud and the fundamental nature of the mistake.)

(b) This is a simple case of mutual mistake. Generally, the reasonable person will favour one side's interpretation of events. If a figure of £1,250 is mentioned then, objectively speaking, it may more obviously relate to one of the two necklaces. If the reasonable person is truly confused then the contract will become void for mutual mistake (i.e. no correspondence of offer and acceptance—*Raffles v Wichelhaus* (1864) 2 H & C 906).

(c) Fraudulent misrepresentation will not avail Barker as third party rights have already accrued (Setter has bought the necklace). Barker must therefore argue that the contract is void for unilateral mistake of identity. As mentioned in **Chapter 8**, this area has undergone a fundamental revision in the light of the House of Lords' decision in *Shogun Finance v Hudson* [2003] UKHL 62, [2004] 1 All ER 215. Emphasize the need for an objective appraisal of the facts, adopting the terminology of offer and acceptance in order to decide whether Barker intended to contract with Rex or Rover. On the facts this issue is relatively easy to resolve as the Law Lords in *Shogun* accepted that where A and B contract with each other face-to-face there is almost an irrebuttable presumption that A intends to deal with B whatever the circumstances. Before *Shogun* you would have been required to draw subtle distinctions between the decisions in *Phillips v Brooks* [1919] 2 KB 243, *Lewis v Averay* [1972] 1 QB 198, and *Ingram v Little* [1961] 1 QB 31, based on the perceived attributes and identity of Rex. Thankfully, such complicated analysis is no longer required in these types of circumstances.

(d) As the robbery is post-contractual the doctrine of frustration would be relevant. In a commercial sense, as the subject matter is irreplaceable, it no longer exists. However, is Barker insured against theft? Was this a foreseeable event? Was Barker at fault in not protecting his shop window more effectively? Affirmative answers would suggest that frustration is inappropriate, in which case Barker is in breach of contract. If so, Rex would claim his money back as well as damages for loss of bargain, provided such damages were not too conjectural. Specific performance would be refused provided it is not in Barker's power to locate an identical necklace.

Question 8

ProPump & Co (PPC) orders a consignment of '3mm diameter copper pipes' from C-U-Later Ltd (CUL), to be delivered on 1 August. The online order form completed by PPC states that all orders are subject to CUL's standard terms, one of which excludes CUL from any liability for late delivery of orders. Consider the legal position in each of the separate following sets of circumstances:

(a) CUL delivers the pipes on 20 August. By this time, PPC, desperate to obtain copper pipes in order to continue its manufacturing operations, had purchased a slightly higher grade of copper pipe from another supplier, costing £1,000 more than the originally agreed contract price with CUL. PPC no longer needs any more pipes from CUL for the foreseeable future and wishes to recover the additional cost of £1,000 from CUL. CUL remind PPC of the exclusion clause.

(b) CUL delivers the pipes on time. However, whereas PPC had assumed that the pipes would be made from 100% pure copper, they are made from 98% copper and 2% zinc. PPC point out that, before the order was sent, a CUL representative had orally confirmed that the pipes were made of 'pure copper'.

(c) While delivering the pipes by road, CUL's sole delivery lorry was stopped by the police, found to have faulty tyres, and impounded. CUL has insufficient funds to purchase or hire alternative transport and therefore declares itself bankrupt, claiming that the contract has been frustrated.

Suggested answer

This question covers exclusion clauses, damages, misrepresentation, breach of contract, and frustration.

(a) At common law CUL will need to establish that reasonable notice of the clause was given to PPC before the contract was formed (*Thornton v Shoe Lane Parking Ltd* [1971] 2 QB 163). Was PPC able to view the relevant terms before sending in its order (*Chapelton v Barry UDC* [1940] 1 KB 532)? Is the clause so onerous that it required special highlighting (*Interfoto Picture Library Ltd v Stiletto Visual Programmes Ltd* [1989] QB 433)? Has PPC and CUL dealt with each other on previous occasions (*Spurling (J) Ltd v Bradshaw* [1956] 1 WLR 461)? Assuming the common law tests have been satisfied, we need to consider the relevant sections within the **Unfair Contract Terms Act 1977 (UCTA 1977)**. On the facts, the following sections may be relevant: ss. 3, 11, 13, and **Sch. 2. Section 3** potentially applies as the parties are businesses dealing on standard terms and CUL appears to be in breach of contract. If so, is the clause reasonable? The question of reasonableness will be resolved by applying s. 11 and the guidelines contained in **Schedule 2** of UCTA 1977, such as equality of bargaining power. With regard to the latter, the good student may point out that if the parties were not of unequal bargaining strengths, the court may assume that they should be allowed to apportion the risks as they think fit (e.g. strong *obiter* comments in *Photo Production Ltd v Securicor Transport Ltd* [1980] AC 827). If the clause is held to be unreasonable then it will be void. A similar approach can be adopted in part (b), although note that it is **UCTA 1977, s. 8**, that addresses any exclusion of liability for misrepresentation.

Damages for breach of contract normally represent the victim's loss of bargain (see *Robinson v Harman* (1848) 1 Ex 850) whereby the party is placed in the position he would have occupied if no breach had occurred. However, where this is difficult to establish (e.g. what profits would PPC have lost if it had been unable to perform its contractual obligations with its customers?) a court will allow reliance damages to be claimed, as here (e.g. *McRae v Commonwealth Disposals Commission* (1951) 84 CLR 377).

Secondly, the remainder of your answer on this point should concentrate on the rules of remoteness and mitigation. Begin by referring to cases such as *Hadley v Baxendale* (1854) 9 Exch 341 and *Victoria Laundry (Windsor) Ltd v Newman Industries Ltd* [1949] 2 KB 528. Consider whether PPC is claiming 'normal' or 'exceptional' losses (representing the two branches of the *Hadley v Baxendale* remoteness principle). It is likely that a court will focus on 'special' loss, requiring some evidence that CUL realized the consequences of delaying delivery of the pipes. For example, did PPC inform CUL at the time of contracting that its stock of copper pipes was extremely low? If such losses were in the reasonable contemplation of the parties, did PPC adopt a reasonable course of action to mitigate its losses? Could it have bought identical pipes at a lower price, rather than pay £1,000 more for a slightly better quality of pipe. Refer to *British Westinghouse Electric & Manufacturing Co. Ltd v Underground Electric Railways Co. of London Ltd* [1912] AC 673 and *Bacon v Cooper (Metals) Ltd* [1982] 1 All ER 397, the latter suggesting that PPC might not have to account for this benefit if all other suppliers were only selling the higher quality pipe.

(b) Start by considering whether CUL's representative misrepresented the quality of the pipes—does the word 'pure' represent a statement of fact (i.e. 100% copper)? Was PPC induced to enter the contract as a consequence of the statement? If so, was the misrepresentation fraudulent (proof of absence of honest belief) or is it covered by s. 2(1) of the Misrepresentation Act 1967, viz. absence of reasonable grounds. Also consider a possible breach of contract action: was 100% purity of the pipes intended by CUL to be a term of the contract? Was it clear to CUL that PPC attached importance to this comment (e.g. *Bannerman v White* (1861) 10 CB (NS) 844). Moreover, can PPC claim the protection of the Sale of Goods Act 1979: were the pipes of 'satisfactory quality under s. 14(2)? Did the pipes conform to their description under s. 13? Finally, if the pipes that had been delivered represented either a breach of contract or a substantially different performance from that which PPC could reasonably have expected, apply s. 3 of UCTA 1977 in order to determine the reasonableness of the exclusion clause (see also above).

(c) This involves a possible frustration of the contract. Has there been a radical change in circumstances? Clearly the pipes cannot be delivered as CUL does not have access to appropriate transport; arguably making the contract physically incapable of performance (e.g. *Taylor v Caldwell* (1863) 3 B & S 826). However, there are three reasons why CUL's frustration claim will fail. First, the impounding of the lorry simply increases the costs to CUL of performing the contract—such inconvenience and hardship are not sufficient grounds for frustrating the contract (e.g. *Tsakiroglou & Co. Ltd v Noblee Thorl GmbH* [1962] AC 93). Secondly, it is clearly CUL's fault that the lorry was impounded by the police and, therefore, the 'event' that occurred was induced by CUL (refer to *Lauritzen (J) A/S v Wijsmuller BV, The Super Servant Two* [1990] 1 Lloyd's Rep 1 which assumed that if the party had 'control' over the events then its failure to act constituted self-induced frustration). Thirdly, it is unlikely that the exclusion clause could be used to support CUL's claim: for a clause to support or undermine any possible frustration claim requires the utmost clarity in its wording, which is patently lacking on the facts (see *Metropolitan Water Board v Dick, Kerr & Co.* [1918] AC 119). Nevertheless, if a court rules that the contract has been frustrated, what are the effects? If PPC was required to make a pre-payment, a court is entitled to exercise its discretion to allow CUL to retain all or part of that sum on grounds of expenses incurred in performance of the contract (see s. 1(2) of the **Law Reform (Frustrated Contracts) Act 1943**—note that as no pipes were delivered there is no valuable benefit under s. 1(3)). Finally, if the contract has not been frustrated, CUL will be in breach of contract—allowing PPC to recover its losses, subject to issues of remoteness and mitigation.

Index